Strategies for College Writing

Sentences, Paragraphs, Essays

Jeanette Harris

Texas Christian University

Ann Moseley

Texas A&M University–Commerce

Allyn and Bacon

Boston ■ London ■ Toronto ■ Sydney ■ Tokyo ■ Singapore

For our children and grandchildren

—JH
—AM

Vice President, Humanities: Joseph Opiela
Editorial Assistant: Kristen Desmond
Executive Marketing Manager: Lisa Kimball
Editorial-Production Service: Susan Freese, Communicáto, Ltd.
Text Design and Electronic Composition: Denise Hoffman
Composition Buyer: Linda Cox
Manufacturing Buyer: Suzanne Lareau
Cover Administrator: Linda Knowles
Cover Designer: Susan Paradise

Copyright © 2000 by Allyn & Bacon
A Pearson Education Company
160 Gould Street
Needham Heights, MA 02494

Internet: www.abacon.com

Between the time website information is gathered and then published, it is not unusual for some sites to have closed. Also, the transcription of URLs can result in unintended typographical errors. The publisher would appreciate being notified of any problems with URLs so that they may be corrected in subsequent editions.

Library of Congress Cataloging-in-Publication Data

Harris, Jeanette
    Strategies for college writing : sentences, paragraphs, essays / Jeanette Harris,
    Ann Moseley.
        p. cm.
    Includes index.
    ISBN 0–205–29515–0 (alk. paper)
        1. English language—Rhetoric. 2. English language—Sentences.
    3. English language—Paragraphs. 4. English language—Grammar.
    5. Report writing. I. Moseley, Ann. II. Title.

    PE1408.H3457 2000
    808'.042—dc21   99-051363

Permissions credits appear on page 534, which constitutes a continuation of the copyright page.

Printed in the United States of America

10 9 8 7 6 5 4 3 2 1   RRDV   04 03 02 01 00 99

Contents

Chapter 2
Generating Ideas   9

Chapter 3
Constructing Paragraphs:
Topic Sentences   25

Chapter 4
Constructing Paragraphs:
Supporting Details   39

Chapter 5
Moving from Paragraph to Essay   55

Chapter 6
Achieving Coherence   67

Chapter 7
Revising Your Essay   89

Chapter 8
Gathering and Documenting
Information from Sources   103

Part Two   Methods of Development   119

Chapter 9
Description   121

Chapter 10
Narration   135

Chapter 19
Compound Sentences   279

Chapter 20
Complex Sentences   291

Chapter 21
Sentence Fragments
and Run-On Sentences   311

Chapter 22
Subject–Verb Agreement   329

Chapter 23
Pronoun Usage   341

Chapter 24
Verb Tenses and Forms   355

Chapter 25
Modifiers   373

Chapter 26
Sentence Style   381

Chapter 27
Punctuation and Capitalization   393

Chapter 28
Spelling   405

Part Five   Reading Selections   471

Preface

Strategies for College Writing bridges a gap that often plagues both developmental students and teachers of basic writing courses. Most textbooks emphasize sentence-level skills and writing based on personal experience. Although students can benefit from this type of instruction and perform successfully at this level, they should also be introduced to the types of academic writing and reading experiences required of their other courses. In this textbook, we retain enough of the sentence-level instruction and personal-experience writing needed to reinforce those skills and to make students comfortable with their new status as college students. However, we also introduce them to more academic assignments.

Strategies for College Writing focuses on two basic pedagogical concepts: (1) Students benefit from learning basic strategies and patterns of academic writing, and (2) students need to gain experience in reading and writing academic discourse. Thus, the instruction in this textbook includes not only explanations, exercises, and reading and writing assignments but also patterns that provide students with simple visual representations of the basic forms and concepts that inform academic discourse.

Organization and Scope

Part One: Writing Paragraphs and Essays (Chapters 1–8) provides students with basic instruction in writing—the use of invention strategies, the importance of having a controlling idea, the structure of a paragraph and an essay, the ways in which ideas are arranged and connected, and the process of gathering information not only from personal experiences but also from printed and electronic sources. This unit also includes a chapter on revising.

Part Two: Methods of Development (Chapters 9–17) provides extensive instruction in using traditional patterns of development: description, narration, process, example, comparison/contrast, classification, cause and effect, definition, and persuasion. Each chapter focuses on both the paragraph and the essay and includes examples of student as well as professional writing.

Part Three: Writing and Editing Sentences (Chapters 18–28) focuses on sentence-level concerns and provides students with basic patterns to help them construct different types of sentences. Appropriate instruction about how to punctuate each type of sentence is included, and exercises are provided to reinforce this instruction. A chapter on style encourages students to avoid wordiness and triteness and to strive for sentence variety and effective parallelism. Other chapters in this part focus on major sentence errors, subject–verb agreement, pronoun usage, verb forms and tenses, modifiers, punctuation and capitalization, and spelling. Each chapter includes appropriate exercises to reinforce the instruction.

Part Four: Critical Reading Strategies focuses on critical reading and study skills. Chapter 29 focuses on critical reading, and Chapters 30 and 31 provide useful strategies for outlining, summarizing, and taking essay exams.

Part Five: Reading Selections includes twelve thematically arranged essays by authors who reflect the diversity found in a typical classroom. This thematic arrangement—which groups readings into units on personal identity, education, the media, and race—provides students with the opportunity to make critical connections among related readings.

Outstanding Features

Features that set this text apart from our competition include the following:

- Strategies for academic writing that prepare students to be successful college writers
- Integration of reading and writing instruction
- Flexible organization that accommodates a variety of course structures and teaching styles
- Thematically arranged readings that include textbook discourse as well as literary selections
- A separate section on critical reading, which reinforces study skills as well as critical thinking skills
- Emphasis on the writing process, especially invention and revision
- Collaborative as well as individual assignments
- Many examples of student writing
- A content review, writing assignment, and collaborative activity at the end of each chapter

Conclusion

Strategies for College Writing is the product of our many years of teaching writing—both in the classroom and in writing centers. We hope that other teachers will benefit from our experience and that students will find in this book a way of becoming effective readers and writers.

Acknowledgments

We would like to thank the following individuals, who reviewed an early draft of this book for Allyn and Bacon: Debra Anderson, Indian River Community College; Deborah Andrews, University of Delaware; Deborah Bradford, University of Massachusetts–Dartmouth; Thomas Burns, Butler County College; Ann Higgins, Gulf Coast Community College; and Michael Hricik, Westmoreland County Community College.

Ann Moseley would also like to thank her children, Davy and Christie, for writing such good paragraphs and essays in their college English classes and for giving her permission to use their writing in this book.

Understanding the Writing Process

As a college freshman, you will be writing and reading for every class you take. Your academic assignments during a typical week might include writing an essay for your English composition class, reading an article and writing a summary for your sociology class, and writing an essay examination in your history class. Since writing is an important part of nearly all college classes, you will probably be writing more than you ever have before.

In your previous writing experiences, you probably thought more about *what* to write than *how* to write. Although the content of your writing is very important, we begin this book by discussing the **process** of writing. By understanding this process, you will be able to make better decisions as you write and become a more successful academic writer.

Asked to describe what happens when she writes, one of our students responded:

> *My writing is a process of thinking, writing, thinking, scratching out, thinking, writing again, and sometimes starting the whole process over. Writing is a struggle with the pen to sort out a complex bundle of words.*

This description of one student's writing process is both accurate and perceptive. For most of us, writing is a struggle that involves rewriting as well as writing. And each time we write, the process varies a little because it is not an exact process such as turning on a computer or solving a math problem by using a specific formula. Using a word processor will make this process easier for you, but writing will remain a difficult and demanding— yet also rewarding—task.

The writing process also varies from one person to the next. No two people go through exactly the same process when they write, even if they are writing to the same audience for the same purpose. You should understand that the writing process is not a precise method but rather a general pattern. However, understanding this general process—even though it is sometimes messy and inexact—will help you become a better writer and a better student.

In general, effective writers go through the following three stages of the writing process:

1. Prewriting
2. Writing
3. Rewriting

Although most writers move through these stages in the order in which we have listed them, each stage actually merges with the others. That is, one stage does not have to end completely before another stage begins. When you are writing, you move back and forth among these stages, starting one stage before you complete another or returning to an earlier stage before moving forward again. Or you may work on two stages at the same time, as when you discover new ideas while rewriting or discard an idea even before you actually begin to write. In addition, you usually go through each stage repeatedly. All writers write, read their work, and rewrite, trying to understand their own ideas, to anticipate their readers' needs, and to communicate their ideas clearly and effectively to those readers. Many rereadings and rewritings may be necessary before this process is complete.

The following diagram emphasizes that the various stages of the writing process do not always follow each other in a neat, sequential order:

Even though these stages vary each time you write, you will be a better writer if you understand how these stages relate to one another.

Prewriting

Some of the most important writing you do never reaches the page or is written and then thrown away. When you are given a topic or a writing assignment, you should ideally think about that topic or assignment before you begin to write. If your assignment is a final course project in a psychology or political science class, you will have weeks or even months for the idea to "incubate" or " cook," to use metaphors that other writers have used. If the assignment is a freshman English essay due in a couple of weeks, you will have only a couple of days to consider the topic before you start working on it. In writing an essay examination for your history class, you will have only a few minutes to consider the topic before you begin to answer it—although you should, of course, have prepared by studying the material.

The thinking period that occurs in the earliest stage of prewriting is important, but beware of letting this stage turn into procrastination. Early in this first stage, you should begin to explore your topic in writing; indeed, if your assignment is a general one that allows you to determine your own specific topic, this early prewriting exploration can help you *find* your topic. Therefore, **prewriting** involves not only *thinking* about your topic but also *writing* about it. For example, when his English teacher asked him to write a paragraph about the basic skills course requirements at his university, a student named Jerry made the following list:

English composition
math—basic math and algebra
computer science—not required (I wonder why?)

Specific prewriting strategies include freewriting, journal writing, brainstorming or listing (as shown in Jerry's list), clustering, mapping, questioning, and discussing—all of which are discussed in more detail in Chapter 2. These strategies will allow you to tap into the knowledge and ideas for writing that you already have but that you may not realize you have.

Subject, Purpose, and Audience

An important part of preparing to write is considering not only the **subject** you are writing about but also your **purpose** and your **audience**, those who will read your work. Indeed, the process of writing is, in large part, a struggle to discover the answers to the important questions of *What? Why?* and *Who?* As shown in the following figure, writers and speakers produce a text (anything that is written or spoken) by considering subject (*What?*), purpose (*Why?*), and audience (*Who?*):

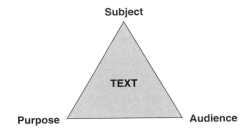

Since these three elements—subject, purpose, and audience—are all basic to the writing process, a writer should consider each of them before and during the writing process. For example, as he thought about his writing assignment, Jerry made the following decisions:

Subject: *I will write about a computer science class as a basic skills requirement.*

Purpose: *I will recommend that a computer science class be added to the list of basic skills requirements.*

Audience: *I will write to college administrators who decide what basic skills courses should be required.*

As Jerry discovered, the elements of subject, purpose, and audience are so dependent on one another that one choice affects, or determines, another. For example, in order to achieve his purpose of trying to get a computer science class added to the list of basic skills courses, Jerry must write to convince a particular audience: college administrators who would make such a decision.

Writing

While **writing** requires preparation, it is also an act of discovery. You may begin with a mental plan—or even an outline (see Chapter 2). Or you may find—as Jerry did in the following draft of his paragraph—that your writing process works better if you just begin writing, discovering the structure of your paragraph or essay as you write and revise:

The ability to use a computer is necessary for college and work. The first day of class this semester, all of my instructors gave assignments that would require me to use a computer. Three out of the four classes that I am taking gave sights on the Internet to access for homework assignments. Since I graduated from high school ten years ago. I have not had one job that has not required me to use a computer. These examples shows that computers play a major role in this world. Therefore, I urge the administrators of our college to add a basic computer science course to the list of basic skills requirements.

Whatever process you use to create your draft, however, you should not hesitate to make changes as new ideas or discoveries come to you. Remember that a good writer is flexible. Do not limit yourself to the ideas you had before you began to write. In both this drafting stage and your final revision stage, you may have new ideas and insights that will strengthen your writing, making it more vivid, more interesting, and more readable.

The number of drafts you write will depend on how many discoveries you make as you write. The writer who requires several drafts is often a better writer than the one who thinks he or she has "gotten it right" the first time. Just as an artist shapes and reshapes, colors and recolors, so a writer writes and rewrites until the finished product achieves its purpose.

Rewriting

As you have already learned, the **rewriting** stage is not limited to the final part of the process but may occur at any point. As you work back and forth through the writing process, you may see your subject, purpose, or even audience in a different light. This act of *revising,* or of "reseeing," your writing then prompts you to rewrite your draft, to make changes in everything from a single word to the focus of your entire composition.

In rewriting, you assume the difficult role of being a reader of your own writing. To rewrite effectively, you must learn to look at your own writing objectively—to *resee* it as your reader will see it.

As illustrated in the following figure, the process of rewriting is both a part of the larger writing process and a process in itself:

As shown here, rewriting includes three different functions: revising, editing, and proofreading. To *revise* means to make important changes in the content, focus, or organization of a draft; to *edit* means to make changes or corrections in sentence structure, usage, and word choice; and to *proofread* means to make minor corrections in the final copy.

For example, as Jerry reread his paragraph, he decided that he had not given enough examples to convince college administrators to consider his recommendation seriously. Therefore, he rewrote it, adding the examples in bold type:

The ability to use a computer is necessary for college and work. The first day of class this semester, all of my instructors gave assignments that would require me to use a computer. <mark>For example,</mark> **my political science, history, and business instructors all** gave sights on the Internet to access for homework assignments. <mark>Furthermore,</mark> **my English instructor explained that I would be required to write and revise my papers on a computer.** Since I graduated from high school ten years ago. I have not had one job that has not required me to use a computer. **The two workplaces where I have used computers the most were a farm supplies store and a law enforcement agency. At the farm supplies store, I used computers for making sales, ordering merchandise, and keeping inventory records. At the law enforcement agency where I am currently working, I use computers for keeping records of offense reports, accident reports, and traffic violations as well as for checking a person's criminal history and driver's license record.** These examples shows that computers play a major role in this world. Therefore, I urge the administrators of our college to add a basic computer science course to the list of basic skills requirements.

In addition to adding specific examples, Jerry also inserted the transitions *For example* and *Furthermore,* which are highlighted.

After Jerry revised his paragraph by adding examples and transitions, he edited and proofread it, making the following changes:

[1]The ability to use a computer is necessary for college and work. [2]The first day of class this semester, all of my instructors gave assignments that would require me to use a computer. [3]For example, my political science, history, and business instructors all
= sites gave ~~sights~~ on the Internet to access for homework assignments. [4]In addition, my English instructor explained that I would be required to write and revise my papers on a computer. [5]Since I graduated from high|school ten years ago. = , I have not had one job that has not required me to use a computer. [6]The two workplaces where I have used computers the most were a farm supplies store and a law enforcement agency. [7]At the farm supplies store, I used computers

for making sales, ordering merchandise, and keeping inventory records. [8]At the law enforcement agency where I am currently working, I use computers for keeping records of offense reports, accident reports, and citations for traffic violations as well as for checking a person's criminal history and driver's license record.

= show [9]These examples <u>shows</u> that computers play a major role in this world. [10]Therefore, I urge the administrators of our college to add a basic computer science course to the list of basic skills requirements.

As shown, Jerry found that in sentence 3 he needed the word *sites,* meaning "location," as in "websites," rather than *sights,* meaning "views" or "visions." He also found and corrected a fragment in sentence 5 and a subject–verb agreement error in sentence 9. Like Jerry, you should wait until your ideas are down on paper and developed fully before you worry about spelling errors and punctuation. If you become too concerned with correctness (editing and proofreading) during your early drafts, you may inhibit your writing process. Knowing that you can attend to matters of style and correctness on later drafts frees you to think more clearly and creatively on early drafts. Save editing and proofreading, as Jerry did, primarily for the final stages. (For more information about rewriting, see Chapter 7.)

Your writing process is uniquely your own, but it is also an evolving process. That is, you probably write best at a particular time—maybe early in the morning or late at night—and in a particular place—perhaps at a computer in the library or propped on a pillow in your room. Yet as your writing process develops throughout your study of this textbook, you will learn new strategies that will make you a better writer. If you take the time to let your writing process work *for* you, you will also become a much more successful college student.

Review

- The writing process involves the three stages of prewriting, writing, and rewriting.

- These three stages of the writing process overlap.

- The writing process is shaped by the elements of subject, purpose, and audience.

- The rewriting stage contains the substages of revising, editing, and proofreading.

■ Writing Assignment

Write a description of your own writing process. How is it similar to or different from the process described in this Introduction?

■ Participating in the Academic Community

Discuss your writing process with a small group of your classmates. Compare your writing processes and discuss how they are similar to or different from the general process described in this Introduction.

Part One

Writing Paragraphs and Essays

This textbook provides effective strategies for the writing you will be expected to do as a college student. The writing instruction includes not only explanations, exercises, and assignments but also patterns that provide you with simple visual representations of the basic forms of most academic writing. Once you have mastered these basic concepts, you will be able to apply them in all your writing assignments.

Part One, Writing Paragraphs and Essays, gives you the foundation you will need to become a better writer. The Introduction included a discussion of the writing process. The eight chapters that form Part One provide you with basic instruction in writing—the importance of a controlling idea, the structure of paragraphs and essays, the ways in which ideas are arranged and connected, and the process of gathering information from written end electronic sources. Most important, Part One includes patterns and strategies to help you construct effective paragraphs and essays.

Chapter 1

Selecting and Limiting a Topic

Selecting an appropriate **topic** and limiting its scope is an important part of any writing project. Occasionally, your instructor will give you a topic and tell you exactly what to write. However, more often your instructor will expect you to come up with a topic on your own. In still other cases, an instructor will give you a general topic and expect you to modify it. This chapter will prepare you for each of these situations.

Your first reaction to a writing assignment may be that you do not know what to write about. Knowing how to select and limit a topic is an important first step to becoming a strong academic writer. In this chapter, you will learn how to get started on a writing assignment by doing the following:

- Selecting a topic on your own
- Modifying an assigned topic
- Limiting, or narrowing, a topic

In selecting, modifying, and narrowing general topics, you should strive for a final topic that allows you to draw on your own knowledge and interests even if the assignment also requires you to engage in some type of research.

Selecting Your Own Topic

Sometimes an instructor, especially in a composition course, will give you a writing assignment but not a topic. The instructor will say something like this: "Write a three- to five-page essay on any topic that interests you" or "Write a one-page definition of something." If you receive this type of open-ended assignment in a writing course, you are indeed free to choose any topic you like. However, you should be aware that certain topics will be valued more than others. If you write about a clichéd topic—such as what you did on your summer vacation or why you do not like living in the dorm—you may satisfy the requirements of the assignment but will probably not produce an essay that earns a very good grade.

Even more constraints are involved when the instructor in a history or sociology course tells you to write a five- to ten-page paper on any topic that interests you. In this situation, there are definite constraints. The instructor assumes that you will write about something associated with the course. You are not free to write about what you did on your summer vacation or even how you feel about the pollution problems created by increasing traffic in your city. Your history instructor will expect you to write on a topic related to history, and your sociology instructor will assume you will write about some sociological issue. So you need to realize that in almost every situation, your choices are somewhat limited. But these limitations can actually be helpful because they focus your thinking and provide you with insight into your instructor's intentions yet allow you to personalize the topic.

Guidelines for Selecting a Topic

The following guidelines will help you select a topic for a writing assignment:

1. *Focus on your own experiences, interests, and attitudes.* In selecting your specific subject, do not concentrate on the instructor's likes or dislikes. For example, if your freshman composition instructor tells you to write an essay about anything that interests you, do not try to think of a topic that will impress her. Sure, she is interested in politics and classical music, but you may know very little about these subjects and have practically no personal experience with either. Instead, select a topic that you know something about and are interested in—something, if possible, with which you have had extensive, firsthand experience. For example, you may know a great deal about cars, small children, or country and western music. If you write on one of these topics, your instructor may learn something by reading your paper. Each writing assignment is an opportunity to demonstrate what you know. If you choose a topic that you know nothing about, have had no experience with, and have little interest in exploring, you cannot hope to write intelligently about it. Your primary concern in selecting a topic for a writing assignment, therefore, should be to choose something you know well and in which you are interested. For example, you might write about what you learned about responsibility while working at a job, how tennis shoes have changed, or why you think grades should be abolished. These topics are not earth shattering but can be the subjects of thoughtful, academically appropriate essays.

2. *Tailor your topic to the class for which the assignment is required.* The kinds of topics you explore and the types of sources you use will vary in different classes. For instance, your English composition instructor

may encourage you to rely primarily on your personal experiences. Your history and political science classes will probably require you to write about topics primarily based on background reading. Your sociology and psychology classes, however, will probably allow you to select writing topics—such as family problems or ways to achieve self-esteem—that will allow you to combine your personal experience and your reading. In selecting topics for any of these classes, however, remember that you can write most intelligently and convincingly about subjects that you know well and in which you are interested.

As you will discover in Chapter 2, Generating Ideas, the tasks of choosing and focusing a topic go hand in hand with invention strategies such as freewriting and brainstorming, which help you not only discover topics for writing but also generate ideas for developing these topics.

EXERCISE

1.1

Brainstorm for a few minutes on a list of topics that are of interest to you (see pages 13–14). Be as inclusive and exhaustive as possible. Do not be concerned with whether these topics are appropriate or safe or interesting to anyone else. The list should reflect *your* interests and preferences—not what you think anyone else might be interested in.

Modifying an Assigned Topic

If your writing assignment stipulates a certain topic, you must focus on that subject. For example, if a history instructor tells you to write about John F. Kennedy, you cannot write about Abraham Lincoln instead (even if you know more about Lincoln). However, you can focus on Kennedy and still use what you know about Lincoln by comparing Kennedy to Lincoln in some way. Even when the assignment is fairly explicit, you can usually modify the topic to take into account your own interests and knowledge.

In fact, instructors usually expect and encourage you to personalize the topics they assign. While you should not radically change the assigned topic or completely ignore it, you can certainly shape it to conform to your own interests. If you are in doubt about modifying an assigned topic, speak with your instructor. Of course, drastic changes in an assignment always need to be approved.

EXERCISE

1.2

The following five writing assignments stipulate topics. Modify and focus each assignment by selecting a topic that reflects your own interests and knowledge yet conforms to the assignment.

1.2 continued

1. Argue for or against an environmental issue.

   Your topic: _____

2. Evaluate some product with which you are familiar.

   Your topic: _____

3. Compare two movies that have the same theme.

   Your topic: _____

4. Analyze a problem that exists in your community.

   Your topic: _____

5. Explain how some aspect of popular culture has changed in your lifetime.

   Your topic: _____

Limiting a Topic

Whether your topic has been assigned or invented by you, it likely needs to be limited, or narrowed. For example, suppose you are free to choose a topic on your own and decide to write about your experiences on a certain job you held. You still need to narrow this topic so that it focuses on one particular aspect of your experience—say, what you learned, how the working conditions created problems, or why the job was stressful. Following are several examples of the process of limiting a topic. Notice that as you move down each list, the topics become increasingly more specific:

1. *Transportation*
   vehicle
   trucks
   domestic versus foreign pickups
   Chevrolet versus Mazda pickups

2. *Music*
   popular music
   jazz
   Nat King Cole's influence on jazz
   Cole's influence on a particular type of modern jazz

3. *Deafness*
   congenital deafness
   attitude of people who are congenitally deaf toward
       people who can hear
   attitude of one congenitally deaf person toward the hearing

Although you may fear that you will not have enough to say if you choose a limited topic, you will discover that you actually have much more information to draw on if you write on a narrowed topic that you know something about and then focus on providing your reader with lots of specific details. Narrower topics invariably result in stronger compositions.

If an instructor gives you a general topic, it is especially important for you to narrow it. For example, if you are asked to write about nutrition, you might narrow this topic to nutrition for a particular age group, perhaps your own. Then you can further tailor the topic to fit your knowledge and experiences by narrowing it to an even more specific topic, such as how good nutrition can benefit college students or the difference between the diets of male and female students.

EXERCISE

1.3

Limit each of the following topics so it is appropriate for a three- to five-page writing assignment.

1. Using the Internet

   _____

2. How to be a good consumer

   _____

3. Current language trends

   _____

4. How education has failed

   _____

5. Causes of stress

   _____

EXERCISE

1.4

The following topics are typical of freshman composition assignments. Narrow each to a limited subject on which you could write an essay.

1. An autobiography about your reading and writing experiences

   _____

2. Profile of a family member

   _____

1.4 continued

3. Campus crimes

_____

4. Problems caused by television

_____

5. Modern heroes

_____

EXERCISE

1.5

Choose one of the topics you included in your brainstorming list in Exercise 1.1, and brainstorm again on this topic. Create a list of your new ideas, and then again choose one. Repeat this process of brainstorming and then selecting a topic from your new list until you have a limited topic that would be appropriate for a three- to five-page essay.

Chapter Review

- When selecting a topic of your own, write on a subject (1) that interests you and that you know well and (2) with which you have had some experience.
- When possible, modify assigned topics to reflect your own interests, expertise, and experience.
- Narrow _all_ topics.

■ Writing Assignment

Select one of the topics you arrived at in Exercise 1.3, 1.4, or 1.5 and write a discovery draft, in which you tell what you know about this subject. Do not worry about organization or structure at this point. The purposes of a discovery draft are to get your ideas on paper and to generate as much information on the subject as possible.

■ Participating in the Academic Community

Meet with others members of your class who have chosen to write about the same general topic for the preceding writing assignment. Compare your limited topics, and share the information you have generated.

Chapter 2

Generating Ideas

Once you have selected or been assigned a topic, you need to explore that topic to decide what you want to say about it and how you want to say it. Although you will need to research some academic topics (see Chapter 8), you can use your own knowledge, your reading, and your experience to generate ideas for most of your writing assignments. As this chapter will show, you can also use specific strategies during the prewriting stage to find and focus (or refocus) your topic, discover your ideas for writing, and plan possible ways of organizing these ideas. These strategies can be helpful not only in your composition class but also in other academic classes.

Using Invention Strategies

The task of thinking of what you have to say, of generating ideas, is often called **invention.** Of course, you do not "invent" ideas that have never existed before. What you actually do is use strategies for tapping into knowledge and experiences that you already have, rediscovering them, so to speak, by making connections between these ideas and your topic and by seeing these ideas as possible subjects for writing. Some of the most helpful invention strategies used in the prewriting stage are freewriting, journal writing, brainstorming, clustering, mapping, questioning, and discussing.

Freewriting

As a beginning writer, you may be intimidated by the task of "getting started." You might be interested to know that even famous writers often share this fear. Truman Capote, for example, once admitted that he hated "facing that blank piece of paper every day and having to reach up somewhere into the clouds and bring something down out of them" (Jon Winokur, *Writers on Writing,* Philadelphia: Running Press, 1986, p. 101). One of the most helpful techniques for getting ideas down on paper is **freewriting.**

To freewrite, simply write rapidly for five or ten minutes without stopping and without worrying about form or correctness. If you do not have a particular topic in mind, or if you are writing to discover a general topic, write whatever comes to mind, repeating words or phrases if you cannot think of something else to write. The key is to keep writing without stopping for several minutes, letting the ideas flow freely, as Shana did in the following example:

> *Well, here is the first day of freshman English and what a suprise! The teacher asks me to write. But write what? Freewrite, she says, so OK. Write, write, write. It seems as if that is what I've done all my live, and I've never liked it. What should I write about? School is writting, and I guess college is writting too. I guess if I have to write about something I can write about writting—why I don't like it. Maybe it goes back to my third grade teacher Mrs. Kibell who never liked my stuff. Worst teacher I ever had. Put red marks all over my papers. Never said anything nice about it. Wonder what this teacher will say when I—*

When you finish freewriting, reread to see if certain words and ideas are especially interesting to you or related to one another, and then underline those ideas. For example, as shown in the following underlined phrases, when Shana reread her freewriting, she discovered that she had actually found a possible idea for an essay:

> *Well, here is the first day of freshman English and what a suprise! The teacher asks me to write. But write what? Freewrite, she says, so OK. Write, write, write. It seems as if that is what I've done all my live, and I've <u>never liked it.</u> What should I write about? School is writting, and I guess college is writting too. I guess if I have to write about something I can write about <u>writting—why I don't like it.</u> Maybe it goes back to my third grade teacher Mrs. Kibell who <u>never liked my stuff.</u> Worst teacher I ever had. Put <u>red marks all over my papers.</u> <u>Never said anything nice about it.</u> Wonder what this teacher will say when I—*

As shown by the words she underlined, Shana has started to focus on her own attitude toward writing and reasons for that attitude.

Helpful variations of freewriting are **looping** and **focused freewriting.** In looping, you take an idea that surfaced in one freewriting and do a focused freewriting on it, writing whatever comes to mind about that particular topic. For example, Shana could develop her ideas further with a focused freewriting on her attitude toward writing. You can open up almost any topic through focused freewriting. (*Note:* Focused freewriting can be part of the looping process or a separate activity.)

EXERCISE

2.1

Do a five- to ten-minute freewriting about your most memorable teacher—perhaps your best or worst one. Remember not to worry about form or correctness and not to stop writing until time is up. When you are finished, reread your freewriting and underline phrases that particularly interest you or that form a connected pattern. Write these phrases here.

_____

_____

_____

If you wish, you may do a more focused freewriting on one of the ideas about your teacher that emerged in your first freewriting.

Journal Writing

Although a **journal** entry has more structure and order than freewriting, it is similar to freewriting in that one of its purposes is to generate ideas. Because your primary audience for your journal is yourself, this format allows you to discover—to question and explore, to think critically, and to write freely about your thoughts, observations, questions, and feelings. In the following journal entry, Housein explores the idea of a special teacher:

> A special teacher, or "mentor," becomes a _leader_ for the students and is not seen as a _boss_ who is always right. Looking back in my past high school years, I had a few teachers that taught me by using this leadership approach. These were the only classes in which I got A's and A+'s, primarily because I liked going to class.
> I remember being in my geometry class just waiting for time to go, as I looked forward to my Anatomy and Physiology class. This class was considered the hardest course at Emporia High School and even had a harder grading scale than regular

classes. I was asked by my geometry teacher why I was failing her class when I had an A in my Anatomy class. I didn't have the answer for her then. I knew only that I liked going to the Anatomy and Physiology class because it was fun, and because the class was fun, I did the best I could without even questioning the amount of work I was putting into the class.

Unlike my geometry class, where I just sat there bored out of my mind and getting in trouble for talking and getting out of my seat. I thought my lack of interest in geometry was just because I couldn't do math, and I dropped her class. My theory for having failed the class changed, as the next year (my Junior year) I got a different teacher and a B + in Geometry. In my new Geometry class, I had a teacher who was also my Track and Field coach. I thought he was the craziest teacher, he was very funny and expected us to do the best we could, because we could.

These two teachers made me feel part of their classes and if I missed or did poorly in class it would affect the whole group. As mentor teachers, they focused on a student centered education.

Housein's journal entry is thoughtful and well developed, but you may have noticed that it has some errors in sentence structure. Although most instructors react to journal entries with written comments, they usually do not evaluate them in the same way they evaluate other written assignments. Thus, you should not be overly concerned with correctness in a journal. Instead, you should feel free to experiment not only with new ideas but also with new words, forms, and styles of writing.

You may write about anything you wish in your journal—your feelings about a relationship, your doubts about college, what you did over the weekend, your baby's first steps. Journal entries focused on topics assigned by an instructor, however, can also provide excellent ideas for academic writing. Rereading one of your academic entries a few days later can remind you of ideas you had about the assignment that you might otherwise have forgotten; rereading one of your personal entries a few years later can remind you of special events and feelings in your life. Here are just a few topics that you might explore in your journal:

1. Tell about a time that you did something right.
2. Write about a day when everything seemed to go wrong.
3. What person do you admire most in the world? Why?
4. What is your favorite book or movie? Why?

5. If you could change identities with another person, who would you choose? Why?
6. Where do you see yourself in ten years?
7. If you could relive any part of your life, what would it be and why?
8. How would you change your life if you could?
9. If you had only a year to live, what would you do with the time left you?
10. If you could live in another time, past or future, when would it be?

Writing in a journal can become an enjoyable routine if you have a particular time and place to write. Many people like to write in their journals just before they go to bed. You may buy a special notebook, or you may create a computer file for your journal. You may write in your journal as often as you wish, but you may find the task easier and more enjoyable if you write in it for ten or fifteen minutes each day. As you get used to writing in your journal, you may spend more time with it, and your journal entries may grow to be as long as Housein's.

EXERCISE

2.2

Write a journal entry on one of the ten topics just listed. Feel free not only to tell about your experience, real or imaginary, but also to describe your feelings and to comment on the importance of the experience.

Brainstorming

Like freewriting, **brainstorming** is a quick and easy method for getting ideas down on paper. To brainstorm, you simply jot down rapidly in list form whatever words, phrases, names, details, or ideas come to mind. Although you can do an unfocused brainstorming to generate—or invent—ideas about a topic, you will get more helpful ideas for writing if you do a focused brainstorming on a particular topic you have already chosen. In the following brainstorming, for example, Amy focused on problems in public schools:

drugs	violence
failure	shootings in Oregon
fights in classroom	shootings in Arkansas
kids don't pay attention	discipline problems
teachers don't care	math classes too hard
kids don't care	not enough money
bomb threat at Emory HS graduation	need more books

As you can see, brainstorming is an effective technique for gathering ideas for writing. You can even use a form of brainstorming when you are taking an in-class essay examination, jotting down main points or examples in the margins of your examination sheet. By writing down ideas for a paper or an exam as soon as you think of them, you can avoid the memory block that sometimes occurs because of writing anxiety.

EXERCISE

2.3

Brainstorm for about five minutes on the goals that you have for your life. What would you like to accomplish right away? What would you like to achieve in the future? In the following spaces, write a list of ideas that come to mind about this topic.

_____

_____

_____

_____

Clustering

When you brainstorm, one idea leads to another so that many of the items you list are connected in some way. If you draw circles and lines to show connections among these related ideas, you will have a **clustering** of ideas to use in a paragraph or an essay. In the following example, notice how Amy created a cluster from her earlier brainstorming:

drugs   (_violence_)

failure   (_shootings in Oregon_)

(_fights in classroom_)————————(_shootings in Arkansas_)

kids don't pay attention   _discipline problems_

teachers don't care   _math classes too hard_

kids don't care   _not enough money_

(_bomb threat at Emory HS graduation_)   _need more books_

As you can see, Amy noticed that she had listed in her brainstorming several items about violence in the public schools. She identified these items and grouped them together. Later, she can add ideas and examples to this original cluster to make a plan for writing about this topic.

EXERCISE

2.4   Review the brainstorming about your goals that you created in Exercise 2.3. Then draw circles and lines to cluster related ideas.

Mapping

If you are a visual learner, you may find the technique of **mapping** particularly helpful. Just as a road map helps you to find your destination and gives you information about the stops on the way when you are on a trip, a visual idea map helps you know where you want to go in your writing and how you can get there. Just as one road leads to another, one thought will lead to another and take you to interesting ideas for writing that you might never have thought of without this exercise. To map an idea for writing, write your general topic in the middle of a piece of paper and then branch out from the topic with related ideas, examples, and details, as shown in Jerry's mapping on the subject of educational methods:

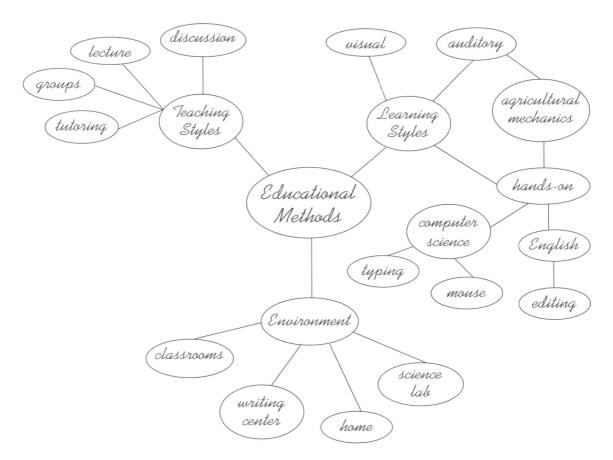

In Jerry's map, you can immediately see a visual diagram of how ideas are related. From such a map, you can often determine which ideas have the potential for development and which do not, thus helping you identify your best choices for writing. In Jerry's map, for example, hands-on learning style emerges as a good topic.

2.5

Add subtopics and examples as necessary to complete the following map on the benefits of a college education. (Use a separate sheet of paper.)

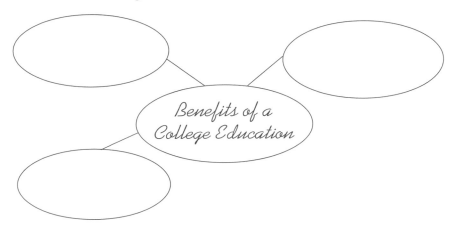

Questioning

To generate ideas for writing, you can also use the technique of **questioning.** When newspaper reporters cover an event or do an interview, they often use questions to be sure they get all the information they need. You can also use these "reporters' questions" to help you select a topic and gather information to develop that topic. You can remember them as the 5-W questions—*Who? What? When? Where? Why?*—and *How?*

Notice how Tomas adapted these questions to explore the topic of an influential teacher:

Who influenced you?   *Mrs. Roberts, my English teacher when I was a junior in high school.*

What did she do?   *She showed an interest in me as a person. She also showed an interest in my culture when she assigned our class Rudolfo Anaya's <u>Bless Me, Ultima</u> to* read. As we talked about this book she helped other students to understand about Mexican American culture.

When did she do this?

She talked about _Bless Me, Ultima_ and Mexican American culture when I was sixteen years old and a high school junior.

Where did she do this?

She discussed this book in my English class. It was in a small town somewhere in southern California, but my family was moving around so much that year that I don't remember the name of the town.

Why did she do this?

At first I wondered why Mrs. Roberts, an Anglo, would teach a Mexican American book in an American literature class. I thought books like this should be taught, but at other schools teachers just talked about Poe and Twain and stuff like that. I think Mrs. Roberts tried to find a book that the Mexican Americans in the class could relate to. But she also seemed to really like the book herself. I think she thought it was just as good as I did.

How did she influence you?

Reading that book got me a lot more interested in school. I saw that I could explain about some of the customs in the book that others didn't know about, and I felt smart. Before we moved, Mrs. Roberts even talked to me about going to college. If it hadn't been for her, I don't think I would have enrolled in this class.

2.6

Use the questioning technique to explore the college major or career that you plan to pursue.

What is your intended career
or major?

_____

_____

Who influenced you to make
this decision?

_____

_____

When did you decide on this career
or major?

_____

_____

Where do you hope to work?

_____

_____

Why did you choose this career
or major?

_____

_____

How do you plan to achieve
your goal?

_____

_____

Discussing

Discussing your writing with your classmates, with a tutor, or with your instructor can also help you think of new ideas for your writing. Moreover, "testing" your own ideas against the ideas of others—comparing and evaluating these ideas—is important for developing the critical thinking skills necessary for all of your academic writing and reading assignments.

Consider the following transcription of a class discussion on the value of classic or great books such as Homer's *The Odyssey* and Nathaniel Hawthorne's *The Scarlet Letter*:

Clay: I disagree with the great books approach. People need to be able to think for themselves. How is all of this classical reading going to prepare students for the "real world"? The answer is, it isn't.

Maggie: But isn't college about a well-rounded education? Reading the classics is a good way to learn about literature, science, art, and mathematics. And it certainly isn't boring!

Cherie: Well, Charles Dickens's *A Tale of Two Cities* is supposed to be a classic, isn't it? I had an English teacher in high school who made us read it, and I didn't even read the whole book. I bought the *Cliff Notes* and read enough to pass my tests. What did I get from that? It's not that I was bad at reading, but the book could not keep my interest long enough for me to gain anything from it.

Maggie: I had a different experience in a summer college class in science fiction. We read books like *Brave New World, Flatland,* and *War of the Worlds.* In class we talked about scientific advances in each book and how far technology has come today to catch up with the fiction. I learned more about physics in this class than in my high school physics class.

Housein: Also, the classics help us learn about life, not just learn for a piece of paper that says we have sat through so many classes to qualify us for a specific job. I like the idea of the classics, but the problem is that it's hard to define a classic or a "great book." Is a book great just because it's on somebody's list? And why aren't there more books by Hispanics and African Americans on the list of classics?

Cherie: Yeah, that's a problem, too. Just who says a book is great? But mostly I agree with Clay that these books just don't apply to my life today. And I don't appreciate being forced to read a long, boring book I have no interest in. I didn't like it in high school, and I don't like it now, especially when I have to pay for it.

Housein: Maybe books don't have to be long and hard to be great. I even think Dr. Seuss's books are great because they teach kids to read and to love language, and they are fun. I think that's really great!

After participating in this discussion, these students may be better prepared to write a paper on some of the advantages and disadvantages of requiring students to read the classics. A discussion such as this enables you to clarify and sharpen your ideas and exposes you to the ideas of others.

EXERCISE

2.7

With a small group of your classmates, discuss the freewriting that you did on your best or worst teachers in Exercise 2.1. What conclusions can you draw about effective teaching from these examples? Write two or three of these conclusions in the following space:

1. _____

2. _____

3. _____

Using Informal Planning Outlines

Outlining is a method of organizing ideas by indicating their relationship to one another. Like a diagram, an outline is a blueprint or plan of a completed work. It is a skeleton that allows you to see the essential framework of a piece of writing.

Since an outline visually represents general and specific relationships, you must understand how to distinguish between general and specific concepts in order to outline. For example, *tree, grass,* and *flower* are three general categories. Thus, on an outline, you would arrange them as three equal headings:

▶ EXAMPLE

tree

grass

flower

Then, if you wanted to include some specific examples of each of these three general categories, you could place them under the appropriate headings. For example, if you wanted to list *oak, elm, pine,* and *fir* under *tree,* you would list these four specific types of trees under the general heading *tree:*

▶ EXAMPLE

Tree

oak

elm

pine

fir

You could also add letters or numbers to your outline to make the relationships more clear:

▶ EXAMPLE

1. Tree

a. oak

b. elm

c. pine

d. fir

Or you could use a different system of representation, as shown here, as long as you continued to indicate that *tree* is the most general term and that *oak, elm, pine,* and *fir* are specific examples or types of trees:

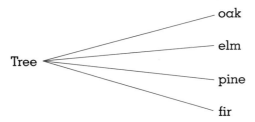

Outlines can appear in various forms as long as they communicate accurately the relationships that exist among the different items of information included. The outline form that is probably most familiar to you is the **formal outline.** Writers use formal outlines to give their readers information about the material being outlined. Formal outlines are most appropriately used as tables of contents. They are frequently included with long reports, research papers, and proposals as a guide to the contents. Since formal outlines must communicate clearly to a reader, the writer uses a traditional form that is familiar to everyone. A formal outline is illustrated here:

<u>Main idea:</u> Literature has traditionally been divided into three categories.

    I. Fiction
      A. Novel
      B. Short story
   II. Drama
      A. Tragedy
      B. Comedy
        1. Low comedy
        2. High comedy
 III. Poetry

This outline could serve as an effective introduction to a chapter or essay on the types of literature. As a reader, you can determine from this formal outline that the three main types of literature are fiction, drama, and poetry. You can also see that fiction can be divided into the subcategories of novel and short story and that drama can be divided into tragedy and comedy. Further, you can see from this outline that comedy can be divided into low comedy and high comedy. Not only do the numbers and letters assigned to the different entries on the outline and the system of indentation indicate the relative importance of the entries and their relationships to one another, but the use of numbering and capitalization is also consistent. (For information on using outlines for studying, see Chapter 30.)

When you are planning a paragraph or an essay, however, you may find a formal outline too limiting. Whereas a formal outline usually requires at least two items in each category, you may find that in some categories you have only one point to make. In addition, the fact that a formal outline is so neat and balanced may discourage you from making changes in your plan as you work. For these reasons, writers usually find that some type of **informal outline** is more helpful for planning purposes.

Since you are the only person who will be using your planning outline, you should select the format that is most helpful for you. Indeed, your planning outline may simply be scratches on a piece of paper—what is called a *scratch outline*—if these scratches communicate to you. However, you may find it helpful to learn several possible formats for planning outlines. Following are four different formats for exploring the topic of hands-on learning:

▶ EXAMPLE A: INFORMAL TOPIC OUTLINE

1. English class (editing)
2. agricultural mechanics class
   —plumbing (copper pipe and PVC pipe)
   —wiring
   —carpentry
3. computer science class (typing and mouse skills)

▶ EXAMPLE B: FLOW DIAGRAM

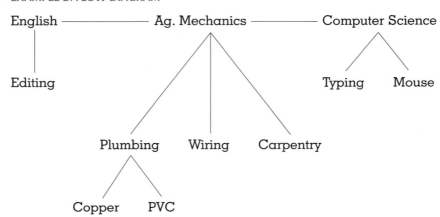

▶ EXAMPLE C: MAPPING

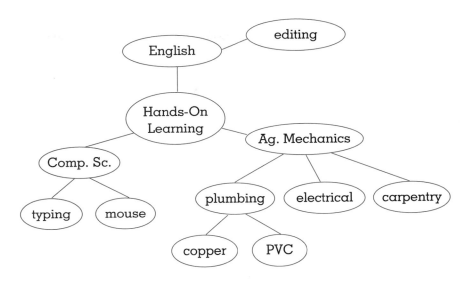

▶ EXAMPLE D: INFORMAL SENTENCE OUTLINE

1. In my English class we practice hands-on editing.
2. In my agricultural mechanics class we get hands-on practice.
    —We plumb with both copper and PVC pipe.
    —We install electrical wiring.
    —We practice carpentry skills.
3. In my computer science class we use both keyboard and mouse skills.

Any one of these planning outlines can help you write a paragraph or brief essay on learning with a hands-on approach. Or, you may want to experiment with two or three different planning formats to determine which ones work best for you.

EXERCISE

2.8   Write an informal outline based on the brainstorming you did about your goals in life in Exercise 2.3 or on one of the other prewriting exercises you have completed. Use whichever planning format you prefer.

Chapter Review

■ Invention strategies help you discover what you have to say about an idea or topic.

1. Freewriting is writing your thoughts rapidly for a few minutes without worrying about form or correctness.

2. Journal writing allows you to explore your thoughts and feelings in depth.

3. Brainstorming is a rapid listing of ideas.

4. Clustering identifies and shows connections among ideas generated by brainstorming.

5. Mapping creates a visual diagram of your ideas.

6. Questioning gathers information from the queries *who, what, when, where, why,* and *how.*

7. Discussing allows you to compare your ideas with others.

■ Informal planning outlines, which can occur in various forms, can be helpful working plans for writing.

Writing Assignment

Write a paragraph, journal entry, or brief essay using the planning outline you created for Exercise 2.8.

Participating in the Academic Community

Compare the planning outline you created in Exericise 2.8 with the outlines of a small group of your classmates. Discuss why you each chose the type of format you used.

Chapter 3

Constructing Paragraphs: Topic Sentences

As a college student, you will be assigned a variety of writing tasks. Instructors will ask you to write such things as memos, reports, essays, research papers, critiques, reviews, and response papers. Most instructors will assume that you know what is involved in writing these types of assignments. One of the purposes of this book is to provide you with the strategies you need to produce a variety of writing assignments. Rather than focusing on each type of assignment individually, this book emphasizes the basic patterns and concepts that inform most academic writing assignments. If you master these concepts, you will know the general shape of all academic discourse and be able to adapt the basic patterns to different assignments. One of the most important of these concepts is the paragraph.

Basic Structure of a Paragraph

A **paragraph** consists of a series of sentences that are related to a single concept, which is identified in the **topic sentence.** In very simple terms, the topic sentence tells the reader what the paragraph will be about. It is usually stated at the very beginning of the paragraph, as in the example that follows:

> As the population of the United States becomes more diverse, and people of color and differing cultures and lifestyles become more visible, there has been a corresponding rise in intolerance.

Continuing anti-Semitic acts, Japanese bashing, gay bashing, and racially motivated hate crimes indicate that intolerance is still smoldering in our nation. Neo-Nazi activities, Ku Klux Klan and skinhead demonstrations, and the growth of extremist religious and cult activity are signs that bigotry and hatred are still present. Cross burnings, religious desecrations, death threats, and actual murders indicate the seriousness of these social problems. Hatred and bigotry divide communities and shatter the social, educational, legal, political, and economic bonds between people. Such actions lead to deterioration in our spiritual, social, and psychological health.

—Rebecca J. Donatelle and Lorraine G. Davis, *Health: The Basics*, 2nd ed.

Notice that this paragraph begins with a general statement, which serves as the topic sentence for the paragraph, establishing the idea that intolerance seems to be increasing in our society. This sentence serves as the introduction and establishes the controlling idea for the paragraph. The next four sentences in the paragraph support the topic sentence by providing specific examples of different types of intolerance. These specific details further explain and reinforce the topic sentence. Then the final two sentences in the paragraph explain the results, or effects, of intolerance and function as a conclusion.

Model of a Basic Paragraph

The following diagram shows the form and proportions of a model paragraph. Notice that the first word in the paragraph is indented several spaces (usually five to ten) from the margin. Notice, too, that the body of the paragraph is much longer than either the introduction or the conclusion:

Introduction: Topic sentence (main idea)
Body: Specific supporting statements
Conclusion: Restatement of main idea (optional)

This paragraph model is just that—a model, or pattern, to help you visualize the shape and proportions of a well-developed paragraph. Other patterns exist, but in general they are variations of this basic model. If you observe paragraphs in books, magazines, and newspapers, you will notice that professional writers often write paragraphs that do not follow this pattern. Experienced writers may omit topic sentences or place their main ideas in the middle or at the end of the paragraph if that arrangement suits their subject and purpose. However, in learning to write and read academic discourse, you will find this pattern useful.

EXERCISE

3.1

The following paragraphs follow the pattern of the model paragraph with the exception that the topic sentence has been omitted. For each paragraph, you are given three sentences, each of which could function as a topic sentence. However, only one of the sentences is really appropriate. Read each paragraph carefully, examining the supporting details and the conclusion. Then select the topic sentence that best expresses the main idea. Write the sentence in the space provided.

PARAGRAPH A

1. Movies are more emotional than recorded music or books.

2. Audiences prefer movies to other forms of entertainment.

3. Movies have a hold on people, at least while they are watching one, that is more intense than any other medium.

Topic sentence: _____

_____

It is not unusual for a movie reviewer to recommend taking a handkerchief, but never will you hear such advice from a record reviewer and seldom from a book reviewer. Why do movies have such powerful effects? It is not movies themselves. With rare exception, these evocative efforts occur only when movies are shown in a theater. The viewer sits in a darkened auditorium in front of a giant screen with nothing to interrupt the experience. The rest of the world is excluded. Movies, of course, can be shown outdoors at drive-in theaters and on television, but the experience is strongest in the darkened cocoon of a movie house.

—John Vivian, *The Media of Mass Communication,* 4th ed.

3.1 continued

PARAGRAPH B

1. College students often face a challenge when trying to eat healthy foods.

2. Most college students do not make the effort to eat a healthy diet.

3. College cafeterias do not provide the variety of foods required by a healthy diet.

Topic sentence: _____

_____

Some students live in dorms and do not have their own cooking or refrigeration facilities. Others live in crowded apartments where everyone forages in the refrigerator for everyone else's food. Still others eat at university food services where food choices are limited. Most students have time constrains that make buying, preparing, and eating healthy food a difficult task. In addition, many lack the financial resources needed to buy many foods that their parents purchased while they lived at home. What's a student to do? While we can't come in and guard your refrigerator to make sure your roommates don't eat your food, we can offer some suggestions for choices that may make your eating experience more healthy.

—Rebecca J. Donatelle and Lorraine G. Davis, *Health: The Basics*, 2nd ed.

EXERCISE

3.2

After reading the three specific statements for each of the following potential paragraphs, supply an appropriate topic sentence.

1. *Topic sentence:* _____

_____

Specific statement: Smoking can cause permanent stains on teeth.

Specific statement: It also contributes to heart disease.

Specific statement: The most significant health risk for most smokers is lung cancer.

2. *Topic sentence:* _____

_____

Specific statement: In the past, a college education prepared people for professional degrees or for a position in a family business.

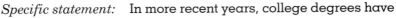

Specific statement: In more recent years, college degrees have increasingly been perceived as the best way to prepare for a career.

Specific statement: Most recently, people have begun to view college degrees as preparation for life.

Writing Effective Topic Sentences

Academic writing nearly always begins with a single, well-defined idea that is expressed in a clear, forceful sentence. You have already learned in this chapter that this statement of the main idea is referred to as a *topic sentence* if you are writing a paragraph. You have also learned that the topic sentence expresses a general concept, which is then supported by more specific ideas—other sentences that elaborate, explain, or expand on it. Now you are ready to learn how to write effective topic sentences.

An effective topic sentence consists of a **topic** (what you are writing about) and an **assertion** (the point you are making about the topic). In other words, the assertion makes a statement about the topic. It may express an attitude or opinion (*Recycling should be enforced by law*), or it may simply indicate what is to follow (*We should recycle for three reasons*). Together, the topic and assertion let your reader know the point you are making or the idea you are developing in your paragraph.

Please keep these points in mind:

- Statements of fact do not usually serve as topic sentences because such statements need no further development or support.

- Titles cannot take the place of topic sentences because they tell what the paragraph is about (*Recycling*) but not what you are going to say (assert) about your topic (*Recycling can be an important step toward an environmentally sound conservation policy*).

Narrowing Topic Sentences

Although a topic sentence is a general statement in relation to the other sentences in the paragraph, it should not be so broad that you cannot develop the idea it expresses in a page or less. Often a statement that is too general to serve as an effective topic sentence can be narrowed by the addition of more specific information. Consider the following sentence:

1. Conservation is important.

This statement is so broad that it cannot possibly be developed adequately in a single paragraph. If you narrow the statement by specifying a particular type of conservation, you will have a more workable topic sentence:

2. Recycling is an important form of conservation.

If you narrow further, you will have an even more effective topic sentence:

3. Local efforts to recycle paper help us conserve our natural forests.

Notice that as you narrow your topic sentence by adding more specific details, it becomes not only a longer sentence but also a stronger topic sentence—one that could be developed in a paragraph. Notice also that both the topic and the assertion are more specific in sentence number 3.

Topic	Assertion
1. Conservation	is important.
2. Recycling	is an important form of conservation.
3. Local efforts to recycle paper	help us conserve our natural forests.

EXERCISE

3.3   Working individually or with your classmates, identify the topic and assertion of each sentence in the following list. Then evaluate the effectiveness of each as a topic sentence by writing several specific statements that could be used to support it.

1. Learning a foreign language can be difficult for adults.

   Topic: _____

   Assertion: _____

   Specific supporting statements:

   (1) _____

   (2) _____

   (3) _____

   Conclusion: _____

   _____

   _____

2. Telephones intrude into the privacy of our daily lives.

   Topic: _____

   Assertion: _____

   Specific supporting statements:

   (1) _____

   (2) _____

   (3) _____

   Conclusion: _____

   _____

   _____

3. Many gun-related accidents involve children.

   Topic: _____

   Assertion: _____

   Specific supporting statements:

   (1) _____

   (2) _____

   (3) _____

   Conclusion: _____

   _____

   _____

EXERCISE

3.4   This exercise will provide you with practice in narrowing statements so that they will be effective topic sentences. As you revise these sentences, keep in mind the following guidelines:

■ A topic sentence should always be a complete sentence.

■ A topic sentence should not merely state a single fact.

■ A topic sentence should be a general statement but should not be so broad or vague that it cannot be developed adequately in a paragraph of five to ten sentences.

3.4 continued Rewrite each of the following statements, narrowing both topic and assertion. (*Note:* You will need to change words and add new words.)

1. Education is important.

   _____

2. Exercise improves a person's health.

   _____

3. Technology has changed the way we live.

   _____

4. Personal relations are often difficult.

   _____

5. Young people ignore rules.

   _____

Identifying Topic Sentences/ Main Ideas in Paragraphs

Much academic reading depends on your ability to identify main ideas and
to distinguish them from supporting details in order to summarize what the
writer is saying. Understanding the various patterns in which topic sentences occur in paragraphs will help you to identify the main ideas when you
read.

Topic Sentence as First Sentence

Often, the main idea appears only once in a paragraph. Most frequently, the
topic sentence, or main idea statement, occurs at or near the beginning of
the paragraph, usually as the first sentence. Remaining sentences, then,
give explanations, examples, and details. This pattern (general to specific) is
illustrated in the figure and the sample paragraph that follow. (The topic
sentence in the paragraph is set in bold type.)

Topic sentence
Specific detail
Specific detail
Specific detail

The American breakfast has changed dramatically in the past few decades. In the first fifty or sixty years of the twentieth century, a typical breakfast consisted of bacon and eggs or cereal. Although some people occasionally liked a gooey donut or a sweet roll for breakfast, most Americans preferred the standard fare—day after day. Since the 1960s, however, breakfasts have become increasingly exotic. Traditional breakfast fare seems rather dull compared with Belgian waffles, French omelettes, or huevos rancheros (eggs topped by a spicy Mexican salsa). Breakfasts have also become healthier. Yogurt, granola, and fruit are considered better for people than bacon and eggs accompanied by buttery hot biscuits smothered in gravy.

Topic Sentence as Last Sentence

The topic sentence can occur as the last sentence of a paragraph. In this case, the paragraph starts with details or examples and concludes with the main idea. This paragraph pattern (specific to general) is illustrated in the figure and the sample paragraph that follow:

Specific detail
Specific detail
Specific detail
Topic sentence

In the early 1980s, prosperity seemed to be our birthright. Jobs were plentiful, money was easy to borrow, and the stock market was on a steady upward course. Then, in the last part of the decade, the economic picture changed. The homeless became a familiar sight on city streets. Some people lost their jobs, and graduates had more difficulty finding employment. And on at least one occasion, the stock market dipped low enough to make even the most optimistic investors nervous. Savings-and-loan associations, banks, and even insurance companies began to fail. By the end of the decade it was clear that the nation was in a significant recession. **The 1980s were a time in which the nation moved from economic optimism and prosperity to economic pessimism and hard times.**

Topic Sentence as First and Last Sentences

Some writers state the topic sentence at both the beginning and the end of a paragraph. In this case, the final statement of the main idea is not merely a restatement of the topic sentence. The last sentence reinforces the main idea but also reflects the conclusions that the writer has reached. This pattern (general to specific to general) is illustrated in the figure and the sample paragraph that follow:

Topic sentence		
	Specific detail	
	Specific detail	
	Specific detail	
Concluding topic sentence		

> **The weather in West Texas is completely unpredictable.** Winter often brings warm, sunny days while summer and spring may surprise residents with periods of cool, cloudy weather. The wind may blow fiercely one day and be completely calm the next. Drought may plague the region at times, only to be followed by heavy rainfall and even flooding. At one time or another, and in no particular order, West Texans experience blinding dust storms, record-breaking heat waves, tornadoes, hail, thunderstorms, and "blue northers"—those sudden cold spells that sweep across the Panhandle and into the state from the north. **The climate throughout West Texas is often dramatic, sometimes disagreeable, but seldom dull.**

Topic Sentence as Second/Middle Sentence

The topic sentence may also be stated in the second (or even the third or fourth) sentence of a paragraph. In this pattern, the first sentence or sentences serve as an introduction to the main idea. Or the first sentence(s) may function as a transition, linking the paragraph to the preceding one.

This paragraph pattern (introduction/transition to general to specific) is illustrated in the figure and the sample paragraph that follow:

Introduction/transition
Topic sentence
Specific detail
Specific detail
Specific detail

In the past few years, millions of Americans have begun to exercise. **Unfortunately, many of these energetic but amateur athletes have sustained serious injuries.** Tennis players have ruined their elbows, joggers their knees, and aerobic dancers their ankles. More serious injuries are often sustained by those who play competitive sports such as basketball or football. Even lifting weights involves certain risks to muscle tissue and bones.

Implied Main Idea

In some paragraphs the topic sentence is not stated. Rather, it is suggested or *implied* throughout the paragraph. In the following sample paragraph, the main idea is implied rather than stated. Read the paragraph carefully and then state the main idea in your own words. Key words that provide you with clues to the main idea of the paragraph appear in bold type.

On his **inauguration day, Andrew Jackson** mounted his horse and rode to the White House, followed by a **crowd** of 10,000 visitors. The people **pushed** into the White House, **climbing on delicate furniture** to see the new president. **Excited supporters trod on valuable rugs** with muddy boots, **turned over pieces of furniture,** and **broke expensive glassware.** They **pushed and shoved** to get next to the new president, who, after being backed helplessly against a wall, climbed out a back window.

Main idea: _____

_____

_____

Although this paragraph does not have a stated main idea (topic sentence) each sentence is an important detail that suggests or implies the main idea. One way to state the main idea would be *On Andrew Jackson's inauguration day his excited supporters destroyed valuable White House property and even endangered the president.*

In your reading you will sometimes find paragraphs in which the main idea is implied rather than stated. When you read a paragraph with an implied main idea, you must use the supporting details to help you determine—or infer—the main idea. The main idea you formulate from these details is an inference. The process of inferring a main idea from the details within a paragraph is similar to the process of inferring the meaning of an unfamiliar word from its context. In both situations, you use the information given to help you infer what the writer implies.

As a writer, you may occasionally write a paragraph with an implied main idea. If you choose not to include a topic sentence, however, you should keep your main idea clearly in mind, being sure that each detail develops the main idea so clearly that your reader will have no difficulty understanding it.

EXERCISE

3.5

In the three paragraphs that follow, the main idea is implied rather than stated. Read each paragraph carefully and then state in your own words its main idea.

PARAGRAPH A

He was the only non-American student in the history class. Since most of the discussions focused on American history and culture, he had little to contribute. He was also very shy, especially when he was called on to answer a question. To make matters even worse, he had to work on a group project with three girls, a situation that only increased his normal shyness.

Main idea: _____

_____

PARAGRAPH B

In the distant past, writers labored with quill pens and ink, carefully forming each letter by hand. The fountain pen, when it appeared on the writing scene, was viewed as a marvelous convenience. Then the typewriter provided writers with a much more efficient method of writing, a method that for many years was viewed as the ultimate in writing convenience. When the correcting typewriter came along, writers thought they had died and gone to heaven. Today, however, writers who write with computers and word-processing programs scorn "old-fashioned" typewriters.

Main idea: _____

_____

PARAGRAPH C

Daytime television is dominated by soap operas and silly quiz shows. Newscasts are brief, sports events are rare, and first-run sitcoms are nonexistent. After the morning shows, which end about the time people's workdays begin, the tube emits the shrieks of quiz show contestants. These ridiculous shows are followed by the high (but seldom serious) drama of the soap operas, with their endless crises and passionate sex. In contrast, nighttime television provides viewers with newscasts, sports events, situation comedies, serious dramas, and documentaries. Viewers can choose from movies, comedies, news stories, musical variety shows, and numerous "specials," all designed to appeal to a more mature, intelligent audience.

Main idea: _____

_____

Chapter Review

- A paragraph consists of a series of sentences that develop a single idea, which is usually stated in a topic sentence.

- A topic sentence usually occurs at the beginning of a paragraph.

- An effective topic sentence includes both a topic and an assertion that makes a statement about the topic.

- A topic sentence should be limited so that it can be developed adequately in a single paragraph.

- Knowing the placement options for topic sentences helps readers identify main ideas in paragraphs.

- A main idea is occasionally not stated in a topic sentence but is implied.

■ Writing Assignment

Limit the following topic sentence by making the idea more specific, and then write five specific sentences that support it.

Topic sentence: Dating is (or is not) the best way to find a mate.

Limited topic sentence: _____

_____

Specific supporting sentences:

1. _____
2. _____
3. _____
4. _____
5. _____

■ Participating in the Academic Community

Meet with a group of your classmates to discuss the topic sentences you have written. Evaluate each topic sentence to determine if it is sufficiently limited and includes both a topic and an assertion.

Chapter 4

Constructing Paragraphs: Supporting Details

You learned in Chapter 3 that a topic sentence expresses the general idea of a paragraph. But it is the specific details in a paragraph that develop the general idea, providing the information that readers need to understand what the writer means. Good writers not only state the main ideas of their paragraphs clearly but also support them with specific facts and details. Read the following paragraph carefully, noticing the details that are used to support the main idea:

> It was a land tortured by weather. There were wet springs when days of pouring rain put creeks out of banks and washed away cotton and corn. At times, before the water could drain off, dust storms blew down from the western plains, clouding the sky and making mouths gritty. Summers were long, hot, dry—worst in the dog days of August, when creeks ran low and scummy and the earth cracked in the sun. The people learned to be grateful for the first cool days of fall, and to bundle up in hard winters when blue northers swept down across Kansas and Oklahoma. They shivered in their shacks and said there was "nothing between them and the North Pole but a bobbed-wire fence."
>
> —William Owens, *This Stubborn Soil*

Identify three specific details from this paragraph that support the main idea that the land was "tortured by weather."

1. _____

2. _____

3. _____

These specific details about the weather make the main idea vivid and meaningful. The details tell *how* the land was tortured by weather—that it was not floods, hurricanes, or earthquakes the people feared but rather heat, dust storms, rain, and "blue northers." The general statement that introduces William Owens's paragraph tells very little about the land or the weather. The details that support the main idea, however, offer a vivid image of the effects the weather had on the people and the land.

Using Specific Details to Support Topic Sentences

Inexperienced writers often construct paragraphs that have too many general statements and too few specific details. A paragraph that consists of a series of general statements is very difficult for a reader to understand, but a paragraph that consists of a general statement supported by specific details is much easier to comprehend.

Thus, a well-constructed paragraph usually consists of one general statement, which functions as the topic sentence, and a series of specific statements, which support the topic sentence. This pattern—general idea plus supporting details—is an important one to remember.

Our young Egyptian guide was lovely. **[general statement]** She was of medium build with a pleasant face lit by enormous brown eyes and framed by long, gently curling hair that was so dark it looked blue-black in the bright desert sunlight. Her voice was soft but distinct, never harsh and commanding as are the voices of many guides. As she led us in and out of tombs and pyramids, she was unfailingly encouraging and reassuring.

4.1

Write three or more sentences that include specific supporting details for each of the following topic sentences.

▶ EXAMPLE   Traffic has become a serious problem in Dallas.

[1]Central Expressway is constantly under construction because it always needs additional lanes. [2]The major interstate highways that transect the city have been inadequate for years. [3]Recently, even the tollway has become a speedway with pick-up trucks, sports vehicles, and every type of automobile imaginable competing for space.

1. College teachers usually expect students to be independent and self-motivated.

   _____

   _____

   _____

   _____

   _____

2. A college education has become very expensive.

   _____

   _____

   _____

   _____

   _____

3. A high school education doesn't insure success in today's world.

   _____

   _____

   _____

   _____

   _____

Factual and Sensory Details

Supporting details may be factual or sensory. **Factual details** help readers by giving them exact information. They usually answer questions such as *Who? What? When? Where? Why? How?* and *How many?* Often these details provide names, dates, places, numbers, measurements, or statistics. In contrast, sensory details appeal to the senses of sight, hearing, smell, taste, or touch. These details help readers not only to visualize the writer's words but also to hear, feel, smell, and taste what the writer is expressing. The following sentence includes both factual and sensory details:

> The runner had completed the race in less than three minutes but was so exhausted that her legs were trembling and her breath came in short, painful gasps.

Write the factual detail.

_____

Write the two sensory details.

_____

_____

In supporting your topic sentences, use both types of specific details. Factual details help your readers understand your meaning, while sensory details help them experience that meaning. Together, these two types of details enable you to communicate more precisely and effectively.

EXERCISE

4.2

For each of the following general statements, write two supporting sentences—one that includes factual details and one that includes sensory details.

1. Child-care programs often fail to provide an ideal environment for children.

_____

_____

_____

_____

_____

2. Math is a difficult subject for many young people.

_____

_____

_____

_____

_____

3. Technology has been a mixed blessing.

_____

_____

_____

_____

_____

4. Sports heroes are overvalued in our society.

_____

_____

_____

_____

_____

5. Americans have less privacy than they once did.

_____

_____

_____

_____

_____

Patterns for Structuring Supporting Details

The specific sentences you use to support a topic sentence may be structured in a variety of ways. Two common ways to structure supporting details are to use patterns of coordination and subordination. **Coordinate**

details are equally specific, whereas **subordinate details** are increasingly specific.

COORDINATE PATTERN	SUBORDINATE PATTERN
Topic sentence	*Topic sentence*

CEORDINATE PATTERN
Topic sentence
  Supporting sentence
  Supporting sentence
  Supporting sentence
  Supporting sentence

SUBORDINATE PATTERN
Topic sentence
  Supporting sentence
    Supporting sentence
      Supporting sentence
        Supporting sentence

As these patterns suggest, in the coordinate pattern each sentence supports the topic sentence and is equally specific. In the subordinate pattern, although all the sentences support the topic sentence, each one is increasingly specific. Thus the first supporting sentence is more specific than the topic sentence; the second is more specific than the first; the third is more specific than the second; and so on.

Using the Coordinate Pattern

To develop the main idea of a paragraph using coordinate, or equally specific, details, you will need to think of a series of sentences (usually three to five), each of which supports your topic sentence. The details in the following paragraph are coordinate:

> [1]Mexico offers visitors a world of contrasts. [2]Its pyramids and ancient ruins give us a glimpse of the past while its modern cities provide us with the best of today's technology. [3]Its mountains offer cool weather and majestic peaks while, only a few miles away, its beaches tempt us with brilliant sun and white sand. [4]Its elegant restaurants serve the most sophisticated continental cuisine while, across the street or down the block, sidewalk vendors sell the simplest of native foods. [5]Thus the traveler to Mexico is faced with a series of delightful decisions.

In this paragraph, the topic sentence is supported by three equally specific, or coordinate, supporting details. This paragraph can be diagrammed as shown here:

Topic sentence (sentence 1)
Coordinate detail (sentence 2)
Coordinate detail (sentence 3)
Coordinate detail (sentence 4)
Concluding sentence (sentence 5)

4.3   Write a paragraph describing a place you know well—a place where you have lived or worked or visited often—using coordinate details. Use the block form shown in the following diagram to write your rough draft, writing a different sentence in each block.

Topic sentence
Coordinate detail
Coordinate detail
Coordinate detail
Concluding sentence

Expanding Coordinate Details

If you want to write a longer paragraph, you may simply expand your coordinate details by adding related but more specific details to support them. This pattern is illustrated for you in the following paragraph. This paragraph contains three major coordinate details, each of which is further supported by a more specific detail. As you read the paragraph, try to decide which sentences express the major coordinate points and which express the more specific details.

> [1]My father's death, which occurred when I was nine years old, had several important effects on me. [2]First of all, I felt great sadness and loneliness. [3]For the first few months, my loneliness was so great that I often dreamed that my father would miraculously return. [4]In addition, throughout the rest of my childhood, I was afraid of losing

someone else whom I loved. [5]Whenever my mother was away from home, I was always nervous until she returned. [6]Finally, the loss of my father caused me to develop a greater sense of responsibility. [7]For example, I believed that with my father gone I was responsible for helping my mother with her chores. [8]My father's death, therefore, left me lonely, frightened, and responsible—a young child with adult feelings.

In this paragraph, the main idea is stated in sentence 1: the major coordinate details are stated in sentences 2, 4, and 6; the more specific supporting details occur in sentences 3, 5, and 7; and sentence 8 briefly summarizes the paragraph. This paragraph pattern can be diagrammed as shown here:

| Topic sentence (sentence 1) |
| Coordinate detail (sentence 2) |
| Supporting detail (sentence 3) |
| Coordinate detail (sentence 4) |
| Supporting detail (sentence 5) |
| Coordinate detail (sentence 6) |
| Supporting detail (sentence 7) |
| Conclusion (sentence 8) |

A variation of this pattern is illustrated in the following paragraph, which also contains three major coordinate details. However, in this pattern, each coordinate detail is supported by not one but two specific details. As you read the paragraph, try to determine which sentences contain the major coordinate details and which contain the more specific supporting details.

[1]The older woman who returns to school faces a number of problems. [2]For one thing, upon enrolling in college, she immediately becomes a minority. [3]She is no longer surrounded by her peers—other women who have shared experiences—but by young people, many of whom are the ages of her own children. [4]Very often, the only person in a class who is her age is the instructor (and even he or she may be much younger). [5]In addition, an older woman who re-enters the academic world assumes the double burden of managing a household while being a student. [6]She may still have children at home or a husband who makes demands on her time. [7]If she is

divorced or widowed, she faces problems such as managing finances, maintaining a car, and mowing the lawn. [8]Finally, a woman middle-aged or older who decides to complete her education faces the challenge of developing a new image of herself—one that is not related to her roles as wife and mother. [9]This problem may prove to be the most difficult of all, for it is not easy to assume a new identity, especially if the former one has been comfortable and secure. [10]To make the transition from housewife to student, a woman must think of herself as an individual rather than as a person whose identity depends on her relationships to other people. [11]Although her maturity may well prove to be an asset as she continues her studies, the older coed initially finds herself in a challenging situation.

In this paragraph, the main idea is stated in sentence 1; the major co-ordinate details are stated in sentences 2, 5, and 8; more specific supporting details are stated in sentences 3 and 4, 6 and 7, and 9 and 10; and the concluding statement comes in sentence 11. This paragraph can be illustrated as shown here:

| Topic sentence (sentence 1) |
| Coordinate detail (sentence 2) |
| Specific detail (sentence 3) |
| Specific detail (sentence 4) |
| Coordinate detail (sentence 5) |
| Specific detail (sentence 6) |
| Specific detail (sentence 7) |
| Coordinate detail (sentence 8) |
| Specific detail (sentence 9) |
| Specific detail (sentence 10) |
| Conclusion (sentence 11) |

EXERCISE

4.4   Write a paragraph telling why you want a college degree. Structure your paragraph according to one of the patterns given for expanded coordinate details. Use two or three coordinate details, developing each with one or more specific details. Use the following block form, writing a different sentence in each block. (*Note:* You may not need to use all of the blocks.)

4.4 continued

(Topic sentence)

(Coordinate detail)

(Specific detail)

(Specific detail)

(Coordinate detail)

(Specific detail)

(Specific detail)

(Coordinate detail)

(Specific detail)

(Specific detail)

(Conclusion)

Using the Subordinate Pattern

To develop a topic sentence using the subordinate pattern, you must write a series of sentences that express increasingly specific details. In this pattern, each detail is more specific than and subordinate to the one before it.

> [1]Global warming is increasingly viewed as a very real threat rather than an academic theory or the ranting of alarmists. [2]Last summer most of the states in the United States experienced temperatures that were above normal. [3]The Southwest especially suffered from intense heat and drought most of the summer. [4]In Texas, for example, the temperature hovered around 110 degrees for weeks, and there was no rain for nearly two months. [5]As a result of these experiences, many people are now taking global warming seriously for the first time.

In this paragraph the main idea, which is stated in sentence 1, is a general statement about global warming. Sentence 2 is more specific, narrowing to the experience of the United States with global warming last summer. Sentence 3 is still more specific, focusing on the Southwest—a particular region of the United States. Finally, sentence 4 is limited to the effects in a single state. Sentence 5 concludes the paragraph by reinforcing the topic sentence. A diagram of this pattern is shown here:

| Topic sentence (sentence 1) |
| Specific detail (sentence 2) |
| More specific detail (sentence 3) |
| Most specific detail (sentence 4) |
| Conclusion (sentence 5) |

EXERCISE

4.5   Write a paragraph about some characteristic of your generation. Develop your paragraph with details that are increasingly specific. Use the following block form to write your rough draft, placing a different sentence in each block.

4.5 continued

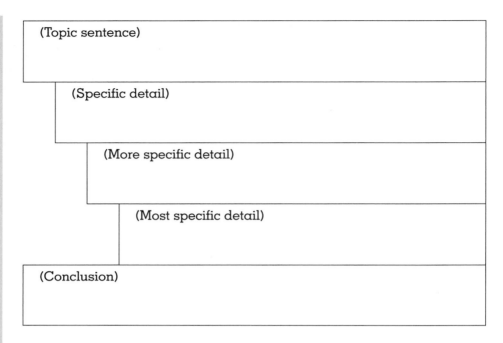

You will find these patterns helpful not only in structuring details but also in generating ideas—that is, in thinking of additional details. These patterns are therefore strategies for gathering as well as organizing information because they encourage you to write more detailed, better-developed paragraphs. These patterns can also be used when you write longer compositions

EXERCISE

4.6

To test your knowledge of the relationship between topic sentences and supporting details, read the following two paragraphs and answer the questions that follow each.

PARAGRAPH A

How do you write a rough draft? There is no simple way to do it; there are several approaches, including no doubt some which no one has tried yet. You will find some writers who say they begin by writing and rewriting their introduction until they get their thesis, purpose, and plan stated clearly and their relationship with their readers established. They believe that once they get the opening in reasonably good shape they can write the rest of the paper relatively easily. You will find other writers who state that they try to write the end of their paper first in the belief that it is easier to write the rest once they know the final idea they want to lead up to. You will find still others who say that they begin anywhere they can in the hope that once they start writing they can more easily pull their best ideas from the unconscious. They are all right—up to a point. Writers write rough drafts just about any way they can.

—Thomas E. Pearsall and Donald H. Cunningham.
The Fundamentals of Good Writing

1. What is the main idea of this paragraph?

    _____

    _____

2. In the following spaces, rewrite in your own words the major supporting ideas.

    a. _____

    _____

    b. _____

    _____

    c. _____

    _____

PARAGRAPH B

Against Britain's armies of well-trained regulars, the Patriots seemed ill-matched. For one thing, the soldiers of the Continental Army had little experience in military tactics and fighting in open battle. Their training had been limited largely to frontier warfare against the Indians and the French. Their officers, too, had little experience compared to British officers. What is more, the Continental Army was loosely organized. Patriots had joined up, not because they had been ordered to do so, but of their own free will. Such volunteers felt free to return to their homes whenever their short terms of service were finished. As a result, the leaders of the army could hardly tell from day to day how many troops were under their command. Also, the colonies had no real navy. Against the strongest navy in the world the Americans could send not one first-class fighting ship.

—Howard B. Wilder et al., *This Is America's Story*

1. What is the main idea of this paragraph?

    _____

    _____

4.6 continued

2. This paragraph includes both coordinate and more specific supporting details. How many major coordinate details does it include?

_____

3. What are the coordinate details?

_____

_____

_____

_____

4. What more specific details support the first coordinate detail?

_____

_____

_____

_____

5. What more specific details support the second coordinate detail?

_____

_____

_____

_____

Relevant and Irrelevant Details

In general, good writing is detailed writing. The more specific details you use to support your main ideas, the easier it will be for a reader to understand your paragraph. However, you should be sure that the details you include in a paragraph actually support the main idea of that paragraph.

Inexperienced writers often include details that do not clearly relate to the topic sentence they are trying to develop, as in the following paragraph:

[1]Two benefits of using a computer are its speed and accuracy. [2]A computer can perform repetitive functions with great accuracy. [3]For example, a robot can be used to perform a task on an assembly line. [4]A person might get tired of doing the same thing for eight hours a day, but a computer-driven robot never gets tired. [5]However, robots cannot solve problems the way humans can. [6]On the other hand, humans often miss work because of illness.

This paragraph has a number of specific details, but few of them directly support the topic sentence, sentence 1. The writer gets sidetracked and begins writing about robots versus humans, failing to address the issues of accuracy and speed on which the topic sentence focuses. The details correspond loosely to the topic stated in the topic sentence, but they do not clearly develop the assertion that the two main benefits of a computer are its speed and accuracy

In writing a paragraph, be sure that each detail you include directly supports—is relevant to—your topic sentence. Details that do not support the main idea will distract and confuse your readers. In contrast, a paragraph that includes details that clearly support the topic sentence is unified and communicates clearly. In order to check a paragraph for unity, you can turn the topic sentence into a question and then see if each detail answers this question. If a detail does not answer the topic sentence question, it is probably irrelevant—off the subject—and should be omitted. For example, if you turn the topic sentence of the paragraph about computers into a question (*How are a computer's speed and accuracy beneficial?*), you can see that sentences 3, 4, 5, and 6 are irrelevant.

EXERCISE

4.7 The following paragraphs are not unified because each includes a sentence that does not develop the topic sentence. In each paragraph, determine which sentence should be omitted by turning the topic sentence into a question and then seeing if the other sentences answer this question. Underline the sentence that is irrelevant.

PARAGRAPH A

Students need to know the process for appealing a grade. This process usually begins with a conference with the teacher who gave the grade that is being appealed. Often this conference can resolve the problem. If so, the process is over. However, if a student still wants to appeal his or her grade after talking with the teacher, making an appointment with the department chair or program director should be the next step. Department chairs are often busy people with very little time to spare. When the student meets with the chair, the chair may make a decision about the grade that is acceptable to the student or may convince the student that the grade in question is appropriate. However, if the student is not satisfied with the outcome of this meeting, he or she may appeal to the dean or the academic vice president. At this point, the appeal is usually made in writing and may or may not include a conference.

4.7 continued

PARAGRAPH B

The term *rhetoric* has several different meanings. In the ancient Greek and Roman civilizations, rhetoric was the main discipline studied in school. Being able to construct effective arguments and deliver clear, convincing speeches was considered a valuable skill. Only males were given an education in these societies. Rhetoric was understood to be the study and practice of effective discourse. Today, however, the term *rhetoric* is often applied to highly emotional discourse, both oral and written. It is even used to describe discourse that is considered dishonest or to mean effective but empty and bombastic speaking and writing.

Chapter Review

- Topic sentences should be supported and developed by specific details.
- Details may be factual or sensory.
- Coordinate and subordinate patterns are useful ways of structuring supporting details.
- Supporting details must be directly relevant to the topic sentence if the paragraph is to be unified.

◼ Writing Assignment

Write a unified paragraph on a topic that interests you. Decide in advance whether you will use a coordinate or subordinate pattern for your paragraph, and be sure to include both factual and sensory details.

◼ Participating in the Academic Community

Working with a partner or peer group, evaluate the paragraphs you have written. Is the topic sentence clear and well supported by specific details? To determine if the paragraph is unified, turn the topic sentence into a question and then read each sentence aloud to be sure it answers that question.

Use the suggestions you receive from your classmates to revise your paragraph.

Chapter 5

Moving from Paragraph to Essay

As a college student, you are frequently required to read and write compositions longer than a paragraph, such as reports and essays. Because the basic structure of reports and essays is very similar to that of paragraphs, your knowledge of paragraph structure will be very helpful to you as you begin to work with these longer compositions.

This chapter focuses on the **essay** because it can serve as a pattern for all types of discourse. As a college student, you will be asked to write various types of reports, book reviews, case studies, essay exams, and research papers. Although each of these different types of academic discourse has its own distinguishing characteristics, especially in terms of format, all are related to the essay. An essay is, very simply, the elaboration of a single idea. Other types of academic discourse may not look like an essay, but they nearly all consist of a central idea that is developed and supported by the writer's arguments and evidence just as an essay is. If you can write a well-constructed, well-developed essay, you can write almost any type of academic discourse.

Most essays, like most paragraphs, consist of an introduction, a body, and a conclusion. However, whereas a paragraph consists of a series of related sentences, an essay is composed of a series of related paragraphs. A good essay is composed of well-developed paragraphs that develop the main idea, or thesis, of the essay.

Many readers and writers make the mistake of ignoring the structure of the paragraph once it is part of an essay. Although the paragraphs that make up the body of an essay may not be able to stand alone as compositions, they often have essentially the same structure as paragraphs that are meant to stand on their own. Therefore, as you read and write essays, you will continue to use your knowledge of paragraphs.

The essay illustrated in the following diagram consists of five paragraphs: an introductory paragraph, three body paragraphs, and a concluding paragraph. Of course, the number of paragraphs varies widely from one essay to another. Some essays are very brief; others are quite long. But the five-paragraph essay serves as a convenient model.

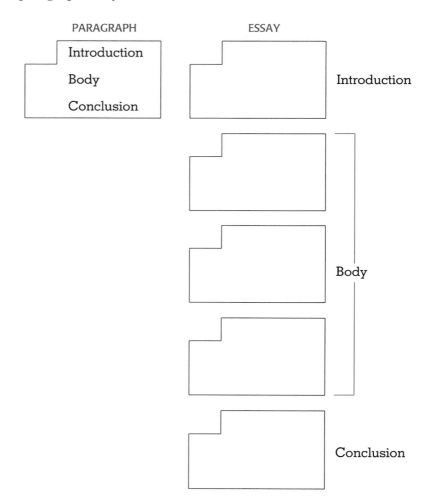

Introduction: Stating the Thesis

Essays, like paragraphs, develop one main idea. The main idea of an essay is called a **thesis statement,** and it is usually expressed at the end of the introduction. Like the main idea of a paragraph, a thesis is a general statement. It is usually more general than the topic sentence of a paragraph but not as general as the thesis of a book.

TOPIC SENTENCE OF A PARAGRAPH

My sixth-grade teacher was a strict disciplinarian.

THESIS OF AN ESSAY

Discipline problems created a poor environment for learning in my high school.

THESIS OF A BOOK

One of the major problems with the U.S. system of education is its failure to deal effectively with discipline problems.

Notice that the topic sentence of the paragraph is limited to a particular person (sixth-grade teacher) and to a specific aspect of that person (role as disciplinarian). The paragraph that develops this topic sentence will not merely describe the sixth-grade teacher but will focus on how he disciplined the class. In contrast, the thesis of the essay is broad enough to include a discussion of several problems that contributed to a lack of discipline in the high school, but it is limited to a particular high school at a particular time and to the experience of one person. The essay that develops this thesis will not discuss every aspect of the writer's high school experience—just the problems associated with discipline in the school. The thesis of a book, however, is much broader, allowing for a complex, complete discussion of how a lack of discipline affects the entire school system of the United States.

A very broad, vague, overly general statement is inappropriate as the thesis of an essay. In fact, many times, the same idea that served as the topic sentence of a paragraph can be used effectively as the thesis of an essay. If you narrow your main idea so that your focus is fairly limited, you will have less difficulty writing your essay and will write a better essay.

Writers usually place their thesis at the end of their introduction because this is where readers expect to find it. The introduction of an essay may consist of a single paragraph or of several paragraphs, depending on the length of the essay. Whatever its length, the introduction usually concludes with a statement of the writer's main idea.

Writing Introductions

An introduction serves as a contract between a writer and his or her readers. In the introduction, a writer makes specific commitments that must then be fulfilled. The most important of these is the thesis statement, which commits the writer to a specific focus. In effect, it provides the reader with an accurate expectation of what the writer plans to do—the main idea that the writer plans to develop.

In general, a good introduction accomplishes three purposes:

1. It attracts the reader's interest.
2. It provides the reader with background information.
3. It focuses the reader's attention on the main idea of the essay.

The following paragraph could serve as an introduction to an essay on the discipline problems that affected one person's high school education:

> From 1982 to 1986, I attended an inner-city high school in Chicago. The school was located in an area that was rapidly changing from residential to commercial. It was an old, respected school that had educated the children of the families in the neighborhood for over fifty years. Many of the teachers were dedicated, competent professionals who had taught in this school all of their professional lives. Others were inexperienced, young teachers who were encountering their first students. However, neither the experienced nor the inexperienced teachers were able to handle the undisciplined, unmotivated students who attended the school in the 1980s. As a result, discipline problems created a poor environment for learning in the high school.

Notice that the writer devotes several sentences to background information, supplying the reader with a context for what is to follow. The sentence about the problems the teachers had in controlling the students serves as a transition, focusing the reader's attention on the thesis statement that follows. The writer and the reader are now ready to explore this thesis statement in the body of the essay.

As a writer, you want your introduction to be not only clear but also interesting. A dull or trite introduction can discourage a reader from continuing to the main part of the essay. Beware, however, of attempts at cuteness and cleverness; they often fail, resulting in an introduction that is not only unclear but also embarrassingly inappropriate.

SUGGESTIONS FOR WRITING EFFECTIVE INTRODUCTIONS

- Be clear and direct. (Clarity is more important than cleverness.)
- Provide the background information your reader needs to understand your subject.
- Avoid trite expressions, such as *in the world today* or *for as long as man has existed.*
- End your introduction with a clear statement of your thesis.

EXERCISE

5.1

Revise the following sentences so that they are strong, effective thesis statements. Also, narrow each thesis statement so that it can be developed adequately in a brief essay.

1. Some students prefer a different grading system.

   _____

   _____

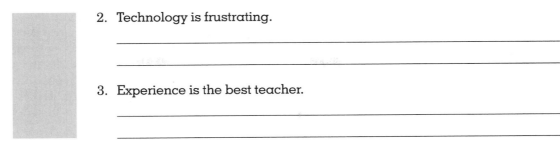

2. Technology is frustrating.

_____

_____

3. Experience is the best teacher.

_____

_____

Body: Developing the Thesis

The body of a unified, coherent essay consists of a number of related paragraphs that develop the thesis. The individual sentences within each paragraph support the main idea (topic sentence) of the paragraph, and the paragraphs support the main idea (thesis) of the essay, as shown in the following diagram:

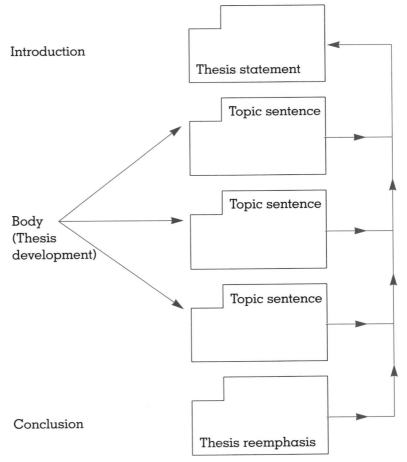

A writer develops the topic sentence of a paragraph by discussing, explaining, and expanding the idea that it expresses. A writer develops the thesis of an essay in the same way. Both topic sentences and thesis statements are general statements that must be supported by specific facts, details, and examples. In an essay, a writer usually devotes a paragraph to each major supporting point. Each of these supporting points is directly related to the thesis and helps develop it. But each major supporting point is also developed individually as a paragraph.

Writing Body Paragraphs

The paragraphs you write in the body of your essay should be well structured and well developed. Most, if not all, of these paragraphs should begin with a topic sentence, which is then supported and developed by five to eight sentences. These sentences should be less general (more specific) than the topic sentence but should all relate directly to the topic sentence.

The primary difference between an independent paragraph and one that is in the body of an essay is that body paragraphs require conclusions less often. Whereas you will frequently include a concluding sentence if you are writing an independent paragraph, you will seldom need to include one in the body paragraph of an essay. If you do include a conclusion in a body paragraph, it should function primarily as a transition to the next paragraph.

Remember that all paragraphs need not only a main idea but also lots of supporting details. These details can be arranged in a variety of ways—in order of importance, in chronological order, and so on. Remember also the patterns of subordination and coordination that you learned in Chapter 4. These patterns are very useful in structuring body paragraphs in an essay. You may also want to consult the chapters in Part Two (Chapters 9 through 17) for additional patterns of development that can be used for body paragraphs.

SUGGESTIONS FOR WRITING EFFECTIVE BODY PARAGRAPHS

- Keep your thesis in mind at all times; each paragraph in the body of your essay should support and develop your thesis.
- Structure each paragraph so that it has a topic sentence (stated or implied) that is fully developed by supporting details.
- Avoid paragraphs of only one or two sentences. (Such paragraphs are usually underdeveloped or unnecessary.)
- Vary the structure of the paragraphs in the body of your essay so that the topic sentence is not always the first sentence.
- Vary the number of paragraphs in your essays. (Every essay does not have to have exactly five paragraphs.)

Conclusion: Reemphasizing the Thesis

The conclusion of an essay, like the conclusion of a paragraph, gives the reader a sense of completion. Conclusions usually refer to the introduction or at least reemphasize in some way the thesis stated in the introduction. Often the conclusion briefly summarizes the thesis and the major supporting points. A good conclusion always confirms the audience's understanding of what they have read by reminding them of the writer's purpose. Like an introduction, a conclusion often provides readers with an overview. The following paragraph would effectively conclude the essay on discipline problems in the Chicago high school:

> Recently I visited my parents in Chicago and drove past my old high school. Now a warehouse for textbooks, the building looks abandoned and dilapidated. Crude, obscene messages remain scrawled on the walls, and many of the windows are broken or missing. Evidently, the discipline problems finally defeated the valiant but discouraged teachers. I am glad the school is now closed, for learning had become impossible in that environment.

Conclusions should not be cute or trite or obvious. The best conclusions are appropriate, clearly written, and straightforward. They do not strain for an effect they cannot achieve (such as humor, cleverness, or brilliance). If you have not written a good essay, your conclusion cannot save it; however, a good essay can be damaged by an ineffective or inappropriate conclusion.

Writing Conclusions

Just as an introduction can be viewed as a contract between you and your reader, a conclusion reassures your reader that you have fulfilled your contract. Your closing paragraph should leave your reader with a sense of completion—with the feeling that you have done what you intended to do and have finished what you had to say. Several types of conclusions accomplish this purpose:

1. *Restatement of main idea.* You may choose to reemphasize or reinforce the main idea in your conclusion. If you choose this type of conclusion, however, be sure not to merely repeat your thesis. You should vary the wording so that your conclusion is not too similar to your introduction, and you should also try to get beyond your thesis statement—to express an appropriate conclusion and to give your reader a sense of closure.

2. *General impression.* If your essay is basically a description of an experience or of a person, place, or thing, an effective conclusion might consist of a statement of the dominant impression you have attempted to convey. For example, if your essay about your high school is largely a description of what occurred to you when you were there, you might conclude with what you remember most clearly about the whole experience.

3. *Evaluation.* An essay may also conclude with a judgment based on the information presented. For example, you might end an essay on your high school by evaluating whether the experience was essentially negative or positive.

4. *Recommendation.* An essay can be concluded with a suggestion for some action the writer feels should be taken. This type of conclusion is especially appropriate if the main idea is a controversial statement or one that is persuasive in nature. For example, you might conclude your essay about your high school's discipline problems by recommending that a new administration be hired or a new school board be elected.

5. *Prediction.* Even though a conclusion is the final part of an essay, it can be used to make a prediction on the basis of the major points made in the essay. This prediction should be closely related to the content of the essay, giving a reasonable explanation of what may happen. For example, you might predict in the conclusion to your essay about your high school's problems that the school will be closed in the near future.

6. *Implications.* In a conclusion you can discuss the implications of the arguments and evidence you have presented. In other words, you can explain why what you've written is important.

Regardless of the type of conclusion you choose for your essay, the conclusion should be a clear signal to your reader that you have completed what you had to say. Following are some suggestions that will be helpful to you in writing conclusions.

SUGGESTIONS FOR WRITING EFFECTIVE CONCLUSIONS
- Do not contradict the point you have made.
- Do not introduce a new topic or new information.
- Do not conclude with a cliché (such as *You can't teach an old dog new tricks*).
- Do not apologize for lack of knowledge, ability, or resources.
- Do not use obvious transition words or phases such as *in conclusion*, *in summary*, and *as I have attempted to show.* You may, however, use less obvious transition words, such as *therefore*, *finally*, and *consequently*.

■ Do make your conclusion brief and to the point.

■ Do make the tone (serious, humorous, clever, straightforward, and so on) consistent with the overall tone of your essay.

From Paragraph to Essay

Read the following paragraph, which focuses on a common myth about college students. Note especially the topic sentence and the major supporting points.

> Although most people think the college years are carefree and irresponsible, many college students are depressed, overwhelmed, and in debt. Separation from friends and family may cause severe depression in some students; others may suffer depression because they have reached a time in their lives when, for the first time, they feel they must solve their own problems and make their own decisions. Others are simply overwhelmed by new pressures on their time and tougher competition in their courses. And, increasingly, college students are in debt—sometimes seriously in debt. The happy-go-lucky college student is all too often simply a myth.

EXERCISE

5.2   Answer the following questions about the paragraph you have just read.

1. What is the main idea of the paragraph?

   _____

   _____

2. Is the main idea expressed in a topic sentence? _____

3. Underline the topic sentence.

4. What are the major supporting points developed in the paragraph?

   a. _____

   b. _____

   c. _____

Now read the following essay, which has the same main idea as the paragraph you have just read. As you read, notice that the main difference

5.2 continued

between the paragraph and the essay is that the writer uses different paragraphs for each of the three major supporting points in the essay and that she uses many more details and examples to support each major point.

¹College students are often stereotyped as irresponsible, carefree, happy-go-lucky young people who are still supported by their families. It is commonly thought that their parents pay most of their bills; their teachers provide them with interesting, stimulating lectures; and student-life organizations or social clubs arrange for them to have active, exciting social lives. But this pretty picture often conflicts with the real situation in which most college students find themselves. For many students, their college years are not filled with checks from home, supportive professors, and endless parties. In reality, many college students are depressed, overwhelmed, and in debt.

²Depression is as common among college students as it is among the general population. Antidepressants, such as Prozac and Zolaf, are routinely prescribed by college medical personnel in an effort to deal with the large numbers of students who suffer from depression. Some students experience only mild depression as a result of being away from home for the first time, but others suffer from severe, debilitating forms of depression. Although depression is often genetic in origin, it can also be situational. And the situation in which college students often find themselves—on their own without familiar support systems and facing much tougher academic competition than they are accustomed to—can easily lead to depression.

³Nearly all college students feel overwhelmed at one time or another, but many of them experience this feeling all the time. They may feel overwhelmed because they are trying to work and go to school; because their courses are demanding; or because they are trying to pay their own bills, do their own laundry, and manage their own lives for the first time. Or they may even be overwhelmed by the number and variety of social activities from which they may choose. This sense of being overwhelmed creates a lot of anxiety and stress. Rather than setting priorities or getting help from a counselor, a student may simply become too overwhelmed to function effectively. In fact, the stress caused by having too much to do often leads students to give up and drop out of school.

⁴Perhaps the most serious problem facing many college students today is the amount of debt they have incurred. For a long time, students have gone into debt to finance their education by taking out

government-financed student loans. These loans can add up to a significant amount over the four or five years that most people spend in college. However, many students today are not only going into debt as a result of student loans but also running up enormous credit card debts. Whereas student loans usually have relatively low interest rates and many lenders allow them to defer repayment until they have finished their degree, credit card companies charge very high interest rates and insist on monthly payments from the time the debt is incurred. Many students attempt to avoid going too deeply in debt by working while they are in school. In fact, some students hold two or more jobs. Unfortunately, even if they do manage to hold down their debts, these students often drop out of school because they are overwhelmed by having too much to do.

[5]Being a college student may be a wonderful experience for a minority of privileged young people who have strong academic backgrounds and parents who are able and willing to pay their bills. But for most people it is a struggle. After years of dealing with depression, stress, and indebtedness, most students understand the real cost of an education.

EXERCISE

5.3

Answer the following questions about the essay you have just read.

1. What is the main idea of the essay?

   _____

   _____

2. Is the main idea expressed in a thesis statement? _____

3. If the main idea is expressed in a thesis statement, underline it.

4. What are the major supporting points developed in the essay?

   a. _____

   b. _____

   c. _____

5. Does each of these major supporting points serve as a topic sentence of a paragraph? _____

5.3 continued

6. Underline each of the topic sentences.

7. Compare these topic sentences with the three major supporting points of the original paragraph. Are they the same? _____

8. List several details the writer uses in the essay but not in the paragraph.

a. _____

b. _____

c. _____

Chapter Review

- A good essay is composed of well-developed paragraphs that, in turn, develop the main idea of the essay.

- A good essay consists of three major parts: introduction, body, and conclusion.

- The introduction of an essay usually concludes with the thesis statement.

- The body of a unified, coherent essay consists of a number of related paragraphs that develop the thesis.

- The conclusion of an essay, like that of a paragraph, gives the reader a sense of completion, usually reemphasizing in some way the thesis stated in the introduction.

Writing Assignment

Write a paragraph about a topic that interests you. Then expand the paragraph into a fully developed essay, restructuring and adding details as needed.

Participating in the Academic Community

Meet with a group of your classmates to read and evaluate your essays. Identify the thesis statement and major supporting points in each essay.

Chapter 6

Achieving Coherence

For a train to run smoothly on a railroad track, its cars must be securely balanced and carefully linked so that the entire machine runs evenly and efficiently. Similarly, for your writing to communicate clearly to your audience, your sentences and paragraphs must be smoothly linked so that they cohere, or hold together. That is, your ideas must be logically arranged and connected so that your audience understands why they occur as they do. A paragraph or an essay is coherent if the different ideas in it function as a unit, or as a unified whole, and not as a series of individual, unconnected sentences or paragraphs. In this chapter, you will learn more about **coherence**—about how ideas relate to one another and about the transitions that writers use to communicate these relationships to their readers.

Arranging Ideas

One of the primary ways that writers achieve coherence is by using logical patterns of **arrangement** that are familiar to their readers. As discussed in Chapters 3 and 4, the most common pattern is simply from general to specific, in which a writer begins with a general idea and then supports this idea with specific details. But additional patterns are often needed. Three of the most frequently used patterns are **time order, space order,** and **order of importance.** As you read this chapter, you will find that you are actually already familiar with these patterns, but the following explanations and exercises will help you see how writers use them to communicate effectively.

Time Order

Most narratives (compositions that tell a story, relate a series of events, or describe a process) are arranged in chronological order; that is, they are arranged in the order in which the events of the narrative occurred. Compositions arranged in chronological order often include references to the time of day, day of the week, or specific dates. Or they include transition words such as *first, then, next,* and *last* to indicate the passage of time. As you read the following paragraph, notice not only the time order in which the events are arranged but also how the bolded words and phrases make this order clear to the reader:

> [1]The **beginning** of each school term marks a period of rebirth for college campuses. [2]**Before the term begins**, the campus is strangely vacant and quiet. [3]**Then** students begin to move into the dorms, carrying suitcases, trunks, and boxes from their cars to their assigned rooms. [4]Shouts of laughter, yells of greeting, and squeals of excitement ring across the campus as students resume their interrupted relationships and establish new ones. [5]**Meanwhile,** maintenance crews move busily around the campus trimming, repairing, painting, and generally refurbishing the campus and buildings. [6]**A few days later,** teachers arrive, coming to their offices to plan for their classes, going to the library to complete a last bit of research, exchanging stories with colleagues. [7]**Finally, on the day classes begin,** commuting students flood the campus, fighting for parking spaces, joining resident students as they scurry to classes, and generally adding to the growing sense of confused activity. [8]**A new semester has begun,** and the campus is alive **once more.**

Clearly, this paragraph begins with events that occur before the new semester starts and ends with the actual beginning of the semester, moving in time order from first to last.

EXERCISE

6.1

Each of the following groups of sentences may be rearranged in a logical paragraph based on time order. Study each group of sentences, looking for the logical time sequence and for transition clues. Then number the sentences in what you believe is the best order. (The topic sentence, or the first sentence in the paragraph, has been identified for you.)

PARAGRAPH A

TS: ___*1*___ I was impressed by a television commercial I saw when I was little.

_____ The camera then moved slowly up the Native American's body, showing his clothes and markings.

_____ In the beginning of this commercial, the camera was focused on pieces of trash lying on the roadside—cans, bottles, candy wrappers, and cigarette butts.

_____ Then, the camera completed its journey, showing the pain and disturbance clearly visible in his face.

_____ With a pause after each item of trash, the camera slowly moved to a pair of moccasin-covered feet.

_____ When the camera reached the lower part of his face, I noticed the drops of tears rolling down his fleshy, strong cheeks.

_____ The Native American's tears were falling because of the contamination of the land.

—Dave McNish, student (adapted)

PARAGRAPH B

TS: __1__ Motion pictures became another form of entertainment for the American people.

_____ A second landmark was in 1927, when Al Jolson's *The Jazz Singer* successfully introduced motion pictures with sound.

_____ The widespread popularity of television after World War II reduced the number of moviegoers.

_____ Pioneered in America by Thomas Edison, the earliest motion pictures were different from those we see today.

_____ However, through the years to the present, "going to the movies" has continued to be the favorite recreation of millions of Americans.

_____ Then, during the 1930s, pictures in color added to the enjoyment of moviegoers.

_____ In the thirties and forties, as many as 100 million people went to the movies each week.

_____ In 1915, the success of *Birth of a Nation* (which has recently been criticized for its racism) encouraged the building of silent-movie theaters in cities and towns throughout the country.

—Adapted from Howard B. Wilder et al., *This Is America's Story*

EXERCISE

6.2

Write a paragraph in which you narrate your typical morning or evening routine. Use time order to arrange your details.

Space Order

Many compositions, especially those that describe places or people, are arranged in space order; that is, the objects or details are arranged in the order in which they are observed in space. In a description of a room, for example, the writer may describe objects from left to right, from floor to ceiling, or from the outside walls to the center of the room. In describing a landscape scene, the writer could move visually from far to near or from near to far. Compositions arranged in space order often include references to directions, such as *right, left, up, down, east, west, under, over, beyond, in front of, behind,* and so on. The following paragraph illustrates space order. As you read this paragraph, pay particular attention to the order in which the author describes the spatial view. The bold words and phrases indicate this order.

> [1] The view **from the front door** was breathtaking. [2] Immediately **in front of** the house, **to the west,** was a small dirt road, and **beyond this road** the land dropped sharply so that the entire valley was visible. [3] This broad valley was cut **down the center** by the Snake River, a curving blue-white scar **across the pale green sage brush** that covered most of the valley. [4] **On the far side of the valley,** sandstone cliffs rose abruptly from the gently rolling valley floor. [5] **Rising above the cliffs** were the **distant mountains,** majestic peaks crowned with snow and ice.

As shown by the transition words indicating space order, this paragraph is arranged from near to far.

EXERCISE

6.3

Each of the following groups of sentences may be rearranged in a logical paragraph based on space order. Study each group of sentences, looking for the logical spatial sequence and for transition clues. More than one arrangement may be possible for the sentences in each group, but in Paragraph A the best order is from the house outward, and in Paragraph B the best arrangement is from bottom to top. Number the sentences in the clearest, most logical order. (The topic sentence, or the first sentence in the paragraph, has been identified for you.)

PARAGRAPH A

TS: __/__ Skillful landscaping distinguishes the professor's white stucco house.

_____ A low trellis separates these flowers from the evenly manicured lawn, which is broken only by a circular planter.

_____ In front of the brick wall of the courtyard is a carefully shaped box hedge.

_____ This circular planter is filled with more geraniums and centered with a fountain.

_____ At the edge of the street, this lawn drops sharply three feet to a street-level sidewalk.

_____ Directly in front of the house is a small brick courtyard in which cacti and yucca plants have been attractively arranged.

_____ Next to this hedge grow rows of brightly colored flowers—red geraniums and white periwinkles.

PARAGRAPH B

TS: __/__ College Hall was one of the oldest and most used buildings on campus.

_____ The maps that covered the dusty chalkboards of classrooms on that floor reflected the history courses that occupied them.

_____ Above, on the second floor, was the English Department, one of the largest departments on campus.

_____ The third floor of the building housed the overflow from the English Department plus the Sociology Department.

_____ On the first floor, the History Department coexisted peacefully with the Dean's office.

_____ On this top floor were also most of the classrooms used by the English and Sociology Departments.

_____ Two programs related to the English Department, the computer lab and writing center, were also on this floor.

EXERCISE

6.4 Write a paragraph in which you describe a room or building that you see daily. Use space order to arrange the details of the place you are describing.

Order of Importance

The details in a composition may also be arranged according to their order of importance. Writers may begin with the most important supporting point and end with the least important. Or they may begin with the least important and end with the most important, which allows them to build to a high point, or climax. In either arrangement, writers may help their readers by emphasizing the major points with transition words such as *first*, *second*, and *finally* or with transition phrases such as *more important* and *most important*. As you read the following paragraph, notice not only the transition words that are in bold type but also how the details are arranged to indicate their relative importance to the writer:

> [1] Several considerations should influence your choice of a career. [2] **First,** you should choose a career that will provide the lifestyle you want. [3] If living in an expensive house and driving a big car are your goals, you should not decide to be a schoolteacher or a paramedic. [4] Although it is possible to make a good living in these professions, most teachers and paramedics make rather modest salaries, especially at the beginning of their careers. [5] **Second, and more important,** you should choose a career for which you have an aptitude. [6] Even though you may love art, if you have no talent as an artist, you will not be successful. [7] **Finally, and most important,** you should choose a career you will enjoy. [8] Deciding to be a mechanic because you are good at repairing cars is not wise if you do not find car maintenance interesting or enjoyable. [9] Becoming a lawyer is a mistake if you do not enjoy writing briefs or researching legal issues. [10] You will spend countless hours working at whatever career you choose. [11] Those hours will be more rewarding and less tiring if they are spent in work you enjoy.

To emphasize the writer's most important point, the reasons in this paragraph are arranged from least important to most important.

EXERCISE

6.5

Each of the following groups of sentences may be rearranged in a logical paragraph based on the order of importance. Study each group of sentences, looking for the most logical order and for transition clues that indicate that order. Number the sentences in the clearest chronological order. (The topic sentence, or the first sentence in the paragraph, has been identified for you.)

PARAGRAPH A

TS: ___*1*___ During the Middle Ages, England had a very strict class structure based on the manor, a self-supporting landed estate.

_____ Above the serf and below the lords was a large group of freemen, including tenants, shop owners, craftsmen, clergymen, soldiers, and lesser nobles.

_____ Finally, at the very top of the class structure was the king, to whom the nobleman owed his allegiance.

_____ The least important member of the class system was the serf, a servant who was bound to the soil of the manor and to the nobleman who owned it.

_____ Near the top of the hierarchy was the lord who owned the estate.

PARAGRAPH B

TS: ___*1*___ All organisms can be classified on the basis of their specializations into more or less well-defined categories.

_____ Within a phylum, the next highest rank is the class.

_____ Within the living world as a whole, the highest taxonomic rank usually recognized is the kingdom.

_____ Using criteria of likenesses and differences among and within groups, one may recognize orders within a class, families within an order, genera within a family, and species within a genus.

_____ The species normally is the lowest unit.

_____ The next highest rank within the kingdom is the division, or the phylum.

—Adapted from Paul Weisz, *The Science of Biology*

EXERCISE

6.6   Write a paragraph in which you list and briefly describe three to five tasks that you need to complete. Arrange these tasks according to their order of importance.

The methods of arranging ideas discussed in this chapter—time order, space order, and order of importance—are also closely related to the various methods of development discussed in Part Two. For example, space order is an ideal method of arrangement for descriptive paragraphs and essays, time order is the logical way to arrange events in a narrative or a process, and order of importance is an effective way to arrange a paper developed by examples.

Connecting Ideas

Logical arrangement of ideas is one important way of achieving coherence in your writing. Readers and writers generally agree that certain arrangements, or patterns, are logical. For example, it is logical to discuss how to dress for an interview before discussing what to say (time order), to describe the front of a house before describing the rear of the house (space order), and to consider the most important reason for choosing to attend a certain college after you have considered the less important reasons (order of importance). But readers often need help to see your logic as a writer. Even though you arrange your ideas in a familiar, logical pattern, a reader may not perceive the pattern or the logic. Thus, a second important method of achieving coherence is to use various types of transition to connect your ideas clearly and logically.

Transition can be defined as the clues, or signals, a writer provides to help a reader see the connections between ideas. That is, transition is the oil that greases the wheels of your writing. If the connections between your ideas are quite clear, transitions are less necessary; if these connections are less obvious, clear transitions become essential. Good writers are sensitive to the needs of their readers and give them as much assistance as possible.

The three basic methods of connecting ideas, or providing transition, are (1) **repetition of key words and ideas,** (2) **repetition of structure,** and (3) use of **transition words and phrases** to indicate the appropriate relationships.

Repetition of Key Words and Ideas

One of the most common means of providing transition is to repeat key words and ideas. This repetition reinforces the main idea and connects supporting details to the main idea and to one another. In writing, you may reinforce, clarify, or elaborate a key word or idea by (1) repeating the same word, (2) using a more specific word or phrase for the same idea, (3) using a word or phrase with a similar meaning (a synonym), or (4) substituting a pronoun. Here are examples of each of these types of repetition:

1. *Repetition of exact word:* The *sea* can be beautiful, but the *sea* can also be dangerous.
2. *Repetition through more specific words:* In literature, *birds* often appear as symbols. For example, the *robin* may symbolize hope and the *raven* death.
3. *Repetition through synonyms:* The candidate made an *attempt* to convince voters, but his *try* was unsuccessful.
4. *Repetition through pronouns:* The *professor* started her lecture on the Constitution, but *she* was unable to finish it before the bell rang.

Much of the coherence of the following paragraph comes from the effective use of various types of repetition to reinforce the main topic, *dangerous chemicals*. Key words and phrases that repeat or reinforce this topic have been highlighted for you. In addition, marginal notes indicate how the author has used repetition to make the paragraph cohere, or "stick together."

Topic sentence	¹For the first time in the history of the world, every human being is
Key phrase	now subjected to contact with dangerous chemicals from the moment
Repetition through pronoun	of conception until death. ²In the less than two decades of their
Repetition through synonym	use, the synthetic pesticides have been so thoroughly distributed
	throughout the animate and inanimate world that they occur
Repetition through pronouns	virtually everywhere. ³They have been recovered from most of the
Repetition through more specific phrase	major river systems and even from streams of groundwater flowing
	unseen through the earth. ⁴Residues of these chemicals linger
Repetition through pronouns	in soil to which they may have been applied a dozen years before.
	⁵They have entered and lodged in the bodies of fish, birds,
	reptiles, and domestic and wild animals so universally that
	scientists carrying on animal experiments find it almost
Repetition through related word (synonym)	impossible to locate subjects free from such contamination.
Repetition through pronoun	⁶They have been found in fish in remote mountain lakes, in
	earthworms burrowing in soil, in the eggs of birds—and in man
Repetition through exact word	himself. ⁷For these chemicals are now stored in the bodies of the
	vast majority of human beings, regardless of age. ⁸They occur
Repetition through pronoun	in the mother's milk, and probably in the tissues of the unborn
	child.

—Rachel Carson, *Silent Spring*

As you read the preceding paragraph, did you notice that the writer reinforced the key words *dangerous chemicals* with all four types of repetition of key words and ideas? If she had used only one type of repetition—through exact words or through pronouns, for example—the paragraph would be repetitious and dull. To see how different the effect would have been, reread the paragraph and substitute the exact word *chemicals* for each boxed word. You will discover that it is not just repetition but repetition with variation that provides the most effective transition.

6.7   The coherence of the following paragraph comes primarily from the effective use of repetition. Study the paragraph and underline all the words and phrases that refer to the subject *language*.

> Americans speak many languages. There is English, our mother tongue and the official language of the United States, which most of us speak more or less well. But there are other languages that many of us also speak. Spanish, Chinese, and Japanese, for example, are increasingly spoken in this country. In addition, there are different dialects spoken in the major geographical regions of the country. Southern English is not the same language as the Northeastern and Midwestern varieties of English. And Cajun English differs from every other language spoken in this country. Then there are the jargons that characterize different language communities. For example, lawyers speak their own version of English, whereas teen-agers, truck drivers, and musicians speak still others. Thus, our official language has many variations.

Repetition of Structure

Repetition of structure can also improve transition and coherence. When writers present information in obviously similar, or parallel, structures, they help their readers focus on their ideas and on the relationships among those ideas. In contrast, when writers present related details and ideas in forms that have different, or nonparallel, structures, the awkward presentation of those ideas may keep readers from understanding them. For example, which of the following sentences is easier to read and understand?

1. A successful pilot must have education, experience, and is courageous.
2. A successful pilot must have education, experience, and courage.

Do you agree that the second sentence is clearer? The first sentence is awkward because the writer has not used parallel forms in a situation in which the reader expects similar forms or structures to be repeated. In contrast to the first sentence, which shifts from noun forms (*education* and *experience*) to an adjective (*courageous*), the second sentence clearly emphasizes three necessary attributes of a pilot by repeating them in parallel noun forms.

As a writer, you can add coherence by repeating parallel (1) word forms, (2) phrases, (3) clauses, and (4) sentences. As a reader, you can use such repetition of structure to help you identify important supporting details and their relationships to one another. Following are examples of the four major types of structural repetition:

1. *Repetition of word form:* The coach *fired* the punter, *traded* a running back, and *hired* a new wide receiver.　(repetition of verbs of similar structure)

2. *Repetition of phrases:* The child looked everywhere for the missing ball—*in the closet, behind the door,* and *under the bed.*　(repetition of phrases of similar structure)

3. *Repetition of clauses:* It was obvious *that I had failed* and *that she had succeeded.*　(repetition of clauses of similar structure)

4. *Repetition of sentences: I was tired I was hungry. I was lost.* And, suddenly, *I was afraid.*　(repetition of sentences of similar structure)

Now read aloud the following paragraph. As you read, notice how the writer repeats similar structures to make his paragraph more coherent, more readable, and more rhythmic. As you read the paragraph, notice especially the repetition of the word *it* and the repeated structure of *it* plus a verb, which occurs throughout the paragraph. The repeated, parallel structures have been underlined and noted for you in the margins.

Repetition of phrases
　from dawn
　to dusk
　to dawn

Repetition of sentences
　It trembles
　It moves
　It is

Repetition of *who*
clauses
　who gaze
　who jump
　who lumbers
　who cross
　. . . smash,
　. . . shortchange,
　. . . get jammed up

[1]In New York from dawn to dusk to dawn, day after day, you can hear the steady rumble of tires against the concrete span of the George Washington Bridge. [2]The Bridge is never completely still. [3]It trembles with traffic. [4]It moves in the wind. [5]Its great veins of steel swell when hot and contract when cold; its span often is ten feet closer to the Hudson River in summer than in winter. [6]It is an almost restless structure of graceful beauty which, like an irresistible seductress, withholds secrets from the romantics who gaze upon it, the escapists who jump off it, the chubby girl who lumbers across its 3,500-foot span trying to reduce, and the 100,000 motorists who each day cross it, smash into it, shortchange it, get jammed up on it.

—Gay Talese, "New York"

By repeating the same structures, the writer is able to emphasize the various activities of the different people who use the bridge. Indeed, his repetition of structure creates a rhythm that reminds us of traffic rushing back and forth across the bridge. By repeating similar structures but varying the content of those structures, you can make your writing clearer and more interesting for your reader. Moreover, you can improve the sound and rhythm of your writing and learn to be more aware of the rhythms in your reading.

6.8

The following paragraph also makes effective use of repetition of structure. Read the paragraph aloud and listen to its rhythm. Then reread the paragraph and look for structures that are repeated. Finally, fill in the blanks in the outline that follows the paragraph.

> On Wednesday morning at quarter past five came the earthquake. A minute later the flames were leaping upward. In a dozen different quarters south of Market Street, in the working class ghetto and in the factories, fires started. There was no opposing the flames. There was no organization, no communication. All the cunning adjustments of a twentieth century city had been smashed by the earthquake. The streets were humped into ridges and depressions, and piled with the debris of fallen walls. The steel rails were twisted into perpendicular and horizontal angles. The telephone and telegraph systems were disrupted. And the great water mains had burst. All the shrewd contrivances and safeguards of man had been thrown out of gear by thirty seconds' twitching of the earthcrust.
>
> —Jack London, "San Francisco Earthquake"

1. Repetition of phrases

   a. In _____

   b. in _____

   c. in _____

2. Repetition of sentence structures and *no* phrases

   a. There _____

   b. There _____

3. Repetition of sentence structures

   a. All _____

   _____

   _____

   b. All _____

   _____

   _____

4. Repetition of sentence structures, phrases, and word forms

   a. The streets _____

      and _____

   b. The steel rails _____

      _____

   c. The _____ and _____

      _____

   d. And _____

      _____

Transition Words and Phrases

Probably the most common type of transitional device is the use of specific transition words and phrases to indicate relationships within and among sentences and paragraphs. These words and phrases signal changes and thus alert readers to "shift gears" or to take a new direction. For example, the word *however* signals contrast, and the words *next* and *then* signal progression.

Transition within the following paragraph is clear because signal words indicate specific relationships among ideas. As you read the paragraph, be sure you understand the appropriateness of each transition word. The transition words have been bolded, and the relationships that they indicate have been noted in the margin.

	Bessie Delaney was one remarkable woman. In 1918, she was turned down by New York University's dentistry program
Cause, contrast	**because** she was a woman. **However,** she enrolled at Columbia University in 1919 to pursue her dream of becoming a dentist. She
Cause	also encountered prejudice in that program not only **because** she
Cause	was a woman but also **because** she was an African American.
Condition	Bessie would never have reached her goal of becoming a dentist **if**
Addition, contrast	she had not been both brave **and** determined. **Nevertheless,** Bessie
Addition, result	studied hard **and** didn't give up. **As a result**, she graduated from
Time clue	Columbia University in June of 1923. **After** practicing dentistry for
	many years, she died in 1995 at the age of 104.

—Based on Sarah Delaney and Elizabeth A. Delaney, *Having Our Say*

As you have seen, the writer's effective use of transition words makes this paragraph easier to read.

As readers, we know to expect a contrasting idea when we see the word *nevertheless*, a similar—or additional—idea when we see *and*, and a condition when we see *if*. As writers, we can use transition words such as these to guide our readers from one idea to another. However, be careful not to rely too heavily on transition words, and be sure to use these words carefully to indicate the appropriate relationships among ideas. If you arrange your sentences and paragraphs so that one idea follows another in a logical progression, your transition words will serve primarily to reflect and reinforce the natural order and connections among your ideas.

The following lists suggest some of the most common transition words and phrases. Notice that they are divided into categories that not only reflect the relationships they share but also suggest the order of arrangement or method of development.

TIME ORDER

after	meanwhile	when
afterward	next	whenever
as	now	while
before	sometime(s)	finally
first, second, etc.	soon	gradually
last	then	immediately
later	until	suddenly

SPACE ORDER

above	under	at the top
around	outside	at the bottom
before	upon	to the north
behind	where(ever)	to the south
in	in front	to the east
out	in back	to the west
outside	to the left	up / down
over	to the right	through

ORDER OF IMPORTANCE   **ADDITION**

first, second, etc.	foremost	in addition	also
especially	primarily	moreover	too
less (important)	more (important)	furthermore	and
least (important)	most (important)		

ILLUSTRATION	CAUSE/EFFECT	RESULT
for example	because	accordingly
for instance	for	as a result
to illustrate	hence	consequently
such as	since	therefore
that is	so	thus

COMPARISON	CONTRAST	
and	but	although
also	yet	even though
as	however	though
just as	nevertheless	whereas
like	on the contrary	while
likewise	on the one hand	instead
similarly	on the other hand	rather
too	in contrast	still

ALTERNATE	CONDITION
or / nor	if / as if / unless

EXERCISE

6.9

For practice in using transition words, read the following paragraphs carefully and then use the preceding lists to help you choose appropriate transition words to fill in the blanks. (The relationship is indicated in parentheses under each blank.) Be sure to read the paragraphs completely before you start to fill in the transition words, and reread as many times as necessary to determine the relationships among the ideas.

PARAGRAPH A

Some influences on consumer behavior can be directly

observed and measured. _____ others must be inferred.
              (contrast)

_____, the impact of a retailer placing a large "sale" sign
(illustration)

in the window of his or her store can be an important influence in

6.9 continued

triggering the start of the purchase decision process for consumers

walking by the store. Many of these consumers will notice the sign

_____ quickly begin the problem recognition stage, stopping
     (addition)

and entering the store to obtain information about the sale item.

The sign is, _____, a very direct influence on consumer
              (result)

behavior.

—Thomas C. Kinnear and Kenneth L. Bernhardt,
Principles of Marketing

PARAGRAPH B

    Many consumers, especially those between the ages of twelve

and thirty, have been observed in recent years wearing short-sleeved

shirts with alligators on them. _____ they are asked why they
              (condition)

bought that kind of shirt, they may cite the quality of the materials or

the shirt's excellent fit. Many students of consumer behavior,

_____, would attribute the choice of the particular shirt to
    (contrast)

such social factors as a desire for prestige and acceptance by

one's peers. It is extremely difficult to measure these influences,

_____ their importance can only be inferred, _____
(cause and effect)   (contrast)

they are no less important to an understanding of consumer

behavior. Marketers must thoroughly understand both inferred

and direct influences on consumer behavior, which include

demographic factors, marketing mix factors, and situational

factors.

—Thomas C. Kinnear and Kenneth L. Bernhardt,
Principles of Marketing

Unifying Ideas

In addition to arrangement and transition, a third important method of achieving coherence in writing is **unity.** That is, each of your major points should relate clearly to your main idea (your topic sentence or your thesis), and each detail should be clearly connected to the point it is intended to develop.

In the following paragraph, for example, the bolded sentence introduces an irrelevant idea that destroys the unity of the paragraph:

> [1] Several important advances toward democracy have occurred under trees. [2] King John signed the Magna Carta under the giant Arkenwyke Yew at Runnymede, England. [3] To save their charter from their cruel governor, the people of Hartford, Connecticut, hid it in what has come to be known as the Charter Oak. [4] **My own grandfather was born under an oak tree as his family traveled to California.** [5] Finally, it was under an elm tree, later known as the Washington Elm, that George Washington accepted the command of the Revolutionary Army that fought for the colonies' independence.

The writer of the bolded sentence may have thought that the detail about his grandfather belonged in the paragraph because the event it describes, like the other relevant events, occurred under a tree. However, unlike the other supporting sentences in the paragraph, this sentence does not develop the paragraph's main idea that *Several important advances toward democracy have occurred under trees.* Therefore, this irrelevant sentence should be omitted from the paragraph (see also pages 52–54).

EXERCISE

6.10   Read each of the following paragraphs. In each paragraph, underline the irrelevant sentence that destroys the unity of that paragraph.

PARAGRAPH A

[1] Many beautiful elm trees have been attacked by Dutch elm disease, which is caused by a fungus that probably originated in Asia. [2] This fungus not only produces toxic substances within the tree but also gums up the water vessels of the tree. [3] Similar fungi often attack other trees, such as the live oak. [4] The inner deterioration of the elm tree soon produces visible effects. [5] The disease first causes the leaves to turn yellow. [6] Next, the elm's branches begin to die, with the

6.10 continued

twig ends drawing up until they look like shepherd's crooks. [7]The disease almost always results in the death of the affected elm tree—sometimes within the annual season.

PARAGRAPH B

[1]A tree is composed of three basic parts: its crown, its trunk, and its roots. [2]The crown, which may be rounded or pointed, is composed of smaller branches, twigs, and leaves. [3]A large tree branch is an excellent place to hang a rope swing. [4]The leaves absorb the sunlight and use it to make food for the tree. [5]The trunk contains several layers of wood, including the heartwood, the sapwood, the growing layer, the inner bark, and the outer protective bark. [6]The main functions of the trunk are to support the crown and to transport food and water from the roots to the rest of the tree. [7]Finally, the roots provide the tree's foundation. [8]Though hidden underground, the roots may be longer and have more divisions than the upper branches. [9]The root system is vitally important to the health of a tree because it is the source of much of the organism's food and water.

Achieving Coherence in Essays

Thus far in this chapter, you have practiced arranging and connecting ideas within paragraphs. However, logical arrangement, transition, and unity are just as important—if not more important—in essays. That is, good writers connect their ideas effectively *between* paragraphs as well as *within* paragraphs.

The same principles for arranging and connecting ideas that apply to paragraphs also apply to essays. Thus, you may organize entire essays as well as paragraphs according to time order, space order, or order of importance. Moreover, you should use repetition of key words, repetition of structure, and transition words to connect ideas in essays just as in paragraphs.

As you read the following essay-length passage from an American government textbook, notice the annotations. Then answer the questions that follow the essay.

Presidential Leadership in Congress

[1]The job of president is ever-expanding, a trend that makes it more and more difficult for any one individual to govern well enough to meet the rising expectations of the American public. Yet ability to

govern comes down to a president's ability to get his programs through Congress. According to one political scientist, **a president has three ways to improve his role as a legislative lobbyist to get his favored programs passed.**

Thesis
Key word *way(s)*

[2]The first way involves the traditional political avenue of using jobs, or other special favors or rewards, **to win support.** Invitations to the White House and campaign visits to districts of members of Congress running for office are two ways **to curry favor with legislators.** Inattention to key members can prove deadly to a president's legislative program. House Speaker Thomas P. O'Neill reportedly was quite irritated when the Carter team refused O'Neill's request for extra tickets to Carter's inaugural. This did not exactly get the president off to a good start with the powerful Speaker.

Transition/key word
Repetion of structure

Repetition of structure

[3]A second political way a president can bolster support for his legislative package is to call on his political party. As the informal leader of his party, he should be able to use that position to his advantage in Congress, where party loyalty is very important. This strategy works best when the president has carried members of his party into office on his coattails, as was the case in the Johnson and Reagan landslides of 1964 and 1984, respectively. In fact, many scholars regard LBJ as the most effective legislative leader. Not only had he served in the House and as Senate majority leader, but he also enjoyed a comfortable Democratic Party majority in Congress.

Transition/key word

[4]The third way a president can influence Congress is a less "political" and far more personalized strategy. A president's ability to lead and to get his programs adopted or implemented depends on many factors, including **his personality, his approach to** the office, others' perceptions of **his ability** to lead, and **his ability** to mobilize public opinion to support his actions. Many call this **his "style."**

Transition/key word

Repetition of structure

[5]Frequently, the difference between great and mediocre presidents centers on their ability to grasp **the importance of leadership style. Truly great presidents,** such as Lincoln and Franklin D. Roosevelt, understood that the White House was a seat of power from which decisions could flow to shape the national destiny. They recognized that their day-to-day activities and how they went about them should be designed to bolster support for their policies and to secure congressional and popular backing that could translate their intuitive judgment into meaningful action. Mediocre

Clue to order of importance

presidents, on the other hand, have tended to regard the White House as "a stage for the presentation of performances to the public" or a fitting honor to cap a career.

—Adapted from Karen O'Connor and Larry J. Sabato,
The Essentials of American Government: Continuity and Change, 3rd ed.

The introduction to this passage clearly states the writers' thesis, and each of the three body paragraphs develops one of the main points of the essay. Each of these main points is arranged logically and introduced with a clear transition that not only connects each main point to the thesis but also shows the clearly unified relationships among the main points in the essay. As shown in the annotations, further coherence is given to the essay through effective repetition of structure, key words, and ideas.

EXERCISE

6.11

Answer the following questions about the essay you have just read, refer-ring back to the essay as necessary.

1. What is the thesis, or main idea, of the essay?

   _____

   _____

2. What are the three main supporting points of the essay?

   a. _____

   b. _____

   c. _____

3. What method of arrangement have the writers used for the three main points of the essay (time order, space order, order of importance)?

   _____

   _____

   _____

4. What words provide clues to the primary method of arrangement in the essay?

   _____

   _____

   _____

5. What words and phrases provide transitions between paragraphs?

   _____

   _____

   _____

6. What other method(s) of achieving transition, or coherence, have the writers employed? Give examples.

   _____

   _____

   _____

   _____

7. Which of the following passages would be more clearly relevant to the essay and why? That is, which idea could be included in the passage without marring its unity?

   a. As commander-in-chief, the president also has authority over the various military branches. In this capacity, he can (within the limitations outlined by the Constitution) simply command support from the military branches.

   b. A president can also gain favor with members of his party in Congress by promoting laws that aid constituents traditionally supportive of the party and its issues. For example, a Democratic president can win points with his party by promoting laws favorable to labor.

Chapter Review

- Coherence in writing is achieved through effective arrangement, transition, and unity.

- Three useful patterns of arrangement are time order, space order, and order of importance.

- Three effective ways of connecting ideas are repetition of key words and ideas, repetition of structure, and use of transition words and phrases.

- Logical arrangement, effective transitions, and unity of ideas are important not only within paragraphs but also between paragraphs in essays.

■ Writing Assignment

Select one of the paragraphs that you wrote for Exercise 6.2, 6.4, or 6.6 and develop it into an essay. Be sure to arrange your major points in logical order, to include various types of transition, and to avoid irrelevant ideas so that your essay will be unified and coherent.

■ Participating in the Academic Community

With a classmate, exchange drafts of the essays you wrote for the previous assignment. Underline examples of transition (repetition of key words, repetition of structure, and transition words) on each other's papers, and identify places that need additional transition and where irrelevant ideas should be omitted.

Chapter 7

Revising Your Essay

An essential part of the writing process is rewriting. Rewriting includes the tasks of revising, editing, and proofreading. This chapter will focus primarily on revising, or "reseeing," what you have written in terms of focus and unity, content and development, and organization and coherence, but it will also encourage you to consider your purpose and audience as you revise. You should always deal with these larger elements of your writing before you focus on editing and proofreading. (Part Three will provide instruction to help you edit and proofread your writing.)

Revising consists primarily of adding, deleting, or changing what you have written. For example, you may need to add specific details or clearer transitions. You may need to delete unnecessary repetition or ideas that do not support your thesis. Or you may need to sharpen your focus, clarify your thesis, or change your conclusion to meet the needs of your audience.

Revising for Focus and Unity

Since one of your first tasks in writing a paragraph or an essay is finding a focus and a purpose for writing, you actually begin to revise, or resee, your writing from the very first. In the prewriting stage, you consider various topics and purposes, rejecting some immediately and exploring others until you find a good starting point for writing. As you write your first draft, you may find that your initial focus continues to change and develop—that you are actually revising your original ideas and discovering more clearly your focus, or what you want to write about. Hence, this first draft is often called a *discovery draft*.

After brainstorming and then freewriting about her hometown of Biloxi, Mississippi, Karen wrote the following discovery draft:

> *In Biloxi, my hometown, tourists, sunbathers, and fishermen leave the harbors in route to the Barrier Island. They make their living by shrimping and oystering.*
>
> *Sunbathing at any of the islands and boating is a popular activity along the coast. Yahats of all sizes travel to the islands for beach and sun. During the summer, the heat blisters the sand and bakes the decks. ~~On a boating trip, the salty air may blow, but it does not stop the~~ ~~The warm salty water off the coast of the islands also attracts boaters. The water is salty, but many sunbathers like to swim.~~ As the sunbathers swim in the salty water, they baste in the sun. ~~The salty water attracts the sun so a high sun protection must be used.~~ After about 2 hours the sunbathers turn a rosy red color. One can find the rosy red humans spread out on the white sandy beaches or on top of yahats and shrimp boats. These tourists also like to go out on the gambling boats along the Biloxi shore.*

—Karen Mikovich Freeman, student

In this first draft, Karen tried to focus on the tourists who are sunbathing and boating—but her false starts, repetitions, and strike-throughs show that she isn't going anywhere with this topic. Actually, it is not until the last sentence of her discovery draft that Karen found her subject: the gambling boats on the Biloxi shore.

In her next draft, then, Karen sharpened her focus by limiting her topic to the gambling cruise ships that had recently been approved for the Mississippi Gulf Coast. She also discovered her initial purpose: to inform readers about the new tourist attraction in Biloxi. However, even at this early stage in her writing process, Karen decided to delete a couple of sentences from her draft:

> A taste of Las Vegas has settled in the backyard of the Mississippi Sound. Gambling ships are now allowed to cruise along the coast. Two years ago, ships were not allowed to pass through the Sound area. Many conflicts occurred between citizens of the coast about these gambling ships. ~~The citizens couldn't agree~~

~~about the gambling issue.~~ Turmoil arose between political leaders and church organizations. Political leaders stressed that ships would boost the economy and tourism of the surrounding area. Church organizations stressed moral values of individuals who gamble along the coast.

Despite efforts to sink operations in the Sound, the House of Representatives approved a bill to allow any vessel of 150 feet or more to conduct gambling operations in the Sound. ~~The Sound is a 8 to 12 mile-wide stretch of water between the beach along U. S. 90 and the barrier islands.~~ This particular bill would allow vessels to operate anywhere in the Sound as long as the boat is moving.

The gambling boats have certainly changed the Biloxi-Gulfport coast.

—Karen Mikovich Freeman, student

EXERCISE

7.1

Writers delete words and sentences for several reasons. For example, the deleted material may be irrelevant, repetitious, or awkward.

1. Why do you think Karen made the first deletion?

   _____

   _____

2. Why do you think she made her second deletion?

   _____

   _____

Revising for Content and Development

One of the most common problems that writers have is lack of adequate development. Adding specific examples, details, and facts to your essay during the revision stage can greatly improve your writing. In her next draft, therefore, Karen not only revised her essay to clarify her focus and organization but also added more specific supporting details to develop her focus, as described in the annotations.

A Taste of Las Vegas

Added definition of Mississippi Sound.

Added thesis sentence.

[1]A taste of Las Vegas has settled in the backyard of the Mississippi Sound. The Sound is an 8- to 12-mile-wide stretch of water between the Biloxi and Gulfport coastline and the barrier islands. After much disagreement about gambling in this area, tourists now ride the gambling ships that cruise the Sound on daily excursions and make an important contribution to the economy of the Biloxi area.

Started new paragraph and added topic sentence about conflict over gambling.

Clarified position of churches and added details about conflict.

[2]**Two years ago, a debate began about whether gambling ships should be allowed in the Sound.** Many conflicts occurred between citizens over the decision of legalized gambling. In particular, turmoil arose between political leaders and church organizations. Political leaders stressed that ships would boost the economy and tourism of the surrounding area. Church organizations, on the other hand, stressed the immorality of gambling and tried to block gambling ships along the Mississippi Gulf Coast with state and federal regulations. Many Baptist and Catholic organizations were especially concerned with the gambling issue.

Kept paragraph/topic sentence about bill.

[3]**Despite the churches' efforts to sink gambling operations, the state House of Representatives approved a bill to allow any vessel of 150 feet or more to conduct gambling operations in the Sound.** This particular bill would allow vessels to operate anywhere in the Sound as long as the boat is moving. Cruise ships as small as 150 feet with a passenger capacity of two hundred can now offer the full array of casino games.

Added detail about ships that can offer gambling.

Added paragraph/topic sentence about area economy.

Deleted repetitious sentence.

[4]**The gambling cruise ships have certainly improved the economy of the Mississippi Gulf Coast.** The ships depend on the citizens and tourists of the area for financial support of their industry. ~~To keep the ships of entertainment alive, their financial needs must be met by the community and tourists of the area.~~ Furthermore, the tourists who arrive from the surrounding states show that casino gambling is popular and profitable in the area. For example, hotels and restaurants in the Biloxi-Gulfport area have shown an increase in service since the ships arrived.

Clarified conclusion and purpose.

[5]The gambling ships make a significant contribution to the economy of the community. Therefore, I hope the public will continue to support legalized gambling in Mississippi because it will bring more tourists to this area.

—Karen Mikovich Freeman, student

Answer the following questions about the focus, content, and development of Karen's essay.

1. What is Karen's thesis statement? _____

_____

_____

2. What detail does Karen add to paragraph 2? _____

_____

3. What detail does Karen add to paragraph 3? _____

_____

4. Explain why Karen deleted the third sentence in paragraph 4. That is, how is it repetitive?

_____

_____

5. The introduction and conclusion of this draft clarify Karen's purpose and suggest her audience.

   a. What is her purpose? _____

   _____

   b. Who is her audience? _____

   _____

Revising for Organization and Coherence

If you begin your paragraph or essay with a logical plan, you may not have to make major changes in your organization. Many students, however, simply write ideas down in the order in which they think of them and then realize that these ideas must be rearranged in a more logical order. After Laura wrote the following first draft of her essay, she reread it and created an effective plan for revision by analyzing the essay and then renumbering and highlighting separate subtopics in different colors. (See also page 101, Exercise 7.5, in which you edit and proofread part of Laura's essay to correct errors in spelling, capitalization, and punctuation.)

Broad Expectations

[1]John Henry Newman suggests in his essay "The Idea of a University" that a student's education is best served by a broad based curriculum. I see this argument as valid in helping a student [B]understand the relationships among subjects, [A]select a major and a career, and [C]develop critical thinking and respect for knowledge.

Thesis (reorder major points)

Move to point C (paragraph 4)

[4][A well-rounded education challenges students to think critically and to respect knowledge for its own sake.]

Delete

~~Newman states that the educated person "is at home in any society" (42). He knows when to speak and when to be silent; he is able to converse, he is able to listen; he can ask a question pertinently, and gain a lesson seasonably" (42). In any situation you will be able to have conversations with people that you might not have been capable of before.~~

Point B (switch paragraphs 2 and 3)

[3]Newman states that "all branches of knowledge are connected together, because the subject matter of knowledge is intimately united in itself. . ." (42). This statement suggests that each discipline of the academic world will lend itself to the others. ~~I want to be able to function in any social situation.~~ The disciplines are all related, each one will help support the next. Learning math will assist a student in science and computer science classes. The basics of english will prepare a student to construct better papers and organize thoughts for other colledge courses. ⌃*For example,* in english I have already learned new methods to decipher main ideas from what I read, which has carried over into history and will assist me in all future classes.

Delete

Add transition

Point A (switch paragraphs 3 and 2)

[2]A broad-based colledge experience will help you find a major and a career in which you are interested. While at colledge I met a

student who told me that when she first started going to school, she thought her major would be journalism. She later discovered photography, and it really caught her attention. ∧*Therefore,* she changed her major and is much happier with her present choice. This student would have never stumbled onto photography had she not delved into different ideas. On a related note, more careers are available to students who have a diverse education. ∧*For example,* courses in psychsology, speech, and business management will make my computer science degree more marketable.

⁴[**A well-rounded education challenges students to think critically and to respect knowledge for its own sake.**] A colledge education should make students test their previous ideas and seek new ones. In my history class, we have learned about other forms of government such as socialism and communism. In my english class, we began with an essay by the early Catholic writer John Henry Newman. We ∧*then* read one essay on education by a conservative thinker, Allan Bloom, and another by a liberal thinker, Bell Hooks. The different ideas of these writers challenged me to decide what I thought myself. These ideas have also challenged me to make use of my God given intelligence and to continue to ask questions and to seek knowledge and wisdom even after I graduate. Those who don't ask "why" are doomed never to know any answers. The realm of knowledge is unlimited.

⁵The more an educated person knows, the more questions will arise. The truly educated realize they know even less than they thought when they started the venture of knowledge. Only the foolish would dare profess to be satisfied with what they know. ∧*Only* the ignorant dare not venture outside what is safe. What they know—or what they don't know— is comforting. But a narrowly focused education that keeps students from asking questions and seeking broad knowledge is a bad education.

—Laura Steelman, student

Add transition

Add transition

Point C
(add sentence)

Add transition

Conclusion

Add transition

7.3

Answer the following questions about the revisions Laura made to improve her organization and coherence.

1. Why do you think Laura reordered her three major points as she did? What order of arrangement does she achieve with her reordering?

   _____

   _____

2. More specifically, why does Laura switch paragraphs 2 and 3?

   _____

   _____

3. Laura moved the sentence in the first box to paragraph 4, which develops the same idea introduced in this sentence. Why do you think she deleted the material in the second box?

   _____

   _____

4. The three major types of transition are repetition of key words, repetition of structure, and transition words and phrases. What type of transition does Laura use most often? Give examples.

   _____

5. What word does Laura add in paragraph 5 to create repetition of structure?

   _____

Strategies for Revising

The drafts of "A Taste of Las Vegas" and "Broad Expectations" have illustrated several areas in which you may need to revise, or resee, your writing—areas of focus and unity, content and development, organization and coherence. Moreover, in revising these essays, these writers—especially Karen—also considered purpose and audience. In addition to actually seeing revision at work as you have in these essays, however, you also need to know some specific strategies for revising your own writing. The following sections provide you with guidelines for revising your work with the aid of your peers or on your own.

Revising in Groups

One of the most helpful strategies for revising your writing can be to work with a group of your peers to read and respond to one another's paragraphs or essays. For these peer group sessions to be successful, however, you and your classmates need to keep in mind the responsibilities you have in preparing for and participating in the sessions. First of all, when a peer revision session is scheduled for class, you and your peers have a responsibility to one another—as well as to yourselves and your instructor—to come to class with complete drafts for discussion. Second, you and your peers are responsible for respecting one another and one another's writing during the session. On the one hand, you should be encouraging rather than overly critical of your peers' efforts; on the other hand, you will not be able to help your peers revise their writing effectively if you do not provide them with specific and honest suggestions for improvement. Just telling classmates that their drafts are fine (*all* writing can be improved in some way) is cheating them of the serious response that you owe them. Third, you have a responsibility to share the allotted time fairly among the members of the group. In a forty-minute session, for example, a group of four students can spend ten minutes on each draft. You may even want to appoint one member as timekeeper to let you know if you are spending too long on one student's writing.

Even if you follow all of these suggestions, you may still find that a peer revision session flounders if you do not have specific guidelines to follow. The questions in the Peer Revision Guide (page 98) should provide direction and purpose to your group.

You may not want to apply all of these questions during a single peer review session. However, if you and your peer review group follow this guide—which can itself be revised and adapted for different assignments—you should receive feedback that will help you revise your writing effectively. However, you should always remember that you—not your group members—are ultimately responsible for the decisions that you make in your final draft. However well intentioned your group members are, they do not have the same experience with and knowledge about your topic that you have, and so they may sometimes give you bad suggestions as well as good ones. You are responsibile for evaluating the responses that you receive in your peer review group and deciding what advice to accept and what to reject. Both the authority and the responsibility for the final decisions about your writing rest with YOU.

Peer Revision Guide

Writer's Name: _____

Names of Peer Reviewers: _____

INSTRUCTIONS TO PEER REVIEWERS: First, read through the following questions. Then, give the writer time to read his/her essay (or paragraph) aloud while you listen carefully (and follow along on a copy if available). After the writer finishes reading, take a few minutes to respond individually to each question on this guide. Then use these questions as the basis for a discussion about the essay. Be sure to give the writer an opportunity to respond and to ask you questions.

1. What do you like best about the essay (or paragraph)?

2. What is the writer's main idea (topic sentence for paragraphs, thesis sentence for essays)? Underline the main idea if you have a copy of the paper. How can this main idea be made clearer?

3. Does the essay (or paragraph) include clear subtopics or major supporting points? What are these supporting points? List these points below and put a plus or a minus beside each to indicate whether or not it clearly supports the paper's main idea. Does the writer need another major supporting point? If so, what would you suggest?

4. What specific supporting examples, details, and facts has the writer used? In the following space, list three of the most effective of these. Where does the writer need additional examples, details, and facts? What suggestions do you have for additional support?

5. What principle of organization has the writer used in arranging the major supporting points (time, space, importance)? Can you suggest a better method of organization or arrangement? What?

6. What transitions has the writer used? (If you have a copy of the paper, circle these transitions.) Where does the writer need additional transitions? (Insert arrows at these points.) What additional suggestions do you have for improving the coherence and unity of the paper?

7. How effective are the introduction and the conclusion? Does the introduction capture the reader's attention and state the writer's purpose? Does the conclusion bring the writer's main points together and refer back to the thesis or topic sentence? How can the introduction and conclusion be improved?

8. If you could give the writer only one suggestion for improving this paper, what would it be?

Revising Independently

Receiving feedback about your writing from your peers can be very helpful. However, you won't always have the opportunity to participate in a peer revision group, and even when you do have this opportunity, you must make the final decisions on your own. Therefore, you should find the following suggestions for independent revision helpful:

1. *Allow some time to pass between writing your draft and revising it.* If you try to make revisions immediately after you finish your draft, you will be so close to your writing that you will not see problems in it. You need some distance to "resee" your writing and make effective revisions.

2. *Pretend that you are a reader who is seeing the draft for the first time.* In order to revise effectively, you must be able to switch roles from that of the writer to that of the reader, looking at your writing from the point of view of someone who doesn't have the knowledge or experience you had in writing it.

3. *Reread your draft several times, selecting a different focus for each reading.* Most of us have trouble keeping several tasks in mind at the same time. Therefore, you may find it helpful to read your essay once to be sure everything in it relates to your focus as stated in your thesis, once to be sure you have included specific support for each major point, once to be sure that your organization is clear, and once to be sure you have included effective transitions.

4. *Read your draft aloud.* Sometimes hearing your words aloud will bring to your attention problems in focus, content, organization, development, and coherence that you would not have otherwise noticed.

5. *Ask a tutor (or even your instructor) to respond to your draft.* If your college or university has a writing lab, a tutor will be happy to read and respond to your draft. Also, most instructors will take the time to answer specific questions before you submit your essay for evaluation.

EXERCISE

7.4   Work both independently and with a group of your peers to revise a paragraph or an essay you have written recently. Which method(s) of revising do you find most helpful? Why?

Editing and Proofreading

After you have made whatever revisions are needed in the larger areas of focus and unity, content and development, and organization and coherence, it is time to edit and proofread your essay. In the earlier stages of your revision process you have been primarily concerned with what you had to say, or with substance; at this point in your revision process you will concentrate more on how you express your ideas, or on style and correctness. That is, you will edit and proofread your draft for problems in sentence style; for major sentence structure errors; and for errors in grammar, usage, punctuation, spelling, and capitalization.

The following suggestions will help you edit and proofread your writing more effectively:

1. *Ask a friend or tutor to read your draft aloud while you follow along on another copy.* Often when you read your own writing—even orally—you read incorrect sentences correctly without even realizing it. Hearing another person read *exactly* what is on the page often helps you to identify these problems.

2. *Read your draft aloud yourself.* When a friend or tutor is not available to read your draft orally for you, it is still a good idea to read it aloud yourself. Hearing your essay orally—whoever reads it—will not only help you identify and correct errors in grammar, usage, and sentence structure but also give you a sense of the essay's natural rhythms and help you smooth out rough places in your style.

3. *As you read your draft, use a pencil or your finger to point to each word.* This process slows your reading down and forces you to notice each word and mark of punctuation. Therefore, you are more likely to notice errors.

4. *Read your draft backward, beginning with your last sentence and concluding with your first sentence.* Since the reading process involves predicting, you often "read into" your essay what you meant to write or what you think you wrote rather than what is actually on the page. Reversing the order in which you read your sentences helps you to interrupt this process of prediction and to see problems more clearly.

5. *Reread your draft several times, focusing on only one or two editing or proofreading concerns at a time.* Since it is difficult to keep several language tasks in your mind at the same time, your proofreading will be more effective if you read your essay once for sentence fragments and run-ons, a second time for grammatical problems such as errors in subject–verb agreement and tense, a third time for errors in punctuation and capitalization, and a fourth time for errors in spelling and word usage.

7.5   Edit and proofread the following paragraph from Laura's essay. Use the questions following the paragraph to guide your editing.

> Newman states that "all branches of knowledge are connected together, because the subject matter of knowledge is intimately united in itself. . . " (42). This statement suggests that each discipline of the academic world will lend itself to the others. The disciplines are all related, each one will help support the next. Learning math will assist a student in science and computer science classes. The basics of english will prepare a student to construct better papers and organize thoughts for other colledge courses. For example, in english I have already learned new methods to decipher main ideas from what I read, which has carried over into history and will assist me in all future classes.

1. This paragraph includes a major sentence structure error—a comma splice (a type of run-on sentence). Locate this error and correct it below (see Chapter 21):

   _____

   _____

   _____

2. Underline the error in capitalization in this paragraph. Write the correction below.

   _____

3. Circle the misspelled word in this paragraph. Write the correct word below.

   _____

(*Note:* Part Three provides specific instructions for identifying and correcting errors in your writing.)

Chapter Review

■ Rewriting includes three functions: revising, or "reseeing," the larger elements as well as editing and proofreading for problems in style and correctness.

- Revision involves adding, deleting, or changing what you have written.

- Good writers initially concentrate on focus and unity, content and development, and organization and coherence when they revise.

- Good writers also consider purpose and audience during the revision stage.

- Two effective methods of revision are revising in groups and revising independently.

- Editing and proofreading involve rereading your writing to correct problems in sentence style, sentence structure, grammar, and usage.

Participating in the Academic Community

Select a paragraph or essay that you have written recently and discuss this essay with a group of your classmates. Use the Peer Revision Guide on page 98 as the basis for your discussion.

Writing Assignment

After you have used the Peer Revision Guide to discuss one of your essays with a group of your peers, revise it carefully. Then write a journal entry about your experience with peer revision. How does your experience in this class compare with previous experiences you have had? How helpful is the Peer Revision Guide? What changes or improvements could you make in this guide? (If you find a way to improve the guide for your purposes, incorporate this change in your next peer revision session.)

Chapter 8

Gathering and Documenting Information from Sources

In gathering information for writing assignments in various academic classes, you will need to use information available in print or electronic form. Your instructors will certainly expect you to use material from your textbooks in your writing assignments, and many professors will also require you to gather information from the library. It is important for you to be able to use and document your sources properly.

Using Textbooks and Magazines

The sources that you will probably use most frequently in your writing assignments are your **textbooks.** For example, you may be asked to write a summary of a case study in your sociology book or a response to an article in your history book. You may even be able to use a textbook from one class in another class. For an open response assignment in her biology class, for instance, one of our students was able to use information from a set of readings on using animals for medical research that she found in her sociology textbook.

While you should consider your textbooks important resources, you should not overlook the value of **magazines** that you have in your home or that you can buy at a newstand. In *Time* or *Newsweek*, for example, you will find recent articles on political campaigns, important bills before Congress, and military conflicts that may be helpful in writing assignments for history and political science classes. Remember, too, that many magazines and journals such as these are available online.

Textbooks and magazines are necessary tools for your academic classes, but you should not rely totally on these sources. For many assignments, you will need to pursue a more deliberate research process involving both print and electronic sources.

EXERCISE

8.1

Following is a list of article citations from recent popular magazines. Beside each citation, write one or more classes in which you might find this article helpful (only titles and source information are given; authors are omitted). Possibilities include biology, earth science, geography, physics, astronomy, sociology, psychology, history, political science, or computer science.

1. "Trying to Stand on Two Feet [Women's Rights in China]." <u>Newsweek</u> 29 June 1998: 48–49.

   _____

2. "Final Analysis: An Unquiet Mind, Two Years Later: The Aftermath of Revealing Battles with Manic Depression." <u>Psychology Today</u> 31.1 (1998): 88+.

   _____

3. "Mountains of Fire: Spewing Ash, Rubble, and Gases, Volcanoes Explode with Awesome Fury." <u>National Geographic World</u> 271 (1998): 32+.

   _____

4. "The Vanishing Prairie Dog: Shoot Them or Save Them?" <u>National Geographic</u> 193.4 (1998): 116+.

   _____

5. "Trapped in the Web: Are You an On-Line Addict? A New Look at the Lure of Cyberspace and How to Log Off." <u>Psychology Today</u> 31.2 (1998): 66+.

   _____

EXERCISE

8.2

Select one of the following topics and find at least one textbook chapter or magazine article on that topic. Make a copy of the article or chapter. Then write a journal entry evaluating the usefulness of your chapter or article in addressing the topic you chose.

1. What is one of the biggest problems facing families today?

2. What is your position on a recent major political issue?

3. Identify one of the greatest scientific challenges we will face in the twenty-first century, and explain why you think this issue will be so important.

Using Library Resources

You will learn more about **library resources** by actually using them than by reading about them. Thus, the best advice that we can give you is to go to the library with a topic or question for research and ask the reference librarian for help when you encounter a problem. You can also ask your instructor for specific suggestions on sources available on your topic. Although you should not expect your teachers to do your research for you, they are, after all, experts in their subjects and may be able to suggest a recent or particularly helpful book or article.

Despite the help that librarians and instructors may give you, however, you need to know some basic research strategies and terms to get started.

1. *Begin your search with the card catalog.* The **card catalog** includes individual listings for books and other materials, such as manuscripts, housed in the library. Until recently, all card catalogs were actually card files, with each book being filed at least three times, categorized under the author, title, and subject. More recently, however, many libraries have put this information into computerized card catalog systems with separate computer files for each of these categories. Both card files and computer files also include other information such as publication information (place, publisher, date), a list of other subjects under which the book is indexed, the number of pages in the book, and so on. In addition, the computerized card catalog will tell you instantly whether the book is already checked out or available for your use.

2. *Identify and use the most helpful search tools.* **Search tools** are reference works that give you information about other books, magazines, and journals to help you to find the particular books and articles that

you need for your specific research topic. Common search tools include **indexes** and **bibliographies.** One of the oldest and most helpful index is the *Readers' Guide to Periodical Literature*, which is a cumulative author–subject index to several hundred of the most important general interest periodicals (publications that come out "periodically," or at set intervals such as weekly or monthly) published in the United States. Following is a sample entry on the subject *College Education:*

Saving for college. D. W. Englander. il <u>Parents</u> v70
p157-9 S '95

This citation directs you to an article entitled "Saving for College" that was written by D. W. Englander and published on pages 157 through 159 of the September 1995 issue of *Parents* magazine. The citation also tells you that this article includes illustrations (il) and that, when bound, the issue can be found in volume 70.

Many more specialized indexes are available for various disciplines. To find the most helpful subject index or bibliography for your particular area, ask your reference librarian.

3. *Photocopy and then annotate helpful articles that you cannot check out from the library.* Before you decide to copy an article, skim through it to be sure it has information that is relevant to your particular topic. Then, copy the article carefully, being sure that words and page numbers are not cut off by the copying process. Also, be sure that all relevant bibliographic items (author, title of article, title of journal, volume and number, and all page numbers) have been copied. If some of this information is omitted on your copy, write it at the top of the article so you will have it for use in your Works Cited list, or page of bibliographic references.

When you have time to reread the photocopied article more carefully, **annotate** it by underlining statements of thesis and purpose in the article as well as relevant and interesting facts, details, and examples. If an article on the topic of divorce lists several causes or effects of divorce, underline and number these items. It is also a good idea to write your own ideas and questions in the margins so you can retrieve them for later use in your paper. Finally, you can make the material you have annotated your own by rewriting or condensing it in your own words on a note card or in a computer file, always being sure to put in quotations any phrases or sentences that you quote directly from the original source. These paraphrases or summaries will be very helpful when you begin to write your paper.

4. *Take careful notes on material that you think might be useful in your paper.* Although you might be able to rely on your annotations in a photocopied article, you will find that you cannot locate and organize material from books if you haven't taken individual **notes** on that material. As you are reviewing the sources you find, you will need to use careful judgment about what and how much information to record in your notes. If you have a definite topic in mind at the beginning of your search process, you will have a better idea of which notes you need to take. You may record your notes on traditional 4" × 6" note cards, in a notebook, or on a computer file. Whatever system you use, however, be sure to include with each note the specific source of your information (including page number) and a notation about the topic or subtopic with which the note belongs (e.g., *Model-A—original price*). In addition, always be sure to record the information accurately. If you are quoting material directly, be sure to quote carefully and exactly; if you are summarizing (condensing) or paraphrasing (rephrasing), be sure to rewrite the information completely in your own words while preserving the author's meaning. If you have difficulty paraphrasing some individual phrases or sentences, remember that you can combine paraphrase and quotation as long as you carefully enclose the quoted phrases in quotation marks.

5. *Be sure to record the bibliographic information for any source that you use.* As an academic writer, you have a responsibility to *cite,* or give credit to, the *works,* or sources, you use (hence, the name *Works Cited* for your list of bibliographic references). You can give proper credit, however, only if you have complete and accurate **bibliographic information.** Since it is both frustrating and time consuming to go back to the library to look up a citation that you forgot to record, you should be sure to photocopy or record, perhaps on separate 3" × 5" cards, the complete citation information for each possible source. For books, include author(s), title, place of publication, publisher, and date; for articles, include author(s), title of article, title of journal or magazine, volume and number, complete date, and inclusive pages. Sometimes you may not initially take notes from a source but may keep the citation in case you want to return to it later.

6. *Don't overlook the possibility of using government documents.* Since these materials are often awkward to use, students sometimes overlook their potential. **Government documents** are often helpful in political science or sociology classes because they provide a wealth of information about how the government works and about the laws of our nation. For example, you can read transcriptions of actual debates on the floor of the House or the Senate, and you can later read the actual law that was passed by Congress and signed by the president.

8.3   Select one of the following topics (or another topic relevant to one of your classes), and locate at least three library resources for this topic. Record the bibliographic information for your sources and at least one interesting note from each.

1. school violence

2. interracial adoption

3. the Great Depression

4. global warming

Using Electronic Resources

Electronic resources generally provide speed and convenience, but you should know not only how these resources differ from one another and from print sources but also some of their potential problems. The three major types of electronic resources are (1) computerized bibliographies, indexes, and databases; (2) CD-ROM materials; and (3) Internet resources and tools.

Computerized Databases

Computerized databases combine the reliability of their printed versions with the speed and convenience of a computer. For example, you can input a particular subject into the computerized database for the *Readers' Guide to Periodical Literature,* and in a matter of seconds you can have a printout of all works written on this topic in the past thirty years. The *Readers' Guide* citation for the article "Saving for College" looks like this in its electronic form:

AUTHOR:	Englander, Debra Wishik
TITLE:	Saving for college
SOURCE:	Parents (ISSN: 0195-0967) 1095-0967 v 70 P 157-9 September 1995
CONTAINS:	illustration(s)

SUBJECTS COVERED:
College education/Costs
Saving and savings

Electronic databases, which include bibliographies and indexes, can be very helpful, but a certain amount of knowledge and training is necessary to be able to use them effectively. In addition, some of these databases are incomplete, covering only a specified number of years, usually the most recent. Your librarian can direct you to the best sources—printed or electronic—for your subject.

EXERCISE

8.4

Use a computerized database (bibliography, index) to look up the topic that you researched in Exercise 8.3. Record bibliographic information for three sources whose titles look interesting and relevant to you.

CD-ROM Materials

Since **CD-ROM materials,** such as computerized dictionaries and encyclopedias, have usually been transferred from printed to electronic form, these materials are usually equally reliable in either form. Sources such as *Infopedia*, which includes *Webster's New Biographical Dictionary* and *Funk and Wagnall's Encyclopedia*, and Microsoft *Bookshelf*, which includes *The American Heritage Dictionary of the English Language* and *The Concise Columbia Encyclopedia,* are regularly updated in new editions. You should check the date and source of these resources just as you would those of a printed version to be sure you are using a recent edition written and published by a reliable source. As long as you have recent and reliable CD-ROM titles and a working computer, these materials should save you time and effort over comparable printed versions.

EXERCISE

8.5

Use a CD-ROM source (encyclopedia, etc.) to look up the topic that you researched in Exercise 8.3. Record bibliographic information for three sources whose titles look interesting and relevant to you.

Internet Resources and Tools

The **Internet** is a global network that you can access with a computer. Researching on the Internet is convenient, quick, current, interactive, and inexpensive. You may be able to communicate by e-mail with a corporation executive with expertise in the business topic that you are researching, or you can access news on CNN Interactive just as the story is breaking.

You should know, however, that it is especially important to check the quality and reliability of sources that you access on the Internet. Literally anyone can create a web page and put it on the Internet. Therefore, while it is important to consider the quality and reliability—the knowledge and possible bias—of the source of any publication (whether printed or electronic), it is even more essential to consider the source of Internet information. Thus, while student Davy found several websites on Model A automobiles as he was researching that topic, he wisely chose to include in his finished paper information only from the web page prepared by the Model A Ford Club of America, a source that he knew to be reputable.

The most convenient way to access the Internet (or the "Net") is through the World Wide Web (WWW) system. A number of search tools are available for searching the Internet. A few of the most popular are listed here:

1. Yahoo! <http://www.yahoo.com>
2. AltaVista <http://altavista.digital.com>
3. Excite <http://www.excite.com>
4. Magellan <http://www.mckinley.com>
5. Webcrawler <http://www.webcrawler.com>

Search procedures vary with these tools, and you may want to experiment with them to see which one you prefer. After accessing Yahoo, for example, you can click on the appropriate category and subcategories until you get to a list of websites that you want to explore, or you may type a specific subject on the Yahoo main screen and press Enter. The search engine will then search its database and display a list (sometimes quite long) of relevant Internet sites.

EXERCISE

8.6   Use one of the Internet search tools listed to look up the topic that you researched in Exercise 8.3. Find and record the Internet address for at least two sites relevant to your topic. (You should visit each of these sites.)

EXERCISE

8.7   Write a brief report on the topic you researched in Exercises 8.3, 8.4, 8.5. and 8.6. Which type of source provided you with the most helpful information on this topic? Which provided the least helpful information?

Documenting and Citing Sources

Several documentation styles exist. Two of the most popular are MLA style, as explained in *MLA Handbook for Writers of Research Papers* by Joseph Gibaldi, and APA style, as described in the *Publication Manual of the American Psychological Association*. Since MLA style is the one most often recommended by teachers of freshman English, that is the one we will illustrate here.

Citing Borrowed Material within Your Text

Twenty or thirty years ago, MLA style required the use of footnotes or endnotes. Today, however, the recommended format is the much simpler internal documentation style in which you insert into your text only enough information to identify the source you are using. For example, if you are using only one work by a single author, you can give the last name of the author either in your text or in parentheses following the borrowed information. You must also include the specific page number from which the material is taken (see the following example). If you have more than one source by the same author, or if the source does not have an author, you must give a short title.

You should remember that you are responsible for crediting not only quotations but also all original information and ideas from your sources. In general, you should know how to document three different kinds of borrowed material: (1) ideas that you have paraphrased (rewritten) or summarized (condensed); (2) short quotations of four lines or fewer that are enclosed in quotations marks and typed as regular text; and (3) long quotations of more than four lines that are indented ten spaces from the left and not enclosed in quotation marks. Each of these three ways of crediting information is illustrated here:

1. *Citing and crediting short quotations (four lines or fewer)*

According to Roger Caras, many researchers "are against vivisection in spirit but believe that today's research protocols require—and grant money goes to—research involving animals" (57).

2. *Citing and crediting long quotations (more than four lines)*

> Jane McCabe cites several types of animal research
> that have helped children with cystic fibrosis:
> > Three times a day my daughter uses enzymes
> > from the pancreas of pigs to digest her food.
> > She takes antibiotics tested on rats before
> > they are tried on humans. . . . If she ever needs
> > a heart-lung transplant, one might be possible
> > because of the cows that surgeons practiced
> > on. (388)

3. *Using and crediting summarized or paraphrased material*

> Children with cystic fibrosis are only expected to live
> about thirteen years, but with current research gains,
> children are living longer (McCabe 387).

Note: The ellipsis, or three dots, in the top example indicates that material has been omitted.

EXERCISE

8.8   Use the article or chapter that you copied for Exercise 8.2 to practice citing borrowed material. Write a brief response to the research question for which you found the article, including in your response at least one short quotation, one long quotation (more than four lines), and one paraphrase or summary from the article or chapter. Follow the instructions above for citing this material.

Preparing Your Works Cited List

Your Works Cited list is just what its name suggests: a list (**alphabetized**) of the works, or sources, that you have cited (quoted or otherwise **used**) in your paper. Although the *MLA Handbook* includes sample citations for many kinds of sources, we include here examples of only a few types of citations that we believe you are most likely to use. (The first line of each Works Cited entry begins at the left margin of your paper, but succeeding lines are indented five spaces.)

1. *Book*

   Collier, Peter, and David Horowitz. <u>The Fords: An American Epic</u>. New York: Summit, 1987.

   Donovan, Frank. <u>Wheels for a Nation</u>. New York: Crowell, 1965.

2. *Essay or Article in an Edited Anthology (or Collection)*

   McCabe, Jane. "Is a Lab Rat's Fate More Poignant Than a Child's?" <u>Interactions: A Thematic Reader</u>. Ed. Ann Moseley and Jeanette Harris. 3rd ed. Boston: Houghton, 1997. 386–89.

3. *Essay or Article in a Magazine*

   Caras, Roger. "We Must Find Alternatives to Animals in Research." <u>Newsweek</u> 26 Dec. 1988: 57.

4. *Essay or Article in a Scholarly Journal*

   Harris, Jeanette. "Student Writers and Word Processing: A Preliminary Evaluation." <u>College Composition and Communication</u> 36 (1985): 323–30.

5. *Item or Article in a Reference Book*

   "Behaviorism." <u>The American Heritage Dictionary of the English Language</u>. 3rd ed. 1994.

   Bolt, Bruce A. "Earthquakes." <u>The New Encyclopaedia Britannica: Macropaedia</u>. 15th ed. 1993.

6. *Newspaper Article (with no author)*

   "Historic Farm Bill Ends Link of Farm Prices, Gov't Subsidies." <u>Country World</u> 4 April 1996: A1+.

7. *CD-ROM Materials*

   "Henry Ford." <u>Webster's New Biographical Dictionary</u>. <u>Infopedia</u>. 1994. CD-ROM. New York: Merriam-Webster, 1983.

   Note: In this citation, the original 1983 publication appeared in CD-ROM format in 1994.

8. *Internet (Online Materials)*

"Model A Story." <u>Model A Ford Club of America Website</u>. 1996. Model A Ford Club of America. 20 May 1998 <http://www.ford.com/archive/ModelA.html>.

9. *Personal Interview*

Jones, Andrew. Personal interview. 15 May 1999.

Remember that all entries in your Works Cited should be alphabetized. (See sample Works Cited, page 116.)

EXERCISE

8.9

Write Works Cited entries for five of the sources that you found in Exercises 8.3–8.6. Include one article, one book, and one Internet site in your group.

Applying the Research Process

While he was a freshman at Texas A&M University–Commerce, Davy wrote the following essay. He used internal documentation style and various types of resources, including a personal interview, library resources (books), and electronic resources (CD-ROM and Internet articles).

The Model A

[1]Beginning with the original Model A in 1902 and continuing for twenty-five years, Henry Ford created a number of automobile models, including the famous Model T. However, the best was yet to come. The "new" Model A, first produced in 1927 but based on the original 1902 model, provided service and style to many early automobile owners, including my own grandfather.

[2]The Model A was both practical and popular. It was a family car with all the extras usually found on much more expensive models. This car was designed to "deliver speed, power and comfort" ("Model A Story" 1). It had a four-wheel braking system plus an independent safety brake, four-wheel hydraulic shock absorbers, wire spoke wheels, an electric starting and generating system, two-sheet safety glass for the front windshield, two-tone paint, and many body styles to choose from. The unveiling of this new car was second in popularity only to Lindbergh's flight across the Atlantic. In New York an estimated ten million people saw the car in the

first thirty-six hours it was on display, and about fifty-thousand deposits were made on new Model A's (Collier and Horowitz 126).

[3]People today probably find it difficult to imagine just why this seemingly slow and boxy "poor man's" car made such a huge impression. The car's large buxom fenders, thin bicycle tires, and forty-miles-per-hour speed don't begin to suggest what the car really stood for to the American people. The car portrayed the coming age of luxury, convenience, and efficiency. Everyone wanted to be able to get what everyone else already had, and the Model A made that possible. Its low price allowed nearly anyone, from Franklin Delano Roosevelt to "Ole Joe" at the fish market, to own one. Nearly five million Model A's were made from late 1927 to 1931, when the Model A was again discontinued. The Model A, however, became a symbol for the success of the ordinary man. In so doing, it paved the way for luxury and efficiency at an affordable cost.

[4]Anyone could own a Model A—even poor young farmers. Thus, on December 23, 1928, my grandfather Fred Moseley purchased a very special Model A Roadster at the local Ford dealership in Sulphur Springs, Texas. Model A's were so much in demand at the time that the dealers could not keep them on the lot. At the time of sale the purchaser would take his receipt to the closest Ford assembly line—which for my grandfather was at the East Grand Ford Plant in Dallas, Texas—and exchange the receipt for a bright, shiny new car. So my grandfather, with his neatly folded white receipt tucked safely into the pocket of his old worn "Sunday go to meet'n" jacket, boarded a noisy, faded red passenger train to Dallas (Moseley).

[5]When my grandfather got off the train, he found waiting his independence, prestige, excitement, and happiness represented in a brand new 1928 dark blue Model A Tudor Roadster. His heart jumped into his throat at the sight. It would have been difficult to find a prouder man than the one who drove off the East Grand Ford assembly line that afternoon (Moseley). The next day, on Christmas Eve, my grandfather was wed to Arlena Belle Lewis in the Sulphur Springs courthouse, and afterward the happily married couple climbed joyously into their day-old roadster and "headed for home" (Moseley).

[6]Henry Ford would have been proud of the good use to which my grandfather put his new automobile. My grandfather used the car for everything from pulling bales of cotton to the cotton gin to delivering the mail to making the Saturday drive to town for supplies. In fact, he had gotten so much use out of the car that by the early forties, the roadster body—now faded, dented, and hopelessly rusted—had to be replaced

by a two-door sedan body. For several more years, the Model A faithfully executed all the jobs required by this hard-working farmer—but all things have their time. Shortly after the birth of my father, the trusty old relic simply could not keep up as it used to. Sadly, my grandfather retired it to the shed behind the house where the worn-out Model A Tudor would sit for several decades (Moseley). In 1991, after both my grandparents had died, I began the difficult task of returning this 70-year-old rusted automobile to its original state.

[7]The Model A represents a time when life was simpler, safer, brighter. All around, the world was growing and changing and building and improving. As preserved today, the Model A makes the period of the late 1920s and early 1930s so vivid that one could almost reach into the history books and grab it. Even though Henry Ford has been dead for over fifty years ("Henry Ford" 1), he would have been very proud of the good use my grandparents made of that one special Model A as well as the great effort that my family and I are making to restore a once great automobile.

- -

Works Cited

Collier, Peter, and David Horowitz. <u>The Fords: An American Epic</u>. New York: Summit, 1987.

Donovan, Frank. <u>Wheels for a Nation</u>. New York: Crowell, 1965.

"Henry Ford." <u>Webster's New Biographical Dictionary</u>. <u>Infopedia</u>. 1994. CD-ROM. New York: Merriam-Webster, 1983.

"Model A Story." <u>Model A Ford Club of America Website</u>. 1996. Model A Ford Club of America. 20 May 1998 <http://www.ford.com/archive/ModelA.html>.

Moseley, Jr., Fred. Personal interview. 24 April 1998.

—Davy Moseley, student

Underline or highlight the internal documentation in Davy's essay. How many parenthetical references did he use? Remember that it is usually better to paraphrase or summarize most of your source material, as Davy did, using quotations sparingly for distinctive passages or statements by important authorities.

8.11   Davy used five citations in his Works Cited list. For each citation, identify the type of source credited.

Chapter Review

- Instructors expect their students to know how to use various resources in academic writing.

- Textbooks and magazines can be helpful resources for academic research.

- Tools for identifying and using library resources include the card catalog, indexes, and bibliographies.

- Good research methods include recording bibliographic citations accurately and taking careful, accurate notes.

- The most important types of electronic resources are computerized databases, CD-ROM materials, and the Internet.

- Good writers give full and accurate credit in their essays and their lists of Works Cited for material that is summarized, paraphrased, or quoted.

Participating in the Academic Community

Working in small groups of three or four, find at least one textbook or magazine source, one library source, and one electronic source for the each of the following topics:

1. bilingual education
2. online dating
3. Alzheimer's disease
4. swing dancing
5. tornadoes

In class, compare your methods and results with those of other groups.

■ Writing Assignment

Narrow the subject your group researched in the previous activity to an appropriate topic. If necessary, research your topic further, and then write an essay on your narrowed topic. Be sure to cite information appropriately and to include a Works Cited list. You may work individually or in a small group.

Part Two

Methods of Development

Several methods of development provide you with strategies for organizing and presenting your ideas in paragraphs and essays. Methods of development such as narration and description go back to the beginning of speech and the stories of hunting and fighting told around ancient campfires. Other methods of development, such as definition and comparison, originated over two thousand years ago with the ideas of the Greek philosopher Aristotle. Still others, such as process and cause and effect analysis, appear to be more modern in nature. And the ability to use persuasion, to use evidence to convince others to act or believe as you wish, is timeless.

In Part Two, you will see how other writers have used various methods of development in their writing and learn how to use these methods yourself. As you concentrate on each chapter, remember that many paragraphs and essays use these methods in combination. However, each writing example in this unit is clearly based on a primary method of development. Learning to understand and use these strategies can be extremely helpful to you in generating and organizing ideas for writing. Indeed, you will often be required to use certain methods of development—such as example, classification, definition, comparison and contrast, or cause and effect—in answering essay examination questions for classes such as history, sociology, and biology.

Chapter 9

Description

Description is one of the most common methods of development in both paragraphs and essays. You can describe how a person looks, how a glass of lemonade tastes, how a headache feels, how cinnamon rolls smell, or how a rock concert sounds. Description can be part of many different types of writing—fiction, poetry, history, science, biography, and business. Description is used heavily in technical manuals and advertising copy, but it can also be found in the most sophisticated novel and the simplest story, in the most formal speech and the most casual conversation. Although many works are primarily descriptive, description is also used to support other methods of development, especially narration.

To describe someone or something effectively, you must be a good observer. You must see people, places, objects, and events with a sharp eye and be able to relate your impressions clearly. Thus, writing an effective description involves more than using many adjectives and adverbs. It requires noticing, selecting, and ordering images and details so that they communicate effectively to a reader.

Understanding Description

In the following paragraph, Sandra Cisneros provides an effective description of a house in which she lived as a child. In her description, she enables you to share her experience—to see and feel what she saw and felt:

> **But the house on Mango Street is not the way they told it at all.** It's small and red with tight steps in front and windows so small you'd think they were holding their breath. Bricks are crumbling in places, and the front door is so swollen you have to push hard to get in. There is no front yard, only four little elms the city planted by the curb. Out back is a small garage for the car we don't own yet and a small yard that looks smaller between the two buildings on either

side. There are stairs in our house, but they're ordinary hallway stairs, and the house has only one washroom. Everybody has to share a bedroom—Mama and Papa, Carlos and Kiki, me and Nenny.

—Sandra Cisneros, *The House on Mango Street*

Qualities of Effective Description

As illustrated in Cisneros's paragraph, effective description contains the following qualities:

1. *A clear purpose and main idea.* The main idea of a description may be stated or it may be implied. In either case, however, it holds the description together and gives it meaning. In her topic sentence, which is set in bold type, Cisneros suggests that her feelings about the house on Mango Street are negative. However, it is through her details, especially through her emphasis on the smallness of everything in or around the house, that Cisneros creates the impression of stuffiness and confinement that she wants to give her readers.

2. *Sensory details.* Writers most often use details that appeal to the sense of sight, but good description also appeals to the other four senses—to hearing, taste, smell, and touch. In describing the red color of the house, the small "tight steps," the "small garage," and the "small yard that looks smaller between the two buildings on either side," Cisneros appeals primarily to the sense of sight. However, she also appeals to the sense of touch in describing the soft, crumbling brick and the front door that is "so swollen you have to push hard to get in."

3. *Factual details.* Factual details give exact information about a subject. For example, Cisneros tells us that there are "only four little elms" by the curb in place of a yard and that there is "only one washroom" to support her impression that the house is small. Working together, factual and sensory details can provide strong support for the main idea of a description.

4. *Effective comparisons.* Using comparisons that create images in the reader's mind is also an effective way to develop a main impression. Cisneros describes the windows as being "so small you'd think they were holding their breath" to emphasize the impression of tightness and confinement. (*Note:* Many comparisons begin with *like* or *as*.)

5. *A clear and consistent method of arrangement.* Finally, good description consistently uses a clear method of arrangment, such as space order, time order, or order of importance. Cisneros arranges the details in her paragraph according to space order, beginning with the front ("tight steps in front," "front door," "front yard"), moving to the back ("Out back"), and then moving from the outside to the inside ("ordinary hall stairs," "only one washroom," "share a bedroom").

EXERCISE

9.1   Read the following paragraphs, and answer the questions that follow each:

PARAGRAPH A

Desert landscapes frequently appear stark. Their profiles are not softened by a carpet of soil and abundant plant life. Instead, barren rocky outcrops with steep, angular slopes are common. At some places the rocks are tinted orange and red. At others they are gray and brown and streaked with black. For many visitors desert scenery exhibits a striking beauty; to others, the terrain seems bleak. No matter which feeling is elicited, it is clear that deserts are very different from the more humid places where most people live. As we shall see, arid regions are not dominated by a single geologic process. Rather, the effects of . . . running water, and wind are . . . apparent. Because these processes combine in different ways from place to place, the appearance of desert landscapes varies a great deal as well.

—Edward J. Tarbuck and Frederick K. Lutgens, *Earth Science*, 7th ed.

1. What is the main idea of the paragraph? _____

_____

2. To what sense(s) do most of the details appeal? _____

3. What are some of the most effective factual and sensory details?

_____

_____

PARAGRAPH B

It was a nice piece of toast, with butter on it. You sat in the sun under the pantry window, and the little boy gave you a bite, and for both of you the smell of nasturtiums warming in the April air would be mixed forever with the savor between your teeth of melted butter and toasted bread, and the knowledge that although there might not be any more, you had shared that piece with full consciousness on both sides, instead of a shy awkward pretense of not being hungry.

—M. F. K. Fisher, *The Art of Eating*

1. What is the implied main idea of the paragraph? _____

_____

9.1 continued

2. To what sense(s) do most of the details appeal? _____

3. What are some of the most effective factual and sensory details?

    _____

    _____

Writing Descriptive Paragraphs

Whether your descriptive paragraph describes a place, a person, an object, or an action, you should try to include the qualities of effective description you studied in the previous section: a clear main idea or overall impression, specific sensory and factual details, effective comparisons, and a clear and consistent method of arrangement. Your method of arrangement will vary according to the subject you choose and the point of view that you take toward your subject. For example, in describing a fishing pier, you could arrange details in space order from the back of the pier to the docks on the edge of the sea; in time order based on the view at different times of the day; or in order of importance from the deserted warehouses to the bustling unloading docks.

Describing a Place

In the following paragraph about his parents' kitchen, Alfred Kazin states his main idea clearly in a topic sentence (which is in bold type) and arranges his details in space order, moving outward from the table in the center of the room. Words that provide spatial cues are highlighted with color bars:

> **The kitchen held our lives together.** My mother worked in it all day long, we ate in it almost all meals except the Passover *seder*, I did my homework and first writing at the kitchen table, and in winter I often had a bed made up for me on three kitchen chairs near the stove. On the wall just over the table hung a long horizontal mirror that sloped to a ship's prow at each end and was lined in cherry wood. It took up the whole wall, and drew every object in the kitchen to itself. The walls were a fiercely stippled whitewash, so often rewhitened by my father in slack seasons that the paint looked as if it had been squeezed and cracked into the walls. A large electric

bulb hung down the center of the kitchen at the end of a chain that had been hooked into the ceiling; the old gas ring and key still jutted out of the wall like antlers. In the corner next to the toilet was the sink at which we washed, and the square tub in which my mother did our clothes. Above it, tacked to the shelf on which were pleasantly arranged square, blue-bordered white sugar and spice jars, hung calendars from the Public National Bank on Pitkin Avenue and the Minsker Progressive Branch of the Workmen's Circle; receipts for the payment of insurance premiums, and household bills on a spindle; two little boxes engraved with Hebrew letters. One of these was for the poor, the other to buy back the Land of Israel.

—Alfred Kazin, "Brownsville: The Kitchen," *A Walker in the City*

Kazin uses effective factual details ("square tub") and sensory details ("fiercely stippled whitewash," "blue-bordered white sugar and spice jars") and makes an effective comparison when he describes "the old gas ring and key" that "jutted out of the wall like antlers."

Describing a Person

In the following paragraph, N. Scott Momaday describes his Kiowa grandmother as he remembers her. Although a paragraph describing a person could also be organized by space order, moving from the person's feet to her head, or vice versa, Momaday's paragraph is organized by order of importance. That is, in describing the "several postures that were peculiar" to his grandmother, he builds to the most important posture: that of prayer. As you read this paragraph, notice the boldfaced statements that suggest Momaday's main idea that his grandmother's prayers carry her somewhere beyond this earth. Notice also the highlighted phrase that suggests that the posture of prayer is the most important to her.

Now that I can have her only in memory, I see my grandmother in the several postures that were peculiar to her: standing at the wood stove on a winter morning and turning meat in a great iron skillet; sitting at the south window, bent above her beadwork, and afterwards, when her vision failed, looking down for a long time into the fold of her hands; going out upon a cane, very slowly as she did when the weight of age came upon her; **praying.**

> **I remember her most often at prayer.** She made long, rambling prayers out of suffering and hope, having seen many things. I was never sure that I had the right to hear, so exclusive were they of all mere custom and company. The last time I saw her she prayed standing by the side of her bed at night, naked to the waist, the light of a kerosene lamp moving upon her dark skin. Her long, black hair, always drawn and braided in the day, lay upon her shoulders and against her breasts like a shawl. I do not speak Kiowa, and I never understood her prayers, but there was something inherently sad in the sound, some merest hesitation upon the syllables of sorrow. She began in a high and descending pitch, exhausting her breath to silence; then again and again—and always the same intensity of effort, of something that is, and is not, like urgency in the human voice. Transported so in the dancing light among the shadows of her room, **she seemed beyond the reach of time.** But that was illusion; I think I knew then that I should not see her again.
>
> —N. Scott Momaday, *The Way to Rainy Mountain*

In this paragraph, Momaday appeals to the senses of sight ("the light of a kerosene lamp moving upon her dark skin," "long, black hair . . . drawn and braided," "dancing light among the shadows of her room") and sound ("high and descending pitch," "urgency in the human voice"). He also makes an effective comparison in the "long, black hair" that "lay upon her shoulders and against her breasts like a shawl."

Describing an Object

As shown in the impression of age and usefulness that his father's hammer has for him, the following paragraph certainly has personal relevance for Scott Russell Sanders. However, it also has many qualities in common with the kind of technical description you might be asked to write in a business course. Like a technical description, which would give the exact length and width of the hammer, this description is very specific and concrete. Early in the paragraph, Sanders describes how the hammer looks ("scratched and pockmarked," "dull sheen") and how it feels ("about the weight of a bread loaf"). Then he provides additional details in spatial order, moving from the head of the hammer to its handle. Notice also the effective comparision of the hammer to "an old plowshare" and of its sheen to "fast creek water in a shade."

The hammer had belonged to him and to his father before him. The three of us have used it to build houses and barns and chicken coops, to upholster chairs and crack walnuts, to make doll furniture and bookshelves and jewelry boxes. The head is scratched and pockmarked, like an old plowshare that has been working rocky fields, and it gives off the sort of dull sheen you see on fast creek water in the shade. It is a finishing hammer, about the weight of a bread loaf, too light, really, for framing walls, too heavy for cabinet work, with a curved claw for pulling nails, a rounded head for pounding, a fluted neck for looks, and a hickory handle for strength.

—Scott Russell Sanders, "The Inheritance of Tools"

Describing an Action

Although a paragraph describing an action is similar to a narrative (indeed, narration and description are often used together), the following paragraph is primarily descriptive. As shown in the boldface sentences, this paragraph not only makes the point that nature may conceal some of its most beautiful and miraculous scenes but also creates a feeling of awe in the presence of such a natural scene. Appropriately, since this paragraph describes the action of the red-winged blackbirds flying out of the Osage orange tree, it is arranged according to time order (see highlighted words and phrases).

For nature does reveal as well as conceal; now-you-don't-see-it, now-you-do. For a week this September migrating red-winged blackbirds were feeding heavily down by Tinker Creek at the back of the house. One day I went out to investigate the racket; I walked up to a tree, an Osage orange, and a hundred birds flew away. They simply materialized out of the tree. I saw a tree, then a whisk of color, then a tree again. I walked closer and another hundred blackbirds took flight. Not a branch, not a twig budged: the birds were apparently weightless as well as invisible. Or, it was as if the leaves of the Osage orange had been freed from a spell in the form of red-winged blackbirds; they flew from the tree, caught my eye in the sky, and vanished. When I looked again at the tree, the leaves had reassembled as if nothing had happened. Finally I walked directly to the trunk of the tree and a final hundred, the real diehards, appeared, spread, and vanished. How could so many hide in the tree without my seeing them? The Osage orange, unruffled, looked just as it had looked from the house, when three hundred red-winged blackbirds cried from its crown. I looked upstream where they flew, and they were gone. Searching, I couldn't spot one. I wandered upstream to force them to play their hand, but they'd crossed the creek and scattered. One show to a customer. These appearances catch at my throat; they are the free gifts, the bright coppers at the roots of trees.

—Annie Dillard, *Pilgrim at Tinker Creek*

Notice that the details in this paragraph appeal not only to the sense of sight ("red-winged blackbirds," "whisk of color," "bright coppers") but also to the sense of sound ("the racket," "cried from its crown").

Writing Topic Sentences for Descriptive Paragraphs

Each of the preceding descriptive paragraphs has a stated or implied topic sentence that includes both a topic and an assertion (see Chapter 3, pages 29–32). The topic sentence of Dillard's paragraph about the red-winged blackbirds in the Osage orange tree can be analyzed in this way:

TOPIC | ASSERTION
For nature | does reveal as well as conceal.

The rest of the paragraph, then, clearly supports this topic sentence, showing how the blackbirds are at first invisible in the Osage orange tree and then how they flash into sight.

Kazin's topic sentence also clearly states his paragraph's topic ("the kitchen") and his assertion ("held our lives together"). In their partially implied topic sentences, Momaday asserts that his grandmother (topic) seemed "beyond the reach of time" (assertion) when she was at prayer, and Sanders suggests that his father's hammer (topic) reminds him of the strength, the work, and the closeness that he and his father had shared (assertion).

The assertion in a descriptive paragraph often suggests an impression, effect, or feeling that the writer wants to create. For example, Kazin's description of his family's kitchen and Sanders's description of his father's hammer suggest feelings of love and closeness, whereas Momaday's description of his grandmother at prayer and Dillard's description of the red-winged blackbirds in the Osage orange tree create feelings of awe and wonder.

9.2

For each of the following topics, write a topic sentence that includes both a topic and an assertion. Then list two or three sensory or factual details that you could use to support that topic.

▶ EXAMPLE: *Topic:* Ringing of the office telephone

Topic sentence: <u>*The ringing of the office telephone is*</u>
<u>*annoying.*</u>

Sensory and factual details: <u>*Rings at least four times*</u>
<u>*before I can reach it. Ringing is loud and harsh and*</u>
<u>*seems to go on forever. A bright light flashes every time*</u>
<u>*the phone rings.*</u>

1. *Topic:* A hamburger

    Topic sentence: _____

    _____

    Sensory and factual details: _____

    _____

    _____

2. *Topic:* Rain on the roof

    Topic sentence: _____

    _____

    Sensory and factual details: _____

    _____

    _____

3. *Topic:* One of the rooms in your house

    Topic sentence: _____

    _____

    Sensory and factual details: _____

    _____

    _____

Using Transitions in Descriptive Paragraphs

Written by a student like you, the following paragraph combines the description of a place with an event that occurred at that place. As you read this paragraph, notice how the highlighted words and phrases show space order.

STUDENT PARAGRAPH

Yellowstone National Park is filled with a fabulous array of underground streams and geysers. These natural springs are not only beautiful, but fascinating as well. As I began my hike through the park, I noticed in front of me the constant gurgling and popping of the boiling spring water. The steam from these underground streams created a musical effect as they poured into the sky. As I stood amidst the geysers admiring their beauty, the ground suddenly began to shake beneath my feet. I quickly turned around, just in time to see the eruption of Old Faithful, the grandfather of all geysers. Water and steam shot up 150 feet into the sky, creating an awesome display.

—Byron Black, student

This paragraph includes not only a clear topic sentence (bolded) and sensory details ("gurgling and popping," "musical effect," etc.) but also effective transitions. Although Byron uses *as* to show the events occurring in time, his transitions primarily show the space order by which he has arranged the paragraph—*in front of, into, around,* and *up into.* The following chart lists words that indicate space order, which is common in descriptive writing:

above	over, through	at the top
around	under	at the bottom
between	upon	to the north
behind	within	to the south
before	in front	to the east
in, into	in back	to the west
out	to the left	up/down
inside, outside	to the right	through

See Chapter 6, page 80, for a list of transition words that show time order and order of importance. Remember to use transitions to help readers follow the arrangement of ideas in your descriptions.

EXERCISE

9.3   Select a place, person, object, or action that you would like to describe. Then fill in the following plan to help you write a paragraph about this topic:

1. *Topic:* _____

   Assertion: _____

   Topic sentence: _____

   _____

2. What method of arrangement will you use to arrange your details?

   _____

3. Write several details that support your topic sentence. Be sure to include both factual and sensory details. (If possible, include details that appeal to more than one of the five senses.)

   _____

   _____

   _____

4. Now, go back and review your details to be sure they all develop your topic and assertion. Cross out any irrelevant details. Then decide on the method you want to use to arrange your details (space order, time order, order of importance). Number your details to fit this arrangement, and write here the transition words that you might use to connect these details.

   _____

   _____

5. Finally, use the information that you have generated in this exercise to write a paragraph about your chosen topic.

Writing Descriptive Essays

Although a descriptive essay can explore a topic more fully than a descriptive paragraph can, it includes the same basic elements. The main idea of a descriptive essay occurs in a thesis statement in the introduction rather than in a topic sentence, but specific factual and sensory supporting details arranged in a logical order with effective transitions are just as important in an essay as in a paragraph.

In the following essay written for an English composition class, Sherri George describes her visit to St. Simons Island in Georgia, where she had lived as a child. Although this essay is primarily descriptive, it also contains some narration. Such a combination of description and narration is quite common in both personal and academic writing.

St. Simons Island, Georgia

[1]It has been said, "You can never go home again, and you can't relive your childhood through your children." Five years ago for one week I did both. I took my two boys on vacation to St. Simons Island, Georgia, my childhood hometown. St. Simons Island is a small island, just barely finding a spot on the map, off the southeastern tip of Georgia's coast. It is one of several islands that make up the Golden Isles of Georgia. You will find it south of Savannah, Georgia, north of Jacksonville, Florida, and nestled deep within my heart of memories. On this visit, which I will recreate for you below, I recaptured the feeling of being home and relived many moments of my own discoveries as I watched my boys make these same discoveries.

[2]Leaving the mainland, we cross the salt-water marsh and intracoastal waterway to reach the island. The tide is coming in, filling the marsh with the damp, salty smell of the ocean. It has a peculiar smell to the boys' senses, but to me it smells like coming home. Anticipation grows as we cross the two "singing bridges," or drawbridges that raise and lower to let the shrimp boats and barges pass under. When the car crosses the bridge, it makes a singing, humming sound on the tires. We are almost on the island now.

[3]The giant oak trees are the first welcoming sight. These trees have stood like sentries on guard for generations. Their branches are dripping with Spanish moss, reaching out like a canopy over the road. The moss is colored like cold ashes left from a fire. It is thick and hangs off the branches like an old sea captain's beard. The road bends and narrows, and the oak trees crowd each side of the road making a first-comer think of southern plantations and mint juleps.

[4]We come to the red light marking the center of town. The heartbeat of St. Simons is the downtown ending at the pier. Main Street is only four or five blocks long, full of character and adventure. The hardware store, office supply, drugstore, and Roberta's Dress Shop have been there seemingly forever. The smell of coffee comes from the coffee and tea shop. T-shirts are hung in nearly every shop window. Everything we see beckons us to stop and shop, but we are headed to the pier.

[5]When we finally arrive at the pier, it looks, smells, and feels the same as it did when I was a little girl. The pier juts out over the greenish gray ocean for half the length of a football field. Thick barnacle-covered beams hold the pier steady against the tide. The roof covers the first one-third of

the pier, so we can escape the sun or occasional rain shower. A long wooden bench lines the pier railing. The bench is perfect for romantic couples sitting, looking out over the ocean, or for the more serious business of fishing and crabbing. The signs of both are everywhere. Sweethearts' initials are carved in the railing posts. The railing is lined with fishing poles, bait buckets, crab lines, ice chests, and bushel baskets to put your catch of crabs in. The smell of fish carcasses, day-old chicken necks for crab bait, and tanning lotion mingles with the ocean breeze. To my boys, who had never seen the ocean before, everything is new, fresh, and exciting. They hurry from one fisherman to the next crabber and back again. They stick their curious noses in every bucket and ask a thousand questions. To me, however, these sights and sounds are familiar because I spent hours on this pier while growing up.

[6]That week in St. Simons, with my boys, I did go home again. I relived a part of my childhood through my children. I watched their excited faces and knew how they felt with each new discovery. I discovered for myself that although I had left the island, the island would never leave me.

—Sherri George, student

EXERCISE

9.4

1. What is the thesis, or main idea, of this descriptive essay? (*Hint:* Reread the introductory and concluding paragraphs to identify the writer's topic and assertion.)

   _____

   _____

2. What is the method of arrangement used in this essay?

   _____

3. What are some of the most effective details in the essay?

   Factual details: _____

   _____

   Sensory details that appeal to sight: _____

   _____

   _____

   Sensory details that appeal to senses other than sight: _____

   _____

   _____

9.4 continued

4. What are some effective comparisons used in the essay? (*Hint:* Comparisons often use *like.*)

_____

_____

Chapter Review

- A good descriptive paragraph or essay has a main idea, which may be implied or stated in a topic sentence or thesis statement.

- The main idea in a descriptive paragraph or essay includes both a topic and an assertion about that topic.

- Effective description includes both factual and sensory details.

- Sensory details appeal to the five senses: sight, hearing, taste, smell, and touch.

- Good description often includes comparisons, many of which use the word *like* or *as.*

- Descriptive paragraphs and essays may be organized according to space order, time order, or order of importance.

◼ Writing Assignment

Rewrite the paragraph that you wrote for Exercise 9.3, developing it into an essay. Be sure that your essay contains a clear thesis (topic and assertion), a clear and consistent method of arrangement, and specific factual and sensory details.

◼ Participating in the Academic Community

After you finish a draft of your descriptive essay, meet with a group of your classmates to read one another's essays. Use the Chapter Review to make suggestions for improvement. First, check each essay to be sure it has a thesis statement that states the main idea clearly. Second, read each essay to be sure it has specific factual and sensory details that support the thesis. Third, determine how the supporting details are arranged (space, time, importance) and evaluate the effectiveness of that arrangement.

Chapter 10

Narration

Most simply, **narration** is a story. Stretching back into ancient times when the only entertainment was telling stories around a campfire, narration is probably the oldest and is certainly the best known of all methods of development. We have all had experiences with stories—listening to them, telling them, watching them on television or movie screens—even before we learned to read and write.

Narration, however, is useful not only for entertaining readers but also for informing them. It is often combined with other methods of development, especially description. Because narration may also be used to explain a process or illustrate a point, it is often used in academic writing. For example, you may use narration in your sociology class to describe an instance of discrimination or in your history class to explain a historical event.

Understanding Narration

The following narrative by Scott Russell Sanders about the sequence of events that occurred on the day his father died will help you to understand the qualities of effective narration:

> At just about the hour when my father died, soon after dawn one February morning when ice coated the windows like cataracts, I banged my thumb with a hammer. Naturally I swore at the hammer, the reckless thing, and in the moment of swearing I thought of what my father would say: "If you'd try hitting the nail it would go in a whole lot faster. Don't you know your thumb's not as hard as that hammer?" We both were doing carpentry that day, but far apart. He

was building cupboards at my brother's place in Oklahoma; I was at home in Indiana, putting up a wall in the basement to make a bedroom for my daughter. By the time my mother called with news of his death—the long distance wires whittling her voice until it seemed too thin to bear the weight of what she had to say—my thumb was swollen. A week or so later a white scar in the shape of a crescent moon began to show above the cuticle, and month by month it rose across the pink sky of my thumbnail. It took the better part of a year for the scar to disappear, and **every time I noticed it I thought of my father.**

—Scott Russell Sanders, *The Paradise of Bombs*

Qualities of Effective Narration

Like Sanders's paragraph, good narration contains the following qualities:

1. *A clear purpose and main idea.* Although some stories are written primarily for entertainment, most narratives make a point or reveal a truth about life. This point, or purpose, may be implied, or it may be clearly stated in a topic sentence or thesis statement. Sanders's paragraph about the death of his father, for example, suggests both the closeness between the father and son who shared a love of carpentry and the loss that the son felt for many months after his father's death. Although this main idea is clearly implied throughout, it is most clearly suggested in the bolded part of the last sentence of the paragraph. Like Sanders's paragraph, most narratives in academic writing do more than entertain. They illustrate a point, explain a process, develop an idea, or provide information.

2. *Use of relevant details and dialogue.* The use of vivid details makes a narrative come alive, but these details should contribute clearly to the main point, help to set the context, or move the narrative along to its climax (high point of action). For example, Sanders's details about the ice emphasize the winter setting of his father's death; his swearing at hitting his thumb, which initially seems unrelated, actually brings to mind what his father would have said and therefore connects the son to the father; and the details about the transformation of the white scar not only emphasize the symbolic meaning of the scar—like a scar of grief—but also show the passing of the months. Well-chosen dialogue also makes a narrative more effective. For example, Sanders's memory of what his father would say makes the father seem real and the son's grief more poignant.

3. *An appropriate and consistent point of view.* Point of view should remain consistent throughout a narrative. Because his narrative was personal, Sanders chose to use the first-person point of view (*I, we,* etc.) throughout his paragraph. For many narratives, however, the more objective third-person point of view (*he, they,* etc.) is preferred; for example, third person is used in most academic writing (see examples in Exercise 10.2).

4. *Clear chronological organization and effective transitions.* A narrative tells what happened. That is, it relates a sequence of events, usually in chronological order, or time order. That is, these events are arranged in the order in which they occurred. Sanders's narrative, for example, progresses clearly from what happened at the hour when his father died to what happened weeks and then months afterward. He uses not only transition words such as *when* and *soon after* but also longer phrases such as "at just about the hour" and "by the time" to show how the events are related to time and its passing.

EXERCISE

10.1   Read the following paragraph about the assassination of President John F. Kennedy, and then answer the questions that follow it.

> When they arrived at Love Field, Congressman Henry Gonzalez said jokingly, "Well, I'm taking my risks. I haven't got my steel vest yet." The President, disembarking, walked immediately across the sunlit field to the crowd and shook hands. Then they entered the cars to drive from the airport to the center of the city. The people in the outskirts, Kenneth O'Donnell later said, were "not unfriendly nor terribly enthusiastic. They waved. But were reserved, I thought." The crowds increased as they entered the city—"still very orderly, but cheerful." In downtown Dallas enthusiasm grew. Soon even O'Donnell was satisfied. The car turned off Main Street, the President happy and waving, Jacqueline erect and proud by his side, and Mrs. Connally saying, "You certainly can't say that the people of Dallas haven't given you a nice welcome," and the automobile turning on to Elm Street and down the slope past the Texas School Book Depository, and the shots, faint and frightening, suddenly distinct over the roar of the motorcade, and the quizzical look on the President's face before he pitched over, and Jacqueline crying, "Oh, no, no. . . . Oh, my God, they have shot my husband," and the horror, the vacancy.
>
> —Arthur M. Schlesinger, Jr., *A Thousand Days*

10.1 continued

1. The main idea in this narrative paragraph is implied rather than stated. Underline the phrases that most clearly suggest this main idea, and then write it in a sentence of your own.

    _____

    _____

    _____

2. What clues are provided to the order of the events in the narrative? Circle, and then write below, transition words and other phrases that show chronological order in the narrative.

    _____

    _____

3. Schlesinger's choice of details emphasizes the irony, or apparent unexpectedness and lack of appropriateness, of the shooting. What are two details that suggest the contrast between what the participants expected and what actually happened?

    _____

    _____

4. Schlesinger's narrative builds suspense to a high point, or climax. What is this climax?

    _____

5. Is the point of view first person or third person? Why is this choice effective in this paragraph?

    _____

    _____

    _____

Since a narrative is a sequence of events, it can be a historical account, a scientific process, or a case study as well as a novel or short story. In relating what happened, a narrative can tell what happened to you, to someone else, or to something else. A novel tells you what happens to the characters in the story. Your history text tells you what happened at Valley Forge or during the Great Depression. And your biology text tells you what happens when trees lose their leaves or a cell divides.

EXERCISE

10.2   Following are examples of narrative paragraphs from two different academic disciplines, or subjects. As you read each paragraph, identify the subject area it represents: literature, history, or science.

PARAGRAPH A

After paralyzing the tarantula, the wasp cleans herself by dragging her body along the ground and rubbing her feet, sucks the drop of blood oozing from the wound in the spider's abdomen, then grabs a leg of the flabby, helpless animal in her jaws and drags it down to the bottom of the grave. She stays there for many minutes, sometimes for several hours, and what she does all that time in the dark we do not know. Eventually she lays her egg and attaches it to the side of the spider's abdomen with a sticky secretion. Then she emerges, fills the grave with soil carried bit by bit in her jaws, and finally tramples the ground all around to hide any trace of the grave from prowlers. Then she flies away, leaving her descendant safely started in life.

—Alexander Petrunkevitch, "The Spider and the Wasp"

Academic subject: _____

PARAGRAPH B

Eight children were there at play, seven sisters and their brother. Suddenly the boy was struck dumb; he trembled and began to run upon his hands and feet. His fingers became claws, and his body was covered with fur. Directly there was a bear where the boy had been. The sisters were terrified; they ran, and the bear after them. They came to the stump of a great tree, and the tree spoke to them. It bade them climb upon it, and as they did so it began to rise into the air. The bear came to kill them, but they were just beyond its reach. It reared against the tree and scored the bark all around with its claws. The seven sisters were borne into the sky, and they became the stars of the Big Dipper.

—N. Scott Momaday, *The Way to Rainy Mountain*

Academic subject: _____

Writing Narrative Paragraphs

You may write a narrative paragraph as a complete composition or as part of a longer essay. The following narrative paragraph by Annie Dillard, for example, is part of a larger narrative.

One night a moth flew into the candle, was caught, burnt dry, and held. I must have been staring at the candle, or maybe I looked up when a shadow crossed my page; at any rate, I saw it all. A golden female moth, a biggish one with a two-inch wingspan, flapped into the fire, dropped her abdomen into the wet wax, stuck, flamed, frazzled and fried in a second. Her moving wings ignited like tissue paper, enlarging the circle of light in the clearing and creating out of the darkness the sudden blue sleeves of my sweater, the green leaves of jewelweed by my side, the ragged red trunk of a pine. At once the light contracted again and the moth's wings vanished in a fine foul smoke. At the same time her six legs clawed, curled, blackened, and ceased, disappearing utterly. And her head jerked in spasms, making a spattering noise; her antennae crisped and burned away and her heaving mouth parts crackled like pistol fire. When it was all over, her head was so far as I could determine, gone, gone the long way of her wings and legs. Had she been new, or old? Had she mated and laid her eggs, had she done her work? All that was left was the glowing horn shell of her abdomen and thorax—a fraying, partially collapsed gold tube jammed upright in the candle's round pool.

—Annie Dillard, "The Death of a Moth," *Holy the Firm*

Notice that Dillard states her main point clearly in the bolded topic sentence at the beginning of the paragraph, organizes the sequence of events in clear chronological order, and uses vivid descriptive details in narrating the sequence of events. She also uses effective transitions, such as *when, at once,* and *at the same time* (see highlighted words and phrases), and maintains consistency in point of view (first person) and tense (past). Finally, Dillard employs vivid action verbs (*flamed, frazzled, curled, crisped,* etc.).

Writing Topic Sentences for Narrative Paragraphs

Although the topic sentence of a narrative paragraph may be implied, many writers—student writers as well as professional writers such as Dillard—find it helpful to state a topic sentence near the beginning of the paragraph. Remember that a good topic sentence includes both a topic (what you are writing about) and an assertion (what point you are making) (see pages 29–30 and 128). The following exercise gives you practice in writing topic sentences for narrative paragraphs.

EXERCISE

10.3   For each of the following topics, write a topic sentence that you could develop into a narrative. (Be sure your topic sentence includes both a subject and a "point," or an assertion.) Then, in the space provided, list the major events to be included in the narrative.

1. An experience that helped you to grow up

   Topic sentence: _____

   _____

   Major events: _____

   _____

   _____

   _____

2. A historical event

   Topic sentence: _____

   _____

   Major events: _____

   _____

   _____

   _____

3. An emotional experience

Topic sentence: _____

_____

Major events: _____

_____

_____

Using Transitions in Narrative Paragraphs

The following paragraph was written as a composition assignment by a college student like you. Notice that the student, Melissa, not only stated her point clearly in her topic sentence and included specific events, details, and even dialogue but also used a logical arrangement and effective transitions.

STUDENT PARAGRAPH

My misjudgment nearly turned into tragedy on a day that was supposed to be special for my seven-year-old daughter Taylor. It was a beautiful Friday morning when I left home; the sun was shining, and the sky was crystal blue. My daughter Taylor and I both looked forward to that evening because her friends, Falon and April, were coming over for a slumber party. After work that day, I picked Taylor up when she got out of school at 3:00. Then, we rushed to pick up the other girls. When we got to Falon's school, I talked with Falon's mother while the girls played on the playground. Taylor played on the monkey bars while the other children played on the slide. Across the playgound, I saw Taylor hanging from the monkey bars and heard her yell, "MOMMA! HELP!" Thinking at first that she was only playing, I didn't pay much attention to her. She then called out again even more urgently, but I still didn't rush to her because she had always been able to climb and rescue herself like the monkey for which the bars were named. However, the next time Taylor called out, she went crashing to the ground. Running frantically to get to her, I saw her arm bent backward at a horrible angle. I saw that the bone was broken, but she wasn't bleeding. Falon's mother and I carried Taylor to the car, and I rushed her to the hospital. The operation took three long hours. When the doctor came out of surgery, he explained that he had put six pins in her arm but that it would heal. Taylor's accident could have been much worse, but I learned never to take my child and her safety for granted.

—Melissa White, student

As shown by the highlighted words, this paragraph—like those of professional writers—includes effective transitions. To help you in writing your own narrations, several transition words indicating time order are listed here:

after	when(ever)	as
first, second, etc.	while	at the same time
next	meanwhile	finally
then	soon	eventually
before	later	last
until	now	sometime(s)

EXERCISE

10.4   Think of something that happened to you that caused you to have a strong emotional feeling, such as anger. Then, write a sentence in which you identify this event. (*Note:* You may be able to use some of your ideas from Exercise 10.3.)

1. I was angry when _____

_____

2. Now list what happened—the specific events that led to your anger.

_____

_____

_____

_____

_____

_____

_____

10.4 continued

3. Now, think for a moment about what happened to you and why it made you angry. Was it the only time this sort of thing made you angry, or do you frequently respond with anger when something similar happens? Do you think your anger was justified, or were you later sorry that you became angry? Can you reach some conclusion, or generalization, about this incident and why it made you angry? Write your generalization here.

_____

_____

_____

4. Rewrite your conclusion, and use it as the topic sentence for a paragraph in which you tell what happened when you became angry. Be sure to include effective transitions.

Writing Narrative Essays

Narration is used as the primary method of development in essays as well as in paragraphs. For an essay examination in your history class, for example, you might be asked to relate the sequence of events leading up to the Revolutionary War. Or for a case study in your sociology class or education class, you might be asked to observe and write a narrative of the activities of an emotionally disturbed child. Or, as illustrated in the following student essay, you might simply be asked to write a personal experience narrative for your composition class.

As you read Liz's essay, notice that she provides background information in her introductory paragraph. Also, try to identify the main point of the narrative and other qualities of effective narration that you have already studied:

The River

¹It was late spring and my family and I were on our way to meet friends at my favorite campground in Arkansas: Camp Albert Pike. Since I was a child, I had always looked forward to these trips with great anticipation. This particular trip, however, would be quite adventuresome.

²By the time we reached the campgrounds, it was just turning dark. Our friends had already spent the day on the river and were just about to eat supper. My father and I listened to the stories of an exciting day that the adventurous part of our group had spent on the river. We then planned to go tubing as soon as possible the next day. To our dismay, however, we awoke the next morning to the sudden and spontaneous flashes of

lightning. This light was the only tear in the thick blankets of rain that covered the morning sky. The loud booming of thunder crashed in my ears like a band of cymbals. We would have to wait patiently before we would be able to go tubing.

[3]I spent most of the day in that old familiar cabin. The pot-bellied stove in the corner, the soft warm bed, and the ceiling fan that made a slight tink-tink-tink sound when it ran all gave me such a comforting glow inside. A friend finally mentioned that he thought the rain had died down enough that he could take us down the river, where the group had gone only the day before. Looking out the window at the strength of the river and the still threatening skies, I had very strong doubts as to whether I really wanted to take part in the "fun."

[4]My father must have read my mind, because just as I was about to try and get out of this, he turned to me and said, "Don't even think of trying to back out, young lady; you got us into this, and we've come too far to back out now." At this time, all the others turned to me and began giving me their reassurances as to the condition of the river and my ability to tame it.

[5]We drove up the river until we came to the spot where we were to put the tubes into the water. All of a sudden, the sky began to fall down on us. The rain felt like bricks, and we found ourselves in the midst of a terrible storm. Despite this and the extreme cold temperature of the river, our friends decided to go ahead and tube back to the cabin and safety. The whole thought of this was terribly frightening, but instead of taking the most logical route back, I allowed our friends (who, I might add, were mostly in their 50s and should have known better) to persuade me to follow them down the river.

[6]To fully understand what I was about to do, it is important to remember that at the river's calmest state, there are huge boulders scattered throughout, averaging about four feet tall and approximately five feet wide. These rocks were almost fully covered by raging water from the earlier rain. As I went over the first rapid, I felt my heart pounding harder than ever before, and I was gasping for breath. It was then that I fully realized my foolishness. The next few rapids went by fine, but as I approached one farther down the river, I noticed that there was quite a bit of bare rock showing above the water. For an instant, I thought that I had fully cleared the rapid safely, until I felt the tube begin to slip out from under me. Somehow, the tube had gotten hung on the rock, and I had been thrown into the water, helpless.

[7]From this point on, my legs often got caught in the rocks so that at one time I was stuck with water rushing over my head. I tried to remain calm as I attempted to reach the side of the river. I reached for tree limbs

above my head, only to have them break off in my hands. I looked farther ahead and saw a huge rock coming up to my right. I realized that if I could hang on to that, I could probably get over to the side, and that's just what I did. After I realized I was safe, I turned around to see just exactly how far I had been dragged. My heart sank to my stomach. The rushing water overpowered the boulders, and at that moment I felt that I was extremely lucky not to have been seriously injured. Despite bruised legs and some cuts here and there, I had come out of it fairly unscathed (only a few scars remain). Later, we found out that at the time this event was happening, a tornado was tearing down everything in its path less than a mile away.

[8]Even though I cannot look back on this experience as a pleasant one, it has taught me many things. I learned that I should listen to what my instincts and common sense tell me, for they are usually right. I also learned that I have the ability to keep my head in very stressful and frightening situations. But most important, I learned that at any time our lives can be taken from us. This experience has truly shown me just how precious life can be.

—Liz Doughty, student

10.5

1. What is the main point, or thesis, of this narrative essay? (*Hint:* Read the introduction and conclusion carefully.)

   _____

   _____

   _____

2. What are the major events in the narrative? Write these events in the space provided. (*Hint:* Look for a major event in each paragraph of the body of the essay.)

   Paragraph 2: _____

   Paragraph 3: _____

   Paragraph 4: _____

   Paragraph 5: _____

   Paragraph 6: _____

   Paragraph 7: _____

3. What is the climax, or high point, of the story?

    _____

    _____

4. Circle ten transition words or phrases that indicate time order in the
    essay. Then write these words here.

    _____

    _____

    _____

5. What is the effect of the dialogue in paragraph 4?

    _____

    _____

6. What are three of the most effective sensory details in the essay?

    _____

    _____

    _____

7. What point of view (first person or third person) and tense (present or
    past) does Liz use?

    _____

Chapter Review

- A narrative is a story, a retelling of a sequence of events or of "what happened."
- Effective narration has a clear point, which is usually stated in a topic
  sentence or a thesis sentence but which may be implied.
- Good narration is usually organized in chronological (time) order and includes clear transitions.
- Good narration includes specific, relevant details and may include
  dialogue.
- In narration, point of view and tense should be consistent.

◼ Writing Assignment

Write a narrative essay based on one of the topics from Exercise 10.3, or revise the paragraph you wrote for Exercise 10.4 by expanding it into an essay, adding additional details and, if relevant, dialogue. As you write your essay, keep in mind the qualities of effective narration listed in the Chapter Review.

◼ Participating in the Academic Community

Meet with a group of your classmates to discuss the draft of your narrative. As you discuss each essay, you should first tell the writer what you like best about the narrative. Then, use the qualities of effective narration listed in the Chapter Review to analyze your classmates' essays and make suggestions for improvement.

Chapter 11

Process

A **process** is a series of actions that brings about a particular end or result. When you are involved in a process, such as writing an essay, you will be more successful if you analyze the process, or divide it into its various steps or stages. The same is true for writing a description of a process. Because good process writing gives a detailed description of the actions involved, this method of development has elements in common with descriptive writing. Process writing is even more closely linked to narration, however, because it is structured chronologically, or in time order.

Although process writing has elements in common with descriptive, narrative, and even cause and effect writing (to be discussed in Chapter 15), it is nevertheless a unique kind of writing. It differs from both description and narration in that it focuses on a sequence of actions—such as those involved in changing a tire, baking a cake, or bathing a baby—that does not occur just once but is repeatable and even somewhat predictable.

Understanding Process Writing

As illustrated in the following examples, process writing is divided into two general types. The first **instructs** the reader about how to complete, or duplicate, a specific process; the second **explains** how a process is completed so the reader can understand the process itself more fully.

INSTRUCTIONS FOR COMPLETING A PROCESS

Freewriting is the easiest way to get words on paper and the best all-around practice in writing that I know. To do a freewriting exercise, simply force yourself to write without stopping for ten minutes. Sometimes you will produce good writing, but that's not the goal. Sometimes you will produce garbage, but that's not the goal either. You may stay on one topic, you may flip repeatedly from one to another: it doesn't matter. Sometimes you will produce a good record of your stream of consciousness, but often you can't keep up. Speed is not the goal, though sometimes the process revs you up. If you can't think of anything to write, write about how that feels or repeat over and over "I have nothing to write" or "nonsense" or "No." If you get stuck in the middle of a sentence or thought, just repeat the last word or phrase till something comes along. The only point is to keep writing.

—Peter Elbow, *Writing with Power*

EXPLANATION FOR UNDERSTANDING A PROCESS

When the grave is finished, the wasp returns to the tarantula to complete her ghastly enterprise. First she feels it all over once more with her antennae. Then her behavior becomes more aggressive. She bends her abdomen, protruding her sting, and searches for the soft membrane at the point where the spider's leg joins its body—the only spot where she can penetrate the horny skeleton. From time to time, as the exasperated spider slowly shifts ground, the wasp turns on her back and slides along with the aid of her wings, trying to get under the tarantula for a shot at the vital spot. During all this maneuvering, which can last for several minutes, the tarantula makes no move to save itself. Finally the wasp corners it against some obstruction and grasps one of its legs in her powerful jaws. Now at last the harassed spider tries a desperate but vain defense. The two contestants roll over and over on the ground. It is a terrifying sight and the outcome is always the same. The wasp finally manages to thrust her sting into the soft spot and holds it there for a few seconds while she pumps in the poison. Almost immediately the tarantula falls paralyzed on its back. Its legs stop twitching; its heart stops beating. Yet it is not dead, as is shown by the fact that if taken from the wasp it can be restored to some sensitivity by being kept in a moist chamber for several months.

—Alexander Petrunkevitch, "The Spider and the Wasp"

Qualities of Effective Process Writing

Good process writing, as illustrated in the paragraphs by Elbow and Petrunkevitch, has the following characteristics:

1. *A clear purpose and main idea.* The general purpose of process writing is either to give instructions that the reader can follow or to explain a process so a reader can understand it. In the first paragraph, composition specialist Peter Elbow shows that freewriting is "the easiest way to get words on paper" by giving instructions on how to freewrite. In the second paragraph, naturalist Alexander Petrunkevitch explains for his readers the natural process in which the wasp attacks and captures a spider to provide food for her young.

2. *Inclusion of all steps, details, and definitions necessary for duplicating or understanding the process.* The process may be rather simple, as in freewriting, or quite complex, as in the wasp's paralyzing of the spider. In either case, however, good process writing includes all the essential steps of the process. Good process writing also includes all details necessary for describing those steps—but no irrelevant or distracting details. Some necessary details are those that explain reasons for certain steps in the process and explanations of options that may occur during the process. Thus, Elbow describes results that may occur in addition to just getting words down on paper, and he explains what to do if you "get stuck." In addition, good process writing defines or explains the significance of any terms that may be unfamiliar or confusing to readers. For example, Petrunkevitch explains that the membrane for which the wasp searches is "the only spot where she can penetrate the horny skeleton."

3. *A chronological sequence and clear transitions.* For readers to be able to understand or reproduce a process, the description must follow a clear chronological sequence. Thus, Petrunkevitch cannot describe the wasp thrusting her sting into the soft spot of the spider before he describes her preparations for this sting. In addition, writers can help their readers to understand the processes they are describing by providing clear transitions. For example, Petrunkevitch begins his paragraph with what the wasp does *first*, proceeds to what she does *then*, and concludes with those events that occur *finally* or *at last*.

EXERCISE

11.1
The following paragraph describes how stalactites are formed. Read this paragraph and then answer the questions that follow it.

Of the various **dripstone,** or cave deposit, features found in caverns, perhaps the most familiar are stalactites. These iciclelike pendants hang from the ceiling of the cavern and form where water seeps through cracks above. When water reaches air in the cave, some of the dissolved carbon dioxide escapes from the drop and calcite, or a crystalline form of natural calcium carbonate that forms limestone, begins to precipitate. Deposition occurs as a ring around the edge of the water drop. As drop after drop follows, each leaves an infinitesimal trace of calcite behind, and a hollow limestone tube is created. Water then moves through the tube, remains suspended momentarily at the end, contributes a tiny ring of calcite, and falls to the cavern floor. The stalactite just described is appropriately called a *soda straw.* Often the hollow tube of the soda straw becomes plugged or its supply of water increases. In either case, the water

11.1 continued

is forced to flow, and hence deposit, along the outside of the tube. As deposition continues, the stalactite takes on the more common conical shape.

—Edward J. Tarbuck and Frederick K. Lutgens, *Earth Science*, 7th ed.

1. What process is described in this paragraph?

    _____

    _____

2. Does this paragraph give instructions for completing a process or explain a process so readers can understand it?

    _____

3. List the four or five major steps in this process.

    a. _____

    b. _____

    c. _____

    d. _____

    e. _____

4. Circle the transitions in the paragraph. Then write three of these transitions here.

    _____

5. The authors of this paragraph define three terms that might be unfamiliar to readers. Identify two of these technical terms and provide their definitions.

    Term: _____ *Definition:* _____

    _____

    Term: _____ *Definition:* _____

    _____

EXERCISE

11.2

Following are a topic sentence and a brainstorming list of steps for the process of making maple syrup. However, several of these steps are out of order. Number the steps in the logical sequence.

Topic Sentence: Since colonial days New England farmers have been making maple syrup from the sap of the sugar maple tree.

_____ When the water is gone, only pure maple syrup is left in the containers.

_____ First, they drill a two-inch hole into the trunk about three or four feet from the ground.

_____ The syrup is then strained, graded according to color, and bottled for shipment to grocery stores and supermarkets.

_____ In late winter or early spring, they begin tapping the maple trees.

_____ After the sap is collected each day, the farmers take the containers to the "sap house" where the water is boiled away into steam.

_____ They then insert a spout into the hole and attach a container to the spout to catch the sap.

Writing Process Paragraphs

The subject of a process paragraph should be limited enough to allow it to be developed clearly in a single paragraph. For example, describing the complete process you go through every morning to get ready for classes or work is too broad for a paragraph. The simpler process of brushing your teeth would be more appropriate for a paragraph.

The outline that follows lists the major steps in the process of *making a vegetable garden:*

1. Select and prepare the ground.
2. Select and buy the plants.
3. Set the plants in the ground.
4. Care for the garden as the plants grow.
5. Harvest the vegetables and enjoy eating them.

The entire process of making a garden would be appropriate for an essay. As shown in Keith's paragraph on page 154, however, the more limited task of actually planting the garden is a better topic.

Writing Topic Sentences and Using Transitions in Process Paragraphs

Ideally, a process paragraph begins with a topic sentence that includes both the topic the writer wants to discuss and the assertion, or point, the writer wants to make. Thus, Keith begins his paragraph with the sentence that *Setting plants in a garden* (topic) *involves four important steps* (assertion).

STUDENT PARAGRAPH

Setting plants in a garden involves four important steps. First, plan carefully where the plants will go in the garden. Be sure to keep plants of the same type in same section of the garden so they do not block the sun from each other. For example, keep viney plants such as zucchini, squash, and cucumbers in the same area. Second, be sure to space the plants according to the instructions on the plastic stick that comes in the plant box. If you ignore this information, your plants may grow too close together and may not mature enough to produce fruit. Third, place your plants in the ground carefully. For each plant, dig a hole deep enough to hold the complete root structure. Then put the plant in the hole and cover the plant to the base of the stem, making sure all the roots are covered. Fourth, after you finish setting your plants, water your garden until it is well soaked with some water still standing on the soil.

—Keith Casey, student

As shown by the highlighted words, Keith uses clear transitions to show the sequence of setting plants in a garden. He also divides this process into four primary steps and describes each.

EXERCISE

11.3

1. Reread Keith's paragraph and list the four steps for setting out plants:

   (1) _____

   (2) _____

   (3) _____

   (4) _____

2. Why is the first step important?

   _____

   _____

3. What may happen if a gardener ignores the second step?

   _____

   _____

As you write your own process narratives, you will find the following list of transition words helpful in indicating order and sequence:

after	as	at the same time	before
eventually	finally	first, second, etc.	immediately
last	later	meanwhile	next
now	often	sometimes	soon
then	until	while	when(ever)

EXERCISE

11.4

Use the following questions to help you plan a paragraph describing a simple process, such as brushing your teeth, doing a push-up, shampooing your hair, shaving, painting your fingernails, or making a peanut butter and jelly sandwich.

1. What specific process will you explain?

   _____

   _____

2. Will your purpose be to provide instructions so that the reader can perform the process or to explain the process so the reader can understand how it works?

   _____

   _____

3. After considering your main point, write a topic sentence.

   _____

   _____

   _____

4. List the steps needed to complete this process.

   a. _____

   b. _____

   c. _____

   d. _____

   e. _____

11.4 continued

Review these major steps to be sure you have listed them in the correct time order. If necessary, renumber the steps so they are arranged in the correct order.

Now write a paragraph based on the plan you have made but adding details as necessary to develop your plan. Be sure to include effective transitions to show the relationships among the steps in your process. When you have finished your paragraph, look back at the qualities of effective process writing listed on pages 150–151. Use this list to help you evaluate and revise your paragraph.

EXERCISE

11.5

Look through one or more of your academic textbooks and locate a process explained by the author(s). For example, in your geology textbook you might read about the development of a weather phenomenon, such as a tornado or a hurricane; in your psychology or health book you might find an explanation of a particular mental process (sleep, memory); in your sociology textbook you might find a description of the process of aging; and in the introduction to this textbook you will find an analysis of the writing process. Find a process in one of your textbooks, and write a paragraph describing it.

Writing Process Essays

A process essay is similar to a process paragraph in that it can either give instructions for duplicating a process or an explanation of how a process works. In an essay, however, the writer has room to discuss a more complex process. Usually a process is clearly divided into major steps, with each major step being developed in a separate paragraph. As a college student, your political science professor might assign you an essay examination question asking you to explain how a bill becomes law, or your English or business writing instructor might ask you to write an essay giving instructions for completing a particular process.

In the following student essay, Andy responded to an assignment similar to the one just described. Notice that this essay includes the same qualities of effective process writing as the paragraphs you have studied in this chapter—a clear main idea statement (thesis), effective supporting steps and details, a logical arrangement, and clear transitions. Indeed, Andy explains the process of making chili so well that you could actually make it yourself.

Texas Chili

[1] Some people identify Texas with cowboys, horses, oil, or even J. R. Ewing—but not me. I think of the great food of Texas, and that food is chili. A staple dish in my household, chili is a dish with a long history. From the

"pioneer" days of the early West to today, chili remains a favorite among many in the West, but particularly in Texas. My chili recipe is based on the contributions of friends, relatives, and a hometown chili parlor. Prepared with its own special ingredients, my Texas Chili will make your guests' eyes and mouths water and leave them with a satisfied appetite.

[2]First, you will need to get the equipment and ingredients you will need to make Texas Chili. Several pieces of equipment are necessary: an electric skillet (with cover), a small wooden spatula, a can opener, a set of measuring spoons, a measuring cup, a glass plate, a microwave, 4–6 medium-sized bowls, and 4–6 spoons. A lengthy but appetizing set of ingredients is also vital to this heavenly dish: 1 pound of lean ground beef, two 16-oz. cans of Del Monte whole peeled tomatoes, 4 tablespoons of Gebhart chili powder, 1 tablespoon of garlic powder, 2 teaspoons of ground black pepper, 1 teaspoon of ground cayenne pepper, 2 teaspoons of ground cumin, 1 teaspoon of table salt, and 1/2 cup of water. Now that the equipment and ingredients are clear, let's really get started.

[3]When you have obtained all of the specified equipment and ingredients listed above, the next step is to prepare your ingredients. Measure each individual dry ingredient and pour it into separate small bowls. Open the cans of tomatoes and leave them in their cans. Measure the water and leave it in the measuring cup until you need it. If the beef is frozen, defrost it in the microwave for approximately 8 minutes. When it is thawed, unwrap it and place it on a glass plate. Now, place all the measured ingredients, the ground beef, and the tomatoes on the counter and place the electric skillet next to them. Plug the skillet in and turn the dial to 225 degrees. You are now ready to begin the actual cooking.

[4]When the temperature light goes off the electric skillet, or when the inside of the skillet feels warm to a quick touch, it's time to start cooking the beef. Place the ground beef in the skillet and break it apart with the spatula until it covers the bottom of the skillet. Stirring with the spatula every 30 seconds, cook the ground beef approximately 6 minutes, or until each piece of beef turns grey inside and out. At the moment the ground beef reaches this stage, pour the garlic powder over the ground beef and stir with the spatula until the garlic is dissolved (approximately ten times around the skillet). When this step is completed, there will be a strong "sinus healing" smell that will tickle the inside of your nose. The garlic makes its presence known.

[5]After the garlic powder is dissolved, add the tomatoes and remaining spices. Pour the tomatoes, including the juice, into the skillet. Using the spatula, cut up the tomatoes into small pieces and stir them around with the spatula until they are evenly distributed in the skillet along with the ground beef and garlic powder. At this point, add the chili powder and cayenne pepper to the mixture and stir with the spatula to dissolve these

spices. Next, pour the table salt, ground black pepper, and ground cumin into the skillet and stir until these ingredients are also dissolved in the mixture. Add the water to the skillet mixture and stir it approximately twenty times around. After these ingredients are combined, the chili will appear a dark red color and will provide a mixed aroma of sweet-smelling tomatoes and spicy hot chili powder along with its cayenne cousin. Now, raise the heat to 350 degrees by turning up the dial on the skillet.

[6]In the final stage of cooking, the chili will start to boil. This is easy to see because the chili will resemble a miniature lava pool with its dark red mixture giving off steam by its bubbling and belching. Let the mixture boil (and belch) for 3 minutes, stirring with the spatula every 15 seconds. Then, turn the dial on the skillet to "simmer" and put the cover on top of the skillet. Let the chili simmer for 8 minutes, stirring with the spatula every minute and reapplying the cover each time. At the end of 8 minutes, turn the dial on the skillet to "off" and take the cover off the skillet. The finished product will be a thick, spicy-smelling red mixture filled with chunks of beef halfway submerged in a hot tub of spicy juices.

[7]The chili is now ready to eat! This recipe serves four Texas-sized portions or six regular portions. With the spatula, place the chili in bowls, and then tell everyone to use a big spoon and "dig in." This chili is spicy and even hot at times, but its combination of sweet and sour flavors is both unique and delicious. A bottle of Corona, twenty crackers, and a big pickle are optional.

—Andy Savage, student

EXERCISE

11.6

1. What process is described in this essay?

   _____

2. What is the thesis, or main idea, of this process essay? Underline the thesis and then rewrite it here.

   _____

   _____

3. What is the purpose of this essay? That is, does it give instructions for completing a process or explain a process so readers can understand it?

   _____

   _____

4. List the five major steps of the process described in this essay.

   a. _____

   b. _____

   c. _____

   d. _____

   e. _____

5. This essay uses transition effectively to move from one major stage to the next. List two or three transitions found in each of the paragraphs listed.

   Paragraph 2: _____

   Paragraph 3: _____

   Paragraph 4: _____

   Paragraph 5: _____

   Paragraph 6: _____

   Paragraph 7: _____

6. This essay is an excellent example of a process essay that combines description with process narration. What are some of the most effective sensory details (appealing to taste, touch, sight, smell, and hearing) in the essay?

   _____

   _____

   What are some of the factual details?

   _____

   _____

Chapter Review

- A process is a series of actions that brings about a particular end or result.

- Process writing often uses narration, description, and cause and effect; however, it is unique in that it focuses on a typical, representative, or repeatable action or process.

- Process writing may either give instructions so readers can duplicate a process or provide an explanation of a process so readers can understand how it works.

- Good process writing includes all of the following elements:
  1. A clear main point that implies the writer's purpose
  2. All essential steps and details for completing or understanding the process
  3. A clear chronological sequence
  4. Effective transitions
  5. Definitions of unfamiliar terms

▨ Writing Assignment

Write a process essay on a topic involving from three to five major steps or stages. You may either give instructions for completing a specific process or explain how a particular process works. You might explain how to complete a process necessary for college, home, or work, such as applying for financial aid, taking notes in class, studying for an examination, changing a tire or changing the oil in your car, doing a load of laundry, applying for a job, running a cash registrar at Wal-Mart, or cleaning up (or closing up) at McDonald's. Or, you might—like Andy—give directions for preparing one of your favorite foods.

Begin your essay with an introductory paragraph that explains your purpose and gives your thesis. Focus a separate paragraph on each major step, being sure to arrange these steps in chronological order and to provide transitions to help your readers move from one step to the next. Include all the relevant details necessary for your reader to follow your instructions or understand the process being explained, and explain any terms that might be unclear or confusing to your readers.

▨ Participating in the Academic Community

When you have finished your process essay, meet with a small group of your classmates and use the Chapter Review to help you evaluate and revise your essays.

Chapter 12

Example

Writers frequently develop their main ideas by using **examples,** or the method of exemplification. Indeed, whatever the primary method of development, a writer nearly always finds it helpful—even necessary—to use examples for support. But exemplification is used not just as a secondary means of development but also as the primary method of development in both paragraphs and complete essays.

Examples are frequently employed in academic writing. Your history textbook gives examples of inventions that brought about the Industrial Revolution, your sociology textbook gives examples of racial or gender discrimination, and your biology textbook gives examples of types of mammals. Moreover, in writing an explanation of stress for your psychology class or a personal essay on the same topic for your English composition class, you will need to give examples of the stress you have observed and experienced.

Understanding Examples

Two major types of exemplification exist. In the first type, several brief examples are given to support the main idea (topic sentence or thesis sentence). In the second type, one extended example develops the main idea. As you read the two paragraphs that follow, notice that the first one uses several brief examples and the second one uses one extended example. The topic sentences of these paragraphs are set in bold type.

BRIEF EXAMPLE

There is even a geography of smells. Certain places have an aroma that becomes an integral part of their profile; for me, there will always be a Baltimore smell. For a colleague, there will always be the smell of the manicured cemetery across the road from his home in Champlain, New York. Sri Lanka is known for the fragrance of palm oil, Jakarta for the pervasive aroma of cloves. The smells of cheap gasoline and inferior cigarettes will forever recall the Soviet Union. You can often tell where in the world you are simply by breathing. This is particularly true of the Third World and in any place where primary crops are processed.

—George J. Demko, *Why in the World: Adventures in Geography*

EXTENDED EXAMPLE

In a society in which many people are socially mobile and may live as adults in a social or cultural environment very different from the one in which they grew up, old forms of discipline may be wholly unsuited to new situations. A father whose family lived according to a rigid, severe set of standards, and who was beaten in his boyhood for lying or stealing, may still think of beatings as an appropriate method of disciplining his son. Though he now lives as a middle-class professional man in a suburb, he may punish his son roughly for not doing well in school. It is not the harshness as such that then may discourage the boy even more, but his bewilderment. Living in a milieu in which parents and teachers reward children by praise and presents for doing well in school— a milieu in which beating is not connected with competence in schoolwork—the boy may not be able to make much sense of the treatment he receives.

—Margaret Mead and Rhoda Metraux, *A Way of Seeing*

Qualities of Effective Exemplification

A paragraph or essay developed by examples should have the following characteristics:

1. *A clear purpose and main idea.* Like all other effective writing styles, a paragraph or essay should have a clear main idea, usually stated in a topic sentence or a thesis statement. Demko's topic sentence "There is even a geography of smells" gives the main idea of his paragraph and prepares for the examples that follow.

2. *One extended example or several brief examples that clearly support the main idea.* Supporting examples, whether one fully developed example or several shorter ones, should clearly relate to the main idea. Each example in the paragraph from Demko's *Why in the World* clearly shows how particular smells are associated with specific places, and the extended example from Mead and Metraux's *A Way of Seeing* directly supports the main idea that "old forms of discipline may be wholly unsuited to new situations."

3. *A clear and logical arrangement of examples.* Examples may be arranged in various ways, such as in the order in which they occur in space or in time, in the order of increasing or decreasing importance, or in other logical orders. Demko arranges his examples from the more personal smells that he and his colleague associate with particular places to smells associated with Third World countries. Mead and Metraux develop their illustration chronologically from the father's experience to the son's experience. Indeed, a narrative is often used as an extended example.

EXERCISE

12.1   The two paragraphs that follow have been taken from a college history textbook. Read each paragraph and then answer the questions that follow it.

PARAGRAPH A

Though often thought of as outposts of rugged individualism, many early agricultural settlements depended heavily on family and kinship networks and communal cooperation. Sugar Creek on the Sangamon River in central Illinois exemplified this cooperative spirit. The white settlers who arrived in 1817 named the settlement for its sugar maples, tapped first by the Kickapoos and then by the American settlers. Although the settlement was based on private land ownership, most newcomers over the next decade were members of kin networks who assisted each other in clearing land and turning temporary dwellings into permanent cabins. Whether raising hogs or children, Sugar Creek families depended on kin and friends for support. In crises, too, they rose to the occasion. When someone "would be sick with chills or jaundice, or something else," Sugar Creek farmer James Megredy recalled, "his neighbors would meet and take care of his harvest, get up wood, or repair his cabin, or plant his corn." Neighbors set up a "borrowing system" whereby scarce tools and labor constantly circulated through the neighborhood. Settlers who came without previous ties, if they stayed, did not long remain strangers.

—Mary Norton et al., *A People and a Nation*, 5th ed.

1. Underline the topic sentence that states the main idea of this paragraph. Then restate the main idea in your own words.

_____

_____

_____

12.1 continued

2. Is the paragraph developed by several brief examples or one extended example?

_____

3. Write the example(s) here.

_____

_____

_____

PARAGRAPH B

   Dorothea Dix described the nether [lower] world she had uncovered in her investigation of the treatment of the insane in the previous two years. She reported appalling conditions in Massachusetts towns: men and women in cages, chained to walls, in dark dungeons, brutalized and held in solitary confinement. In a surprise visit to a Newburyport almshouse in the summer of 1842, Dix expressed her surprise at the comfortable conditions for the "one idiotic" and seven insane inhabitants. On the grounds she discovered, however, one man residing in a shed whose door opened to the local "dead room" or morgue; the man's only companions were corpses. Shocked, she heard from an attendant about another insane inmate whom no one spoke of: "a woman in a *cellar*."
                              —Mary Norton et al., *A People and a Nation*, 5th ed.

1. Underline the topic sentence that states the main idea of this paragraph. Then restate the main idea in your own words.

_____

_____

_____

2. Is the paragraph developed by several brief examples or one extended example?

_____

3. Write the example(s) here.

_____

_____

_____

Writing Example Paragraphs

In writing an example paragraph, you should keep in mind each of the three qualities of effective illustration. That is, (1) you should begin your paragraph with a topic sentence that clearly states your main idea, (2) you should use one extended example or several shorter ones that clearly support your main idea, and (3) you should arrange your examples clearly and logically.

Writing Topic Sentences and Using Transitions in Example Paragraphs

In addition to beginning an example paragraph with an effective topic sentence (see pages 29–30 and 128), you should also include clear **transitions** that clarify your organization or your method of arrangement. The following paragraph, for instance, is organized according to order of importance. The topic sentence is in bold type and the transition words that indicate examples or order of importance are highlighted with color bars.

STUDENT PARAGRAPH

A college freshman who displays good study habits will be a successful student. For example, a responsible college freshman will make sure she gets to class on time every day. My roommate Pam, for instance, gets to her classes ten to fifteen minutes early. She wants to be prepared for the daily lecture or any pop quizzes. Even more important, a good student is always alert in class. Pam pays close attention to her teacher so she can take good study notes. She also tries to catch key words and hints that he may give during lectures that might help her with her homework or tests. Finally, and most important, Pam always begins her assignments early and spends plenty of time on them. She sets aside certain hours to do her homework, and she disciplines herself so that she never turns in a late or a sloppy assignment. As a result of these good study habits, Pam and students like her make good grades.

—Jill Kerr, student

Jill begins her paragraph with a clear topic sentence stating her main point that good study habits (topic) help a student succeed in college (assertion). She then illustrates her point by providing examples of study techniques that her roommate has used to become a successful student. The organization of Jill's paragraph is also effective, moving from less important to more important examples of study habits. Finally, Jill uses effective transitions between her supporting examples. The following list shows not only the transition words that Jill uses but also other transitions that you will find helpful in writing example paragraphs and essays:

for example	also	more/most important
for instance	in addition	less/least important
to illustrate	furthermore	next
such as	moreover	then
that is	first, second, etc.	finally

EXERCISE

12.2

Write a topic sentence for each of the following subjects. Then list three examples to support this topic sentence.

1. Your favorite type of movie

   Topic sentence: _____

   _____

   Examples: a. _____

   b. _____

   c. _____

2. Teachers who have influenced you

   Topic sentence: _____

   _____

   Examples: a. _____

   b. _____

   c. _____

3. Problems on your college campus

   Topic sentence: _____

   _____

   Examples: a. _____

   b. _____

   c. _____

12.3

Select the topic that interests you most in Exercise 12.2. Then use the topic sentence and examples that you wrote for that exercise and the following questions to plan a paragraph on this topic.

1. What is the topic? _____

2. What is your topic sentence? (*Note:* You may want to revise the topic sentence you wrote for Exercise 12.2.)

   _____

   _____

3. Decide on the order in which you want to arrange your examples. Then rewrite these examples in the order you have chosen and add additional details to support each example.

   Example 1: _____

   Details: _____

   _____

   Example 2: _____

   Details: _____

   _____

   Example 3: _____

   Details: _____

   _____

12.3 continued

Use this plan to write a paragraph developed by examples. You may develop your paragraph by using three brief examples or by developing one example fully. In either case, be sure to use clear transitions. You may find especially helpful the transition words listed earlier.

Writing Example Essays

While examples occur to some degree in nearly all writing, they are often used as the primary method of development in essays as well as paragraphs. Like a paragraph, an essay may develop one long example or use several briefer examples. Each paragraph within an essay may develop a single example or include several examples. The possible variations are nearly endless. As you read the following student essay, notice the different ways that Christie uses examples. Notice also that her essay includes a clear main idea (thesis statement), a logical arrangement of the primary supporting examples, and effective transitions.

Who's in Charge? Man or Machine

[1] As I dialed the number to order a cassette tape I'd seen advertised on television, I was hoping that I would get an answer. After all, it was fifteen minutes after 5 o'clock, and I had some questions about the free gift that I would receive for purchasing *George Strait's Greatest Hits.* "Hello," I said when I heard the click of a phone being picked up. "I am calling about the George Strait cassette, and I have some questions about . . ." While I was trying to blurt out my question, I heard this strange monotone thanking me for calling and telling me what a great deal this offer was. The voice was slow and had an eerie similarity to Darth Vader's voice from *Star Wars.* The voice continued to brag about the George Strait tape but with about the same enthusiasm I'd have if I were eating oatmeal in a prison. "Dang computers!" I screamed as I slammed down the phone. I'm not much on ordering over the phone, but when I do, I at least want to talk to a real person since I'm sending in real money.

[2] This instance with telephone ordering is just one of many negative experiences I have had with computers. In my opinion, the world is becoming so computerized that there is real danger of the human element being lost. Many businesses such as colleges, banks, and car manufacturers are relying more and more on computers rather than on people.

[3]First, computer error occurs frequently on college campuses. For example, when I was a senior in high school, I was also enrolled in History 121 at East Texas State University. After I finished the semester, I couldn't wait to get my grade. I knew I had a B for sure, and I thought I had a chance for an A. I was horrified, however, when my grade report said that I had made a D. That couldn't be right, I thought. The lowest grade I'd made all semester was a 79 on the first and hardest test we had had. My other grades were A's, and I thought I had done well on the final. I called my instructor to check on the grade and try to get it changed. He said I had made a B and that he was sure he had turned in a B. The secretary or the computer had made a mistake. I'm sure that some person had entered the grade wrong, but with the over-reliance on computers, no one wanted to take the responsibility for the error.

[4]Even more frightening is the fact that banks have become almost completely computerized. While this computerization has some advantages for bankers and their customers, my family recently had an experience that shows some of the problems that can be caused by computers in banks. My grandmother has had a life insurance premium automatically deducted from her account each month for several years. After she died last year, we told the bank so there would be no more automatic withdrawals. The lady at the bank said there would be no charge to stop payment. The computer, however, automatically made a $15.00 stop check charge. The account was low since no new deposits had been made since my grandmother's death, so the $15.00 deduction made the account $.88 overdrawn, which caused the computer to go crazy and charge $42.00 in overdraft and nonsufficient fund penalties. The problem was quickly remedied, however, when we talked to a real person at the bank, and all charges were refunded.

[5]Finally, and most disturbing of all, manufacturers of various products are also relying more and more on computers not only to run their businesses but also to produce their products. I hear on television every day that more and more people are laid off from factories because of new engineering and computerized machines doing the work of many people. The factories and manufacturing companies would rather pay for an expensive computerized system than keep human workers to do the same job and provide them benefits and insurance. Car manufacturers are particularly guilty of this practice. For example, the plant for the Saturn car uses many computer robots, and the plant that makes the Ranger pickups is almost completely run by computers. I can see how a company may want to save money in the long run, but this isn't just cutting costs. These are men's and women's lives.

[6]I do believe that the world is becoming too computerized and that the human element is being lost. Many people don't even talk to other people over the telephone anymore. They talk through the Internet, by e-mail, and over fax machines. We are taking computers to the extreme when they start replacing people.

—Christie Welch, student

This essay is a variation of the five-paragraph pattern that you studied in Chapter 5. The first paragraph provides an extended example that captures the interest of the reader and introduces the subject of the essay: the relationship of human beings to computers. The second paragraph, like many introductory paragraphs, places this example in context and states the thesis of the essay, even listing in a logical order the three main examples to be developed (i.e., reliance of colleges, banks, and manufacturers on computers more than human beings). Moreover, each paragraph in the body of the essay begins with a transition that not only connects each main point to the thesis but also shows the relationships among the main points in the essay.

EXERCISE

12.4   Answer the following questions about the essay you have just read, referring back to the essay as necessary.

1. Why does Christie use an example in her introduction?

    _____

    _____

2. Underline the thesis statement, and then rewrite it here.

    _____

    _____

3. Reread the body paragraphs and indicate whether each is based on several brief examples or on one extended example.

    Paragraph 3: _____

    Paragraph 4: _____

    Paragraph 5: _____

4. List the specific example(s) that you believe are most effective in the essay.

_____

_____

_____

_____

5. What method of arrangement does Christie use for the three main points of the essay (time order, space order, order of importance)?

_____

6. What transitions between paragraphs provide clues to the primary method of arrangement in the essay?

_____

_____

_____

_____

7. Individual paragraphs in an essay may be arranged according to a different method of arrangement than that used for the essay itself. What method of arrangement is used in paragraphs 1, 3, and 4?

_____

Chapter Review

- A paragraph or essay developed by example should have a clear main idea (topic sentence or thesis statement).

- Each example in a paragraph or essay should clearly support the main idea.

- The main idea may be supported by several brief examples or one extended example.

- The examples should be logically arranged and clearly connected with effective transitions.

■ Writing Assignment

Expand the paragraph you wrote for Exercise 12.3 into an essay. You may use each of the examples from your original paragraph as the basis for one of your body paragraphs, adding additional details to each example, or you may expand one of your examples into an essay. Whatever your method of expansion, be sure to arrange your examples in a logical order and use appropriate transitions.

■ Participating in the Academic Community

When you have completed a draft of your essay, meet with a peer revision group to evaluate one another's essays. Using the guidelines in the Chapter Review, identify the strong points and the weak points of each essay and make suggestions for improvement.

Chapter 13

Comparison and Contrast

In its broadest definition, **comparison** involves showing both similarities and differences between two people, places, objects, or actions. Thus, you may compare two suits, cars, or houses—looking at differences as well as similarities—before deciding which to buy. In academic writing assignments, however, instructors often distinguish between the processes of comparing and contrasting, using *comparing* to mean "showing similarities" and *contrasting* to mean "showing differences." Thus, your biology professor might ask you to compare two mammals to identify the similarities that place them in the category of mammal, or your history professor might ask you to contrast two presidents. As these examples suggest, **comparison** and **contrast** are extremely useful methods of development in academic writing.

Understanding Comparison and Contrast

Both paragraphs and essays can be developed by comparison, contrast, or a combination of the two. This section will help you recognize effective comparison and contrast writing in your reading, understand how comparison and contrast are organized, and learn how to use them in your own writing.

Although the process of comparison may include both similarities and differences, we will try to avoid confusion in this chapter by using the term *compare* to indicate similarities and the term *contrast* to mean differences. The first of the following paragraphs emphasizes similarities whereas the second focuses on differences.

PARAGRAPH A: Comparing

Barbiturates and tranquilizers are both sedatives. They relax or calm people; and when taken in higher doses, they often induce sleep. *Barbiturates* decrease the excitability of neurons throughout the nervous system. They calm the individual by depressing the central nervous system. The use of barbiturates as sedatives, however, has diminished; they have largely been replaced by another class of drugs—tranquilizers. *Tranquilizers* are a group of drugs that also sedate and calm people. With a somewhat lower potential for abuse, they are sometimes called minor tranquilizers. Valium and Librium are two of the most widely used tranquilizers prescribed by physicians for relief of mild stress. Although tranquilizers are less dangerous than barbiturates, they have also been widely abused by all segments of society because of their availability.

—Adapted from Lester A. Lefton, *Psychology*, 6th ed.

PARAGRAPH B: Contrasting

Moving from Detroit, Michigan, to Hobbs, New Mexico, was not easy because I had to get used to the differences in climate, size, and the attitude toward time. Even though the weather in Michigan is not ideal, it was what I had known all my life, and I was used to the dampness and the cold in winter and the dampness and the heat in the summer. Detroit is a busy, industrial city that never sleeps. In this busy city, time is a valuable commodity, seldom wasted. Thus, everyone in Detroit is on the move—in a hurry, rushed, afraid of being late. Hobbs differs from Detroit in each of these three areas. In the dry climate of Hobbs, any moisture evaporates immediately, and it is sometimes difficult to tell winter from summer since the two seasons are so much alike. Unlike its hectic city neighbor to the north, the town of Hobbs never wakes up. It is so quiet and small that I felt at first as though I were living on the fringe of civilization. But the biggest difference between the two places was the attitude toward time. I don't mean just the fact that Detroit is on Eastern Standard Time and Hobbs is on Mountain Standard Time. I mean fast versus slow. In contrast to Detroit, no one in Hobbs really cares what time it is. No one seems concerned about getting places on time, much less early. But now that I have lived in Hobbs for a year, I find that I too am slowing down. Moreover, I have found that I haven't left civilization. I've just moved to a different type—a drier, warmer, quieter, slower one.

Qualities of Effective Comparison and Contrast

Whether used separately or together, the processes of comparison and contrast have several qualities in common:

1. *A clear sense of purpose.* Like other types of writing, comparison and contrast writing should have a clear sense of purpose. Most of the comparison and contrast writing that you will write or read in your college classes will be either informative or persuasive, but you may occasionally encounter comparison and contrast writing that is intended to entertain. Lefton's paragraph about sedatives is not only informative but also mildly persuasive, concluding that barbiturates are more dangerous than tranquilizers. The paragraph about Detroit and Hobbs uses a rather humorous style to explain the differences to which the writer had to adjust.

2. *Two related and limited subjects.* Comparison and/or contrast writing always presents two subjects that have a close enough relationship to be effectively compared or contrasted. These subjects should also be narrow enough to be developed into a paragraph or essay that is supported with specific details and examples. For instance, because barbiturates and tranquilizers are both sedatives, they clearly have a basis for comparison. Even though Detroit and Hobbs have many differences, these subjects also have a clear basis for comparison because they are both cities. The two subjects in both of these paragraphs are clearly limited and defined.

3. *A clearly stated or implied main idea.* Effective comparison and contrast writing has a clear main idea (usually stated in a topic sentence or thesis statement) that specifies the two subjects and their relationship. That is, the main idea indicates whether the two subjects are primarily similar or different. The topic sentence of the first example paragraph points out that barbiturates and tranquilizers are similar. The topic sentence of the second paragraph explains that life in Hobbs, New Mexico, is quite different from life in Detroit, Michigan.

4. *Clearly identified and balanced supporting points and details.* The number of points to be compared or contrasted and the details and examples used to support each subject should be fairly balanced. Lefton provides effects and uses (and abuses) of both barbiturates and tranquilizers, and the writer of the paragraph about Detroit and Hobbs gives details about living in both cities. Moreover, both writers provide specific examples and details to support their points. Lefton lists Valium and Librium as examples of tranquilizers, and the writer of the paragraph contrasting Detroit and Hobbs gives specific details about the climate, size, and attitude toward time. For example, Detroit is described as primarily cold and damp whereas Hobbs is hot and dry.

5. *A clear organizational structure.* As shown in the next section, this balanced presentation of the two subjects of a comparison or contrast and of the major points and details supporting each subject may be achieved by either of two organizational structures.

Arrangement in Comparison and Contrast Writing

The most common patterns of arrangement for supporting points and details in a comparison/contrast paragraph or essay are the **subject-by-subject** (or block) **method** and the **point-by-point** (or alternating) **method.**

Subject-by-Subject (Block) Method

In the subject-by-subject method used in the sample paragraphs on page 174, the writer presents first one subject and then the other of the comparison or contrast. The following outline illustrates how the details contrasting Detroit and Hobbs are arranged in this subject-by-subject method:

Topic sentence: Moving from Detroit, Michigan, to Hobbs, New Mexico, was not easy because I had to get used to the differences in climate, size, and the attitude toward time.

Subject A: Detroit, Michigan
  Point 1:   Climate
  Point 2:   Size
  Point 3:   Time

Subject B: Hobbs, New Mexico
  Point 1:   Climate
  Point 2:   Size
  Point 3:   Time

Point-by-Point (Alternating) Method

In the point-by-point method, the writer discusses both subjects of the comparison or contrast for the first point, then both sides for the second point, and so on. Using the point-by-point method, the same contrasting information about Detroit and Hobbs would be organized like this:

Topic sentence: Moving from Detroit, Michigan, to Hobbs, New Mexico, was not easy because I had to get used to the differences in climate, size, and the attitude toward time.

Point 1:   Climate
  Subject A: Detroit
  Subject B: Hobbs

Point 2:   Size
    Subject A: Detroit
    Subject B: Hobbs

Point 3:   Time
    Subject A: Detroit
    Subject B: Hobbs

Although the subject-by-subject structure is easier for many students to use, the point-by-point pattern is often more effective in longer paragraphs and essays because readers don't have to wait for the comparisons or contrasts to be completed for one subject before reading about the next subject.

EXERCISE

13.1   The following two paragraphs are taken from college textbooks—the first from a sociology textbook and the second from a history textbook. Read each paragraph and then answer the questions about structure that follow.

PARAGRAPH A

    Differentiated treatment of the two gangs [the Saints and the Roughnecks] resulted in part because one gang was infinitely more visible than the other. This differential visibility was a direct function of the economic standing of the families. The Saints had access to automobiles and were able to remove themselves from the sight of the community. In as routine a decision as to where to go to have a milkshake after school, the Saints stayed away from the mainstream of community life. Lacking transportation, the Roughnecks could not make it to the edge of town. The center of town was the only practical place for them to meet since their homes were scattered throughout the town and any non-central meeting place put an undue hardship on some members. Through necessity the Roughnecks congregated in a crowded area where everyone in the community passed frequently, including teachers and law enforcement officers. They could easily see the Roughnecks hanging around the drugstore.

    —Ian Robertson, *Sociology,* 3rd ed.

1.   Underline Robertson's topic sentence, or main point. Does this main point emphasize similarities or differences?

2.   Does Robertson organize his paragraph subject by subject (block method) or point by point (alternating method)?

13.1 continued

3. Complete the following outline of the relationships expressed in the paragraph:

	Saints	**Roughnecks**
Point 1: Transportation	_____	_____
Point 2: Place of meeting	_____	_____
Point 3: Visibility	_____	_____

PARAGRAPH B

The two men [Paul Revere and John Singleton Copley] must have found the occasion [of Copley's painting Revere's portrait in 1768] remarkable. The artist customarily painted portraits of the wealthy and high born, not of artisans, even well-connected, affluent ones. The subject himself was an artist—a maker of beautiful silver and gold objects, an engraver of cartoons and townscapes. The political sympathies of Copley, the painter, lay primarily with Boston's conservatives, whereas Revere, the sitter, was a noted leader of resistance to British policies. . . . Copley was thirty, Revere thirty-four. Each man had learned his trade from a parent. Revere's father Apollos, who arrived in Boston as a teenage Huguenot refugee early in the century, was an accomplished gold- and silversmith; Paul served as his father's apprentice and took over the family business when Apollos died in 1754. Copley, whose Irish parents had immigrated to Boston in the 1730s, was taught to paint by his stepfather, Peter Pelham, an English artist. The two young tradesmen had undoubtedly known each other for years. In 1763 and thereafter Copley hired Revere to make silver and gold frames for the miniature portraits that were among his earliest works. But their finest collaboration was the painting.

—Adapted from Mary Norton et al., *A People and a Nation*, 5th ed.

1. Underline Norton's topic sentence. Note that this topic sentence points out the "remarkable" connection between the two men but is general enough to allow Norton to discuss both similarities and differences.

2. Does Norton organize her paragraph subject by subject (block method) or point by point (alternating method)?

_____

3. Complete the following outline of the relationships expressed in the paragraph, indicating whether the relationship in each point is treated as a similarity or a difference:

	John Copley	Paul Revere	Relationship
Point 1: Type of artist	_____	_____	_____
Point 2: Politics	_____	_____	_____
Point 3: Age	_____	_____	_____
Point 4: Learned trade	_____	_____	_____

EXERCISE

13.2

Narrow each of the following topics to two subjects that can be effectively compared, and then list three points of comparison, or similarities, for each subject.

▶ EXAMPLE: Two courses

Limited subjects:	A. freshman composition	B. freshman history
Point	1. listening (in student groups)	1. listening (to lecture)
Point	2. writing (essays)	2. writing (essay examinations)
Point	3. reading (student essays)	3. reading (professional essays)

1. Two people (parents, friends, politicians, etc.)

   Limited subjects: A. _____   B. _____

   1. _____   1. _____

   2. _____   2. _____

   3. _____   3. _____

2. Two places (rooms, buildings, vacation spots, etc.)

   Limited subjects: A. _____   B. _____

   1. _____   1. _____

   2. _____   2. _____

   3. _____   3. _____

13.2 continued

3. Two things (cars, computers, animals, plants, etc.)

Limited subjects: A. _____   B. _____

1. _____   1. _____

2. _____   2. _____

3. _____   3. _____

E X E R C I S E

13.3

In the space below, contrast the same narrowed subjects that you compared in Exercise 13.2. List three points of contrast, or difference, for each subject.

▶ EXAMPLE: Two courses

Limited subjects: A. <u>freshman composition</u>   B. <u>freshman history</u>

Point   1. student centered   1. teacher centered

Point   2. emphasizes discussion 2. emphasizes lecture

Point   3. focuses on current   3. focuses on past
                    issues   events

1. Two people (parents, friends, politicians, etc.)

Limited subjects: A. _____   B. _____

1. _____   1. _____

2. _____   2. _____

3. _____   3. _____

2. Two places (rooms, buildings, vacation spots, etc.)

Limited subjects: A. _____   B. _____

1. _____   1. _____

2. _____   2. _____

3. _____   3. _____

3. Two things (cars, computers, animals, plants, etc.)

Limited subjects: A. _____   B. _____

1. _____   1. _____

2. _____   2. _____

3. _____   3. _____

Writing Comparison and Contrast Paragraphs

You will be able to write better comparison and contrast paragraphs if you pay particular attention to three important elements of each paragraph: (1) the topic sentence, (2) the organization, and (3) the transitions.

Writing Topic Sentences in Comparison and Contrast Paragraphs

The topic sentence of a comparison and/or contrast paragraph usually identifies the two subjects and indicates whether the paragraph will discuss their similarities, differences, or both. For example, the following topic sentences provide clear main ideas for paragraphs comparing or contrasting your composition and history classes:

COMPARISON: *My composition and history classes have several similarities.*

CONTRAST: *My composition and history classes are different in several ways.*

Notice that the assertion, or the main point, in these topic sentences is based on whether the two subjects are similar or different. The major supporting points in paragraphs developing these topic sentences would focus on these similarities or differences.

EXERCISE

13.4

In Exercises 13.2 and 13.3, you narrowed three broad topics and listed both similarities and differences for each of these topics. Now, write topic sentences to compare or contrast each of your narrowed topics.

1. People

   Narrowed topic: _____

   Comparison topic sentence: _____

   _____

   Contrast topic sentence: _____

   _____

13.4 continued

2. Places

   Narrowed topic: _____

   Comparison topic sentence: _____

   _____

   Contrast topic sentence: _____

   _____

3. Things

   Narrowed topic: _____

   Comparison topic sentence: _____

   _____

   Contrast topic sentence: _____

   _____

Using Transitions in Comparison and Contrast Paragraphs

Because of the complex relationships among subjects in a comparison and/or contrast paragraph, you need to be especially careful to use appropriate transitions to guide your readers. Although both methods of organizing a comparison or contrast paragraph require effective transitions, you will need to use more transition words with the point-by-point method than with the subject-by-subject method. For example, notice the transition words that Janna uses in the following paragraph contrasting point by point how a wealthy man and a poor man are treated by the legal system:

STUDENT PARAGRAPH

   In the legal system, people are often judged by their financial status. In two parallel cases, a wealthy man and an indigent man were charged with the same type of crime: robbery. The wealthy man had the financial resources to hire three attorneys and an investigator to work on his case. However, the indigent man had only one court attorney appointed to his case and did not have the money to hire a private investigator to spend time on the case. The wealthy man had actually committed the crime of breaking into a store and stealing money from it, but his case was dismissed because he had money to buy his freedom. The poor man, on the other hand, was convicted of robbery and spent three years in jail even though he was innocent. As these instances show, the legal system in the United States is often unfairly biased to the "haves" over the "have-nots."

—Janna Hammons, student

In this paragraph, Janna uses the point-by-point method of organization. She discusses first the financial resources of both the wealthy man and the poor man and then the legal results for both men. Notice that with each point of her comparison, she uses a transition to move from one side of her comparison to the other. Thus, she uses the transition word *however* to show the contrast between the financial resources of both men and the transition phrase *on the other hand* to show the contrast between the results of the cases for the two men. If she had used the subject-by-subject method, she would have needed to discuss both the financial resources and legal results for first one man and then the other.

The following chart lists several helpful transition words to show either comparison or contrast:

COMPARISON		CONTRAST	
and	in addition	but	yet
like	likewise	although	unlike
as	just as	in contrast	nevertheless
as well as	both . . . and	however	even though
also	similarly	whereas	while
both	either, neither	conversely	on the other hand

EXERCISE

13.5

Rewrite Janna's paragraph using the subject-by-subject method of organization. Be sure to provide appropriate transitions.

13.6   Select one of the items that you completed for Exercise 13.2 or 13.3 and write a paragraph about two people, places, or things. Decide what relationship you want to show in your paragraph (comparison or contrast) and write (or select from Exercise 13.4) a narrowed topic sentence that clearly shows that relationship. Then determine the organizational arrangement (subject-by-subject or point-by-point) that you want to use and the details that you want to include. Use the following guide to complete a plan for your paragraph:

Relationship: _____

Topic sentence: _____

_____

Arrangement: _____

SUBJECT-BY-SUBJECT PLAN

Subjects: _____

Side A: _____

    Point 1: _____

    Point 2: _____

    Point 3: _____

Side B: _____

    Point 1: _____

    Point 2: _____

    Point 3: _____

POINT-BY-POINT PLAN

Subjects: _____

Point 1: _____

    Side A: _____

    Side B: _____

Point 2: _____

    Side A: _____

    Side B: _____

Point 3: _____

Side A: _____

Side B: _____

Writing Comparison and Contrast Essays

In addition to writing comparison and contrast paragraphs that can stand alone or function as part of a longer composition, you will occasionally need to write an entire essay that is developed primarily by comparison and contrast. For example, your history professor might ask you to compare Presidents Franklin Roosevelt and Woodrow Wilson, your psychology professor might ask you to compare long-term and short-term memory, or your literature professor might ask you to compare two poems or characters.

The following sample essay develops the main point about the relationship between Detroit and Hobbs that was begun earlier. As you read this essay, look for (and underline) the thesis sentence that states the writer's main point, and pay particular attention to the essay's organization and use of transition.

Moving from Detroit to Hobbs

[1]I was born in Detroit, Michigan, and had lived there all of my life until I married and moved with my husband to Hobbs, New Mexico. The morning that my parents took us to the airport, they cried as if I were leaving the country and moving to a foreign land. Although I felt some apprehension, I thought that surely there could not be much difference between one state or city and another. I felt confident that my life would be much the same. It did not take me long to discover, however, that moving from Detroit to Hobbs was not easy because I had to get used to differences in climate, size, and the attitude toward time.

[2]First, I had to get used to the change in climate. Even though the weather in Michigan is not ideal, it was what I had known all my life. I was used to the dampness and the cold in the winter and the dampness and heat in the summer. I accepted mildew and frizzy hair as facts of life. In Hobbs, however, any moisture that accidentally occurs immediately evaporates. Even in the early morning there is no dew on the grass, and a rainfall is a major event, celebrated and talked about for days. Fog and mist are absolutely unheard of. Day after day the sun shines brightly, even relentlessly, drying out everything. In fact, it is sometimes difficult to tell winter from summer because the two seasons are so much alike.

[3]My next problem was adjusting to life in a small town. Detroit is a busy, industrial city that never sleeps. In contrast, Hobbs never wakes up. It is so quiet and small that I felt at first as though I were living on the fringe of civilization. Instead of several major newspapers, a variety of local radio and television channels, and a choice of big name entertainers and shows, Hobbs has one daily newspaper, a small radio station, and a few movies. By ten o'clock at night almost everyone is at home. And everyone knows everyone else. In Detroit, I could go all over the city and never see anyone I knew, but in Hobbs I rarely see anything but familiar faces. A stranger in town is the source of real excitement—a cause for speculation and curiosity. In Hobbs I don't dare go to the supermarket (there are only a few) with my hair in curlers, for I am sure to see people I know. In Detroit I could be anonymous when I chose; in Hobbs I am part of a small, even intimate, community.

[4]But the biggest problem I had was the difference in time. I don't mean just the fact that Detroit is on Eastern Standard Time and Hobbs is on Mountain Standard Time. I mean fast versus slow. Everyone in Detroit is on the move—in a hurry, rushed, afraid of being late. In Hobbs, on the other hand, no one really cares what time it is. No one seems concerned about getting places on time, much less early. For example, soon after we arrived in Hobbs we were invited to a party. Conditioned by years of living in Detroit, where everyone strives to be punctual, my husband and I arrived at the party on time. The door was opened by a surprised hostess, who, dressed in a robe, was straightening the living room and preparing some last-minute snacks for the party. She very graciously invited us in and explained that the other guests would be arriving soon. ("Soon" turned out to be almost an hour later.) We sat uncomfortably in the deserted living room as the hostess finished dressing and preparing the food. When the other guests finally arrived, an hour after the appointed time, the party began, although guests continued to arrive late into the evening. I now realize that when people in Hobbs say a party begins at a certain time, they don't really mean at that exact time. The attitude toward time is so relaxed that it is almost impossible to be *late*. People just aren't terribly concerned with being punctual.

[5]I have now lived in Hobbs for a year, and I find that I am slowing down, too. I don't drive as fast as I did; I don't worry if I am a few minutes late; and I certainly don't arrive at parties on time. I am also getting used to the climate. On a recent trip back to Detroit I was terribly conscious of the humidity and nearly froze because the weather was so cold and damp. Moreover, I have discovered that moving to Hobbs has not meant that I left civilization. I've just moved to a different type of civilization—one that is drier, warmer, quieter, and slower.

EXERCISE

13.7

1. Are the subjects of this essay (Hobbs and Detroit) compared or contrasted? That is, does the writer show similarities or differences?

   _____

2. What is the thesis sentence of this essay?

   _____

   _____

3. What organizational pattern does this essay follow? That is, is it organized by the subject-by-subject method, discussing first one subject and then the other, or by the point-by-point method, alternating information about Hobbs and Detroit as each point is discussed?

   _____

4. Is each of the writer's main points introduced in a topic sentence? If so, underline these topic sentences and then write the writer's main points about Hobbs and Detroit here.

   a. _____

   b. _____

   c. _____

5. Circle transition words that show the relationship between these two cities. Then write several of these transition words and expressions.

   _____

   _____

6. What conclusion does the writer draw about Detroit and Hobbs?

   _____

   _____

Chapter Review

- To compare means to show similarities between two subjects; to contrast is to show differences between two subjects.

- Comparison and contrast writing, like any other type of writing, should have a clear purpose.

- Two limited and related subjects are essential to good comparison and/or contrast.

- The main point of a comparison or a contrast should be expressed in a topic sentence or a thesis statement that identifies the subjects and indicates whether they will be compared or contrasted.

- Comparison and contrast paragraphs and essays should have clearly identified and balanced supporting points.

- Comparison and contrast paragraphs and essays should be structured according to the subject-by-subject or the point-by-point pattern and should include effective transitions.

- Each side of a comparison or contrast paragraph or essay should be supported with specific details and examples.

Writing Assignment

Choose one of the following options and write an essay comparing or contrasting two people, places, actions, or objects.

OPTION A: Select two comparable subjects that you have studied in one of your academic classes and compare and/or contrast these subjects in an essay. For example, you might compare two presidents, two ancient cities, two weather events, two computers, or two learning styles. Be sure, however, that you limit your subjects, or choose subjects narrow enough that you can develop them fully in an essay.

OPTION B: Select one of the pairs of subjects that you compared or contrasted in Exercises 13.2–13.4 and write a comparison or contrast essay about these subjects.

Before you write your essay, decide on the arrangement that you want to use and list your major points and examples.

Participating in the Academic Community

When you have finished your draft, meet with a small group of your classmates for a peer evaluation of your essays. Read each essay aloud in your group. Then adapt the questions from Exercise 13.7 for discussing and making suggestions about one another's essay.

Chapter 14

Classification

When you organize information by placing items into groups with other items that have similar characteristics, you are classifying. **Classification** is used not only by writers but also by other people who want to organize information clearly. Scientists classify plants, sociologists classify families, and political scientists classify types of government. Students classify their professors according to the subjects they teach (history professors, English professors, psychology professors), and at the end of each semester, teachers often classify students according to their performance in class (A students, B students, and so on).

Understanding Classification

Classifying means organizing items into categories. Thus, while a single subject can be analyzed, or divided into its separate parts (the earth into its crust, the rocky mantle below the crust, the outer core, and the inner core), only plural subjects can be classified. For example, you can classify students, colleges, computers, pizzas, cars, and televisions, but you can't classify a single student, college, computer, pizza, car, or television show. The following paragraph is an example of classification:

> **All rocks can be categorized into three basic types according to how they are formed: igneous, sedimentary, and metamorphic.** The first type, igneous rocks, originate when molten rock material called *magma* cools and solidifies. They may be coarse or fine depending upon the cooling process. For example, granite has large crystals because it was formed deep within the earth and cooled slowly; basalt is a fine-grained or glasslike rock because it cooled quickly near the surface. The second type, sedimentary rocks, are formed from the sediments that result from the decomposition of igneous rocks or of microscopic marine matter. Generally deposited

in layers, sedimentary rocks include sandstone, shale, and limestone. Finally, metamorphic rocks are formed from igneous or sedimentary rocks that are buried deep within the earth and subjected to great pressure and heat. For example, under heat and pressure, shale is transformed into slate and sandstone into quartzite.

Qualities of Effective Classification

The following qualities are present in effective classification paragraphs and essays:

1. *A clear purpose.* Although classification writing can persuade or entertain, most academic classification writing is informative in purpose. For example, the sample paragraph clearly informs readers that rocks are classified into three groups according to how they are formed.

2. *A clear main idea.* Whether stated or implied, good classification writing includes a clear main idea that states the subject of the paragraph or essay and either the basis of the classification or the categories of the classification (or both). In the paragraph about rocks, the topic sentence provides all three of these elements: the subject (rocks), the basis of classification (how they are formed), and the categories (igneous, sedimentary, and metamorphic).

3. *A single basis, or criterion, of classification.* To develop a system of classification, the writer must first determine a basis for classifying—that is, a *criterion* on which to base the classification. Items should be classified on the basis of a single, clear criterion. For example, rocks can be classified according to size, color, or how they are formed—but only one of these bases of classification can be used at a time.

4. *Completeness of classification.* The important point in classification is not *how many* categories you have but *how clearly and fully* the items you are classifying fit into your categories. Ideally, each item within a subject area should fit into one—and only one—category. Thus, all rocks can be classified as igneous, sedimentary, or metamorphic.

5. *Clearly identified and logically arranged subtopics supported with specific examples and details.* The categories of a classification paragraph or essay function as subpoints. Thus, the paragraph about rocks includes the three subtopics of igneous rocks, sedimentary rocks, and metamorphic rocks arranged logically in the order in which the types of rocks were formed chronologically. In addition, effective classification paragraphs and essays also include specific examples and details as well as clear transitions. For example, the model paragraph provides specific examples of each type of rock and clear transitions between subtopics.

EXERCISE

14.1

Each of the following groups has one item that doesn't belong. First, identify the basis of classification into which most of the items fit and write it in the space provided. Then circle the item that does not fit this classification system.

▶ EXAMPLE: Restaurants
    a. Chinese
    b. Mexican
    (c.) fast-food
    d. Italian

    Basis of classification: *national, or ethnic, background*

1. TV shows
    a. situation comedies
    b. dramas
    c. soap operas
    d. popular shows

    Basis of classification: _____

2. Types of government
    a. democracy
    b. American
    c. monarchy
    d. dictatorship

    Basis of classification: _____

3. Types of stores
    a. drug store
    b. grocery store
    c. privately owned store
    d. clothing store

    Basis of classification: _____

EXERCISE

14.2

For each of the following subjects, determine a basis of classification and then list the categories into which the subject can be divided.

▶ EXAMPLE

Pollution

   a. *Basis of classification:* _where pollution occurs_

   b. *Categories:* _air, water, land_

1. Jobs

   a. *Basis of classification:* _____

   b. *Categories:* _____

2. Colleges

   a. *Basis of classification:* _____

   b. *Categories:* _____

3. Foods

   a. *Basis of classification:* _____

   b. *Categories:* _____

4. Movies

   a. *Basis of classification:* _____

   b. *Categories:* _____

Writing Classification Paragraphs

Once you understand how to classify items, you are ready to employ this method of development in your writing. Although classification is also used to develop essays, you will find it much easier to begin by writing a classification paragraph.

Writing Topic Sentences and Using Transitions in Classification Paragraphs

The point, or main idea, developed in a classification paragraph is usually stated in a topic sentence. Whether this main point—the topic and the assertion—is stated or implied, however, it should be clear to the reader. Beginning with a clearly stated point is particularly important in academic writing, as shown in the following paragraph in which Lue answers her biology teacher's question about the major classes of trees. Notice the bold-faced topic sentence.

STUDENT PARAGRAPH

Most trees can be categorized into one of two types: those that keep their leaves throughout the year and those that lose their leaves in the winter. Trees that fit into the first category, or those that keep their leaves, are called evergreens or coniferous trees. These trees produce seeds in cones and have needle-shaped leaves. This type of trees includes pines, firs, and cedars. The second group of trees, those that lose their leaves in the winter, are called deciduous trees. They bear seeds that are encased in a fruit or berry, and their leaves are usually broad and flat. Elms, maples, and oaks, for example, are deciduous trees.

—Lue Kernes, student

In this student paragraph, the topic sentence to be developed by classification states (1) the subject to be classified, (2) the basis of classification, and (3) the categories that result. In this topic sentence, the subject for classification is "trees," the method of classification is "what happens to leaves in winter," and the categories are "those that keep their leaves" and "those that lose their leaves." In addition, Lue's paragraph uses several transition words, which are highlighted, to help you identify the categories of classification and the supporting examples. These transitions and other helpful words for writing classification paragraphs are listed here:

TRANSITION WORDS	VERBS
the first category (class, etc.)	include(s)
the second group (kind, etc.)	fit into (are divided into, etc.)
another type (method, etc.)	can be categorized (classified, etc.)
a final category (finally)	

EXERCISE
14.3

Each of the following items includes (1) the subject to be classified, (2) the basis of classification, and (3) the categories. Use this information to help you write a topic sentence in the space provided. (Your topic sentence should include the subject and either the basis of classification or the categories.)

▶ EXAMPLE

Subject:	restaurants
Basis of classification:	type of napkins
Categories:	those that provide cloth napkins, those that provide paper napkins, and those that provide no napkins

Topic sentence 1: <u>Restaurants can be classified according to the type of napkins they use.</u>   (basis of classification)

Topic sentence 2: <u>Restaurants can be classified according to whether they have cloth napkins, paper napkins, or no napkins.</u>   (categories)

1. *Subject:* schools
   Basis of classification: source of funding
   Categories: public or private

   Topic sentence: _____
   _____

2. *Subject:* literary works
   Basis of classification: genre
   Categories: fiction, poetry, drama

   Topic sentence: _____
   _____

3. *Subject:* economic systems
   Basis of classification: the way wealth is divided
   Categories: capitalist, socialist, communist

   Topic sentence: _____
   _____

Using Other Methods of Development in Classification Paragraphs

A classification paragraph (or essay) often uses other methods of development, such as examples, for the overall purpose of classification. (Later, you will discover that classification is also useful in writing definitions.) The following classification paragraph by Judith Viorst also uses other methods of development. As you read this paragraph, look for both the method of classification and the other methods of development.

There are medium friends, and pretty good friends, and very good friends indeed, and these friendships are defined by their level of intimacy. . . . We might tell a medium friend, for example, that yesterday we had a fight with our husband. And we might tell a pretty good friend that this fight with our husband made us so mad that we slept on the couch. And we might tell a very good friend that the reason we got so mad in that fight that we slept on the couch had something to do with the girl who works in his office. But it's only to our very best friends that we're willing to tell all, to tell what's going on with that girl in his office.

—Judith Viorst, "Friends, Good Friends"

EXERCISE

14.4

1. What is the subject of Viorst's classification?

_____

2. What is Viorst's basis of classification for her subject?

_____

3. What are the the categories of her classification?

_____

(Note that, although the categories of a classification paragraph are often listed in no particular order, Viorst deliberately arranges her categories in a logical order, leading from the least important to the most important.)

4. What is another way that you could classify friends?

_____

5. Underline the topic sentence. Then rewrite this sentence in your own words.

_____

_____

6. What transition words and phrases does Viorst use to show her categories of classification and her examples?

_____

7. What other methods of development does Viorst use in this paragraph?

_____

14.5

On a separate sheet of paper, list as many examples of college students as you can. Then, think about how you can classify these students into categories. Write here both the basis for your classification and the names of your categories. Then, for each category, list appropriate subcategories or examples.

Basis of classification: _____

Category 1: _____

    a. _____

    b. _____

Category 2: _____

    a. _____

    b. _____

Category 3: _____

    a. _____

    b. _____

Write a topic sentence in which you state your subject, the basis of your classification, and the categories you have identified.

_____

_____

Now, write a paragraph in which you develop this topic sentence by briefly describing and providing examples for each of the categories of students you have identified.

Writing Classification Essays

Classification may be used as the primary method of development in essays as well as in paragraphs. In a classification essay, the subject to be classified, the method of classification, and the categories of the classification are usually stated in the thesis statement (main idea). A successful classification essay also includes other qualities of effective classification, such as clear transitions. However, the ideas in a classification essay are more fully developed than those in a classification paragraph. Indeed, classification essays—even more so than classification paragraphs—often employ other methods of development, such as the use of example, comparison, contrast, and definition.

As you read the following classification essay, which has been adapted from a psychology textbook, look for the various qualities of effective classification:

Types of Personality Disorders

[1]People who exhibit inflexible and longstanding maladaptive ways of dealing with the environment that typically cause stress and/or social or occupational difficulties may have one of the **personality disorders.** People with personality disorders are divided into three broad clusters: those whose behavior appears (1) odd or eccentric, (2) fearful or anxious, or (3) dramatic, emotional, and erratic. We will now consider five specific personality disorders: paranoid, dependent, histrionic, narcissistic, and antisocial. Each of these five disorders fits into one of the three major clusters of personality disorders.

[2]Fitting into the first cluster, by showing odd or eccentric behavior, are people suffering from *paranoid personality disorder*, who have unwarranted feelings of persecution and who mistrust almost everyone. They are hypersensitive to criticism and have a restricted range of emotional responses. They have strong fears of being exploited, and of losing control and independence. Sometimes they appear cold, humorless, even scheming. As you might expect, people with paranoid personality disorder are suspicious and seldom able to form close, intimate relationships with others.

[3]Fitting into the second behavior cluster, by acting fearful or anxious, are individuals whose behavior is characteristic of *dependent personality disorder*. Such people are submissive and clinging; they let others make all the important decisions in their lives. They try to appear pleasant and agreeable at all times. They act meek, humble, and affectionate in order to keep their protectors. Battered wives often suffer from the dependent personality disorder. Overprotective, authoritarian parenting seems to be a major initiating cause of dependence.

[4]The third cluster of disorders, those involving dramatic, emotional, and erratic behaviors, includes three sub-categories. The first sub-category includes those people with the disorder called *histrionic personality disorder*. Individuals with this disorder seek attention by exaggerating situations in their lives. They have stormy personal relationships, are excessively emotional, and demand constant reassurance and praise. Closely related to histrionic personality disorder, and also classified in the third cluster, is *narcissistic personality disorder*. People with this disorder have an extremely exaggerated sense of self-importance, expect favors, and need constant admiration and attention.

They show a lack of caring for others, and they react to criticism with rage, shame, or humiliation. Still another disorder of the third cluster, and perhaps the most widely recognized personality disorder, is the *antisocial personality disorder*. An antisocial personality disorder is characterized by egocentricity, behavior that is irresponsible and that violates the rights of other people (lying, theft, delinquency, and other violations of social rules), a lack of guilt feelings, an inability to understand other people, and a lack of fear of punishment. Individuals with this disorder may be superficially charming, but their behavior is destructive and often reckless. A person so diagnosed must be at least 18 years old and usually displays a blatant disregard for others.

⁵Often, these various disorders begin in childhood or adolescence and persist throughout adulthood. People with personality disorders are easy to spot but difficult to treat.

—Adapted from Lester A. Lefton, *Psychology*, 6th ed.

EXERCISE 14.6

1. Underline the thesis sentence. Then write it here in your own words.

   _____

   _____

2. What is the general subject classified in this essay?

   _____

3. What is the basis of classification used in this essay?

   _____

   _____

4. The author divides his subject into three primary categories, which he presents in order from the least to the most severe. What are these three categories?

   a. _____

   b. _____

   c. _____

5. What transitions are used in the essay?

   _____

   _____

6. What methods of development besides classification are used in this essay? Identify two of these methods and give an example of each.

Method 1: _____

Example: _____

Method 2: _____

Example: _____

Chapter Review

- Classification organizes items with similar characteristics into groups, or categories.

- A good classification paragraph or essay has a clear purpose and a clearly stated or implied main idea (topic sentence or thesis statement) that usually includes the subject to be classified and either the basis of the classification or the categories of the classification.

- Good classification writing uses only one basis of classification at a time and includes all items to be classified.

- Good classification writing includes logically arranged subtopics connected with clear transitions.

- Good classification writing includes specific examples and details.

- Classification writing may include other methods of development (example, comparison and contrast, and so forth).

Writing Assignment

Look back at Exercise 14.5. Review your topic sentence and rewrite it as the thesis of an essay on that subject. Be sure that your thesis includes the subject to be classified, the basis of classification, and the categories within the classification.

Thesis sentence: _____

_____

_____

Now, write a topic sentence for each of the categories that you created for your paragraph in Exercise 14.5. Then add supporting examples for each of your categories.

Topic sentence 1: _____

_____

a. _____

b. _____

Topic sentence 2: _____

_____

a. _____

b. _____

Topic sentence 3: _____

_____

a. _____

b. _____

Topic sentence 4 (optional): _____

_____

a. _____

b. _____

After discussing your plan with a group of your classmates, write a brief essay in which you develop your thesis sentence with the three topic sentences you have written. Be sure to develop each topic sentence with subtopics and specific examples.

■ Participating in the Academic Community

Before writing your essay, share your plans with a small group of your classmates. Evaluate one another's thesis sentences to be sure that each thesis clearly states the subject to be classified, the basis of classification, and the categories to be included. Check to be sure that each category follows the basis of classification. Finally, review the supporting examples for each category to be sure they also fit the category clearly.

Chapter 15

Cause and Effect

Another method of developing a main idea is to explore its causes and effects. Whereas process writing focuses on how something is done, **cause and effect** writing focuses on *why* something occurs and on *what results* from the occurrence. You use cause and effect thinking in many academic classes as well as in your everyday life. In your American history class, you may analyze the causes of the Civil War; in an environmental sciences class, you may speculate on the possible effects of global warming; and in your sociology class, you may consider both the causes and effects of divorce. Like the other methods of development, cause and effect is not just a way of writing but also a way of thinking.

Understanding Cause and Effect

The main idea of a cause and effect paragraph or essay can focus on causes, effects, or both. The important thing is to explore the relationship between cause and effect. Thus, a writer can begin with a cause and explain its effect or with an effect and explore its cause. As illustrated here, writers can move in one direction or the other:

CAUSE → EFFECT ▶ EXAMPLE: Smoking *causes* lung cancer.
(effect)

EFFECT → CAUSE ▶ EXAMPLE: Lung cancer is an *effect* of smoking.
(cause)

The following paragraphs are developed primarily by cause and effect. In the first paragraph, Isak Dinesen moves from cause to effect. In the second paragraph, James Thurber begins with the effect and then discusses the cause.

CAUSE TO EFFECT

Once I shot an Iguana. I thought that I should be able to make some pretty things from his skin. A strange thing happened then, that I have never afterwards forgotten. As I went up to him, where he was lying dead upon his stone, and actually while I was walking the few steps, he faded and grew pale, all colour died out of him as in one long sigh, and by the time that I touched him he was grey and dull like a lump of concrete. It was the live impetuous blood pulsating within the animal, which had radiated out all that glow and splendour. **Now that the flame was put out, and the soul had flown, the Iguana was as dead as a sandbag.**

—Isak Dinesen, "The Iguana," *Out of Africa*

EFFECT TO CAUSE

I passed all the other courses that I took at my university, but I could never pass botany. This was because all botany students had to spend several hours a week in a laboratory looking through a microscope at plant cells, and I could never see through a microscope. I never once saw a cell through a microscope. This used to enrage my instructor. He would wander around the laboratory pleased with the progress all the students were making in drawing the involved and, so I am told, interesting structure of flower cells, until he came to me. I would just be standing there. "I can't see anything," I would say.

—James Thurber, "University Days," *My Life and Hard Times*

Qualities of Effective Cause and Effect Writing

The qualities of good cause and effect writing found in the paragraphs by Dinesen and Thurber are listed for you here:

1. *A clear purpose.* The purpose of cause and effect writing may be to inform or persuade. In explaining the causes of his failure in biology, Thurber informs and perhaps justifies the result to his audience—and maybe to himself. In describing the effects of killing the iguana, however, Dinesen subtly argues against shooting an animal to use its skin for decoration. In achieving its purpose, cause and effect writing often employs narration, as well. For example, Dinesen narrates the

events that lead to the death and dullness of the iguana, and Thurber narrates the events that result from his inability to see through a microscope.

2. *A clear main idea that suggests the focus and causal relationship.* As shown in the bolded sentences, both Dinesen and Thurber include main ideas (topic sentences) that state the causal relationships developed in their paragraphs: Dinesen begins with the shooting of the iguana, which causes the effect she will describe in detail; Thurber begins with the primary effect—his failure in botany—then discusses in detail the causes of this effect. However, a cause and effect paragraph may also divide its focus evenly between causes and effects, or it may discuss causes and effects as a chain reaction—moving from a cause to an effect that then causes another effect and so on.

3. *Specific details that develop the causal relationship stated in the main idea.* By including specific descriptions of the effect of shooting the iguana—and its loss of color at death—Dinesen re-creates the experience for her readers and leads them to her implied conclusion that the death of the iguana was a waste—even useless and cruel—because the beautiful skin colors that would have made "pretty things" disappeared with its life. In developing his paragraph, Thurber shows that his inability to see plant cells through a microscope led to his instructor's anger and to the ultimate effect of Thurber's failure. Thus, the details in cause and effect writing may develop a single cause and/or effect, as in Dinesen's paragraph, or multiple causes and/or effects, as in Thurber's.

4. *Logical and relevant support.* Supporting details for cause and effect writing should always be logical and relevant. Writers should avoid oversimplifying events or relying on coincidental occurrences and should limit support to logical and/or proven cause and effect relationships. For example in Paragraph C in Exercise 15.1, the fact that the 1989 World Series was being played in Candlestick Park when the Loma Prieta earthquake hit was omitted because it was coincidental rather than causal.

5. *Effective organization and transition that clearly show causal relationships.* The organization in cause and effect writing should clearly move from cause to effect, as in Dinesen's paragraph, or from effect to cause, as in Thurber's paragraph. Although logical connections between events and feelings are the basis of strong cause and effect writing, transition words that clearly show causal relationships can certainly clarify those relationships. For example, Thurber clearly suggests that he failed botany *because* of his poor laboratory performance. The relationship between Thurber's poor performance and his grade is present even without the word *because*, but the transition provides a valuable clue to this relationship for the reader.

15.1   Read the following paragraphs and answer the questions that follow each.

PARAGRAPH A

The impact of Alzheimer's disease on the patient is enormous; the disease severely damages the quality of life. At the beginning patients are not necessarily stripped of their vigor or strength, but they slowly become confused and helpless. Initially, they may forget to do small things. Later, they may forget appointments, anniversaries, and the like. The forgetfulness is often overlooked at first. Jokes and other coping strategies cover up for memory losses and lapses. The memory losses are not always apparent; some days are better than others. Ultimately, however, the disorder grows worse. Alzheimer's patients start to have trouble finding their way home and remembering their own name and the names of their spouses and children. Sometimes fast retrieval is impaired more than general accumulated knowledge. Patients' personality also changes. They may become abrupt, abusive, and hostile to family members. Within months, or sometimes years, they lose their speech and language functions. Eventually, they lose all control of memory and even of basic bodily functions.

—Lester A. Lefton, *Psychology*, 6th ed.

1. As stated in the topic sentence, what is the main idea of this paragraph?

   _____

   _____

2. Does the development and support in this paragraph focus *primarily* on (a) causes, (b) effects, (c) both causes and effects, or (d) how one cause creates an effect that then creates another effect (chain reaction)?

   _____

3. Does the organization of this paragraph move from cause to effect or effect to cause?

   _____

PARAGRAPH B

The Dust Bowl was an ecological disaster. In the 1920s farmers on the southern plains had bought tens of thousands of tractors and plowed millions of acres. Then, in the 1930s, the rain stopped. Soil that had been plowed was particularly vulnerable to the drought that gripped the plains. Strong winds caused enormous dust storms; from 1935 through 1938, 241 dust storms hit the southern plains. Farmers shuttered their homes against the dust as tightly as possible, but, as a woman in western Kansas recounted in 1935, "those tiny particles seemed to seep through the very walls. It got into cupboards and clothes closets; our faces were as dirty as if we had rolled in the dirt; our hair was gray and stiff and we ground dirt between our teeth." Farm animals lacked all protection. The photographer Margaret Bourke-White observed that "cattle quickly become blinded. They run around in circles until they fall and breathe so much dust that they die."

—Mary Norton et al., *A People and a Nation*, 5th ed.

1. As stated in the topic sentence, what is the main idea of this paragraph?

   _____

   _____

2. Does the development and support in this paragraph focus *primarily* on (a) causes, (b) effects, (c) both causes and effects, or (d) how one cause creates an effect that then creates another effect (chain reaction)?

   _____

3. Does the organization of this paragraph move from cause to effect or effect to cause?

   _____

PARAGRAPH C

The most tragic result of the violent shaking was the collapse of some double-decked sections of Interstate 880, also known as the Nimitz Freeway. The ground motions caused the upper deck to sway, shattering the concrete support columns along a mile-long section of the freeway. The upper deck then collapsed onto the lower roadway, flattening cars as if they were aluminum beverage cans. Other roadways that were damaged during the earthquake included a 50-foot section of the upper deck of the Bay Bridge, which is a major artery connecting the cities of Oakland and San Francisco. The vibration caused cars on the bridge to bounce up and down vigorously. A motorcyclist on the upper deck described how the roadway bulged and rippled toward him: "It was like bumper cars— only you could die! . . ." Fortunately, only one motorist on the bridge was killed.

—Edward J. Tarbuck and Frederick K. Lutgens, *Earth Science*, 7th ed.

15.2 continued

1. As stated in the topic sentence, what is the main idea of this paragraph?

    _____

    _____

2. Does the development and support in this paragraph focus *primarily* on (a) causes, (b) effects, (c) both causes and effects, or (d) how one cause creates an effect that then creates another effect (chain reaction)?

    _____

3. Does the organization of this paragraph move from cause to effect or effect to cause?

    _____

Writing Cause and Effect Paragraphs

You may write a cause and effect paragraph that functions independently or as part of a longer essay. In either case, it should have a clear main idea, logical organization, specific and relevant support, and effective transitions. In the following section, you will learn more about writing topic sentences and using transitions in cause and effect paragraphs.

Writing Topic Sentences and Using Transitions in Cause and Effect Paragraphs

As in other types of paragraphs, the main idea of a cause and effect paragraph is usually stated in a topic sentence. Ideally, the topic sentence will state the basic relationship between causes and effects in the paragraph and will indicate whether the paragraph will focus on the causes or effects of the situation. In the following paragraph, for example, Davy moves from effect to cause, explaining the causes of his poor performance in elementary school:

STUDENT PARAGRAPH

My poor performance in elementary school was caused by weaknesses in the education I had received in the second and third grades. Because my class had twenty-nine students to one teacher for both of these years, I didn't get the help and attention that I needed. More important, however, I didn't learn because my second and third grade teachers were both poor educators. My second grade teacher, Mrs. Myers, expected me and the rest of the class to understand everything the first time it was explained. I was also afraid of her because she lost patience easily and even threw erasers at us. My third grade teacher Mrs. Kivell wasn't interested in teaching the basics of reading, writing, and arithmetic. Instead, she just taught arts, crafts, and foreign holidays. As a result of these factors, I performed very poorly in school until I reached high school and college where I encountered a more effective education.

—Davy Moseley, student

As Davy's topic sentence suggests and as the support in his paragraph confirms, his focus is primarily on the causes of his poor performance in elementary school. He gives two primary causes, class size and poor teachers, and then provides supporting details and examples.

In addition to providing a clear topic sentence and support, Davy also uses effective verbal clues to show the relationships within his paragraph. Notice how the highlighted verb and transition words clarify the cause and effect relationships in the paragraph. The following list shows several additional transition words you can use to show cause and effect relationships in your own writing:

accordingly	because	as a result
consequently	for	hence
in order that	since	so
so that	therefore	thus

In addition to these transition words, you can also use the nouns *causes, reasons, results*, and *effects* and the verbs *caused* and *resulted* to show causal relationships.

EXERCISE

15.2   For each of the following topics, list three causes and three effects. Decide whether a paragraph on this subject would be more effective if it moved from cause(s) to effects (developing the effects) or from effect(s) to causes (developing the causes), and write this relationship in the space provided. Then write a topic sentence that expresses this causal relationship.

Causes	Effects
1. Stress	

a. _____   a. _____

b. _____   b. _____

c. _____   c. _____

d. _____   d. _____

This paragraph will develop (causes or effects):_____.

This paragraph will move from _____ to _____.

Topic sentence: _____

_____

2. Drug or alcohol abuse

a. _____   a. _____

b. _____   b. _____

c. _____   c. _____

d. _____   d. _____

This paragraph will develop (causes or effects):_____.

This paragraph will move from _____ to _____.

Topic sentence: _____

_____

3. Divorce

a. _____   a. _____

b. _____   b. _____

c. _____   c. _____

d. _____   d. _____

This paragraph will develop (causes or effects):_____.

This paragraph will move from _____ to _____.

Topic sentence: _____

_____

Now select one of these topics and use your plan to write a cause and effect paragraph.

Writing Cause and Effect Essays

The principles that apply to writing cause and effect paragraphs also apply to writing cause and effect essays. A cause and effect essay will move either from cause to effect(s) or from effect to cause(s). Although an essay may provide a detailed analysis of a single cause and a single effect, most cause and effect essays are developed by focusing either on several effects of one cause or on several causes of one effect. As you read the following essay by Greg Rogers, determine whether it moves from a single effect to a discussion of several causes or from a single cause to a discussion of several effects.

Starting Out Right

[1]Teenagers should be encouraged to have a part-time job while attending high school. I have held many jobs, but the most important to me was my first job as a dishwasher at an Italian restaurant in Seattle. Because of this job, I learned about responsibility, money values, and human relationships.

[2]One result of my job is that it taught me responsibility. A job and responsibility go hand in hand. Indeed, in most cases, people get paid on the basis of how much responsibility they can handle. Responsibility means being accountable for one's actions or duties, including being at work on time. Before I got my first job, I didn't own a watch, much less keep track of time. This job forced me to get a watch and keep my eye on it. The duties I had to perform included taking out the trash to the large trash can in back. Another one of my duties was to sweep and mop the floor of the entire restaurant. Grotesque is the only way to describe the floor after a booming Friday night. Pizza sauce and pasta covered the fake marble tile floor, and it was my job to scrub the tile until it didn't look fake. Because I began to take great pride in my work, I worked really hard to make the place look good. I came to feel that my work was a mirror of me as a person. Therefore, with this job, I became more responsible.

[3]Another effect of my job was that it helped me to learn more about the value of money. I had to work two weeks before I could get my first pay check, and I was counting every minute. I calculated all the hours that I would have on my check about a hundred times to make sure I knew how much it would be. When that long-awaited Friday came, I got up early, went to school, and went straight to work from there. As I ran inside, the owner met me at the counter with a strange grin, thanked me for my hard work, and handed me an envelope containing my first check. I was excited, but I composed myself and thanked her. All that night at work, I thought of how I was going to spend my hard-earned money. After all the empty trips back from the mall, you'd think I would have narrowed what I wanted to buy down to about ten items, but no, I wanted it all. The next

morning I woke my mom up fifteen minutes before the mall opened, and after ten minutes of tormenting this poor woman, she was up and out of her room—mad as hell, but up nonetheless. I started out with two hundred dollars. As we traveled this mecca of material objects in the mall, I found myself saying, "I wouldn't throw my money away for that." I said that more and more times the longer we stayed. I went home that night with a very tired mom and one hundred ninety-eight dollars and fifty cents. The only things I had bought were two Orange Juliuses that my mom and I had enjoyed very much. Although I don't think I realized it until much later, I learned a lesson that day. If your money is hard earned, it's hard spent also.

[4]A final outcome of my job was that I learned about relationships with others from this first job. The restaurant was like a home away from home, but with better food. One night after work, my bike was stolen, and I was very upset at myself because I had been careless and immature and had forgotten to lock it up. Knowing that I was upset, Frank, a cook, told me to wait around a while after work. Then he told me to get into his Jeep. I thought he was going to give me a ride to my house near his, but he drove past my house, turned down another street, and stopped in front of a local pawnshop. I didn't know what was going on, so I stayed in the Jeep while he went inside. I sat there clueless until Frank came outside and told me to come in. I opened the door and scanned left to right for Frank, but before I saw him, my eyes locked on my bike. "That's mine!" I yelled. Frank stood next to the bike, smiling from ear to ear. He paid the twenty-five bucks for the bike, and we took it outside. Drunk with relief and happiness, I thanked him. Then he said, "Kid, you can't give people a chance to rip you off." As I rode home, I thought that what Frank did was one of the nicest things anyone had done for me. After that I locked my bike up every day and paid Frank back the twenty-five dollars. I've learned that a job is not just a job; it's also relationships with the people you work with.

[5]I loved working at this first job. It taught me how to conduct myself responsibly in a job, how to manage the money I earned, and how to get along with and learn from other people. Every day I went to work and worked hard because everyone around me also worked hard. I may have only made three dollars and eighty-five cents an hour, but I learned a lot about work and the real world from the good people I worked with.

—Greg Rogers, student

1. What is the thesis, or main point, of this essay?

_____

_____

2. Does this essay move from cause to effect(s) or from effect to cause(s)?

   _____

3. Does the body of the essay (its development) focus primarily on causes or effects?

   _____

4. What are the three major supporting points (causes or effects) of this essay?

   a. _____

   b. _____

   c. _____

5. What transition words does the essay use to show cause and effect relationships?

   _____

   _____

6. What are some of the most effective supporting details and examples in the essay?

   _____

   _____

   _____

7. Although this essay is developed primarily by cause and effect analysis, it also employs other methods of development. What are two of these methods, and in what paragraph(s) are they used?

   a. _____

   b. _____

EXERCISE

15.4

Write a paragraph in which you discuss some of the causes of students' dropping out of high school. Then write another paragraph in which you discuss the effects that dropping out of school can have on a young person's life. Finally, combine these two paragraphs into an essay in which you explore both the causes and the effects of this problem. Be sure to begin each of your paragraphs with a clear topic sentence and use effective transitions to show your causal relationships.

Chapter Review

- The purpose of cause and effect writing, which focuses on why something occurs and on what results, may be to inform or persuade.

- Cause and effect writing includes a clear main idea (topic sentence or thesis statement) that states the causes and/or effects to be developed.

- Supporting details in cause and effect writing should clearly develop the causal relationship being discussed; details should never be coincidental or oversimplified.

- The organization of cause and effect writing may move from cause(s) to effect(s) or from effect(s) to cause(s).

- Good cause and effect writing includes not only logical organization but also effective transitions.

Writing Assignment

Write an essay on the causes and/or effects of one of the following topics:

Stress	Obesity or anorexia
Drug or alcohol abuse	Pollution
Divorce	Credit card debt
Success (or failure) in college or a job	Violence in schools

Your thesis sentence should express the relationship between cause and effect found in the topic and clarify your purpose and focus. You will probably have a more coherent essay if you focus on either effects, discussing several effects of a single cause, or on causes, discussing several causes of a single effect. Be sure you include in your essay specific, relevant evidence to support the causal relationship you are analyzing. (*Note:* Because you listed causes and effects for some of these topics in Exercise 15.2, you may find that you have already done some helpful planning for your essay.)

Participating in the Academic Community

After you have completed a draft of your essay, meet with a small group of your classmates and use the Chapter Review to help you evaluate and revise your essays. As you read or listen to each other's essays, be sure that the writer's thesis is clearly stated, that the organizational structure clearly moves from cause(s) to effect(s) or effect(s) to cause(s), and that the writer has used effective transitions.

Chapter 16

Definition

Definition is not really a different method of development as much as it is a combination of all the other methods. Your main concern in defining a subject is to tell what it is. You can give a brief definition as part of a longer composition, or you can devote your entire composition to defining a term or an idea. You can define a subject by describing, illustrating, comparing, or classifying it. You can even define a subject by telling a story about it or analyzing its causes or effects.

Understanding Definition

Clear definitions are essential to the process of communication. When you read a chapter in a textbook, you must understand the basic terminology in order to comprehend the ideas being expressed. For example, since your political science text will frequently refer to "governmental bureaucracy," you need to know that a *bureaucracy* is a set of complex agencies and departments that help a governor or president carry out law and policy. When you write a paragraph or an essay, you must be sure not only that you understand the words you are using but also that you use and define terms so your reader can understand how you are using them.

As you read the following two definition paragraphs, think about why they are successful definitions and try to identify other methods of development that the writers use to develop their definitions.

Robotics is the science that deals with the construction, capabilities, and applications of robots. Most robots are used to perform tedious, dangerous, or otherwise undesirable work in factories. . . . These industrial robots can work where humans cannot, and do not need protective devices. They never need time off; a typical industrial robot is up and running 97 percent of the time! And the quality of work never suffers. Further, management never has to contend with sick, tired, or bored robots. The machines never complain, go on strike, or ask for higher wages.

—Steven L. Mandell, *Introduction to Computers*

Falling in love is an experience that almost everyone has at least once and usually several times. **To fall in love is to fall into a profound set of emotional experiences.** There may be a range of physical symptoms such as dry mouth, pounding heart, flushed face, and knotted stomach. The mind may race, and fantasy, especially about the loved one, is rampant. Motivation to work, play, indeed for anything except the lover, may fall to zero. As the love feelings develop, strong feelings of passion may occur. In fact, passionate love is essentially the same as romantic love, except that the focus is more specifically on the emotional intensity and sexual passion.

—Clyde Hendrick and Susan Hendrick, *Liking, Loving, and Relating*

Qualities of Effective Definition

The qualities of effective definition illustrated in the sample paragraphs defining robotics and falling in love are listed here:

1. *A sense of purpose and audience.* Writers need to have a clear sense of purpose and audience when they define a subject. Definition is most often used to inform, but it may also be used to persuade. For example, the writer of the paragraph on robotics seems to be addressing a scientific or business audience interested in technological efficiency, whereas the authors of the paragraph on falling in love are addressing a more general audience.

2. *A clearly stated or implied main idea.* A good definition paragraph begins with a topic sentence, or main idea, that introduces and makes an assertion about the subject. Often this main idea is stated in the form of a brief introductory definition. In the first example paragraph, for example, the writer initially defines *robotics* by classifying it as a science and then explains that it "deals with the construction, capabilities, and applications of robots." The writer then explores other characteristics of robots, especially their capabilities and applications. In the second paragraph, falling in love is defined briefly in the first two sentences, but the second sentence completes the main point that this situation results in "a profound set of emotional experiences." (The topic sentence may be a formal definition, which is explained in the following section.)

3. *Use of several methods of development in extended definitions.* When writers define a subject, they are free to use any methods of development that will help their readers arrive at a clear understanding of the subject. A writer may describe a subject (using both factual and sensory details), give an example of it, compare or contrast it with something else, or classify it. The main strength of the sample paragraph on falling in love is its extended development through various methods. The authors provide effective descriptive examples of how one feels (having "dry mouth, pounding heart, flushed face, and knotted stomach") and acts ("the mind may race, and fantasy, especially about the loved one, is rampant") when falling in love. The definition also includes effects ("motivation . . . may fall to zero" and "strong feelings of passion may occur") of falling in love.

Formal Definitions

When you look up a word in the dictionary, the definition that you find is usually a formal definition. A **formal definition** places the subject (or term) into a category and then tells how it differs from the other members of that class. For instance, we can define a lullaby by placing it in the general category of songs and then specifying the characteristics that make it different from other songs. We might, therefore, arrive at the definition "a lullaby is a song that is used to encourage babies to sleep." A formal definition is more effective if the term is placed in a category that is not too broad. Thus, the category of *song* is much more effective than that of *music* for defining a lullaby.

Formal definitions are usually brief and to the point. In paragraphs and essays, therefore, they are most often used as part of an extended definition. Formal definitions are also used to define secondary terms within a composition.

EXERCISE

16.1

Read the following definition paragraph and answer the questions that follow it.

An earthquake is the vibration of the earth produced by the rapid release of energy caused when rock plates that are pressure balanced on either side of a fault zone slide past each other, releasing the stored energy in short bursts. This energy radiates in all directions from its source, the focus, in the form of waves analogous to those produced when a stone is dropped into a calm pond. Just as the impact of the stone sets water waves in motion, an earthquake generates seismic waves that radiate throughout the earth. Even though the energy dissipates rapidly with increasing distance from the focus, instruments located throughout the world record the event. On October 17, 1989, at 5:04 p.m. Pacific Daylight Time, for example, strong tremors shook the San Francisco Bay area. Millions of Americans and others around the world were just getting ready to watch the third game of the World Series, but instead saw their television sets go black as the shock hit Candlestick Park. Although this Loma Prieta earthquake was centered in a remote section of the Santa Cruz Mountains, about 16 kilometers north of the city of Santa Cruz, major damage occurred in the Marina District of San Francisco 100 kilometers to the north. Here, as many as 60 row houses were so badly damaged that they had to be demolished.

—Adapted from Edward J. Tarbuck and Frederick K. Lutgens,
Earth Science, 7th ed.

1. This paragraph begins with a formal definition. Analyze the parts of this formal definition in the space provided.

   Term: _____ *Class:* _____

   Differentiation from others in class: _____

   _____

2. This paragraph uses at least four other methods of development besides definition. In the spaces below, identify and give an example of three of these methods.

   Method 1: _____

   Example: _____

   Method 2: _____

   Example: _____

   Method 3: _____

   Example: _____

EXERCISE

16.2

Write formal definitions of the following terms.

1. *Term:* Hurricane

   Class: _____

   How it differs from others in its class: _____

   _____

2. *Term:* Duplex

   Class: _____

   How it differs from others in its class: _____

   _____

3. *Term:* Compact disk

   Class: _____

   How it differs from others in its class: _____

   _____

Informal Definitions

Sometimes writers prefer to use **informal definitions** rather than formal ones. You will often find words defined informally in your reading, especially in your textbooks. Informal definitions are particularly helpful for defining words in definition paragraphs and essays. As discussed in the following sections, informal definitions include restatement through synonyms; contrast, often using antonyms; brief examples and illustrations; and brief explanations.

Restatement and Synonyms

The simplest kind of informal definition provides a synonym for the word being defined. A **synonym** is a word that has the same, or approximately the same, meaning as the word being defined. Thus, the synonym restates the word's meaning in more familiar terms.

▶ EXAMPLE: The millionaire was **magnanimous,** or generous, with his money.

The word *generous* is a synomym that restates the meaning of *magnanimous*, thus defining as well as emphasizing the meaning of the word.

Contrast and Antonyms

A word may also be defined through contrast, usually using an antonymn and/or transition words that show contrast. An **antonymn** is a word that means the opposite of the word in question.

▶ EXAMPLE: Mark was **surly** rather than polite when he accepted the ribbon for being second in the race.

In this example, the words *rather than* indicate the contrast in meaning between *surly* and *polite*, thus helping the reader understand that *surly* means "rude." Other transition words that show contrast include *but, although,* and *however.*

Examples

Another way to define a word informally is to use an example, or examples, of the term to be defined.

▶ EXAMPLE: I do not like **acrid** foods such as sour pickles and
                    green persimmons.

Because sour pickles and green persimmons are both bitter in taste, the reader can infer that *acrid* means "bitter or sharp." Writers often use the transition words *for example* and *such as* to introduce examples.

Explanation

Finally, an informal definition may simply provide an explanation of the word's meaning in the context of its usage.

▶ EXAMPLE: The boy's grandfather was so **parsimonious** with his
                    monthly income that he even refused to buy enough to eat.

Here the explanation that the boy's grandfather was so parsimonious that he wouldn't buy enough to eat suggests that the word *parsimonious* means "thrifty" or "stingy" with one's money to the point of self-denial.

EXERCISE

16.3

Write the definition and the type of informal definition (synonym or re-statement, antonym or contrast, example, explanation) for each of the bold-faced words in the following sentences.

1. The storekeeper was so **avaricious** that he tried to cheat his customers when he gave them change.

   Definition: _____

   Type of informal definition: _____

2. Although our last gardener was lazy, the present gardener is **diligent.**

   Definition: _____

   Type of informal definition: _____

3. **Clairvoyants**—such as fortune-tellers, seers, and prophets—are not always right.

   Definition: _____

   Type of informal definition: _____

Denotations and Connotations

When writers are defining a word—especially when writing an extended definition—they also need to be aware of the difference between a word's **denotation** and its **connotation.** The denotation of a word is its formal dictionary definition; the connotation of a word includes the personal and societal associations that the word brings to mind. The word *fire*, for example, may suggest warmth and romance to a woman who received her engagement ring in front of the flickering fire of her fireplace but remind another woman of the raging fire that destoyed her home and all her family photographs.

EXERCISE

16.4

1. Write the denotation of the word *house.*

   _____

2. Now, write two or three words that have similar denotations to *house* but that have very different connotations. Beside each word, write the connotations, or associations, that the word has for you.

   a. _____

   b. _____

   c. _____

Writing Definition Paragraphs

A definition paragraph may be a separate composition or a part of a longer composition. As illustrated in the following student paragraph, a good definition paragraph may combine formal and informal definitions. Also, a well-developed definition paragraph usually includes various methods of development. As you read Kristy's paragraph, see how many methods of development you can identify.

STUDENT PARAGRAPH

Known informally as "falling sickness," epilepsy is a nervous disorder in which the sufferer experiences a loss of sensory, motor, and psychic functions. An attack of epilepsy, often called an epileptic seizure, occurs when certain nerve cells in the brain suddenly release a large burst of electrical energy. What causes this phenomenon in the brain? Many seizures seem to occur for no other reason than fatigue or emotional stress. The brain of an epileptic patient sometimes is unable to limit or control the large burst of electrical energy. Epileptic seizures can be of different types. In a Petit Mal seizure, a person usually goes blank for a few seconds, during which he or she is unaware of everything. During this type of seizure, the epileptic may appear to be dreaming. In the more serious Grand Mal seizure, the person usually falls down and the entire body stiffens and then twitches or jerks uncontrollably. Often as the person falls, an "epileptic cry" is emitted as the larynx goes into spasm. The muscles contract rigidly, and the person's jaw clamps shut with tremendous pressure. It is not uncommon for the person to bite his or her tongue. As the seizure subsides, the person may fall into a deep sleep. This type of attack often lasts three to five minutes and leaves the victim disoriented or confused and perhaps with a severe headache. Most of the time, the person has no memory of the event. According to "The New Good Housekeeping Family Health and Medical Guide," an estimated 0.5 percent of the population suffer from recurrent seizures—which translates into one million people in the United States.

—Kristy Childers, student

Kristy's paragraph begins with a topic sentence that provides not only a formal definition of epilepsy but also an informal definition ("falling sickness"). Kristy focuses on the formal definition, which states that the condition is a nervous disorder. The methods of development she uses to expand this definition are cause and effect, classification, contrast, description, process, narration, and example.

Because definition involves so many methods of development, no one particular type of transition word is more helpful than another. However, in writing definition paragraphs and essays, you may find yourself overusing the verb *is* in defining terms. Following is a list of verbs that you may find helpful in introducing definitions:

denotes	connotes	indicates
means	suggests	implies

16.5

Write a paragraph on one of the following topics:

1. Select a word that means "a place to live" and write a paragraph defining that word. For example, you might define *house, home, residence, domicile, dwelling, shack, mansion, apartment,* and so on. Begin your paragraph with a clear topic sentence and use clear and varied introductory terms and transitions. You may want to include both formal and informal definitions, and you should pay particular attention to connotation as well as denotation. Also, be sure to use several methods of development, such as description, narration, comparison and contrast, and so forth. (*Hint:* Your brainstorming list from Exercise 16.4 may be helpful prewriting for this assignment.)

2. Choose a subject that particularly interests you and write a paragraph defining that subject. You may define an object, an emotion, an event, or a type of person. Once you have selected your subject, think about the different methods you might use to define it. Can you describe it, compare or contrast it with something or someone else, illustrate it, classify it, discuss its causes or effects, and so on? Decide which of the methods would explain your subject clearly to a reader and use at least two of these different methods in your paragraph. Include a clear topic sentence and a formal and/or informal definition.

Writing Definition Essays

In your academic classes, you may sometimes be asked to write an essay defining a particular term. For example, your sociology instructor might ask you to define *sexual harassment* or *discrimination;* your political science teacher might ask you to define *socialism* or *capitalism;* and your music appreciation teacher might ask you to define *rock* or *baroque* music. Each of these concepts is so complex that you would need to define it in an essay rather than a paragraph.

In the following essay, Joe defines a musical instrument, the French horn.

The French Horn

[1]The French horn is a member of the brasswind family of musical instruments that has an attractive and interesting appearance, a unique shape, and a delightful mellow tone. The French horn resembles a large circular disk made of tubing that has a bright polish. The physical properties of the French horn are essential to the powerful sound that the horn produces.

[2]Physically, the horn is an attractive and interesting instrument. The horn has a finely polished surface, like chrome on a sports car. The horn has four valves at the top—three to the right side and one underneath the tubing for the thumb. The polish, interrupted only by a leather cord added by many musicians, looks as clear as a mirror. The cord is wrapped around the tubing and keeps the finish from being broken down by sweat from the player's hand. The cord starts right after a parallel spot above the thumb valve and continues to the shepherd's crook. The shepherd's crook that cradles the pinkie finger is found on many different instruments and gets that name from its resemblance to the crook of a shepherd's staff.

[3]Physical shape and sound are closely related in the French horn. Thus, the most notable feature of the French horn is the bell at the end of the tubing where sound emanates. One of the qualities that makes a French horn different is that, unlike the bells in other brass instruments, this bell points back behind the horn player. The bell in the French horn is also quite large—about the diameter of a basketball. The horn player puts his or her hand into the bell to control the sound. The player can change positions of his or her hand, either by putting the hand palm up or palm down, and thus change the sound of the horn.

[4]The sound of the French horn is peaceful and pleasant. To the sensitive listener, it creates an image of autumn with all the leaves in colors of red and yellow. The hearer can imagine trees standing in a peaceful state with small animals scampering about them. The long, slow passage of the wind can be heard from the beginning of the horn's whole notes. When the horn hits the high notes in a phrase, listeners may see a mental image of an eagle soaring through the air in search of prey. As the imaginary eagle drops toward a small brook, the horn hits a run of fast notes from high to low. About the time the imaginary eagle snags a small fish out of the water, the horn makes a leap to an upper note that plays clearly and triumphantly. The low notes are the stately ones, reminiscent of a steamboat on the Mississippi. The performance comes to an end by bringing thoughts of winter and a snowy sleep to the listener.

[5]My knowledge of the French horn is firsthand, based not only on my general experience with French horns but also on my knowledge of my own new French horn. Because my French horn is new, it as yet has no dents or scratches and can therefore be distinguished from the older French horns in my college band. The valves of this particular instrument work as smoothly as the sighing of the autumn wind that the instrument recreates each time I play it.

—Joe Johnson, student

1. What is the thesis statement of this essay?

   _____

2. This thesis is also a formal definition. Identify the different elements of this formal definition.

   Term: _____ *Class:* _____

   Distinguishing characteristics: _____

   _____

   _____

3. What are the main points of the thesis statement developed in the essay?

   a. _____

   b. _____

   c. _____

4. This essay uses several different methods of development. Indicate the method(s) of development used in each paragraph and provide supporting examples for each.

   PARAGRAPH 2

   Method(s): _____

   Examples: _____

   PARAGRAPH 3

   Method(s): _____

   Examples: _____

   PARAGRAPH 4

   Method(s): _____

   Examples: _____

   PARAGRAPH 5

   Method(s): _____

   Examples: _____

Chapter Review

- A definition paragraph or essay should have a clear sense of purpose and audience and a clearly stated main idea (topic sentence or thesis statement).

- Extended definitions often employ other methods of development.

- A formal definition places a subject (or term) into a class and then tells how it differs from other members of that class.

- Informal definitions may be synonyms, antonyms, examples, or explanations.

- The meaning of a word includes its connotation (associations) as well as its denotation (formal dictionary definition).

■ Writing Assignment

Write an essay in which you provide an extended definition of a quality or feeling (courage, love, hate, integrity, patriotism, prejudice, success, failure, etc.) or of a type of person (hero, friend, patriot, traitor, leader, etc.). Include a formal definition in your introduction, perhaps as a part of your thesis statement, but write about what the word means to you as well as its formal dictionary definition. That is, consider the word's connotations as well as its denotation. Develop your definition with at least two different methods of development. Finally, include informal definitions of the word where you think they will add to your definition.

■ Participating in the Academic Community

Read the introduction of your essay to a small group of your classmates and ask them to predict, or suggest, how you will define the subject of your essay. Then, compare your classmates' predictions and suggestions with the content of your draft, taking notes on any ideas that you would like to include in your revision of the essay.

Chapter 17

Persuasion

The primary purpose of **persuasion** is to convince readers to agree with a particular position or point of view. In addition, persuasion often encourages readers to act in support of that position. To achieve these purposes, writers must provide effective support for their arguments.

In your academic classes, you will often be asked to take a position on a controversial issue and defend that position in writing. Your biology teacher might ask you to argue for or against using animals in medical research; your sociology professor might ask you to argue for or against capital punishment; and your journalism or computer science instructor might ask you to argue for or against censorship of information available on the Internet. As a student, you will also be required to evaluate persuasive writing to determine if an argument is logical, fair, and effective. For example, in your political science class, you might be asked to evaluate the contrasting arguments of a liberal and a conservative politician.

Understanding Persuasion

Persuasive writing differs from other writing in purpose more than in content. In attempting to persuade readers to accept a particular position or point of view, persuasive writers use many of the same methods of development already discussed in this unit. As illustrated in the following paragraph, one of the most common methods of development in persuasive writing is the use of examples and statistical evidence to support an argument:

> **We are encouraged by conservation success stories, of course, but only the most hopeful among us are optimistic about the long term.** Of earth's 9,000 species of birds, about 1,000 are already at risk. And while the old perils—habitat destruction, pesticide poisoning, shooting, oil spills, migrant-killing TV towers, and others—continue, we are adding new threats. Especially sinister are the gaseous byproducts of advanced technology—carbon dioxide, methane, nitrous oxide, CFCs—the products responsible

for acid precipitation, ozone depletion and the greenhouse effect, developments whose long-term impact on birds (and other life) we are beginning, nervously, to guess at. To what future will man's growing population and attendant technologies take us? Harvard biologist E. O. Wilson, in a recent interview, delivered a stark warning: "Humanity, in the desperate attempt to fit eight billion or more people on the planet and give them a higher standard of living, is at risk of pushing the rest of life off the globe."

—Alan Pistorius, "Species Lost," *Country Journal*

Qualities of Effective Persuasion

As illustrated in the paragraph by Alan Pistorius, the qualities of effective persuasion include the following:

1. *A sense of purpose and a clear main idea stating the writer's position.* A persuasive argument states a position or a solution to a problem. To qualify as persuasion, the statement must be arguable and not a simple statement of fact. In the preceding paragraph, for example, the first sentence states Pistorius's position that "only the most hopeful among us are optimistic about the long term" outlook for many species—a statement with which some people would disagree. In persuasive paragraphs such as this one, the writer's position—or main idea—is often stated at the beginning of the paragraph. In a persuasive essay, however, the writer usually provides some background information or a statement of the problem before stating the thesis, which may appear at the end of the first paragraph or even in the second paragraph.

2. *Strong supporting evidence.* The success of persuasive writing depends on the quality of the writer's support for his or her argument. That is, a writer who convinces readers to agree with his or her position must provide strong reasons and evidence. For example, Pistorius supports his position about the danger of extinction with statistics about the number of birds at risk (1,000), with examples of dangers to different species (habitat destruction, pesticide poisoning, carbon dioxide, etc.), and with a statement from an authority in the field (E. O. Wilson). (These types of evidence are discussed in the following section, Using Persuasive Appeals.)

3. *Recognition and refutation of opposing arguments.* To persuade readers—especially those who disagree—writers cannot ignore opposing arguments. Instead, a writer should recognize the strongest arguments against his or her point of view and refute, or argue against, each of these arguments. In his first sentence, Pistorius recognizes that there are some "conservation success stories" but nevertheless argues that the evidence he has provided suggests a bleak outlook for many species in the future.

4. *A clear and logical structure.* Although the structure of a persuasive argument may vary, the sample paragraph suggests a helpful pattern for writing essays as well as paragraphs. This pattern is outlined here:

   a. Background and statement of persuasive claim
   b. Evidence to support the argument
   c. Recognition and refutation of opposing arguments
   d. Conclusion

   Each of these structural divisions is included in condensed form in Pistorius's paragraph. In an essay, however, the first paragraph would provide background and state the writer's position (main idea), the next two or three paragraphs would give support for the writer's argument, another paragraph would recognize and refute opposing arguments, and the final paragraph would conclude the essay. (This structure is illustrated in Mike Burton's essay on pages 238–239.)

EXERCISE

17.1

Select three arguable topics and write them in the spaces labeled Topic A, Topic B, and Topic C. For each topic, write an assertion that states your position on that topic. Then list three arguments for and three arguments against your position. Topics that you might consider are abortion, affirmative action, AIDS testing of health care employees, capital punishment, drug testing in the workplace, and gun control.

TOPIC A: _____

Position: _____

	For	*Against*
Reason 1:	_____	_____
Reason 2:	_____	_____
Reason 3:	_____	_____

TOPIC B: _____

Position: _____

	For	*Against*
Reason 1:	_____	_____
Reason 2:	_____	_____
Reason 3:	_____	_____

17.1 continued

TOPIC C: _____

Position: _____

	For		*Against*

Reason 1: _____   _____

Reason 2: _____   _____

Reason 3: _____   _____

Using Persuasive Appeals

In order to persuade readers to agree with a particular position on an issue, writers need to think carefully about how they will appeal to their audience and what support they will use. Depending on who their audience is, writers may want to appeal to either their readers' **reason** or their **emotion.** If you are arguing, for example, that taxes in your community need to be raised so better lighting can be added at the city park, you will make different persuasive appeals to different audiences. You could appeal to the emotions of parents who are worried about the safety of their children, but you would want to appeal to the reason of other taxpayers and local government officials, arguing that better lighting in the city park could actually save money by reducing crime in the area.

Martin Luther King, Jr.'s, "Letter from a Birmingham Jail" is an extremely effective argument that uses the persuasive appeals of both reason and emotion. As you read the paragraphs from his letter in the following sections, keep in mind that King wrote them in 1963, when he was in jail for "parading without a permit" in Birmingham, Alabama. In his letter, King was directly addressing eight Birmingham clergymen who "deplored" the demonstrations in their city, but indirectly he was addressing all humanity for the purpose of gaining equal rights and justice for African Americans and, indeed, for all people.

Reason

An appeal to reason presents representative, fair, and logical evidence. As illustrated in the following paragraph, this appeal often relies on an accepted truth, such as the idea that some laws are moral while others are immoral. Once this accepted truth, or premise, is established, the writer can then develop an argument based on this premise.

> You express a great deal of anxiety over our willingness to break laws. This is certainly a legitimate concern. Since we so diligently urge people to obey the Supreme Court's decision of 1954 outlawing segregation in the public schools, at first glance it may seem rather paradoxical for us consciously to break laws. One may well ask: "How can you advocate breaking some laws and obeying

others?" The answer lies in the fact that there are two types of laws: just and unjust. I would be the first to advocate obeying just laws. One has not only a legal but a moral responsibility to obey just laws. Conversely, one has a moral responsibility to disobey unjust laws. I would agree with St. Augustine that "an unjust law is no law at all."

—Martin Luther King, Jr., "Letter from a Birmingham Jail"

From the premise that some laws are just and others are unjust, King reasonably concludes that "one has a moral responsibility to disobey unjust laws."

Emotion

In using an emotional appeal, a writer uses language, examples, and descriptions that make readers react to the argument with their personal feelings. When presented fairly and honestly, as it is in the following paragraph by King, an appeal to the reader's emotions is an effective and justifiable type of persuasion.

> We have waited for more than 340 years for our constitutional and God-given rights. The nations of Asia and Africa are moving with jetlike speed toward gaining political independence, but we still creep at horse-and-buggy pace toward gaining a cup of coffee at a lunch counter. Perhaps it is easy for those who have never felt the stinging darts of segregation to say, "Wait." But when you have seen vicious mobs lynch your mothers and fathers at will and drown your sisters and brothers at whim; when you have seen hate-filled policemen curse, kick, and even kill your black brothers and sisters; when you see the vast majority of your twenty million Negro brothers smothering in an airtight cage of poverty in the midst of an affluent society; when you suddenly find your tongue twisted and your speech stammering as you seek to explain to your six-year-old daughter why she can't go to the public amusement park that has just been advertised on television, and see tears welling up in her eyes when she is told that Funtown is closed to colored children, and see ominous clouds of inferiority beginning to form in her little mental sky, and see her beginning to distort her personality by developing an unconscious bitterness toward white people; when you have to concoct an answer for a five-year-old son who is asking, "Daddy, why do white people treat colored people so mean?" . . . —then you will understand why we find it difficult to wait. There comes a time when the cup of endurance runs over, and men are no longer willing to be plunged into the abyss of despair. I hope, sirs, you can understand our legitimate and unavoidable impatience.

—Martin Luther King, Jr., "Letter from a Birmingham Jail"

King' s emotional appeal in this paragraph is effective because it is based on actual experiences and human feelings with which his readers can identify. However, writers should be careful not to misuse the emotional appeal by unjustly exaggerating or misrepresenting events or situations.

EXERCISE

17.2   Both of the following persuasive paragraphs focus on the controversy of hand gun control. As you read these paragraphs, identify in each the writer's position on the topic and the primary appeal (reason or emotion). (*Note:* The writer's position is clearly stated in one of these paragraphs and clearly implied in the other.)

PARAGRAPH A

Gun control is not an easy issue. But, for me, it is a fundamental issue. My family has been touched by violence; too many others have felt the same terrible force. Too many children have been raised without a father or a mother. Too many widows have lived out their lives alone. Too many people have died.

—Edward M. Kennedy, "The Need for Handgun Control,"
Los Angeles Times

1. What is the writer's position on the topic?

   _____

2. What is the writer's primary appeal?

   _____

PARAGRAPH B

It is clear, I think, that gun legislation simply doesn't work. There are already some 20,000 state and local gun laws on the books, and they are no more effective than was the prohibition of alcoholic beverages in the 1920s. Our most recent attempt at federal gun legislation was . . . intended to control the interstate sale and transportation of firearms and the importation of uncertified firearms; it has done nothing to check the availability of weapons. It has been bolstered in every nook and cranny of the nation by local gun-control laws, yet the number of shooting homicides per year has climbed steadily since its enactment, while armed robberies have increased 60 percent.

—Barry Goldwater, "Why Gun-Control Laws Don't Work,"
Reader's Digest

1. What is the writer's position on the topic?

2. What is the writer's primary appeal!

Evaluating Your Evidence

To persuade readers to agree with a position, a writer must present convincing evidence. That is, a writer must use enough relevant, reliable evidence to prove the persuasive point to the audience. As you plan your persuasive paragraph or essay, be sure to omit weak evidence and use only your strongest support.

Using Effective Evidence

Effective support for persuasive writing includes effective **examples,** accurate **facts and statistics,** and statements from **reliable sources.**

1. *Examples.* Relevant examples provide effective support for an argument. If possible, choose examples that will have a strong impact on readers, and remember that two or three examples are often more persuasive than one.

    ARGUMENT: [G]raphic violence . . . [is] especially damaging for young children because they lack the moral judgment of adults . . . [but] are excellent mimics.

    EXAMPLE: One 5-year-old boy from Boston recently got up from watching a teen-slasher film and stabbed a 2-year-old girl with a butcher knife. He didn't mean to kill her (and luckily he did not). He was just imitating the man on the video.

    —Tipper Gore, "Curbing the Sexploitation Industry," *Raising PG Kids in an X-Rated Society*

    ARGUMENT: I hope, sirs, you can understand our legitimate and unavoidable impatience [for] . . . our constitutional and God-given rights.

    EXAMPLE: But . . . when you suddenly find your tongue twisted and your speech stammering as you seek to explain to your six-year-old daughter why she can't go to the public amusement park that has just been advertised on television, and see tears welling up in her eyes when she is told that Funtown is closed to colored children. . . .

    —Martin Luther King, Jr., "Letter from a Birmingham Jail"

2. *Facts and statistics.* Both facts and statistics are effective in persuasive writing because they provide objective evidence that can be proved (or disproved). Statistics are a particular kind of facts based on numerical evidence. In the first example that follows, the statement that oil spills are a peril for different species is factual because it can be proved or disproved; the statement that 1,000 species are at risk is a statistic. Be sure that the factual evidence you use clearly supports your argument and comes from a reliable source.

ARGUMENT: Modern man has made the Earth unlivable for many other species; and biologists fear a round of extinctions from which the recovery of biodiversity may be impossible.

FACT/STATISTIC: Of earth's 9,000 species of birds, about 1,000 are already at risk. And . . . the old perils—habitat destruction, pesticide poisoning, shooting, oil spills, migrant-killing TV towers, and others—continue. . . .
                                              —Alan Pistorius, "Species Lost," *Country Journal*

ARGUMENT: I hope, sirs, you can understand our legitimate and unavoidable impatience [for] . . . our constitutional and God-given rights.

FACT/STATISTIC: We have waited for more than 340 years. . . .
                                              —Martin Luther King, Jr., "Letter from a Birmingham Jail"

3. *Reliable sources.* Persuasive writing often uses support from reliable sources. As shown in the following examples, support from a credible and respected authority in the field can be convincing evidence. Readers trust a Harvard biologist to know about endangered species, and St. Augustine is a respected scholar and author of the fifth century AD.

ARGUMENT: Modern man has made the Earth unlivable for many other species; and biologists fear a round of extinctions from which the recovery of biodiversity may be impossible.

AUTHORITY: Harvard biologist E. O. Wilson, in a recent interview, delivered a stark warning: "Humanity, in the desperate attempt to fit eight billion or more people on the planet and give them a higher standard of living, is at risk of pushing the rest of life off the globe."
                                              —Alan Pistorius, "Species Lost," *Country Journal*

ARGUMENT: One has a moral responsibility to disobey unjust laws.

AUTHORITY: I would agree with St. Augustine that "an unjust law is
no law at all."

> —Martin Luther King, Jr., "Letter from a Birmingham Jail"

Avoiding Ineffective Evidence

When writers plan support for their arguments, they should be careful to avoid unreliable and ineffective evidence. The four general types of unreliable and illogical support that should be avoided are **oversimplification, irrelevant evidence, unfairly emotional words,** and **distorted or suppressed evidence.**

1. *Oversimplification.* Oversimplification is poor reasoning that weakens a persuasive argument. Oversimplification occurs when a writer draws a conclusion based on insufficient evidence. Concluding, for example, that all women are bad drivers because three women received traffic tickets in one day is oversimplifying the issue and drawing a hasty conclusion. Similarly, writers may make an illogical assumption that one thing causes another simply because these two events occur in succession—as in the superstition that a black cat crossing a road causes an accident that occurs afterward. Writers also oversimplify many situations by assuming that only two choices are possible when several choices may actually exist. Toothpaste advertisers, for example, would have us believe that the only alternative to using their product is to have cavities, when actually several other products can also prevent cavities. Sometimes writers also make comparisons that can be misleading. Comparing life to a chess game creates an interesting metaphor but does not make a logical point. Finally, writers are guilty of circular reasoning—and of proving nothing—when they make a statement such as "Alcohol is intoxicating because it makes you drunk."

2. *Irrelevant evidence.* Politicians are frequently guilty of using irrelevant evidence. One candidate may smear or "sling mud" at another candidate about such things as gambling habits or failure to serve in the military even though such accusations are irrelevant to the political issues being discussed in the campaign. If the accuser has no supporting evidence, he or she may simply hint that the candidate is a racist or an adulterer. If a reporter asks a politician a direct question about his or her opinion or vote on a particular issue, the politician may simply change the subject and give an irrelevant response.

   Of course, politicians aren't the only people who use irrelevant evidence. A beginning writer may be tempted to make a statement because "everybody believes it" rather than search for evidence to support the truth. Another example of irrelevant evidence is quoting someone simply because he or she is famous. To be a reliable authority, the person must have expertise or experience m the subject.

3. *Overly emotional words.* In choosing words, writers should consider the connotations (personal associations) as well as denotations (dictionary definitions). Thus, if a writer wanted to present a positive picture of a celebrity, she would call him *famous;* if she wanted to present a negative picture of the individual, she would call him *notorious.* However, a writer should be careful not to use words just for their emotional impact—either positive or negative. That is, while the emotional appeal is valid, writers should not substitute emotion for reason. In particular, writers should be careful about *name calling (conspirator, racist, chauvinist,* etc.) or about using *glittering generalities (American way of life, decent standard of living).* Such words and phrases have lost much of their meaning from having been used too frequently and thoughtlessly.

4. *Distorted or suppressed evidence.* Finally, good persuasive writing does not distort or suppress evidence. One kind of distortion is taking a quotation out of context. A second kind of distortion is misrepresenting an opposing point of view before refuting it. And finally, suppression of evidence occurs when the opposing view is completely ignored. All of these problems in reasoning ultimately weaken the writer's persuasive argument.

EXERCISE

17.3

Each of the following items is an example of weak reasoning. Write in the blank the kind of weak reasoning it illustrates: oversimplification, irrelevant evidence, overly emotional words, or distorted or suppressed evidence.

1. Let's go see the new movie at the Majestic. Everybody says it's great.

_____

2. He doesn't go to church on Sundays, so he must be an atheist.

_____

3. The third-party candidate for state senator calls herself a "liberal." What she really means is that we should give up free enterprise and the American dream in this country in favor of government ownership and control.

_____

4. Try our new brand of cigarettes. They give you only a fresh menthol taste.

_____

5. All foreign cars have bad engines. I know because I have owned two foreign cars, and the engines blew up in both of them.

_____

Writing Persuasive Paragraphs

The topic sentence of a persuasive paragraph states the writer's position, or main idea. Since you do not have as much space for supporting evidence in a paragraph as you do in an essay, you should be especially careful to select the most persuasive evidence. As you read Davy's paragraph, notice both his organization and the types of evidence he uses.

STUDENT PARAGRAPH

Unless Congress reinstates the support price for the sale of fluid milk, many more family dairy farms will go out of business. Opponents of a dairy support price argue that other businesses don't receive help from the government and that such help is expensive to taxpayers. It is true that few other businesses receive government help, but all business people except farmers can set their own prices to be sure they make a profit. As President John F. Kennedy observed many years ago, "The American farmer is the only person in society who buys at retail, sells at wholesale, and pays the freight both ways." The milk company that buys the dairy farmer's milk sets the price the farmer receives as well as the price the farmer must pay the company to haul his milk. Because fluid milk will spoil, the dairy farmer is forced to take whatever price is offered regardless of his expenses. The American dairy farmer is at a disadvantage both within the United States and with other countries because the governments of most other countries continue to help their dairy farmers. In addition, the actual price of fluid milk in the 1990s declined or remained the same while other farm expenses went up.

For example, a tractor that cost a farmer $15,000 in the late 1970s costs over $50,000 today. Yet, fluid milk that sold for about $14.00 (per hundred pounds) in the late 1970s and for $16.00 in the late 1980s sold for only $13.00 in the mid to late 1990s. As a result of these relatively low milk prices, many dairy farmers have gone out of business. For example, in one major dairying county in Texas, 250 of the county's 500 dairy farms went out of business during the late 1990s. Thus, possible money from taxes is being lost, and a business important to the health of America's citizens—especially to its children—is being destroyed. If the trend continues, several results will occur. Americans will be forced to rely more and more on dairy products from other countries or the production of dairy products by large companies. In either case, the price of dairy products is likely to go up as the quality goes down. Ultimately, the taxpayers must pay a higher price than they would have if they had supported a reasonable governmental price floor to keep small dairy farms in business. Therefore, I encourage you to write your national legislators and encourage them to restore the dairy support price.

—Davy Moseley, student

After beginning with the topic sentence that states his position, Davy gives necessary background about the practice of supporting dairy prices. Then he recognizes and refutes the opposing argument that dairies should not receive government aid because other businesses in the United States do not receive such help. Davy continues by providing evidence to prove the necessity of the dairy support price and to encourage readers to act in support of his position.

Davy uses several kinds of evidence in his paragraph, including a quotation from President Kennedy, an example of the increased cost of tractors, and statistics about the price of fluid milk and the declining number of dairies. Although a persuasive paragraph or essay can include many types of development, the most common methods of development are probably the use of comparison and contrast to present opposing arguments, examples to provide evidence for the writer's argument, and cause and effect to speculate about results. Some of the transition words used in these methods of development, which are highlighted in Davy's paragraph, include the following:

CONTRAST	EXAMPLE/ ADDITION	CAUSE/EFFECT/ CONDITION
although	and, also	as a result
but	first, second, etc.	because
however	for example	consequently
in contrast	for instance	for, hence, if
nevertheless	finally, last	since, so
on the other hand	such as	therefore
yet	ultimately	thus

EXERCISE

17.4

Write a persuasive paragraph on one of the following topics. State your position in your topic sentence and then use fair, reasonable, and effective reasons and evidence to support that claim. Do not forget to refute the opposing argument.

1. Physical education activity courses should (or should not) be required for college graduation.

2. Spanish (or another foreign language) should (or should not) be required for college graduation.

3. The Internet should (or should not) be regulated.

4. Minors should (or should not) buy _____.

5. Candidate _____ for the office of _____ should (or should not) be elected.

Writing Persuasive Essays

The purpose of a persuasive essay, like that of a persuasive paragraph, is to convince the reader to agree with the writer's position and, perhaps, to take action accordingly. However, a persuasive essay requires much fuller development than a persuasive paragraph. Thus, you have space in the introductory paragraph of an essay to provide background before stating your position in your thesis. You can also provide more detailed support of your position and a fuller refutation of the opposing position in an essay. Moreover, in developing your argument, you may use completely different methods of development in different paragraphs. As you read the following essay, look for the thesis; different types of appeals, reasons, evidence, and methods of development; and the refutation of the opposing argument.

Que Es la Problema?

[1]What is bilingualism? It is a method of teaching in which students for whom English is a second language are given the opportunity to learn in their native language. Bilingual education (bilingualism) uses three different methods: *transition*, which helps students move from their native language to English; *enrichment*, which uses their native language to enrich their studies; and *maintenance*, which allows students to continue to learn in their native language throughout their school careers. Of these three types of bilingual education, the maintenance method is the least effective. Indeed, this approach creates several problems. Bilingual maintenance programs in schools in the United States cost additional taxes, isolate students for whom English is a second language, and may even keep these students from becoming productive and successful citizens.

[2]The first problem with the maintenance method is that it is expensive. In contrast to the transition and enrichment programs, which provide extra instruction for only three to five years, the maintenance program requires extra funding for the entire thirteen years that the student is in school. Thus, the maintenance program is approximately three times as expensive as the other methods of bilingual education. With an average teacher's salary of $30,000, the difference in expenses for the school with between one and three teachers would be $60,000. Although a district can often put in a single classroom several students whose native language is Spanish, an even greater problem arises when a district has only two or three French, German, or Japanese students because ideally each group would be placed in a separate classroom. Of course, extremely small bilingual classes are even more expensive to teach than average sized classes.

[3]Another problem with the bilingual maintenance program is that it isolates students in the program from the rest of the student body for their entire school career. School teaches students not only writing and arithmetic but also how to get along with other people and other cultures. Isolating students in the maintenance program requires that they interact only with people from their same culture. Some may argue that this isolation is only in the classroom because students are able to interact with other students at lunch and playtime. However, students are much more likely to socialize with those whom they know from their classroom experiences. The placement of English-as-a-second-language students in separate classrooms may make other children see them as different and ignore or even ridicule them. At my own high school, the Spanish-speaking students always ate at a table by themselves, usually speaking Spanish, and the English-speaking students also ate by themselves. The maintenance program is governmentally supported segregation.

[4]Perhaps the greatest argument against the maintenance program, however, is that it often keeps its students from becoming productive and successful members of society. For example, if children are taught entirely in Spanish, they will never be able to compete in the job market in an English-speaking country. They will have difficulty completing job applications in English, will have trouble communicating on the job, and are likely to remain in a lower paid position while those who have a better command of the English language are promoted.

[5]Supporters of the bilingual maintenance program offer two opposing arguments. First, these supporters argue that English-as-a-second-language students will be more successful in school if they are taught in their native languages. Certainly, these students might initially succeed better in their native languages, but the negative long-term career effects outweigh the short-term classroom effects. Besides, a good bilingual transition program can prepare students to succeed in an English-speaking classroom as well as an English-speaking society. Second, supporters of the maintenance program argue that if students are taught in English, they will soon forget their native language and will lose their cultural heritage. Certainly, students should have the right and ability as well as the desire to hold on to their cultural heritage, but the classroom is not the only, or even the best, place to promote cultural values. English-as-a-second-language students can continue to speak their native language in their homes and communities, thus truly becoming bilingual by using two languages.

[6]Certainly, the public schools have a responsibility to establish reasonable bilingual programs, such as transition or enrichment programs, that allow English-as-a-second-language students to succeed in school. However, the various costs of the bilingual maintenance program are too high. This program costs the taxpayers more money, it isolates and separate bilingual students from other cultures, and, most important, it keeps these students from competing and succeeding in the job market. We must help English-as-a-second-language students become less dependent and more independent and truly bilingual.

—Mike Burton, student

EXERCISE

17.5

1. What is the writer's thesis?

_____

_____

_____

17.5 continued

2. What are the three reasons the writer gives to support his thesis?

    a. _____

    b. _____

    c. _____

3. Identify and give an example of the primary appeal used in this essay.

    Appeal: _____

    Example: _____

    Does the writer of this essay use any other appeals? If so, what and how?

    _____

    _____

4. List two types of evidence used in this essay and an example of each.

    First type of evidence: _____

    Example: _____

    Second type of evidence: _____

    Example: _____

5. The writer of this essay recognizes and refutes two opposing arguments. Identify each of these opposing arguments and the refutation that the writer uses for each.

    First opposing argument: _____

    Refutation: _____

    Second opposing argument: _____

    Refutation: _____

6. Identify the method(s) of development used in each paragraph in the body of this essay.

    Paragraph 2: _____

    Paragraph 3: _____

    Paragraph 4: _____

    Paragraph 5: _____

7. In your opinion, what is most effective about the writer's conclusion?

_____

_____

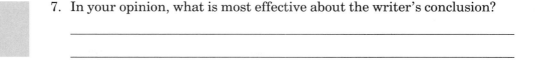

Chapter Review

- Persuasive writing attempts to convince readers to agree with the writer's position on an argument.

- In persuasion, a writer's topic sentence or thesis should be an arguable statement and not a statement of fact.

- Effective persuasion appeals to the reader's reason and emotion.

- Good support for a persuasive claim should be reasonable, fair, and effective; types of support include examples, facts and statistics, and reliable sources.

- Good persuasive writing avoids oversimplification, irrelevant evidence, unfairly emotional words, and distorted or suppressed evidence.

- Good persuasive writing recognizes and effectively refutes opposing arguments.

- Good persuasive writing uses an effective structure:
    1. Background and statement of the writer's position on the subject
    2. Strong evidence for the writer' s position
    3. Recognition and refutation of the opposing argument(s)
    4. A conclusion that restates the writer's position

Writing Assignment

In Exercise 17.1 you brainstormed about three arguable topics, identifying reasons or evidence to support each side of the argument and concluding with a persuasive position statement about the topic. Select one of these topics and develop your thesis into a persuasive essay. Use the following space to plan your essay:

PARAGRAPH 1

Background: _____

_____

Thesis statement: _____

_____

PARAGRAPH 2

Reason 1: _____

Evidence: _____

PARAGRAPH 3

Reason 2: _____

Evidence: _____

PARAGRAPH 4

Reason 3: _____

Evidence: _____

PARAGRAPH 5

Opposing argument(s): _____

_____

Refutation of opposing argument(s): _____

_____

PARAGRAPH 6

Conclusion: _____

_____

■ Participating in the Academic Community

When you finish a draft of your essay, meet with a small group of your peers to evaluate and revise your work. As you read one another's essays, be sure that each essay includes a clear and convincing thesis; that each essay provides fair, reasonable, and effective reasons and evidence to support the writer's position; and that each essay includes and refutes opposing arguments. Also, identify and evaluate the audience appeals used in each essay.

Part Three

Writing and Editing Sentences

As a student, you have repeatedly studied the sentence—its structure, its elements, even its definition. But you may find at this point in your education that you still need to know more about sentences. You may have realized that you need to be able to analyze sentences—to take them apart, understand how they work, and put them back together in different ways. The ability to analyze sentences enables you to be a better editor and proofreader of your own writing.

In Chapter 7 you learned the importance of revising what you write so that the content and organization accurately reflect your ideas and communicate clearly to your readers. But experienced writers also edit and proofread what they have written. Chapters 18, 19, and 20 emphasize how to write effective sentences and how to edit them to make them more readable, more interesting, more graceful, and, ultimately, more correct. Chapters 21–25 focus on errors in sentence structure and usage, while Chapter 26 deals with matters of style. Finally, Chapters 27 and 28 provide instruction in punctuation, capitalization, and spelling.

Chapter 18

Simple Sentences

In order to become a strong academic writer, you need a good basic knowledge of sentence structure. Because academic writing is nearly always directed at readers who value traditional rules of sentence structure and punctuation, you must be able to write sentences that measure up to their expectations.

In terms of their structure, sentences are usually defined as *simple, compound,* or *complex.* Many of the sentences you write are probably simple, but that does not mean they are elementary or simple-minded, merely that they consist of a single subject–verb relationship. In fact, all writers produce an abundance of simple sentences not only because they are easy to read but also because they can be forceful and direct. Because sentence variety is a goal of most experienced writers, simple sentences are also used to provide contrast with longer, more structurally complicated sentences.

Essential Elements of the Sentence

Writers generate an almost endless variety of sentences. But every complete sentence, regardless of how it varies from other sentences, has two essential parts: a **subject** and a **verb.** The subject of a sentence is what you are writing about, and the verb makes a statement or asks a question about the subject. Although a sentence may have other elements, it must have a subject and verb. The following sentence has only these two essential elements:

Maria smiled.

Most sentences, however, are longer and more detailed. Notice in the following sentence pairs that the essential elements (subject and verb) remain the same even though more details have been added. (The subject has been underlined once and the verb twice.)

▶ EXAMPLES

Car rolled.

The battered old <u>car</u> <u>rolled</u> down the hill.

Several stood.

<u>Several</u> of the construction workers <u>stood</u> with their backs to us.

Wind blew.

The hot, dry <u>wind</u> constantly <u>blew</u> the fine sand into our faces.

18.1

Underline the subject once and the verb twice in each of the following simple sentences.

1. The judge allowed the trial to be televised.

2. Each year, the threat of global warming increases.

3. There was a young child alone in the car.

4. Next year's schedule will be posted on the board.

5. The cup of coffee sat on the edge of her desk.

6. The student wearily dropped her backpack onto a chair.

The preceding sentences are all examples of **simple sentences.** That is, they all have a single subject–verb relationship: The verb of each sentence makes a statement about the subject of the sentence. Even in a sentence in which the subject or verb is *compounded* (composed of two or more parts), the sentence is still a simple sentence if both the verbs are making the same statement about both of the subjects.

▶ EXAMPLES

Compound verb:	Maria <u>smiled and nodded</u>.
Compound subject:	<u>Maria and John</u> smiled.
Compound subject and verb:	<u>Maria and John</u> <u>smiled and nodded</u>.

All three examples are still simple sentences because they have only one subject–verb relationship. But if the sentence is changed so that it expresses two subject–verb relationships *(Maria smiled,* and *John nodded),* the sentence is no longer a simple sentence. (*Note:* See Chapter 19 for a more extensive discussion of compound elements.)

EXERCISE

18.2   Write five simple sentences, including at least one with a compound subject or verb. Underline the subject once and the verb twice in each sentence.

1. _____

_____

2. _____

_____

3. _____

_____

4. _____

_____

5. _____

_____

Subjects

Since your subject is what you are talking about, it is often a word that names someone or something. We call such words **nouns.** Look at the following list of nouns:

1. arrangement
2. warning
3. receptionist
4. politicians
5. monkey
6. actress
7. Carlos
8. pride
9. writers
10. lab technician

EXERCISE

18.3   Each of the nouns listed above can function as the subject of a sentence. Write ten simple sentences using each of these nouns as a subject.

1. _____

_____

2. _____

_____

3. _____
   _____

4. _____
   _____

5. _____
   _____

6. _____
   _____

7. _____
   _____

8. _____
   _____

9. _____
   _____

10. _____
    _____

Pronouns are words that refer to nouns. Like a noun, a pronoun can function as the subject of a sentence. For example, the following pronouns could refer to the nouns listed earlier.

1. arrangement—it
2. warning—it
3. receptionist—he
4. politicians—they
5. monkey—it
6. actress—she
7. Carlos—he
8. pride—it
9. writers—they
10. lab technician—she

EXERCISE

18.4

Rewrite five of the sentences you wrote in Exercise 18.3, using an appropriate pronoun as the subject of each sentence.

1. _____
   _____

2. _____

_____

3. _____

_____

4. _____

_____

5. _____

_____

EXERCISE

18.5   Many of the subject nouns and pronouns have been deleted from the following passage. Replace the blanks with appropriate nouns or pronouns so that each sentence has a subject that makes sense. Any word that makes sense in the context is acceptable. Do not worry about right or wrong answers. If the word you choose is appropriate for the context, it is right.

He was raised by his aunt and uncle, who was his father's

brother. _____ had been staying with them when his parents
                (1)

died, and he simply stayed on. _____ slept in a narrow bed
                                      (2)

in a small and dingy room. _____ lived in a sunless ground-
                                (3)

floor apartment in an old five-story red-brick building where his

uncle collected the rents for the owner no one ever saw. The

_____ was the talk of their Brooklyn neighborhood. There was
      (4)

something wrong with it; _____ had gone awry from the very
                              (5)

beginning. The furnace was whimsical and tended to die when it

was most needed; valves stuck, _____ leaked, faucets gushed
                                     (6)

unevenly when turned on, or gave off explosions of air; electrical

_____ shorted mysteriously; _____ of brick worked loose
      (7)   (8)

and tumbled to the sidewalk; the tar paper covering of the roof, no

18.5 continued

matter how recently replaced, became warped, then buckled and cracked. But the rents were low, the _____ were always filled, ___(9)___ and his uncle, who earned an erratic livelihood from the badly organized and decrepit Hebrew bookstore he operated in the neighborhood, was kept very busy. Often his _____ himself fired ___(10)___ up the furnace on those early winter mornings when the janitor was in a drunken stupor from which he could not be roused. _____ ___(11)___ came and went. His uncle's _____ was not an easy one. ___(12)___

—Adapted from Chaim Potok, *The Book of Lights*

Verbs

In addition to a subject, each complete sentence must have a verb—a word or phrase that makes a statement or asks a question about the subject. The verb of a sentence may be a single word (such as *drink)* or a verb phrase (such as *will be drinking).* Each verb has many different forms. The form of a verb changes most often to indicate **tense**—the time at which the stated action or being takes place. Look at the following examples of the different tenses of the verb *dance:*

I **dance** each day to keep in shape.   (present)

I **danced** for several hours last night.   (past)

I **will dance** with you later.   (future)

I **have danced** with her before.   (present perfect)

I **had danced** for hours.   (past perfect)

I **will have danced** every dance.   (future perfect)

I **am dancing** too much.   (present progressive)

I **was dancing** energetically.   (past progressive)

I **will be dancing** in the chorus.   (future progressive)

I **have been dancing** with him.   (present perfect progressive)

I **had been dancing** for many years.   (past perfect progressive

I **will have been dancing** for twenty years next month.   (future perfect progressive)

Most speakers of English do not have to think consciously about using the appropriate tense—the one that communicates the intended relationship between the time of the action expressed in the sentence and the actual time at which the sentence is written or spoken. However, choosing the appropriate verb form is part of a writer's responsibility. Within the range of what is considered correct are many choices, but each choice conveys a different meaning. (See Chapter 24, Verb Tenses and Forms.)

▶ EXAMPLES

I danced all night.   (past tense, occurring in the past at a specified time)

I have danced to that song before.   (present perfect, occurring at some time in the past)

I am dancing too much.   (present progressive, occurring at the present time)

Writers also use auxiliaries (such as *should, would, could, might, may, can, must,* and *do* or *did)* to make other distinctions about verbs. Readers use these auxiliaries as clues to interpret a writer's meaning.

▶ EXAMPLES

I **may** dance.
I **might** dance ⟶ possibility

I **must** dance.
I **should** dance ⟶ obligation

I **can** dance.
I **could** dance. ⟶ ability

I **would** dance. ——— condition

I **will** dance. ——— intent

I **do** dance
I **did** dance. ⟶ emphasis

EXERCISE

18.6   The following four sentences have no main verb. Using the clues provided in each sentence, fill in as many appropriate forms of the verb *speak* as you can.

1. Every day as he walks to work, Michael _____ to her.

   _____

   _____

18.6 continued

2. Yesterday, as he walked to work, Michael _____ to her.

_____

_____

3. Tomorrow, as he walks to work, Michael _____ to her.

_____

_____

4. By then, Michael _____ to her.

_____

_____

E X E R C I S E

18.7

The main verbs have been deleted from each of the sentences in the following passage. Supply a verb for each sentence. Be sure that you choose a verb that reflects the appropriate tense and that the resulting paragraph makes sense.

In March there _____ a death on the island. Like most
　　　　　　　　　　　　　(1)

deaths on Yamacraw, it _____ with unforeshadowed swiftness;
　　　　　　　　　　　　　(2)

there was no lingering or gradual wasting away or bedside

farewells. A heart attack _____ Blossom Smith on a Saturday,
　　　　　　　　　　　　　　(3)

an islander raced to Ted Stone's house, and Stone immediately

_____ for a rescue helicopter from Savannah. Blossom was
　　(4)

_____ to an open field near the nightclub, where half the island
　　(5)

gathered around her wailing and praying. The helicopter appeared,

_____ rapidly and efficiently, received the motionless Blossom
　　(6)

into the dark angel with the rotating wings, _____ into the sky
　　　　　　　　　　　　　　　　　　　　　　(7)

in a maelstrom of debris and air, and then _____ over the top of
　　　　　　　　　　　　　　　　　　　　　(8)

trees. It _____ all very quick, very impressive, and very
(9)

futile. Blossom _____ that night in Savannah surrounded by
(10)

strangers and the ammonia smells of a death ward.

—Pat Conroy, *The Water Is Wide*

18.8

Following are two lists of verbs. One consists of five present tense verbs, and the other consists of the same verbs in the past tense. Use each verb in a sentence that provides the appropriate context for the tense.

PRESENT TENSE VERBS	**PAST TENSE VERBS**
1. walks	2. walked
3. is singing	4. was singing
5. eat	6. ate
7. can study	8. could study
9. does believe	10. did believe

▶ EXAMPLE: He *reads* his lesson every day.

He *read* that novel last weekend.

1. _____

_____

2. _____

_____

3. _____

_____

4. _____

_____

5. _____

_____

6. _____

_____

18.8 continued

7. _____

_____

8. _____

_____

9. _____

_____

10. _____

_____

Basic Patterns of the Simple Sentence

All English sentences are derived from three basic patterns. A knowledge of these three patterns will enable you to analyze the structure of any sentence you read or write:

Pattern 1:   Subject–Verb (S–V)

Pattern 2:   Subject–Verb–Object (S–V–O)

Pattern 3:   Subject–Linking Verb–Complement (S–LV–C)

Pattern 1: Subject–Verb (S–V)

This pattern has only the two essential elements of a sentence: a subject and a verb. However, it may also have modifying words and phrases that describe and/or limit either the subject or the verb. Remember also that the verb of a sentence may be a verb phrase.

▶ EXAMPLES

Students study.   (S–V)

Students will be studying.   (S–V phrase)

Many students in Dr. Goff's chemistry class study together in the evening.   (S–V plus modifying words and phrases)

Although the subject and verb in this pattern usually occur in the order shown (subject preceding verb), the order may be inverted without affecting the pattern.

▶ EXAMPLES

In the stacks, on the top floor of the library, <u>study</u> the most industrious, dedicated <u>students.</u>

(The subject of this sentence is *students,* and the verb is *study.* Even though the word order has been inverted, the pattern is still S–V.)

<u>Did</u> the biology <u>students</u> <u>study</u> for their test?
(Because this sentence is a question, the word order is inverted: The subject *students* comes between the auxiliary verb *did* and the main verb *study.*)

Sentences with inverted word order offer writers additional options for subtle differences in meaning. *The moon we could not see* is not the same as *We could not see the moon.* As a writer, you need to be aware of the options that inversion of word order offers. As a reader, you need to be aware of the problems such sentences present, for they are more difficult to read than sentences in which the elements follow normal word order. A knowledge of basic sentence patterns will help you analyze and understand such sentences.

EXERCISE

18.9

Write three sentences that follow the subject–verb pattern. Include one sentence that has inverted word order.

1. _____

_____

2. _____

_____

3. _____

_____

Pattern 2: Subject–Verb–Object (S–V–O)

This pattern has a third major element—an **object** (often called a **direct object**)—in addition to the essential subject and verb. An object completes and receives the action expressed by the verb. Like a subject, an object is a noun or a noun substitute.

▶ EXAMPLES

Her husband washed the dishes.   (S–V–O)

Her husband was washing the dishes.   (S–V phrase–O)

Silently but efficiently, her husband washed the dirty dishes.
(S–V–O plus modifiers)

The elements in this pattern, like those in the S–V pattern, usually occur in normal order (S–V–O); however, the word order can also be inverted.

▶ EXAMPLES

      O   S   V
That book he had not read.

          O   S   V
This solution she had not considered.

Pronouns as Objects

Personal pronouns, which refer to people or things, assume different forms depending on their function in the sentence. The object form of a personal pronoun should be used when the pronoun is functioning as the object of a verb. Compare the contrasting examples of subject and object forms given here:

▶ EXAMPLES

He caught the frisbee.   (personal pronoun as subject)
The frisbee hit **him.**   (personal pronoun as object)

I met Shawn at the party.   (personal pronoun as subject)
Shawn met **me** at the party.   (personal pronoun as object)

She sent her accountant an invitation.   (personal pronoun as subject)
Her accountant sent **her** to the bank.   (personal pronoun as object)

They visited their friends.   (personal pronoun as subject)
Their friends visited **them.**   (personal pronoun as object)

In the first example, the subject form of the pronoun (*he*) is used because the pronoun is functioning as the subject of the sentence. But in the second example, the object form (*him*) is used because the pronoun is functioning as the object of the sentence. The following chart lists both the subject and object forms of the personal pronouns:

	SUBJECT FORM	OBJECT FORM
First-person singular	I	me
Second-person singular	you	you
Third-person singular	he, she, it	him, her, it
First-person plural	we	us
Second-person plural	you	you
Third-person plural	they	them

Be sure to use the subject form of the pronoun if you are using it as a subject and the object form if you are using it as an object. (*Note:* Some sentences also include an *indirect object*—the one to or for whom the direct object is intended.)

▶ EXAMPLE: I sent **him** a letter.

Him is the indirect object—the one to whom the letter is sent. Pronouns that function as indirect objects are in the objective case.

EXERCISE

18.10

Write three sentences that follow the S–V–O pattern. Use a pronoun as the object of two of your sentences.

1. _____

   _____

2. _____

   _____

3. _____

   _____

Pattern 3: Subject–Linking Verb–Complement (S–LV–C)

Like the S–V–O pattern, this one also has three elements: subject, linking verb, and complement. A **complement,** like an object, completes the meaning of the verb. However, in this pattern the verb is a **linking verb,** and the complement refers to the subject. In fact, the complement is often called a *subject complement.* It can be either a noun or pronoun that renames the subject or an adjective that describes the subject.

Noun

▶ EXAMPLES: Marcus is my friend.   (S–LV–C)

Adjective

Marcus is friendly.   (S–LV–C)

Both of these sentences follow the S–LV–C pattern, but the first has a noun complement (*friend* renames *Marcus,* telling who he is), and the second has an adjective complement (*friendly* describes *Marcus,* telling something about him). Both complements refer to the subject *Marcus* even though they are part of the verb. A complement, in fact, is necessary to complete the meaning of the linking verb.

Linking Verbs

A linking verb connects the subject to the subject complement. The verb *to be* (*am, is, are, was,* and *were*) is the most frequently used linking verb. (Because it is a highly irregular verb, we have listed its main forms on page 363.)

The following verbs may also function as linking verbs. Notice that each of these verbs could be replaced by some form of the verb *to be.*

VERB	EXAMPLE OF VERB IN SENTENCE
act	The dog **acts** sick. (is sick)
appear	The plants **appear** healthy. (are healthy)
become	They **became** unhappy. (were unhappy)
fall	The gorilla **fell** ill. (is ill)
feel	I **feel** great. (am great)
get	My aunt **is getting** old. (is old)
go	The dog **went** crazy. (was crazy)
grow	The child **grew** sleepy. (was sleepy)
keep	My mother **keeps** healthy. (is healthy)
look	The winner **looked** happy. (was happy)

prove	That decision **will prove** a mistake. (will be a mistake)
remain	The mockingbird **remained** quiet. (was quiet)
run	That river **runs** deep. (is deep)
seem	You **seem** sad. (are sad)
smell	That onion **smells** terrible. (is terrible)
sound	That piano **sounds** off-key. (is off-key)
stay	The door **stays** open. (is open)
taste	The apple **tastes** sour. (is sour)
turn	The leaves **were turning** brown. (were brown)

Although each of these verbs could be replaced by a form of the verb *to be*, they are essential to good writing because they are more specific, concrete ways of expressing the overused verb *to be*.

Pronouns as Complements

Personal pronouns as well as nouns can function as complements. When a personal pronoun is used as a complement, it takes the subject form rather than the object form.

▶ EXAMPLES

Personal pronoun as subject: **She** is a good student.

Personal pronoun as object: Her teacher entered **her** in a contest.

Personal pronoun as complement: In fact, the winner of the contest was **she.**

EXERCISE

18.11   Write three sentences that follow the S–LV–C pattern. Be sure to include linking verbs other than the verb *to be* in one of your sentences and to use one personal pronoun as a complement.

1. _____

   _____

2. _____

   _____

3. _____

   _____

Expanding the Simple Sentence

One of the most important ways to expand the basic elements of a simple sentence is by using modifiers—words and phrases that describe, limit, point out, identify, and make more specific the words they modify. Although modifiers are not an essential part of a sentence, they add information to the basic elements of the sentence. Without modifiers writers could communicate only general ideas.

▶ EXAMPLES

Armadillos dig.   (basic elements unmodified)

Two large armadillos dig ruthlessly in my yard every night.
(basic elements modified)

Adding modifiers to the basic elements in the second example makes the sentence much more specific and vivid. We now know how many armadillos, the size of the armadillos, and how, where, and when they dig.

Adjectives

Adjectives are modifiers of nouns or noun substitutes and can be divided into several types.

1. **Indefinite adjectives** limit the nouns they modify, usually by restricting the amount or number. Look at the following list of frequently used indefinite adjectives:

some	every	much
many	each	most
other	all	another
few	any	several

   Notice in the following sentences how the indefinite adjectives limit in some way the nouns they modify.

   ▶ EXAMPLES: **Some** restaurants stay open **all** night.

   Several photographers and a **few** reporters were seen at **each** meeting.

   Few, if **any,** policemen were at the **other** riot.

   Notice also that an indefinite adjective always comes before the noun it modifies.

2. **Demonstrative adjectives** identify or point out. There are only four demonstrative adjectives—*this, that, these,* and *those*—and they, too, occur before the nouns they modify.

   ▶ EXAMPLES: **This** movie is as boring as **that** one.

   These sandwiches are stale and soggy.

   He selected **those** players for his team.

3. **Descriptive adjectives,** as their name implies, describe the nouns they modify. They usually occur before the nouns but may occur in a variety of positions.

   ▶ EXAMPLES: The **loud, rhythmic** music filled the room.

   Loud and **rhythmic,** the music filled the room.

   The music, **loud** and **rhythmic,** filled the room.

   As a writer, you should be aware of the options you have in placing descriptive adjectives. Try to vary your basic sentence patterns by placing descriptive adjectives in different positions. Notice in the examples that the meaning, rhythm, and emphasis of each sentence are altered slightly by the changes in the placement of the adjectives.

4. **Participles** are verb forms used as adjectives. For example, the verb *shake* has a present participle form, *shaking,* and a past participle form, *shaken.* Each of the participle forms can be used as part of a verb phrase that functions as the main verb of a sentence.

   ▶ EXAMPLES: The old man **is shaking** his fist at us.

   The medicine **was shaken** thoroughly.

   As shown here, participles can also be used as adjectives:

   ▶ EXAMPLES: The **shaking** child ran to her mother's waiting arms.

   The child, **shaking,** ran to her mother.

   Shaking and crying, the child ran to her mother.

   The old man, pale and **shaken,** sat down carefully.

   Shaken by the accident, the woman began to cry.

   Notice in these examples the different positions that a participle may take in relation to the word it modifies. In your own writing, try to vary the positions of the participles you use.

In the following **sentence combining** exercises, you are given a series of short simple sentences. Using the first sentence as your base sentence, reduce the sentences that follow to modifiers that can be used to expand the base sentence.

▶ EXAMPLES: The wall stretched for miles.
The wall was granite.
The granite was gray.
The wall was thick.
The miles were endless.

Combinations:

The thick, gray granite wall stretched for endless miles.

Thick and gray, the granite wall stretched for endless miles.

The granite wall, thick and gray, stretched for endless miles.

Notice that several combinations are possible. There is no single correct combination. Try to think of as many different combinations as you can and then choose the one you like best. You may want to say some of the combinations aloud before deciding on your choice. Try to vary the positions of your adjectives so they do not all come before the nouns they modify.

Punctuation Note: Adjectives that do not come before the nouns they modify are set off by commas.

The quilt, **torn** and **ragged,** lay on the bed.

Coordinate (equal) adjectives in a series are separated by commas.

The **torn, ragged** quilt lay on the bed.

However, if adjectives in a series are not coordinate, they are not separated by commas.

The **careless young** man failed to signal as he turned.

To determine if adjectives are coordinate, insert the word *and* between them. If the resulting construction makes sense, the adjectives are coordinate.

The **torn** and **ragged** quilt lay on the bed.

The **careless** and **young** man failed to signal as he turned.

In the first sentence, the insertion of *and* makes sense, so the adjectives are coordinate and should be separated by a comma.

The **torn, ragged** quilt lay on the bed.

In the second sentence, the insertion of *and* does not make sense, so the adjectives are not coordinate and should thus not be separated by a comma.

The **careless young** man failed to signal as he turned.

EXERCISE

18.12

Combine each of the following groups of sentences into a single sentence; discuss punctuation possibilities with your instructor or classmates.

1. The girl slept in the doorway.
   The girl was young.
   The girl was pretty.
   The doorway was cold.
   The doorway was dirty.

   _____

   _____

   _____

2. The groundhog peeked out of its hole.
   The groundhog was shy.
   The groundhog was shaggy.
   The hole was private.

   _____

   _____

   _____

3. The dancers kept time to the music.
   The dancers were moving energetically.
   The music was loud.
   The music was pulsating.

   _____

   _____

   _____

4. The candle went out.
   The candle was sputtering.
   The candle was hissing.

   _____

   _____

   _____

5. The woman was visiting her aunt.
   The aunt was her favorite.
   The woman was middle-aged.
   The woman was dutiful.

   _____

   _____

   _____

EXERCISE

18.13

Replace the blanks in the following passage with appropriate adjectives.

It was a beautiful college. The buildings were _____
(1)
and covered with vines and the roads gracefully winding, lined with

hedges and wild roses that dazzled the eyes in the _____
(2)
sun. Honeysuckle and _____ wisteria hung heavy from the
(3)
trees and _____ magnolias mixed with their scents in the
(4)
_____ air. I've recalled it often, here in my hole: How the grass
(5)
turned _____ in the springtime and how the mockingbirds
(6)
fluttered their tails and sang, how the moon shone down on the

buildings, how the bell in the chapel tower rang out the precious

short-lived hours; how the girls in _____ summer dresses
(7)
promenaded the _____ lawn. Many times, here at night, I've
(8)
closed my eyes and walked along the _____ road that winds
(9)
past the girls' dormitories, past the hall with the clock in the tower, its

windows warmly _____, on down past the _____ white
(10)   (11)

Home Economics practice cottage, whiter still in the moonlight,

and on down the road with its sloping and turning, paralleling the

_____ powerhouse with its engines droning earth-shaking
(12)

rhythms in the dark, its windows _____ from the glow of the
(13)

furnace, on to where the road became a bridge over a _____
(14)

riverbed, tangled with brush and _____ vines; the bridge of
(15)

rustic logs, made for trysting, but virginal and untested by lovers;

on up the road, past the buildings, with the _____ verandas
(16)

half-a-city-block long, to the sudden forking, barren of buildings,

birds, or grass, where the road turned off to the insane asylum.

—Ralph Ellison, *Invisible Man*

Adverbs

Another way of expanding basic sentence patterns is by using **adverbs** to modify the verb of the sentence. Adverbs can also modify other modifiers (e.g., *She spoke **very** slowly*) or even entire sentences, but they usually give additional information about the verb of a sentence. Adverbs that modify verbs tell how (in what manner), when, or where.

> The student entered the classroom **late**.   (when)
>
> They went **home** after the party.   (where)
>
> The judge stood up **slowly** and **majestically**.   (how)

Adverbs do not necessarily occur either immediately before or after the verbs they modify, although they may occur in these positions. Notice that in the third example, the adverbs *slowly* and *majestically* occur after the verb *stood up*. However, these adverbs could be shifted to the beginning of the sentence.

> **Slowly** and **majestically,** the judge stood up.

Adverbs, especially those that end in *-ly*, can be shifted from one position in the sentence to another. However, when adverbs are placed at the beginning of the sentence rather than in their normal position after the verb, they are usually followed by a comma.

18.14 Following is a series of short simple sentences. Using the first sentence as your base sentence, reduce the other sentences to adverbs and use them to expand the basic sentence. Remember to vary the placement of your adverbs. If you are adding -*ly* to a word that ends in -*y*, change the *y* to *i* before adding the -*ly* suffix.

1. The walrus waddled.
   The waddling was comical (ly).
   The waddling was clumsy (ly).
   The waddling was backward.

   _____

   _____

   _____

2. The guitarist played.
   The playing was soft (ly).
   The playing was steady (ly).
   The playing was all evening.

   _____

   _____

   _____

3. The plant grew.
   The growing was unexpected (ly).
   The growing was sudden (ly).

   _____

   _____

   _____

4. The president spoke to the press.
   The press was eager.
   The speaking was serious (ly).
   The speaking was unpretentious (ly).

   _____

   _____

   _____

5. Alice rode the motorcycle.
    The riding was fearless (ly).
    The riding was natural (ly).
    The riding was along the trail.

_____

_____

_____

18.15

Replace each blank in the following passage with an appropriate adverb.

The stern of the vessel shot by, dropping, as it did so, into a

hollow between the waves; and I caught a glimpse of a man

standing at the wheel, and of another man who seemed to be doing

little else than smoke a cigar. I saw the smoke issuing from his lips as

he _____ turned his head and glanced _____ over the
            (1)   (2)
water in my direction. It was a careless, unpremeditated glance,

one of those haphazard things men do when they have no immediate

call to do anything in particular, but act because they are alive and

must do something.

But life and death were in that glance. I could see the vessel

being swallowed _____ in the fog; I saw the back of the man
                        (3)
at the wheel, and the head of the other man turning, _____
                                                            (4)
turning, as his gaze struck the water and _____ lifted along it
                                                (5)
toward me. His face wore an absent expression, as of deep thought,

and I became afraid that if his eyes did light upon me he would nevertheless not see me. But his eyes did light upon me, and looked

_____ into mine; and he did see me, for he sprang to the
        (6)

wheel, thrusting the other man _____, and whirled it round
                                        (7)

and _____, hand over hand, at the same time shouting orders
        (8)

of some sort. The vessel seemed to go _____ at a tangent to
                                                (9)

its former course and leapt almost _____ from view into
                                            (10)

the fog.

I felt myself slipping into unconsciousness, and tried with all

the power of my will to fight above the suffocating blankness and

darkness that was rising around me. A little _____ I heard the
                                                        (11)

stroke of oars, growing nearer and _____, and the calls of a
                                            (12)

man. When he was _____ near I heard him crying, in vexed
                        (13)

fashion, "Why in hell don't you sing out?" This meant me, I thought,

and _____ the blankness and darkness rose over me.
        (14)

—Jack London, *The Sea Wolf*

Prepositional Phrases

Prepositional phrases provide a third way to expand basic sentences. A prepositional phrase consists of a preposition and its object (a noun or noun substitute). The prepositional phrase itself may be expanded by the addition of adjectives that modify the object of the preposition.

▶ EXAMPLES: The nurse smiled **at the child.**
                The nurse smiled **at the small, timid child.**

                The fighter **in the corner** looked mean.
                The fighter **in the far corner** looked mean.

                We caught the bus **at the station.**
                We caught the bus **at the central station.**

The following words are commonly used as prepositions:

aboard	behind	from	throughout
about	below	in	to
above	beneath	into	toward
across	beside	like	under
after	between	near	underneath
against	beyond	of	until
along	but (except)	off	unto
amid	by	on	up
among	down	over	upon
around	during	past	with
at	except (but)	since	within
before	for	through	without

Examples of compound prepositions follow:

according to	due to	instead of
along with	in addition to	on account of
because of	in place of	out of
contrary to	in spite of	

Function

Prepositional phrases function in a sentence as either adjectives or adverbs, depending on whether they modify a noun or a verb. Those that function as adverbs give information (where, how, when, or why) about verbs.

▶ EXAMPLES: The party was held **at the beach.**   (where)

The stunned man wandered about **in a daze.**   (how)

They arrived early **in the morning.**   (when)

They came **for the homecoming party.**   (why)

Prepositional phrases that function as adjectives modify nouns by telling which one(s).

▶ EXAMPLES: The girl **in the red dress** raised her hand.

That book **of mine** caused a lot of trouble.

The room **on the second floor** is vacant.

In the preceding examples, the prepositional phrases function as adjectives because they modify nouns; they tell us which girl, which book, and which room. In other words, they identify as well as describe the nouns they modify.

Placement

Most prepositional phrases that function as adverbs can be moved about freely.

▶ EXAMPLES: **During the morning,** the rain fell steadily.

The rain fell steadily **during the morning.**

Notice the slight difference in emphasis and style that results from the shift in the position of the prepositional phrase. The placement of adverbial prepositional phrases is another option that a writer has. However, prepositional phrases that function as adjectives are placed *immediately after* the nouns or pronouns they modify.

EXERCISE

18.16   In the following sentence-combining exercise, use the first sentence as your base sentence and reduce the others to prepositional phrases that modify a noun or verb in the main sentence. Remember to vary the placement of your adverb phrases but be sure that each adjective phrase follows immediately the word that it modifies.

1. The wilting fern sat.
    The sitting was in a dusty corner.
    The corner was of the waiting room.

    _____

    _____

    _____

2. Jeff swept the dirt.
    The sweeping was in a hurry.
    The sweeping was under his bed.

    _____

    _____

    _____

3. The picture hung.
    The picture was of the church.
    The church was on the hill.
    The hanging was in the office.

_____

_____

_____

4. The banker parked her car.
   The parking was in a no-parking zone.
   The no-parking zone was near a fire hydrant.

   _____

   _____

   _____

5. The father placed the small child.
   The placing was in her crib.
   The crib was beside the big bed.
   The placing was at night.

   _____

   _____

   _____

EXERCISE

18.17   Write appropriate prepositions in the blanks in the following passage.

The distance _____ the earth _____ the moon
                    (1)   (2)

changes every day, even _____ minute _____ minute,
                              (3)   (4)

because both the earth and the moon travel _____ oval orbits.
                                                  (5)

Since the moon's orbit is not circular, but oval-shaped, the moon is

closer _____ the earth _____ some times and farther
            (6)   (7)

away _____ other times. _____ the nearest approach
          (8)   (9)

to the earth, the moon is 360,000 km away. _____ its farthest
                                                  (10)

point, the moon is 404,800 km away. . . .

The moon does not actually change shape. It is the pattern

_____ reflected light that changes. The moon does not give off
  (11)

18.17 continued

light _____ its own. It receives light _____ the sun, just
            (12)   (13)

as the earth and other planets do. The moon's barren surface reflects

much _____ the light into space and some _____ that
            (14)   (15)

light reaches the earth. One half of the moon is always lighted

_____ the sun and one half is always dark, just as the earth
      (16)

is. But the same half _____ the moon is not lighted all
                              (17)

_____ the time because the moon is traveling _____
      (18)   (19)

an orbit _____ the earth while the earth travels around the
              (20)

sun.

—Adapted from William H. Matthews, III, et al., *Investigating the Earth*

Appositives

A final way that basic sentence patterns can be expanded is by the use of appositives. An **appositive** is a noun or noun phrase (noun plus modifiers)
that gives additional information about another noun. Unlike adjectives—
which describe, limit, or identify nouns—an appositive explains or defines a
noun.

▶ EXAMPLES: The picture, **a pastel watercolor,** was for sale.

They served my favorite dessert, **raspberry sherbet.**

An energetic person, Nora Smith is always up before
dawn.

In the first two examples, the appositives follow the nouns they explain. This is by far the most common position for an appositive. In the third
sentence, however, the appositive comes before the noun it explains. In either case, whether the appositive comes before or after the noun it explains,
it must be immediately adjacent to it. Appositives cannot be shifted about in
the sentence pattern as freely as can adjectives and adverbs.

An appositive is usually set off by commas. In instances in which the
appositive is essential to identify the noun it explains (e.g., *my friend Dale*),
commas may be omitted. But most of the time—in fact, any time the appositive could be omitted from the sentence without changing the meaning of
the sentence—it is set off by commas.

18.18   Combine each sentence pair into one sentence by making one of the sentences an appositive that explains a noun in the other sentence.

▶ EXAMPLES: The swing hung from a tree.
The tree was an old live oak with low, gnarled branches.

Combination:
The swing hung from a tree, an old live oak with low, gnarled branches.

1. Dr. Martinez performed the delicate operation.
   Dr. Martinez is a renowned heart surgeon.

   _____

   _____

2. The plants were set in large clay pots around the patio.
   The plants were geraniums and periwinkles.

   _____

   _____

3. They liked the other car.
   The other car was a small foreign model.

   _____

   _____

4. An aardvark was the main attraction at the zoo.
   An aardvark is one of the strangest looking animals in existence.

   _____

   _____

   _____

5. I chose a new color for my bedroom walls.
   The new color was a pale, cheerful yellow.

   _____

   _____

   _____

This sentence-combining exercise contains a series of sentence groups that can be combined in various ways. Using the first sentence as your base sentence, reduce the sentences that follow to modifiers (adjectives, adverbs, or prepositional phrases) or appositives that can be used to expand the base sentence. Try to vary the position of the modifiers. If you are unsure of the correct punctuation, discuss the sentence with your instructor or classmates.

1. The cat stretched.
   The cat was fat.
   The cat was sleek.
   The cat was a Burmese.
   The stretching was lazy (ly).

   _____

   _____

   _____

2. The car rolled.
   The car was a Mercedes.
   The car was expensive.
   The rolling was slow (ly).
   The rolling was arrogant (ly).
   The rolling was to a stop.

   _____

   _____

   _____

3. I read the book.
   The reading was reluctant.
   The book was silly.
   The book was repetitious.
   The reading was to my son.

   _____

   _____

   _____

4. The dancer twirled.
   The dancer was holding his arms up.
   The dancer was lifting his head high.
   The twirling was rapid (ly).
   The twirling was for several moments.

   _____

   _____

   _____

5. The salesperson took the money.
   The salesperson was a young girl.
   The young girl was shy.
   The money was the customer's.
   The customer was complaining.

   _____

   _____

   _____

EXERCISE

18.20

Combine the following sentences. Then rewrite the sentences to create a paragraph.

1. Santa Fe is a town.
   The town has a past.

   _____

   _____

   _____

2. It seems to belong.
   The belonging is to another time.
   The belonging is to another place.
   It is located in the hills.
   The hills are at the foot.
   The foot is of the mountains.

   _____

   _____

   _____

18.20 continued

3. One immediately notices.
   What one notices is the age.
   The age is of the town.
   The age is obvious.
   One leaves the highway.
   The highway is modern.
   The highway is four-lane.
   The four-lane is wide.
   The highway leads to Santa Fe.

   _____

   _____

   _____

4. Some buildings date.
   The dating is back.
   The dating is to the 1600s.

   _____

   _____

   _____

5. Even the buildings are designed.
   The buildings are new.
   The designing is to look old.

   _____

   _____

   _____

6. Everything is built.
   The everything is new.
   The everything is old.
   The building is adobe.
   The adobe is pink.

   _____

   _____

   _____

7. Streets are narrow.
    Streets are unpaved.
    The unpaving is frequent (ly).

    _____

    _____

    _____

8. Dogs wander.
    The wandering is free (ly).
    The wandering is about the plaza.
    The plaza is central.
    The dogs ignore the traffic.
    The dogs ignore the tourists.

    _____

    _____

    _____

9. Women peddle their wares.
    The women are Native American.
    The women are wrapped.
    The wrapping is in shawls.
    The shawls are hand-woven.
    The peddling is along the sidewalks.
    The sidewalks encircle the plaza.

    _____

    _____

    _____

10. They too ignore the traffic.
    They too ignore the tourists.

    _____

    _____

    _____

Chapter Review

- A simple sentence, like any sentence, must have two essential elements: a subject and a verb.

- A simple sentence may have a compound subject and/or a compound verb.

- Subjects are usually nouns or pronouns.

- A verb has different forms that indicate tense—the time at which the stated action or being took place.

- Simple sentences can be classified according to the following patterns: subject–verb, subject–verb–object, or subject–linking verb–complement.

- Simple sentences can be expanded by adding to the essential elements one or more of the following:
  1. Adjectives (indefinite, demonstrative, descriptive, or participial)
  2. Adverbs
  3. Prepositional phrases
  4. Appositives

Writing Assignment

Rewrite a paragraph or an essay that you have written for an earlier assignment, editing carefully. Focus especially on sentence structure. Have you used a variety of patterns for your simple sentences? Does each sentence have a subject and verb? Have you expanded your simple sentences with adjectives, adverbs, prepositional phrases, and appositives?

Participating in the Academic Community

Read a paragraph or essay that one of your classmates has just edited, focusing again on sentence structure. Does each sentence have a subject and verb? Does the writer use a variety of sentence patterns? Are the simple sentences expanded appropriately?

Chapter 19

Compound Sentences

In Chapter 18 you learned that a simple sentence consists of one subject–verb relationship and makes a single statement or asks a single question. In this chapter you will learn about compound sentences. A **compound sentence** consists of two or more simple sentences.

▶ EXAMPLES

Simple sentence: The physician sat down.

Simple sentence: The patient remained standing.

Compound sentence: The physician sat down, but the patient remained standing.

The most common way to connect simple sentences to form a compound sentence is to use a **coordinating conjunction.** For example, in the previous example, the coordinating conjunction *but* not only connects the simple sentences but also indicates the relationship between them. The following chart lists all of the coordinating conjunctions, categorizing them into three groups according to the relationships they indicate:

ADDITION	CONTRAST	CAUSE AND EFFECT
and both . . . and	but or nor yet either . . . or neither . . . nor	for so

Simple sentences are called **independent clauses** when they become parts of a compound sentence. Therefore, a compound sentence can be described as a combination of two or more independent clauses—groups of words that have a subject and verb and can function as a simple sentence.

Notice that the two independent clauses (simple sentences) in the previous example are coordinate. That is, they are equal; each could function as a sentence on its own, each has a subject and verb, and each contributes equally to the meaning of the sentence.

A compound sentence can be diagrammed as shown here:

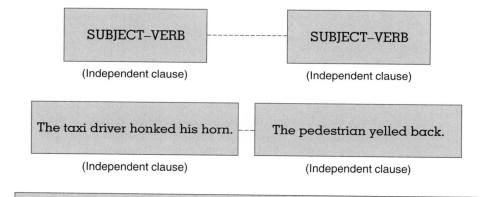

In reading and writing compound sentences, you need to understand the relationship that exists between independent clauses. Like other compound elements, independent clauses are often connected by coordinating conjunctions. These coordinating conjunctions indicate the relationship between the elements they connect. For example, the meaning of each of the sentences that follows is completely altered when the coordinating conjunction is changed.

He was defeated, **but** he kept trying.

He was defeated, **or** he kept trying.

He was defeated, **yet** he kept trying.

He was defeated, **and** he kept trying.

He was defeated, **so** he kept trying.

As a reader, you must be alert to the words that signal the relationship between the two thoughts, and as a writer, you must be careful to choose the connecting word that indicates the appropriate relationship.

In addition to being connected by coordinating conjunctions (*and, or, nor, for, but, yet, so*), the independent clauses in a compound sentence can be connected by **conjunctive adverbs.** These connecting words, like coordinating conjunctions, indicate relationships between the independent clauses. The following chart lists some of the most common conjunctive adverbs and indicates the relationships they express:

ADDITION, EMPHASIS, COMPARISON	CONTRAST	CAUSE/ EFFECT, CONCLUSION	EXAMPLE	TIME
moreover	however	therefore	for example	then
also	nevertheless	accordingly	for instance	later
too	instead	as a result	to illustrate	next
besides	on the contrary	consequently	that is	first, second,
plus	on the other	hence		third, etc.
furthermore	hand	thus		meanwhile
in addition	otherwise	in conclusion		afterward
indeed	in contrast	in summary		finally
in fact		in other words		
likewise		of course		
similarly		then		
certainly				
again				
another				
at the same				
time				

Punctuating Compound Sentences

There are three ways to connect independent clauses and to punctuate correctly the resulting compound sentence.

1. *Use a coordinating conjunction and place a comma before the conjunction.*

   Some students want an education, **but** others simply want a degree.

2. *Use a conjunctive adverb and place a semicolon before the conjunction and a comma after it.*

Some students want an education; **however,** others simply want a degree.

(*Note:* A conjunctive adverb may appear in a sentence in which it does not introduce an independent clause.

Some students, **however,** simply want a degree.

When used in this way, the conjunctive adverb is set off by commas but requires no semicolon because it is not introducing a second independent clause.)

3. *Use no conjunction and place a semicolon between the two independent clauses.*

Some students want an education; **others** simply want a degree.

Notice that the independent clauses in a compound sentence are closely and logically related in thought. If the relationship between them is not apparent, the resulting sentence will be ridiculous.

Some students want an education; teachers should receive higher salaries.

If independent clauses are connected with just a semicolon and no connecting word or phrase that indicates their relationship, the two clauses must be clearly related in meaning. If a coordinating conjunction or a conjunctive adverb is used, the relationship can be less obvious but should, nevertheless, be clearly expressed by the connecting word.

Joan studied hard; _____ she failed the test.

A good choice for the connecting word in this example would be *however* because the relationship here is one of contrast. If a conjunctive adverb such as *moreover,* indicating addition, or *therefore,* indicating result or conclusion, were used, the sentence would not make sense because the relationship between the two clauses would not be logical.

EXERCISE

19.1

In this exercise, all of the coordinating conjunctions and conjunctive adverbs that connect the independent clauses have been omitted. Write in each blank an appropriate connecting word. In making your choice, consider the relationship between the two clauses and the existing punctuation.

Remember that a comma is placed before a coordinating conjunction connecting two independent clauses and a semicolon is placed before a conjunctive adverb connecting two independent clauses.

Many of today's young students have an attention span that

has been conditioned by years of watching television. They focus

their attention on an issue for a very few minutes, approximately

the length of a television commercial; _____ , they expect
                                              (1)

something different, _____ they grow bored. As a result,
                         (2)

teachers must constantly arrange for a variety of learning activities,

_____ they lose the attention of their students. Teachers, in
      (3)

effect, assume the role of entertainers; _____ , students
                                               (4)

assume the role of audience. One of the problems that arises from

this situation is that students who perceive themselves as an

audience tend to be passive. Learning requires active participation

rather than passivity; _____ , these passive students are
                              (5)

often nonlearners.

EXERCISE

19.2

In this exercise, you are given one independent clause and a connecting word, either a coordinating conjunction or a conjunctive adverb. Supply a second independent clause that is related appropriately to the first.

1. The sentimental goodbys were over, **and** _____

   _____

2. The sentimental goodbys were over; **however,** _____

   _____

3. The sentimental goodbys were over; **therefore,** _____

   _____

19.2 continued

4. The airplane must land quickly, **or** _____

_____

5. The airplane must land quickly, **for** _____

_____

6. The airplane must land quickly; **consequently,** _____

_____

7. The airplane must land quickly; **otherwise,** _____

_____

8. Children often disobey, **and** _____

_____

9. Children often disobey; **then** _____

_____

10. Children often disobey, **yet** _____

_____

11. Children often disobey; **for example,** _____

_____

Punctuation Review

Coordinating Conjunction and Comma

Independent clause	, coordinating conjunction	independent clause

▶ EXAMPLES

| Carlos took five courses last semester | , and (addition) | he worked twenty hours each week. |
| Rachel liked most music | , but (contrast) | she didn't like hard rock. |

Conjunctive Adverb and Semicolon

Independent clause	; conjunctive adverb,	independent clause

▶ EXAMPLES

Carlos took five courses last semester	; moreover, (addition)	he worked twenty hours each week.
Rachel liked most music	; however, (contrast)	she didn't like hard rock.

Semicolon

Remember also that if two independent clauses are closely and obviously related, you may connect them by using just a semicolon.

Independent clause	;	independent clause

▶ EXAMPLES

Carlos took five courses last semester	;	he worked twenty hours each week.
Rachel liked most music	;	she didn't like hard rock.

EXERCISE

19.3   Read each of the following pairs of independent clauses carefully to determine the relationship between them. Then, noting the punctuation that is given, write in each blank an appropriate connecting word.

1. The price of oil declined; _____, the economy of the oil-producing states suffered.

2. The politician spoke longer than she was supposed to; _____, her speech was interesting.

3. The money was missing from the cash drawer, _____ the valuables had been taken from the safe.

4. The children behaved badly; _____, one refused to eat.

5. You may want the pecan pie for dessert, _____ you may prefer the cheesecake.

6. His handwriting was barely legible; _____, we could make out the words.

7. First, he opened the door carefully; _____ he peered inside the dimly lit room.

8. The weather was hot and humid; _____, everyone was terribly uncomfortable.

9. The wine tasted sweet and fruity; _____, it went well with the bread and cheese.

10. Somehow they managed to move the huge chest, _____ they were not able to get it through the door.

EXERCISE

19.4

Combine the following pairs of independent clauses into compound sentences. Punctuate each sentence appropriately.

1. The yellow Camaro swerved dangerously.
   The driver remained in control of the car.

   _____

   _____

   _____

2. The young widow lived alone.
   She was occasionally lonely.

   _____

   _____

   _____

3. The rain fell steadily all day.
   By evening the water had risen dangerously.

   _____

   _____

   _____

4. The Yomiko sisters resemble each other.
   They are not twins.

   _____

   _____

   _____

5. Hunting is not permitted in these parks.
   Many animals are killed.

   _____

   _____

   _____

6. The television commercial lasted only a few moments.
   It seemed to last forever.

   _____

   _____

   _____

7. He must pay cash.
   He will lose the merchandise.

   _____

   _____

   _____

8. This is not the first time.
   It will be the last.

   _____

   _____

   _____

19.4 continued

9. Rainfall is scarce.
   Water is precious.

   _____

   _____

   _____

10. The clouds were thick.
    The eclipse was not visible.

    _____

    _____

    _____

EXERCISE

19.5   Write the following types of compound sentences, punctuating each appropriately.

1. Three compound sentences in which the two independent clauses are connected by a coordinating conjunction:

   a. _____

      _____

   b. _____

      _____

   c. _____

      _____

2. Three compound sentences in which the two independent clauses are connected by a conjunctive adverb:

   a. _____

      _____

   b. _____

      _____

   c. _____

      _____

3. Three compound sentences in which no connecting word is used:

a. _____

_____

b. _____

_____

c. _____

_____

19.6

The following paragraph includes a number of compound sentences that have not been punctuated correctly. Edit this paragraph, supplying the correct punctuation for the compound sentences.

¹Students often feel compelled to declare a major when they first arrive at college. ²They are faced with countless forms that ask them to indicate their major and their parents often urge them to make this important decision as soon as possible. ³In addition, their professor and classmates are constantly asking them what their major is. ⁴Students feel they are remiss if they don't declare a major therefore they make this important decision without really knowing where their interests and talents lie. ⁵Thus, they commit to a certain course of study but soon realize they have made a mistake. ⁶They discover they have chosen a path that they do not wish to pursue yet are reluctant to admit they have made a mistake. ⁷Fortunately, a counselor, professor, or classmate usually comes to their rescue and helps them realize they need to reconsider their hasty decision.

Chapter Review

- A compound sentence consists of two independent clauses (or simple sentences).

- There are three ways to connect the independent clauses in a compound sentence:
  1. Use a coordinating conjunction and a comma.
  2. Use a conjunctive adverb and a semicolon.
  3. Use just a semicolon.

Writing Assignment

Revise a paragraph or an essay you have previously written, combining some of the simple sentences into compound sentences.

Participating in the Academic Community

Working with a group of your peers, edit the paragraphs or essays you have revised, focusing on the correct punctuation of compound sentences.

Chapter 20

Complex Sentences

A **complex sentence** consists of a simple sentence (independent clause) that contains within it a **subordinate,** or **dependent, clause.** Whereas coordinate elements are equal, a subordinate element is dependent on another element. Similarly, in an essay, the topic sentences are subordinate to the thesis statement, and in a paragraph, major details are subordinate to the topic sentence.

Unlike the compound sentence, which consists of two equal (coordinate) independent clauses, the complex sentence is made up of two types of clauses: an independent clause and a subordinate, or dependent, clause. The independent clause expresses the main idea of the sentence, and the dependent clause expresses a supporting idea or detail. As shown in the following figure, the dependent clause functions as part of the independent clause:

Independent clause	
	Subordinate clause

Reggie loses a lot of money (Independent clause)	
	when he bets on the horses. (Subordinate clause)

To understand subordinate clauses, you must understand both phrases and independent clauses because a subordinate clause has characteristics of both. The following chart summarizes the characteristics of both phrases and clauses:

PHRASE: to the theater	Does not have a subject and verb	Functions as a unit in a sentence	Cannot stand alone as a sentence
SUBORDINATE CLAUSE: when he went to the theater	Has a subject and verb	Functions as a unit in a sentence	Cannot stand alone as a sentence
INDEPENDENT CLAUSE: he went to the theater	Has a subject and verb	Does not function as a unit in a sentence	Can stand alone as a sentence

As the chart indicates, a subordinate clause, unlike an independent clause, cannot function as a sentence even though it has a subject and a verb. A subordinate clause is like a phrase in that it is part of an independent clause and functions as an adverb, an adjective, or a noun within the independent clause. Thus, the two clauses of a complex sentence are not equal (coordinate) as are the clauses of a compound sentence. In a complex sentence, the subordinate clause is dependent on—or subordinate to—the independent clause.

▶ EXAMPLES

Adverb clause: **Although the forests are old,** much of the undergrowth is recent.

Adjective clause: The actress **who appeared in the second act** had a shrill voice.

Noun clause: The jury concluded **that he was guilty.**

Adverb Clauses

An **adverb clause** is a subordinate clause that functions as an adverb within the independent clause in which it appears. An adverb clause usually modifies the verb of the independent clause. Listed here are some of the transition words, or subordinating conjunctions, that are commonly used to introduce adverb clauses:

after	as if	although	even if
before	as soon as	though	even though
when	if	since	wherever
whenever	unless	because	
while	whether	until	
as	whereas	so that	

The following complex sentences contain adverb clauses. Observe how the placement and punctuation of the adverb clause differ in the two sentences.

▶ EXAMPLES

At beginning of sentence: **Unless you save carefully,** you will run out of money.

At end of sentence: You will run out of money **unless you save carefully.**

Notice in the first sentence the adverb clause comes at the beginning of the sentence and is followed by a comma. In the second sentence, the adverb clause comes after the independent clause and is not separated from it by a comma. An introductory adverb clause is always followed by a comma; an adverb clause that occurs at the end of a sentence, however, require no punctuation.

EXERCISE

20.1

Combine each of the following pairs of sentences into a complex sentence with an adverb clause. Vary the position of your adverb clauses and punctuate correctly. You may wish to refer to the list of transition words for adverb clauses provided earlier.

1. The desert is hot and dry.
   Many flowers grow there.

   _____

   _____

   _____

20.1 continued

2. The spectators were injured at an accident at the race track.
   No one was killed.

   _____

   _____

   _____

3. I looked out the rear window of the car.
   I came to a stop at the busy intersection.

   _____

   _____

   _____

4. The Jacksons escaped from their burning house.
   Their three-year-old son was awakened by the heat.

   _____

   _____

   _____

5. I broke my leg.
   I went skiing in Colorado.

   _____

   _____

   _____

EXERCISE

20.2

Write five complex sentences with adverb clauses. Be sure to vary the position of the adverb clauses you use. Punctuate your sentences correctly.

1. _____

   _____

   _____

2. _____

   _____

   _____

3. _____

_____

_____

_____

4. _____

_____

_____

_____

5. _____

_____

_____

Adjective Clauses

An **adjective clause** modifies a noun or a noun substitute within the independent clause in which it appears. Transition words (relative pronouns) used to introduce adjective clauses are listed here:

who	which
whom	where
whose	when
that	why

Adjective clauses that are needed to identify the words they modify are called *restrictive clauses* and require no punctuation. *Nonrestrictive adjective clauses* must be set off by commas. Both of the following sentences contain adjective clauses. As you read the sentences, notice the difference between them.

▶ EXAMPLES

Restrictive: The woman **who married Hitler** committed suicide to prevent capture by the Allies.

Nonrestrictive: Eva Braun, **who married Hitler,** committed suicide to prevent capture by the Allies.

In the first sentence the word *woman is* identified by the adjective clause *who married Hitler.* In the second sentence the adjective clause is not needed to identify Eva Braun; the clause is therefore nonessential, or nonrestrictive.

20.3   Combine each of the following pairs of sentences into a complex sentence with an adjective clause. Be sure to punctuate each sentence correctly. You may wish to refer to the list of transition words for adjective clauses provided earlier.

1. The city council supports a rapid-transit plan.
    The plan will reduce freeway traffic.

    _____

    _____

    _____

2. The citizens of Buffalo rallied to the defense of the man.
    The man was accused of stabbing his daughter's rapist.

    _____

    _____

    _____

3. The blue lake mirrored the snow-capped mountains.
    The lake was crescent-shaped.

    _____

    _____

    _____

4. I shopped at the new mall with my sister Myra.
    Myra lives in Anaheim.

    _____

    _____

    _____

5. Charles Lindbergh was received in New York with wild enthusiasm.
    He had accomplished a remarkable feat.

    _____

    _____

    _____

20.4   Write five complex sentences that include adjective clauses. Be sure to include at least one sentence with a restrictive clause and one with a nonrestrictive clause. Punctuate your sentences correctly.

1. _____

_____

_____

2. _____

_____

_____

3. _____

_____

_____

4. _____

_____

_____

5. _____

_____

_____

Noun Clauses

A **noun clause** functions as the subject, object, subject complement, or object of a preposition within the independent clause of a complex sentence. Transition words used to introduce noun clauses are listed here:

who	that	whichever	wherever
whom	whoever	whatever	when
which	whomever	where	whenever
what			

The following four sentences illustrate the different kinds of noun clauses. Following each sentence is a second sentence in which a simple noun or pronoun has been substituted for the noun clause. By comparing these sentence pairs, you will be able to see more clearly how the noun clause functions within a complex sentence.

TYPES OF NOUN CLAUSES

1. **As subject: Whoever arrives early** can set up the tables and chairs.   (**They** can set up the tables and chairs.)

2. **As direct object:** He knew **what she wanted to do.**   (He knew her **plan.)**

3. **As subject complement:** The problem was **that we were already late.**   (The problem was **our lateness.)**

4. **As object of preposition:** I will go to the play with **whoever asks me first.**   (I will go to the play with **Fran**.)

(*Note:* Since a noun clause functions as an essential element within a sentence, it requires no added punctuation. If you are not sure whether a clause is a noun clause, substitute a noun or pronoun for the clause. If the substitution makes sense, the clause is functioning as a noun.)

EXERCISE

20.5   Combine each of the following sentence pairs into a complex sentence with a noun clause. You may wish to use the transition words suggested in parentheses.

1. The patient knew something. (that)
   The operation might be fatal.

   _____

   _____

   _____

2. Please select something. (whichever)
   The dessert is your favorite.

   _____

   _____

   _____

3. The disposal of waste was the problem. (for which)
   They were seeking a solution.

   _____

   _____

   _____

4. The candidate is someone. (whoever)
   Someone wins the primary.

   _____

   _____

   _____

5. Please give the package to someone. (whoever)
   Someone answers the door.

   _____

   _____

   _____

EXERCISE

20.6   Write five complex sentences with noun clauses.

1. _____

   _____

   _____

2. _____

   _____

   _____

3. _____

   _____

   _____

4. _____

   _____

   _____

5. _____

   _____

   _____

Signaling Relationships in Complex Sentences

Good readers and writers are able to determine main ideas and supporting ideas within sentences and to understand the relationships between those ideas. One of the best ways to identify supporting ideas in subordinate clauses is to look for the transition words that introduce them. The transition words also indicate the relationship that exists in a complex sentence between the subordinate clause and the independent clause of which it is a part.

In previous exercises you have used transition words to connect independent and subordinate clauses. The following chart not only lists the most common transition words used to introduce subordinate clauses but also indicates the relationships shown by the transition words. Study the words carefully so that you can use them appropriately to connect independent and subordinate clauses.

PLACE	**CONTRAST**		**EXAMPLE**
where	although	whereas	such as
wherever	though	than	as
	even though	except	
	even if	except that	

MANNER, CONDITION	**TIME**	**AGENT**	**CAUSE/EFFECT, CONCLUSION**
if	after	who	so that
unless	before	whom	in order that
as, as if	when	whose	because
lest	while	which	since
provided	until	that	
provided that	whenever	whichever	
in case	as long as	whoever	
just as	as soon as	whomever	
whether	as often as	whosoever	
how		whatever	
		wherever	

Read each sentence carefully and then insert in the blank a transition word or phrase that shows the proper relationship between the main idea expressed in the independent clause and the supporting idea expressed in the subordinate clause.

▶ EXAMPLE: The concert was canceled _*because*_ rain was forecast.

(The relationship here is one of cause and effect, so *because* would be a good choice.)

1. _____ a left-handed child is forced to write with his or her right hand, the child may become confused.

2. The nurse ran into the patient's room _____ he could assist the doctor.

3. Most college students call their parents _____ they run out of money.

4. I wasn't sure _____ had given me the flowers until I read the card.

5. I don't know _____ the test is being given on Tuesday or Thursday.

6. _____ he is no longer a child, a teenager is not an adult.

7. The baby didn't know _____ the stove was hot.

8. _____ the car stopped, I crossed the street.

9. Cats can never be owned; they live with _____ takes care of them.

10. I hope _____ I have time to eat lunch _____ I have to go to my next class.

20.8

In the following paragraph transition words used to introduce subordinate clauses have been omitted. Read the paragraph carefully and write in the blanks appropriate transition words.

Young people _____ choose to teach today are a
(1)

special breed. They are not primarily interested in money or prestige,

for teaching affords neither. _____ they wanted wealth, they
(2)

would choose law or medicine or business as a career. These

aspiring young teachers know _____ teachers work long
(3)

hours and receive little recognition and less pay. But they choose

teaching _____ they want to serve society, or _____
(4)   (5)

they enjoy children, or _____ they love knowledge.
(6)

_____ they make the decision to become teachers, they
(7)

realize _____ they are giving up some important things, but
(8)

they also know _____ they will realize important dreams
(9)

and goals as teachers. Once upon a time young females became

teachers _____ they had few other professional choices.
(10)

Today teaching gives both males and females _____ they
(11)

value most—a sense of satisfaction.

In this exercise, you are given an independent clause and a connecting word. Supply a dependent clause that fits the relationship indicated by the transition word and punctuate each sentence correctly.

1. They left the house before _____

_____

2. They left the house so that _____

_____

3. They left the house although _____

_____

4. They left the house because _____

_____

5. We believe that _____

_____

6. We believe what _____

_____

7. We believe whoever _____

_____

8. We believe whatever _____

_____

9. Because _____

the child sleeps peacefully.

10. After _____

the child sleeps peacefully.

11. Whereas _____

the child sleeps peacefully.

Punctuating Complex Sentences

As you have seen earlier in this chapter, different types of subordinate clauses require different punctuation. Review the following punctuation guide:

1. *An introductory adverb clause is set off by a comma:*

   Because the rain was coming down in torrents, the game was delayed.

2. *An adverb clause at the end of a sentence is not set off by a comma:*

   The game was delayed **because the rain was coming down in torrents.**

3. *A nonrestrictive adjective clause is set off by commas:*

   Jim, **who is president of my fraternity,** is my best friend.

4. *A restrictive adjective clause is not set off by commas:*

   The man **who is president of my fraternity** is my best friend.

5. *A noun clause is not set off by commas:*

   Did you know **that I was here?**

EXERCISE

20.10

Edit the following complex sentences carefully by supplying punctuation where it is needed. Some sentences are correct.

1. When the party is over we'll have our meeting.

2. We took a vacation on Padre Island where there is a good beach.

3. I'll take you to Venice where you can ride in gondolas.

4. You have some very important decisions to make when you graduate.

5. Paul Farrell to whom my sister is engaged graduated from Yale.

6. The cook that the boss hired is very efficient.

7. Mrs. Thomas fired the secretary that Mr. Thomas liked so well.

8. Mr. Crockett who used to be a football player is enormous.

9. When I push this button the motor begins to run.

10. Because it was hot he opened the window.

11. This ball club never won a game until Jack was named manager.

12. When I married Sarah she weighed only ninety pounds.

13. His car skidded around the corner because the tires were slick.

14. When I came home late I entered quietly.

15. I bought him a card because it was his birthday.

16. That I lost my library card caused me many problems.

17. I discovered that I was overdrawn when I balanced my checkbook.

18. Although my sister loves to cook she hates to do the dishes.

19. The horse that broke through the fence did not hurt itself.

20. Your roommate wanted to know what time you got home.

21. Since I am a mountain man I like high places.

22. He visits his parents when he can.

23. The flight attendant who spilled my drink apologized profusely.

24. Their club president who was elected by only one vote resigned yesterday.

25. Although missing one class may not be serious missing a week of classes can hurt your grades.

EXERCISE

20.11   Each of the following groups of sentences can be combined into single complex sentences. Combine the sentence groups, being sure to punctuate each new sentence appropriately. Remember to put main ideas in independent clauses and supporting ideas in subordinate clauses. Then rewrite the sentences to create a paragraph.

1. Tennessee Williams reveals something.
   The revelation is in *The Glass Menagene*.
   The something is that dreams are fragile.

   _____

   _____

   _____

   _____

20.11 continued

2. Laura Wingfield is extremely shy.
Laura is physically disabled.
Laura has retreated from the real world.
Laura has retreated into a world of Victrola music.
Laura has retreated into a world of little glass animals.

_____

_____

_____

_____

3. Her mother is Amanda Wingfield.
Amanda lives in the past.
The living is with her girlhood memories.
The memories are of "gentleman callers."

_____

_____

_____

_____

4. Laura's brother Tom escapes.
Tom works at a job.
The job is drab.
The job is at a warehouse.
The warehouse is for shoes.
He escapes by going to the movies.
He escapes by writing poetry.

_____

_____

_____

_____

5. Tom's dilemma is something.
The something is he feels responsible.
The responsibility is for his family.
He needs freedom.
The freedom is for himself.

_____

_____

_____

_____

6. The situation is brought to a climax.
   The situation is tense.
   The situation is in the Wingfield household.
   Tom brings home a "gentleman caller."
   The "gentleman caller" is named Jim O'Connor.
   The "gentleman caller" is to meet Laura.

_____

_____

_____

_____

7. Jim comes home with Tom.
   Jim is kind.
   The kindness is to Laura.

_____

_____

_____

_____

8. Laura comes out of her world.
   The world is of dreams.
   The coming out is only for a while.
   Laura thinks something.
   The something is that she has found someone.
   The someone is to love her.

_____

_____

_____

_____

20.11 continued

9. However, Jim breaks something.
   The breaking is accidental.
   The something is a unicorn.
   The unicorn is little.
   The unicorn is glass.
   The unicorn is Laura's ornament.
   The ornament is her favorite.
   Jim shatters her hopes.
   Jim tells her something.
   The something is that he is already engaged.

   _____

   _____

   _____

   _____

10. Jim leaves.
    Laura is left with her dreams.
    Laura is left with her animals.
    The animals are little.
    The animals are glass.
    The dreams comfort her.
    The animals comfort her.

    _____

    _____

    _____

    _____

11. Amanda discovers something.
    The something is that Jim is engaged.
    The something is that Laura has no hope.
    The hope is of marrying Jim.
    Amanda accepts reality.
    Amanda admits something to herself.
    The admission is that Laura has a physical disability.

    _____

    _____

    _____

    _____

12. The play ends.
    Tom has joined the merchant marines.
    Tom is looking back at his memories.
    The memories are of his mother.
    The memories are of his sister.

    _____

    _____

    _____

    _____

EXERCISE

20.12   Edit the following paragraph, correcting the punctuation errors in the complex sentences.

[1]Although I had traveled widely in Europe and Mexico I had never been to Egypt. [2]When I arrived at the Cairo airport I immediately knew I had entered an exotic land that was very different from anything I had known before. [3]Most of the men were dressed in long robes and some wore long scarves wrapped around their heads. [4]Some of the women also wore long robes, and nearly all of them wore scarves on their heads. [5]In some cases these scarves also covered all but the center of their faces. [6]As we left the airport and headed toward the center of the city I was struck by the traffic which was incredibly hectic and noisy. [7]All the drivers seemed to use their horns at the slightest excuse. [8]When they were angry they honked. [9]When they were frustrated and impatient they honked. [10]They even honked when they wanted to express appreciation to another driver for letting them go first or squeeze through. [11]From time to time, I could see above all this confusion a minaret or mosque in the distance. [12]But I really knew that I had arrived in Egypt when we crossed the Nile and then, a few minutes later, caught sight of the pyramids at Giza. [13]At that moment I felt as if I had left the modern world and entered a much more ancient and exotic one.

Chapter Review

- A complex sentence consists of an independent clause that includes within it a subordinate clause.

- A subordinate clause cannot function alone as a sentence.

- Subordinate clauses function as adverbs, adjectives, or nouns.

- The transition word that introduces a subordinate clause indicates its relationship to the independent clause.

Writing Assignment

Revise a paragraph or essay you have previously written, converting some of the simple and compound sentences to complex sentences.

Participating in the Academic Community

Working with a group of your peers, edit the paragraphs or essays you have revised, focusing on the correct punctuation of the complex sentences you created.

Chapter 21

Sentence Fragments and Run-On Sentences

Good writing is made up of well-constructed sentences that express complete thoughts. Sometimes, however, writers make major sentence errors that seriously detract from their writing. Two such errors are **sentence fragments** and **run-on sentences.** This chapter will explain these errors and show you how to identify and correct them in your writing.

Sentence Fragments

A fragment is a separated sentence part that does not express a complete thought. To decide whether or not a group of words is a sentence or a fragment, ask yourself these three questions:

1. Does it have a *subject?*
2. Does it have a *verb?*
3. Does it express a *complete thought?*

If the answer to any one of these questions is no, the group of words is not a sentence but a part of a sentence—a fragment.

Observe carefully the differences between the following fragments and complete sentences (in which subjects are underlined once and verbs are underlined twice):

FRAGMENT: The seven-foot basketball player.   (subject but no verb)

FRAGMENT: Tripped and fell on the floor.   (verbs but no subject)

FRAGMENT: The seven-foot basketball player running down the court.   (subject but no verb)

FRAGMENT: <u>As</u> the seven-foot basketball player was running down the court.   (subordinate clause)

SENTENCE: The seven-foot basketball <u>player</u> <u>was running</u> down the court.   (complete sentence with a subject and a verb)

SENTENCE: The basketball <u>player</u> running down the court <u>tripped</u> and <u>fell</u>.   (complete sentence with a subject, two verbs, and an *-ing* modifier)

As these examples show, length doesn't determine whether a group of words is a sentence or a fragment. For instance, the sentence *The player tripped and fell* is actually much shorter than several of the fragments shown. Long fragments that contain several modifiers can easily fool you into thinking they are sentences. Therefore, in order to identify a fragment, you need to be able to analyze a group of words to determine whether it includes all the requirements for a complete sentence.

Many types of fragments exist, but five types occur often enough to need special explanation and practice. The five types of sentence elements commonly mistaken for complete sentences are (1) participial phrases, (2) appositive phrases, (3) prepositional phrases, (4) infinitive phrases, and (5) subordinate clauses.

Participial Phrase Sentence Fragments

A participle is a word formed from a verb but used as an adjective. Participles are frequently mistaken for main verbs, and the phrases in which they appear are frequently mistaken for complete sentences. **Participial phrase fragments** are of two types: **present participial phrase fragments** and **past participial phrase fragments.**

Present Participial Phrase Fragments

Present participles are *-ing* forms of verbs that must have a helping verb, such as *am, is, was, were,* or *has been,* to function as a verb in a sentence. Without such a helping verb, a participle or participial phrase is often a fragment, as shown here:

FRAGMENT: **Reading comic books all the time.**

The *-ing* form of a verb can be especially confusing when it is used with a noun or pronoun subject but without a helping verb, as shown in the following example:

FRAGMENT: Jim **reading comic books all the time.**

This structure is a fragment even though it contains a subject and a word that *looks* like a verb. You can correct this fragment by adding a helping verb, a form of the verb *to be*.

> CORRECT: <u>Jim</u> <u>was reading</u> comic books all the time.

Or, you could add another verb to complete the structure and use the *-ing* phrase as a modifier. In the following revised sentence, the participial phrase functions as an adjective modifying the subject of the independent clause to which it is attached:

> CORRECT: **Reading comic books all the time,** <u>Jim</u> <u>lived</u> in a world of fantasy.

Past Participial Phrase Fragments

Past participles and past participial phrases without the helping verb *to have* or *to be* may also appear as fragments:

> FRAGMENTS: **Hidden in the closet.**
>
> The child **hidden in the closet.**

To correct a past participial phrase fragment, you may complete the verb phrase or you may use the participial phrase as an adjective:

> CORRECT: The <u>child</u> **had hidden** in the closet.   (verb phrase)
>
> The <u>child</u> **hidden in the closet** <u>was playing</u> hide-and-seek.   (adjective)

EXERCISE

21.1   The following five participial phrases are written incorrectly as sentence fragments. Write five complete sentences by adding an independent clause to each of these participial phrases. Be sure the phrase modifies the subject of your independent clause.

1. Seeing the exit sign ahead.

    _____

    _____

2. Working on the project for weeks.

    _____

    _____

21.1 continued

3. Expecting guests soon.

_____

_____

4. Sitting on a bus all day.

_____

_____

5. Forgotten in the confusion of the storm.

_____

_____

EXERCISE

21.2

The following five fragments include a noun and an incomplete verb (or a participial phrase). Rewrite these fragments as complete sentences. You may add a new verb and use the verb form in the structure as a participial modifier of the subject, or you may use a form of the verb *to be* to change the participle into a complete verb.

1. Parents wanting to know.

_____

_____

2. Prisoner seeing no way out.

_____

_____

3. The teenager sneaking in her house through the back door.

_____

_____

4. Tracie's blind date opening his car door.

_____

_____

5. The student watching a PBS special on World War II.

_____

_____

Appositive Phrase Sentence Fragments

An appositive or appositive phrase explains the noun or pronoun it follows. As shown in the following example, neither an appositive nor an appositive phrase can stand alone as a sentence:

FRAGMENT: The eighteen sailors rowed 3,618 miles to Timor. **An island near Java.**

An island near Java is an **appositive phrase fragment** explaining *Timor* and should be joined to the preceding sentence.

SENTENCE: The eighteen <u>sailors</u> <u>rowed</u> 3,618 miles to Timor, **an island near Java.**

Notice that the appositive phrase is set off from the rest of the sentence by a comma or, as in the following sentence, by two commas:

▶ EXAMPLE: <u>Alvin,</u> **one of my best friends,** <u>has left</u> for college.

EXERCISE
21.3

Each of the following items includes both a complete sentence and an appositive or appositive phrase sentence fragment. Correct the sentence fragments by attaching them to the sentences, changing punctuation and capitalization as necessary. You may also need to rearrange word order so that the appositives follow the words they modify.

1. We enjoy playing Parcheesi. A game from India.

   _____

   _____

2. The entrance to the Mediterranean is guarded by a rocky peninsula. Gibraltar.

   _____

   _____

3. Astonomers have recently photographed Saturn. The planet encircled by rings.

   _____

   _____

21.3 continued

4. Thursday was named for Thor. The Norse god of thunder.

_____

_____

5. *The X-Files* was made into a movie. A successful television series.

_____

_____

Prepositional Phrase Sentence Fragments

Less frequently, but occasionally, a long prepositional phrase or series of prepositional phrases will be mistaken for a sentence.

FRAGMENT: **Without the professor's study questions.**
(one long prepositional phrase)

CORRECTED: **Without the professor's study questions,** Joel could
not prepare for the exam.   (subject and verb added)

FRAGMENT: **In the summer around the old swimming pool in the field behind our house.**   (a series of prepositional phrases)

CORRECTED: **In the summer,** we meet **around the old swimming pool in the field behind our house.**   (subject and verb added)

Sometimes a prepositional phrase is attached to an element that could function as a subject or verb in a sentence. The following example is a fragment because, although it has a word that could function as its subject (*dancer*), there is no verb—only a series of prepositional phrases:

FRAGMENT: The young dancer **in the short, pink skirt with the orange ribbon in her hair and purple scarf in her hand.**

CORRECTED: The young dancer **in the short, pink skirt with the orange ribbon in her hair and purple scarf in her hand** won the contest.   (verb added)

In order to recognize **prepositional phrase fragments,** you need to know what words are prepositions. The following chart lists some of the most common prepositions:

about	above	across	after	against
along	among	around	at	before
behind	below	beneath	beside	between
by	down	during	except	for
from	in	inside	into	like
near	next to	of	off	on
onto	out	outside	over	past
through	to	toward	under	until
up	upon	with	within	without

EXERCISE

21.4   Rewrite the following prepositional phrase fragments by adding the essential elements they need to be complete sentences.

1. Without looking in the direction of the traffic on the street.

   _____

   _____

2. My broker at the respected firm of Jones, Jones, and Jones.

   _____

   _____

3. Out of the bushes to the right of the large oak tree.

   _____

   _____

4. Occasionally in the morning after a night out with my friends.

   _____

   _____

5. The fly in my cup of lukewarm coffee on the table before me.

   _____

   _____

Infinitive Phrase Sentence Fragments

The word *to* is often used as a preposition followed by the noun or pronoun that is its object. However, as shown in the following example, *to* can also be used with a verb, in which case it is an **infinitive** instead of a preposition:

▶ EXAMPLE: Arial wanted **to go** (infinitive phrase)
to the dance (prepositional phrase).

Infinitive phrases may be used either as modifiers or as noun substitutes in complete sentences. However, infinitive phrases that are not attached to a subject and a verb are **infinitive phrase fragments,** another type of fragment that you need to avoid.

FRAGMENT: **To get to work on time.**

CORRECTED AS MODIFIER: **To get to work on time,** Kayla drove ten miles an hour over the speed limit.

FRAGMENT: **To dream the impossible dream.**

CORRECTED AS NOUN: **To dream the impossible dream** is the right of all Americans.   (subject)

The right of all Americans is **to dream the impossible dream.**   (subject complement)

EXERCISE

21.5

Rewrite the following infinitive phrase fragments as complete sentences.

1. To move into the house by the time our lease is up.

   _____

   _____

2. To go to college for a degree.

   _____

   _____

3. To get the impossible done.

   _____

   _____

4. To try to make up for the eighteen years since I dropped out of college.

_____

_____

5. To explain to my parents about my low grade.

_____

_____

21.6

The following paragraphs include eight fragments. Rewrite these paragraphs on a separate sheet of paper, correcting the fragments.

[1]The American frontier, if we are to believe the tales that have been handed down, was populated with some amazing personalities. [2]The heroes about whom we hear were always at least six feet tall and often reached the height of giants. [3]Not only were these heroes large; they were also strong and clever. [4]Eating enormous amounts of food, performing astounding feats of strength and courage, inventing miraculous methods of accomplishing difficult tasks, and doing an amazing amount of work. [5]These heroes could out-run, out-jump, out-brag, out-drink, out-shoot, and out-fight anyone foolish enough to challenge them. [6]These giants among men, our folk heroes. [7]Superhumans created to populate and tame the rugged, often dangerous frontier.

[8]These folk heroes tell us something about the people who created them. [9]Faced with countless dangers and constant weariness. [10]The frontier settlers created mythical heroes who were capable of facing dangers and doing work in unusual and often humorous ways. [11]Many mythical supermen, such as Paul Bunyan and Pecos Bill, were entirely the products of the frontier imagination. [12]Pioneers were even able. [13]To create the super folk heroine Swamp Angel, a female Paul Bunyan figure.

[14]However, the early Americans sometimes glorified actual people. [15]Like Davy Crockett and John Henry. [16]In an effort to transform them into larger-than-life heroes. [17]Whether based on fact or fancy, these heroes were projections of the men who created them. [18]Ordinary mortals needing to be superhuman in order to tame the frontier.

Subordinate Clause Fragments

A subordinate (dependent) clause has a subject and a verb but does not express a complete thought. It cannot stand by itself as a sentence but must always be attached to an independent clause. The following diagrams illustrate a subordinate clause that is used correctly as part of an independent clause and one that is used incorrectly as a fragment unattached to an independent clause:

SUBORDINATE CLAUSE AS PART OF
INDEPENDENT CLAUSE (CORRECT)

Independent clause	
	Subordinate clause

▶ EXAMPLE: She knew with certainty

that he was the prowler.

SUBORDINATE CLAUSE AS FRAGMENT WITH
NO INDEPENDENT CLAUSE (INCORRECT)

No independent clause	Subordinate clause

▶ EXAMPLE: **That he was the prowler.**

Subordinate clause fragments may be corrected in one of two ways:

1. Attach the subordinate clause to an independent clause, as shown in the first diagram.
2. Omit the subordinating word that makes the subordinate clause dependent. (Example: *He was the prowler.*)

When a subordinate clause is attached to an independent clause, the subordinate clause functions as an adverb, adjective, or noun in the independent clause:

ADVERB CLAUSE FRAGMENT:	**When Alonzo started college.**
SENTENCE WITH ADVERB CLAUSE:	**When Alonzo started college,** he had to learn to manage his time wisely.
ADJECTIVE CLAUSE FRAGMENT:	**Who makes the highest average.**
SENTENCE WITH ADJECTIVE CLAUSE:	The student **who makes the highest average** will win the scholarship.
NOUN CLAUSE FRAGMENT:	**That his examinations required essay answers.**
SENTENCE WITH NOUN CLAUSE:	Professor Yani explained **that his examinations required essay answers.** (direct object)

The following chart provides a list of subordinating conjunctions that introduce the three kinds of subordinate clauses, or the three types of subordinate clause fragments:

after	although	as	because	before
even though	except	how	if	provided
since	so that	that	though	unless
until	what	whatever	when	whenever
where	wherever	which	whichever	while
who	whoever	whom	whomever	whose

(See Chapter 20 for further explanation and practice with these three types of subordinate clauses.)

EXERCISE

21.7

In the spaces provided, change each of the following subordinate clause fragments into a complete complex sentence including both an independent clause and a subordinate clause.

1. Who broke her glasses.

_____

_____

2. Because the lights on the stage went out during the performance.

_____

_____

21.7 continued

3. That we had made a mistake.

    _____

    _____

4. After the burglar ran away.

    _____

    _____

5. Who is president of the student senate.

    _____

    _____

EXERCISE

21.8   Rewrite the five sentences from Exercise 21.7 as complete sentences by omitting the introductory subordinating conjunction.

1. _____

2. _____

3. _____

4. _____

5. _____

EXERCISE

21.9   The following passage includes twelve fragments, each of which is a subordinate clause incorrectly written as a sentence. Rewrite the passage on a separate sheet of paper, connecting each fragment to a related independent clause.

> [1]Almost every book on art includes a reproduction of the *Mona Lisa*. [2]Which is one of the most famous paintings in the world. [3]The *Mona Lisa* was painted by Leonardo da Vinci. [4]Who worked on it for four years (1503–1506). [5]The painting was never quite finished. [6]After he had worked for several hours. [7]Leonardo would sit down in front of the *Mona Lisa* to quiet his nerves. [8]Some people say. [9]That

Leonardo did not finish the painting. [10]Because he wanted an excuse to keep it with him.

[11]On the face of the woman in the painting there is a mysterious smile. [12]Which has intrigued people for centuries. [13]Although no one knows the true explanation of the smile. [14]Several different legends have grown up about it. [15]One story says that the woman was smiling sadly. [16]When she sat for the portrait. [17]Because her child had died. [18]Another story, however, says that Leonardo hired musicians—flutists and violinists—to play during the sittings. [19]So that he could capture the young woman's rapt expression.

[20]When Leonardo left Italy and moved to France. [21]He took the painting with him. [22]The French king persuaded him to sell the painting. [23]Which now hangs in the Louvre, an art museum in Paris.

Run-On Sentences

Two (or more) independent clauses that are incorrectly joined result in a **run-on sentence** (see also Chapter 19). The two basic types of run-on sentences are the **fused sentence** and the **comma splice**. A fused sentence is two complete sentences, or independent clauses, run together without any punctuation or conjunction to separate them:

▶ EXAMPLES OF FUSED SENTENCES

1. My sister is an **artist she** completely decorated her home.
2. The beef enchiladas were **spicy the** tacos were fresh.
3. My daughter likes rock **songs my son** likes classical music.
4. Our football boys played **hard they** lost by one point.
5. I'm really thankful for spring break this **year it** will give me a chance to catch up on my homework.

A comma splice, or a spliced sentence, is two complete sentences with only a comma to separate them:

▶ EXAMPLES OF COMMA SPLICES

1. My sister is an **artist, she** completely decorated her home.
2. The beef enchiladas were **spicy, the** tacos were fresh.
3. My daughter likes rock **songs, my son** likes classical music.
4. Our football boys played **hard, they** lost by one point.
5. I'm really thankful for spring break this **year, it** will give me a chance to catch up on my homework.

Correcting Run-On Sentences

Run-on sentences may be corrected in several ways, depending on the meaning and relationship of the two sentences involved. Here are five ways to correct run-on sentences:

1. *Two separate sentences.* One of the most common ways to correct run-on sentences is to write them as two separate sentences.

   RUN-ON: My sister is an **artist, she** completely decorated her home.

   CORRECT: My sister is an **artist. She** completely decorated her home.

   Correcting all fused sentences or comma splices in this way, however, results in too many short, choppy sentences. Furthermore, you may need to show the relationship between the two independent clauses more clearly, as is possible with some of the other methods of correcting run-on sentences.

2. *A comma and a coordinating conjunction.* A second way to correct a run-on sentence is with a comma followed by a coordinating conjunction between the two independent clauses. The coordinating conjunction clarifies the relationship between the two clauses.

   RUN-ON: The beef enchiladas were **spicy the tacos** were fresh.

   CORRECT: The beef enchiladas were **spicy, and the tacos** were fresh.

   The coordinating conjunctions are listed in the following chart:

and	but	for
or	nor	so
yet	both . . . and	either . . . or
	neither . . . nor	

3. *A semicolon.* A third way to correct a run-on sentence is to insert a semicolon between the independent clauses. A semicolon is particularly appropriate when the relationship between the two clauses is clear without a transition word, or when the two independent clauses are clearly balanced or parallel.

   RUN-ON: My daughter likes **rock songs, my son** likes classical music.

   CORRECT: My daughter likes **rock songs; my son** likes classical music.

4. *A semicolon and a conjunctive adverb.* A fourth method of correcting a run-on sentence is to use not only a semicolon but also a conjunctive adverb that shows the relationship between the two independent clauses.

RUN-ON: Our football boys **played hard, however** they lost by one point.

CORRECT: Our football boys **played hard; however,** they lost by one point.

Notice that the conjunctive adverb is usually followed by a comma. The following chart lists some of the most common conjunctive adverbs and the relationships they indicate:

ADDITION, COMPARISON	CONTRAST	TIME	CAUSE/EFFECT, CONCLUSION	EXAMPLE
also	however	finally	accordingly	for example
besides	in contrast	first, etc.	as a result	for instance
furthermore	instead	gradually	consequently	in fact
in addition	nevertheless	immediately	hence	that is
indeed	on the contrary	meanwhile	in conclusion	to illustrate
likewise	on the other hand	next	in summary	
moreover	otherwise	sometimes	of course	
similarly	rather	suddenly	therefore	
too	still	then	thus	

5. *Subordination.* A fifth, and final, way to correct a run-on sentence is to make one of the independent clauses subordinate. Sometimes this method is necessary to show the true relationship between the clauses in a run-on sentence.

RUN-ON: I'm really thankful for spring break **this year it** will give me a chance to catch up on my homework.

CORRECT: I'm really thankful for spring break **this year because** it will give me a chance to catch up on my homework.

Subordinating conjunctions include *although, because, since, if, before, after, when, while, unless,* and *until.* For a more complete list of subordinating conjunctions, see the charts on pages 293 and 321.

21.10

Rewrite each of the following run-on sentences as a correctly punctuated sentence.

1. I looked at the paint on the walls, it was scratched and pealing.

   _____

   _____

2. It has been raining all day it is very cold outside.

   _____

   _____

3. College students need to save money, they shouldn't lose credit hours when they transfer from a community college to a university.

   _____

   _____

   _____

4. Change is sometimes very hard, for example it was difficult for my parents to sell their old home and move to a new one.

   _____

   _____

   _____

5. Several years ago the people in my neighborhood helped one another, now people are just interested in themselves.

   _____

   _____

   _____

Notes and Warnings

1. Notice that the little word *then* is a conjunctive adverb that should be preceded by a semicolon when it comes between two independent clauses. NEVER use the word *then* with just a comma to connect two independent clauses because the result will be a run-on sentence.

   RUN-ON: Write a complete draft of **your paper, then** edit and proofread it.

   CORRECT: Write a complete draft of **your paper; then** edit and proofread it.

2. Although it should always be preceded by a semicolon when it separates two independent clauses, a conjunctive adverb is separated only with a comma, or commas, when it appears within a single independent clause.

CORRECT: His **roommate, however,** was wide awake.

His roommate was wide **awake, however.**

EXERCISE

21.11   Each of the following paragraphs contains run-on sentences—both fused sentences and comma splices. Rewrite each paragraph on a separate piece of paper, correcting all the run-on sentences.

PARAGRAPH A

[1]I agree with John Henry Newman all branches of knowledge are connected. [2]Certainly, all sciences are related to one another, for instance medicine uses both plant life and animal life to make discoveries about diseases and to create new treatments. [3]Also, history helps explain literature, literature helps explain history. [4]Even today, studying one subject can help us to understand another subject better. [5]Also, knowledge of different subjects can help us in our careers, for example, the architect needs math to help him plan his blueprints the history teacher needs to understand English, art, and sociology to teach history.

PARAGRAPH B

[1]Many people believe in the idea of a liberal arts curriculum for the first two years of college I don't happen to be one of those people. [2]A general liberal arts education doesn't prepare students directly for their careers, it wastes their time and their money. [3]Students should be allowed to take and pay for the courses that will directly prepare them for their careers in life.

PARAGRAPH C

[1]Ten years ago I dropped out of college I didn't have clear goals for my life and my career. [2]This time I don't intend to take any shortcuts, instead I intend to take all the liberal arts courses I can. [3]These courses will give me a good background in different areas then I can truly find the career area that interests me. [4]Also, I believe that knowing about areas other than my own field will give me more chances to get a good job.

Chapter Review

- A fragment is an incomplete sentence that does not express a complete thought.
- These are the five most common types of fragments:
    1. Participial phrase fragments
    2. Appositive phrase fragments
    3. Prepositional phrase fragments
    4. Infinitive phrase fragments
    5. Subordinate clause fragments
- A run-on sentence results from the incorrect joining of two independent clauses.
- The two basic types of run-on sentences are fused sentences and comma splices.
- Run-on sentences may be corrected in five different ways:
    1. Rewriting the independent clauses as two separate sentences
    2. Inserting a comma and a coordinating conjunction between the two clauses
    3. Inserting a semicolon between the two clauses
    4. Inserting a semicolon and a conjunctive adverb between the two clauses
    5. Changing one of the independent clauses to a subordinate clause

■ Writing Assignment

Select a paragraph or essay that you are writing for one of your academic classes—perhaps your history class or this composition class—and edit it carefully for fragments and run-on sentences. Then rewrite the assignment with the corrected sentences.

■ Participating in the Academic Community

Compare your corrected versions of Exercises 21.9 and 21.11 with those of a small group of your classmates. (Remember that fragments and run-on sentences can be corrected in several different ways.) Or meet with a small group of your classmates to edit one of your writing assignments for major sentence errors.

Chapter 22

Subject–Verb Agreement

For correct **subject–verb agreement,** the subject and verb of a sentence must agree in number. That is, if the subject is singular, the verb must be singular; if the subject is plural, the verb must be plural.

▶ EXAMPLES: **He is** an actor.   (singular subject *he* and singular verb *is*)

They are pals.   (plural subject *they* and plural verb *are*)

This grammatical rule sounds simple enough to follow, and in most instances it is. In fact, with the exception of the verb *to be,* verbs do not change their forms to indicate number except in the present tense.

▶ EXAMPLES: **He walked** home.   (singular subject and verb)

They walked home.   (plural subject and verb)

Therefore, to master subject–verb agreement, you need primarily to study the present tense. Begin by looking carefully at the following chart, which shows the different present tense forms of a typical regular verb:

PRESENT TENSE OF *to walk*	
SINGULAR	**PLURAL**
First person: *I walk*	First person: *we walk*
Second person: *you walk*	Second person: *you walk*
Third person: *he, she, it walks*	Third person: *they walk*

Notice that an *s* is added to the third-person singular form. (*Note:* Adding an *s* or *es* to a noun makes the noun plural. However, an *s* ending on a verb indicates that the verb is singular.)

The boy **walks** to school each day.   (singular verb)

The three boys **walk** to school each day.   (plural verb)

22.1

Supply the correct third-person singular, present tense form of the verbs indicated in the sentences. Be sure that all of your verbs end in an *s*.

1. In the end he always _____ his goals.
   (to reach)

2. He _____ at the library on weekends.
   (to work)

3. Here he _____ now, early as usual.
   (to come)

4. He _____ to be an accountant when he graduates.
   (to plan)

5. He _____ that hard work is always rewarded.
   (to believe)

Now examine carefully the present tense forms of the three irregular verbs shown in the following chart. Note especially the third-person singular, present tense form of each of the verbs.

PRESENT TENSE OF *to be*

SINGULAR	PLURAL
First person: *I am*	First person: *we are*
Second person: *you are*	Second person: *you are*
Third person: *he, she, it* **is**	Third person: *they are*

PRESENT TENSE OF *to have*

SINGULAR	PLURAL
First person: *I have*	First person: *we have*
Second person: *you have*	Second person: *you have*
Third person: *he, she, it* **has**	Third person: *they have*

PRESENT TENSE OF *to do*

SINGULAR	PLURAL
First person: *I do*	First person: *we do*
Second person: *you do*	Second person: *you do*
third person: *he, she, it* **does**	Third person: *they do*

Notice that of these examples (*to be, to have, to do*) the verb *to be* is the most irregular. The other two verbs change their forms only in the third-person singular. Notice also that these irregular verbs also end in *s* in the third-person singular. In fact, the only exceptions to this pattern are the auxiliaries *can, shall, may, will, ought,* and *must.* All other verbs end in *s* in the third-person singular present tense.

EXERCISE

22.2

Supply the correct present-tense form of the irregular verbs indicated in the following sentences. Refer to the charts given earlier if you are in doubt.

1. You _____ in a difficult situation.
   (to be)

2. _____ she commute?
   (To do)

3. They _____ several reasons for voting as they did.
   (to have)

4. She _____ a friend of mine.
   (to be)

5. In the morning, we _____ an appointment with the dean.
   (to have)

6. It _____ not matter where you park your car.
   (to do)

7. They _____ remaining on campus during vacation.
   (to be)

8. _____ he been absent before?
   (To have)

9. She _____ more studying than he does.
   (to do)

10. _____ they in the same class?
    (To be)

Thus far, you have been given sentences with pronouns as subjects. Look now at the following sentences, which all have noun subjects.

▶ EXAMPLES: **Sabrina** has a tough schedule this semester.

Jogging is a popular form of exercise.

Children play in the park around the corner.

Now fill in the blanks in the following sentences, substituting the appropriate pronoun subjects for the deleted noun subjects:

_____ has a tough schedule this semester.

_____ is a popular form of exercise.

_____ play in the park around the corner.

The pronoun *she* can replace the noun *Sabrina* in the first sentence; the pronoun *it* can be substituted for the noun *jogging* in the second sentence; and the pronoun *they* can be used instead of the noun *children* as the subject of the third sentence. All of these pronouns are third-person singular or plural.

If your noun subject is third-person singular, your verb must also be singular. And if you are using a present tense verb, be sure that the verb has an *s* ending. When you are in doubt about subject–verb agreement, substitute a pronoun for the noun subject; you are more likely to recognize errors in subject–verb agreement if the subject is a pronoun.

EXERCISE

22.3

In the following sentences, some of the subjects are nouns and some are pronouns. Supply the correct *present tense* form of the verbs indicated. If you are in doubt about the correct verb form, change the noun subject to a pronoun.

1. Many students _____ in computer courses each semester.
   (to enroll)

2. He _____ as though he is bored.
   (to look)

3. Smoking _____ not allowed in this building.
   (to be)

4. The men _____ after the women leave.
   (to enter)

5. There _____ three new students in our class.
   (to be)

6. The desk _____ three drawers.
   (to have)

7. My room _____ as though a storm hit it.
   (to look)

8. A different lecturer _____ our class each Friday.
   (to visit)

9. Julia, Sam, and Tyrone _____ the same schedule.
   (to have)

10. My teacher _____ promptly at eight o'clock.
    (to arrive)

EXERCISE

22.4

The following sentences have plural subjects and plural verbs. In the space provided under each sentence, rewrite the sentence, changing the subject and verb so that both are singular.

▶ EXAMPLES: The **reports evaluate** the situation.

The **report evaluates** the situation.

1. They have a major problem to solve at the office.

   _____

   _____

2. The computers badly need repairing.

   _____

   _____

3. The account books have many errors.

   _____

   _____

4. The salesmen are frequently late.

   _____

   _____

5. The phones ring almost constantly.

   _____

   _____

EXERCISE

22.5

Errors in subject–verb agreement are more difficult to identify when they occur in the context of a paragraph. Read the following paragraph carefully. In it are ten subject–verb agreement errors. Edit the paragraph by underlining the ten verbs that do not agree with their subjects in number. Then correct the errors you identified.

22.5 continued

[1]Colleges and universities were once attended mainly by young, middle-class students who had just graduated from high school. [2]Today campuses across the United States are populated with a variety of different types of students, many of whom are not young, middle-class, or even American. [3]Some of these new students come from lower economic backgrounds. [4]Government loans enables them to attend college when once they would have been forced to get a job. [5]In addition to students from lower economic backgrounds, U.S. colleges are also accepting increasing numbers of foreign students. [6]A student do not have to be an American citizen to attend a college or a university in this country. [7]One class may have students from several different foreign countries. [8]Students today is also not necessarily young. [9]If an older person decide to start college, he may discover that many of his classmates are also middle-aged or even older. [10]Some of these students have been out of high school for ten to twenty years. [11]Others never completed high school. [12]Yet they seems capable of competing successfully with the young students. [13]In fact, an older student often have an advantage over the young people in his classes because he have more experience and often are more highly motivated. [14]These new students who are poorer, older, or not Americans by birth add variety and interest to our campuses. [15]Although the new student have not replaced the traditional young high school graduate, he bring a new dimension to higher education in this country.

Special Problems with Subject–Verb Agreement

A subject and a verb must always agree in number, but in some cases the rule is difficult to apply. This section addresses some specific problems with subject–verb agreement.

Indefinite Pronoun Subjects

Some indefinite pronouns take a singular verb even though they appear to be plural in meaning. Following is a list of singular indefinite pronouns:

anybody	everything	either
anyone	nobody	neither
anything	none	someone
each	nothing	somebody
everybody	one	something
everyone	another	much

The following sentences have singular indefinite pronouns as subjects. Notice that in each of the sentences the verb is singular to agree with the singular subject.

▶ EXAMPLES: Everyone **studies** before a test.

Nobody **likes** to study.

Neither of them **is going** to the library.

Much of the information **comes** from the textbook.

None of the students **listens** to the teacher.

Other indefinite pronouns, such as *few, many, both, some,* and *several,* are plural and, therefore, take plural verbs.

▶ EXAMPLES: All of them **are** in the class.

Several **attend** the special study sessions.

Many **need** additional help.

A few of the indefinite pronouns can be either singular or plural, depending on their meaning. For example, *all* and *some* are usually considered plural, but if they refer to a mass instead of individual units, they are singular.

▶ EXAMPLES: All of the class **has** that assignment.   (singular)

All of the students **are** motivated.   (plural)

Some of the material **is** boring.   (singular)

Some of the students **are** bored.   (plural)

In addition, the indefinite pronoun *none* is frequently considered plural even though it means *no one.* Usage appears to be changing regarding this pronoun, and many educated speakers and writers now use *none* as a plural as well as a singular pronoun.

▶ EXAMPLE: None of the tests **are** difficult.

22.6

The following sentences have subjects that are indefinite pronouns. Provide the appropriate present tense verbs.

1. Each of us _____ the same teacher.
   (to want)

2. Few really _____ chicken gizzards.
   (to like)

3. Several of the new Chinese restaurants _____ hot, spicy food.
   (to serve)

4. Nothing _____ my boss more than my being late.
   (to upset)

5. Somebody _____ the building at six o'clock each night.
   (to lock)

Compound Subjects

A compound subject is one in which two or more nouns or pronouns are joined by coordinating conjunctions *(and, or, nor)*. Subjects joined by *and* are usually plural.

▶ EXAMPLE: The book and tape **are** both available.

Subjects joined by *nor* and *or* are usually singular.

▶ EXAMPLES: The coach or the trainer **is** with the injured player.

Neither Mary nor Sue **plans** to graduate this semester.

However, if both the subjects joined by *or* or *nor* are plural, then a plural verb should be used.

▶ EXAMPLE: Tapes or books **are** available.

If *or* or *nor* joins one singular subject and one plural subject, the verb agrees with the nearer subject.

▶ EXAMPLES: The teacher or the students **are** always unhappy.

The students or the teacher **is** always unhappy.

22.7

Choose the correct present tense form of the verbs indicated in the following sentences.

1. Both my uncle and my aunt _____ to come to the wedding.
   (to plan)

2. The choir members and their director _____ to Russia each summer.
   (to travel)

3. The mare and colt _____ healthy.
   (to seem)

4. Neither my fears nor my anger _____ justified.
   (to be)

5. The veterinarian or his assistants _____ on the animals each evening.
   (to check)

Intervening Prepositional Phrases

Agreement problems often occur when a subject and a verb are separated by a prepositional phrase, as in the following example:

▶ EXAMPLE: One **of the boys** dates a computer science major.

The subject of this sentence is *one*, not *boys;* therefore, the verb is the singular *dates* rather than the plural *date.* In this type of sentence, it is important to distinguish between the subject of the main verb and any nouns or pronouns that may be part of the phrase that occurs between the subject and verb.

The following chart, which lists common prepositions, will help you to identify prepositional phrases that might cause difficulty in subject–verb agreement:

about	above	across	after	against
along	among	around	at	before
behind	below	beneath	beside	between
by	down	during	except	for
from	in	inside	into	like
near	next to	of	off	on
onto	out	outside	over	past
through	to	toward	under	until
up	upon	with	within	without

EXERCISE

22.8   Supply the correct present tense verb in the following sentences.

1. Toni, rejecting the offers of both Kim and LaKeitha, _____ to class with Dalton.
   (to ride)

2. Another of my friends _____ a new car.
   (to have)

3. Those students, in spite of their teacher's warning, _____ absent again.
   (to be)

4. One of our new neighbors _____ from Micronesia.
   (to come)

5. The noise of the parties _____ the dorm residents much concern.
   (to cause)

Inverted Sentence Order

Sentences in which the subject does *not* come before the verb also present special problems with subject–verb agreement.

▶ EXAMPLES: Where are the vegetables you cooked?   (vegetables *are*)

Where is the shirt you ironed?   (shirt *is*)

In the door flies a bright yellow canary.   (canary *flies*)

In the door fly several small birds.   (birds *fly*)

There are three reasons I can't go.   (reasons *are*)

There is a good reason for his not coming.   (reason *is*)

(*Hint:* You may reverse the order of the sentence to check for agreement problems. Example: *The vegetables you cooked are where?*).

EXERCISE

22.9   In each of the following sentences, locate the subject and underline it. Then choose the correct present tense form of the verb indicated.

1. There _____ several reasons why the plan failed.
   (to be)

2. Under the bed _____ an enormous cat.
   (to sleep)

3. _____ the computers been installed?
   (To have)

4. _____ the captain always obey his orders?
   (To do)

5. Here _____ the bus.
   (to come)

EXERCISE

22.10

The following paragraph contains ten errors in subject–verb agreement. Edit the paragraph by underlining the incorrect verb forms and then replacing them with the correct verb forms.

[1]Science fiction shows on television provides a look into the future. [2]These programs take a writer's dreams about the future and makes them seem real to the television viewers. [3]The remarkable thing about these shows is that what the television audience considered science fiction twenty or thirty years ago is science reality today. [4]In the fifties and sixties, for example, robots and computers began to appear on television. [5]Now everyone consider these marvels of technology rather commonplace. [6]Industry, as well as our homes, are increasingly dependent on computers. [7]And even robots are fairly commonplace in our complex society. [8]They may not look like the ones on the early science fiction shows, but they can do basically the same things. [9]Early television also showed man in space years before he actually accomplished this remarkable feat. [10]Neither television nor its viewers was aware that within a few years our astronauts would actually be able to orbit the earth in space ships. [11]Today movies on television often portrays man moving across the galaxies, visiting various planets. [12]There is several reasons to expect that this fantasy too will come true in the near future. [13]It will not be long before our technology, together with our talented scientists, have us to the point that we are ready to undertake these types of space voyages. [14]Not all the science fiction shows on television becomes a reality, but many of them seem to be a reliable prediction of what the future hold.

Chapter Review

- Subjects and verbs must agree in number: singular subjects take singular verbs; plural subjects take plural verbs.

- The singular form of third-person present tense verbs ends in an *s*.

- Special problems in subject–verb agreement occur with indefinite pronoun subjects, compound subjects, intervening prepositional phrases, and inverted sentence order.

  1. Most indefinite pronouns are singular, but *few, many, both, some,* and *several* take plural verbs.

  2. Subjects joined by *and* are usually plural; subjects joined by *or* or *nor* are usually singular, but if one subject is plural, the verb takes the number of the nearer subject.

  3. When a prepositional phrase occurs between a subject and a verb, the verb always agrees with the subject rather than the object of the preposition.

  4. The subject comes after the verb in some sentences, but reversing the sentence order makes agreement clearer.

Writing Assignment

Write a paragraph in the present tense in which you describe what a friend of yours is doing today. Be sure that all of your subjects and verbs agree.

Participating in the Academic Community

Meet with a group of your classmates to edit your paragraphs about your friends' activities. Read each paragraph orally, checking to be sure the subjects and verbs agree.

Chapter 23

Pronoun Usage

When you are editing your writing, you may encounter several different areas of pronoun usage that need special attention. Some of these areas are **pronoun reference, pronoun agreement,** and **pronoun case.** In addition, you should edit your writing to be sure that your point of view is consistent and that you have avoided using pronouns in a sexist manner.

Pronoun Reference and Agreement

A pronoun is a noun substitute; it stands for a noun or another pronoun. The noun or pronoun to which a pronoun refers is called the **antecedent.** Thus, in the following sentence, *it* and *its* refer to *cat,* so *cat* is the antecedent:

▶ EXAMPLE: The **cat** arched **its** back, and then **it** hissed loudly.

A pronoun should agree with its antecedent in number, gender, and person. The most frequently used pronouns are **personal pronouns,** which have various forms to indicate number, gender, and person.

	SINGULAR	PLURAL
First person	I (me, my)	we (us, our)
Second person	you (your)	you (your)
Third person	he, she, it (him, his, her, its)	they (them)

Agreement in number means that if the antecedent is plural, the pronoun that refers to it must also be plural. And, if the antecedent is singular, the pronoun should be singular.

▶ EXAMPLES: The **computer** was down again, so I called the service
department to have **it** repaired.   (singular)

The **computers** were down again, so I called the service
department to have **them** repaired.   (plural)

For a pronoun to agree in gender with its antecedent, the pronoun should be masculine if the antecedent is masculine and feminine if the antecedent is feminine.

▶ EXAMPLES: The **ballerina** poised gracefully on **her** toes.
(feminine)

Mr. Chiang delivered **his** lecture and left before we
could speak with **him.**   (masculine)

For a pronoun to agree in person with its antecedent, it should be first person (*I, me, my, mine, we, us, our, ours*) if the antecedent is first person, second person (*you, your, yours*) if the antecedent is second person, and third person (*he, him, his, she, her, hers, it, its, they, them, their, theirs*) if the antecedent is third person.

▶ EXAMPLES: **We** lost **our** way in the dense fog.   (first person)

You lost **your** way in the dense fog.   (second person)

They lost **their** way in the dense fog.   (third person)

These agreement rules are usually easy to follow. In fact, you usually follow most of them without really thinking about the rules at all. But occasionally these rules are more difficult to understand and apply. The following sections on indefinite, relative, and demonstrative pronouns explain how to avoid agreement errors in using these types of pronouns.

Indefinite Pronouns

Indefinite pronouns are always third person and have only one form, but problems sometimes arise in using these pronouns if the writer does not know which are singular and which are plural.

The following chart lists both singular and plural indefinite pronouns:

SINGULAR INDEFINITE PRONOUNS

everybody	neither	somebody
everyone	none	nobody
each	one	everything
anyone	someone	nothing
anybody		

PLURAL INDEFINITE PRONOUNS

all	any
some	both
few	none
several	

If an indefinite pronoun functions as the antecedent of another pronoun, that pronoun must agree with it in number.

▶ EXAMPLES

Everyone left **his** or **her** shoes outside the door.   (singular pronouns)

All of them left **their** shoes outside the door.   (plural pronouns)

EXERCISE

23.1   Correct the pronoun agreement errors in the following sentences.

1. Does anybody know their Spanish well enough to translate this joke?

   _____

   _____

2. Both must apply for his own parking ticket.

   _____

   _____

3. Ms. Kowalski gave his annual donation to United Way.

   _____

   _____

23.1 continued

4. The teacher wants everyone to furnish their own paper for the examination.

_____

_____

5. Each of the students has their own opinion about the course.

_____

_____

Relative and Demonstrative Pronouns

The problem in using **demonstrative pronouns** (_this, that, these,_ and _those_) and **relative pronouns** (_who, whom, which, what,_ and _that_) is that sometimes the antecedents are not clear (see also page 295).

▶ EXAMPLE: I had to wait two hours, **which** made me angry.

Two hours is not the antecedent of the pronoun _which;_ rather, the _waiting_ made the writer angry. But because the pronoun does not have a clear antecedent, the sentence is unclear and awkward. The revised sentence below eliminates the pronoun reference problem.

▶ EXAMPLE: Because I had to wait two hours, I was angry.

(_Note:_ In using relative pronouns, it is also important to remember that _who_ refers only to people and _which_ refers only to animals and inanimate objects, whereas _that_ can refer to people, animals, or objects.)

EXERCISE

23.2

Correct the pronoun reference errors in the following sentences.

1. We found the gun in his car which suggests he is guilty.

_____

_____

2. The person which called failed to give his name.

_____

_____

3. Jim told Tom a lie. This caused a lot of trouble.

_____

_____

4. I frequently called home long distance, which annoyed my father.

_____

_____

5. My friend often works in her garden, which is obvious.

_____

_____

EXERCISE

23.3

Edit the following paragraph for ten errors in pronoun reference and agreement.

[1]Three of my early teachers are special to me because they took the time to show an interest in me and to challenge me to work harder. [2]This made me a better student. [3]I remember my English teacher Mrs. Johnson, which always encouraged me with my wriitng. [4]They were always hard to write, but with their encouragement I made them even better. [5]In my history class, Mr. Krelinski pushed me to be a better student by giving me challenging questions and making me rethink and support my answers. [6]In my math class, Dr. Kline gave me the extra time I needed by explaining difficult problems to me. [7]I never would have come to college if she hadn't encouraged me and if he hadn't taught me how to think. [8]A hard-working teacher like this can really make a difference in a student's life. [9]He certainly did in mine.

Pronoun Case

The correct pronoun form, or **case,** of a personal pronoun is determined by its use in a sentence. As illustrated in the following chart, pronouns occur in subjective, objective, and possessive cases:

NUMBER	SUBJECTIVE	OBJECTIVE	POSSESSIVE
Singular			
First person	I	me	my, mine
Second person	you	you	your, yours
Third person	he, she, it who, whoever	him, her, it whom, whomever	his, her, hers its, whose
Plural			
First person	we	us	our, ours
Second person	you	you	your, yours
Third person	they, who whoever	them, whom whomever	their, theirs, whose

1. *Subjective case:* Subjects and complements that rename the subject take the **subjective case:**

   ▶ EXAMPLES: The children and **I** went on a picnic in the park. (subject)

      The winner of the race is **she.**   (complement)

2. *Objective case:* Direct objects, indirect objects, and objects of a preposition take the **objective case:**

   ▶ EXAMPLES: The car nearly hit **us** before it stopped on the median. (direct object)

      Professor Gonzalez gave **him** a B+ on his midterm exam. (indirect object)

      Please give this message to **them** before you leave. (object of preposition)

3. *Possessive case:* Pronouns that show ownership are in the **possessive case:**

▶ EXAMPLES: **His** baseball went through **their** window on **its** way out of the ballpark.

Is this book **yours, mine,** or **ours?**

(*Note:* The simple possessives *my, your his, its, our,* and *their* are normally followed by nouns; the possessives *mine, yours, hers, ours, yours,* and *theirs* refer to nouns or pronouns. See also pages 422–423.)

In determining which case to use in a particular situation, you also need to pay particular attention to the use of *who* (*whoever*) and *whom* (*whomever*), to compound elements, and to comparisons.

Who (Whoever) and *Whom (Whomever)*

The pronouns *who* and *whoever* are subject forms; the pronouns *whom* and *whomever* are object forms. In general, these pronouns function much like other subjective and objective pronouns. As shown here, the two primary uses of these words are as questions or as relative clauses in complex sentences:

QUESTIONS

Who knows the answer?   (subject)

Whom did you call?   (object: rephrase as *You did call* **whom?**)

COMPLEX SENTENCES WITH RELATIVE CLAUSES

The politician **who spends the most** often wins the election.
(subject of relative clause: **who** *spends the most*)

The judge will give the prize to **whomever she chooses.**
(direct object of relative clause: *she chooses* **whomever**)

The manager should hire **whoever will do the best job.**
(subject of relative clause: **whoever** *will do the best job*)

(*Note:* As shown in these examples, the correct pronoun form is determined by how the pronoun is used in the relative clause, not by how the clause is used in the complex sentence.)

Since questions use inverted word order and complex sentences have more than one subject and verb, the use of *who* (*whoever*) and *whom* (*whomever*) can sometimes be tricky. To help you choose the right form of these words, rephrase questions as statements and substitute more common pronoun forms, such as *he* and *him*, for *who* or *whom* in relative clauses.

Compound Elements

A pronoun is often used as one of the elements in a compound subject, a compound direct or indirect object of a verb, or a compound object of a preposition:

SUBJECT:	**Jonikka** and **I** studied until midnight.
DIRECT OBJECT:	The dog followed **Wayne** and **her** all the way home.
INDIRECT OBJECT:	Please give **Deanna** and **him** the book.
OBJECT OF PREPOSITION:	The surprise is just for **Jason** and **me**.

To help you choose the correct pronoun case in a compound element, restate the sentence with only the pronoun. For example, if you are tempted to write *The surprise is just for **Jason** and **I*** in the last example, omit the first item in the compound element (*Jason*) and compare the resulting sentences. Clearly, *The secret is just for **me*** is preferable to *The secret is just for **I***.

Comparisons

Pronouns are often used in implied comparisons such as those in the following sentences:

SUBJECT FORM:	Her father was more upset than **she**. (Her father was more upset than ***she*** *was upset*.)
OBJECT FORM:	The scholarship would mean more to Waylon than **me**. (The scholarship would mean more to Waylon than *it would mean to **me**.*)

EXERCISE

23.4   In each of the following sentences, select the correct form of the pronoun.

1. Shane and _____ go hiking in the Colorado mountains every
   (she, her)
   summer.

2. It's not fair that, as members of the head table, you got _____
   (your, yours)
   dinner an hour before we got _____.
   (our, ours)

3. To _____ did you give the money from the concession stand?
   (who, whom)

4. My younger sister is two inches taller than _____.
                                                            (I, me)

5. _____ boss gave _____ a 10 percent raise.
    (She, her)   (she, her)

6. The district championship will be decided in the final game between

   _____ and _____
   (they, them)   (we, us)

7. The first-place spelling medal should go to _____ earns it.
                                         (whoever, whomever)

8. We watched _____ as _____ waved goodbye to
           (they, them)   (they, them)
   _____ daughter.
   (their, theirs)

9. Jandy said that the loss of the championship hurt the assistant coach

   more than _____.
            (she, her)

10. _____, personally, would like to learn as much as I can
    (I, Me)
   in college.

EXERCISE

23.5   Edit the following paragraph for eight errors in pronoun case.

[1]On the long flight to Hawaii, I sat next to a young mother and her five-year-old son whom were flying home to Jordan. [2]Early in the flight, the attendant distributed peanuts and soft drinks to they and I. [3]The child, whom was named Abdul, quickly gobbled up his peanuts and looked hungrily at mine. [4]Of course, I gave he not only my peanuts but also my soft drink. [5]In fact, in a few hours, after I had shared part of a complete meal with him, Abdul and me were good friends. [6]I was certainly tired and hungry when I arrived in Honolulu. [7]However, I realized that they were more exhausted than me, and I felt sorry for whomever sat next to Abdul on the rest of the flight.

Using Pronouns with -*Self* and -*Selves*

Pronouns with -*self* or -*selves* (*myself, yourself, yourselves, himself, herself, itself, themselves*) can be used as intensives or reflexives. An intensive pronoun is a personal pronoun plus -*self* or -*selves* that emphasizes the noun or pronoun to which it refers:

INTENSIVE PRONOUN: She **herself** won the essay contest.

She won the essay contest **herself.**

A **reflexive pronoun** has the same form as an intensive pronoun but indicates that the subject of the sentence receives the action of the verb.

REFLEXIVE PRONOUN: The child hurt **herself.**

An intensive pronoun functions as a modifier; a reflexive pronoun functions as an object. Remember that a pronoun with -*self* or -*selves* in its spelling can never be used as the subject of a sentence. Remember also that you should never use *hisself* or *theirselves*, which are not legitimate words.

EXERCISE

23.6

Examine each of the following sentences for errors in the use of intensive or reflexive pronouns. Rewrite incorrect sentences correctly. If a sentence has no error in pronoun usage, write *Correct* in the blank.

1. The children wanted to plan their own party by theirselves.

    _____

    _____

2. The governor visited the flooded area himself.

    _____

    _____

3. Herself was late for the meeting.

    _____

    _____

4. The rock singer had made so much money that he gave hisself a new car for his birthday.

    _____

    _____

5. The bank officials were accused of loaning themselves money illegally.

_____

_____

Using a Consistent Point of View

First-person pronouns (*I* and *we*) always refer to the person who is speaking or writing. The second person (*you*), which is the same in the singular and plural, refers to the person spoken to or addressed (the audience). The third-person pronouns (*he, she, it,* and *they*) refer to a person or thing spoken or written about.

▶ EXAMPLES

I need to exercise each day because I feel better when I am active. (first-person point of view)

You need to exercise each day because you feel better when you are active.   (second-person point of view)

People need to exercise each day because they feel better when they are active.   (third-person point of view)

When you are writing, it is important to be consistent in your point of view. If you choose to write from the first-person point of view (*I* or *we*), you must use this point of view throughout your paper. Avoid shifting casually from one point of view to another unless there is a good reason for doing so. In some types of formal writing, first- and second-person points of view are not often used. In fact, it is usually best to avoid using a second-person point of view (*you*) unless you are giving directions or explaining a process.

EXERCISE

23.7   Revise the following sentences to eliminate unnecessary shifts in point of view.

1. I like math because it is easy for me, and you can grasp it on your own.

_____

_____

2. When we had received our sheets and blankets, we were shown how to make one's bed according to army regulations.

_____

_____

23.7 continued

3. I need to improve my writing skills. To be able to express yourself in writing is of great importance.

_____

_____

4. To me, graduation marks the beginning of a new life, a demanding life, from which a person can expect to receive only as much as you give.

_____

_____

5. I want to learn all the rules you need to know in order to stay out of trouble with the authorities.

_____

_____

Using Nonsexist Pronouns

Since pronouns frequently indicate gender, a writer is often faced with a decision about which gender to choose if the sex of the antecedent is not apparent. Traditionally, masculine pronouns were used when the sex of the antecedent was not stated.

▶ EXAMPLE: A **teacher** should motivate **his** students.

However, this solution is increasingly considered unacceptable. A fairer practice is to alternate masculine and feminine pronouns.

▶ EXAMPLE: A **teacher** should motivate **her** students.

Or you can use both the masculine and feminine pronouns.

▶ EXAMPLE: A **teacher** should motivate **his** or **her** students.

Using both pronouns is perhaps fairer, but the result is somewhat awkward and wordy. Another way to solve this problem is to use the plural form of the noun and thus avoid the dilemma completely.

▶ EXAMPLE: **Teachers** should motivate **their** students.

EXERCISE

23.8

Revise the following sentences to eliminate sexist pronouns.

1. A judge usually delivers his decision at the end of a trial.

_____

_____

2. Anyone who arrives late must take his place in line.

_____

_____

3. A secretary should take her notepad with her to meetings.

_____

_____

4. The politician asked everyone to give his best for the campaign.

_____

_____

5. A great writer, like a great actor, must practice his craft.

_____

_____

EXERCISE

23.9

Edit the following paragraphs, correcting the eighteen errors in pronoun usage (reference, agreement, case, -*self* words, point of view, and sexist pronouns). Use the third person consistently.

[1]All teachers need a broad liberal arts education as well as training in a special area of study. [2]This is very important to prepare teachers to face a variety of challenges in a classroom for which a narrow, specialized education is inadequate. [3]For example, a social studies teacher needs to develop his knowledge of literature, art, and music. [4]In my teaching profession, I will use my courses from the university's general studies program as much as the courses in our major fields.

[5]Many colleges require students whom are preparing to teach to work in the field as practice teachers for a year before he graduates. [6]This is probably more helpful to young, inexperienced teachers than to those whom have already worked as substitute teachers. [7]However, being in the classroom theirselves is no doubt helpful to all whom are preparing to teach.

23.9 continued

[8]Teachers cannot be too well prepared because in the classroom students will ask you a variety of questions and expect you to know about the world in general as well as about how to teach your subject. [9]Teachers should realize that the students who they teach will depend on they and the administrators to provide a quality education.

Chapter Review

- A pronoun should have a clear antecedent—a noun or other pronoun to which the pronoun refers.

- A pronoun and its antecedent must agree in number, gender, and person.

- Problems in pronoun reference and agreement often occur with indefinite, relative, and demonstrative pronouns.

- Personal pronouns take the subjective, objective, or possessive case depending on whether they are used as subjects, objects, or modifiers.

- Special problems with pronoun case sometimes occur with *who* and *whom*, compound elements, and comparisons.

- Pronouns with *-self* and *-selves* can be intensive or reflexive, but *hisself* and *theirselves* are not legitimate words and should never be used.

- The point of view of personal pronouns should be consistent.

- Writers should be careful to use nonsexist pronouns.

Writing Assignment

Write a paragraph in which you tell about something that one of your family members has done recently. Be sure to use pronouns clearly, correctly, and consistently in your paragraph.

Participating in the Academic Community

Meet with a group of your classmates to edit your paragraphs. Check each paragraph carefully for correct pronoun usage. (You may want to refer to the Chapter Review as you edit your paragraphs.)

Chapter 24

Verb Tenses and Forms

A good writer must have a clear understanding of verb tenses and forms. **Verb tense** shows the time at which the stated action or being takes place. Each verb has many different tenses (see Chapter 18, pages 250–251), but the tenses that you will probably use most often—and that you will study in this chapter—are listed here:

Present:	I **study** every night.
Past:	I **studied** last night.
Future:	I **will study** tomorrow night.
Present perfect:	I **have studied** all day.
Past perfect:	I **had studied** before I took the test.
Future perfect:	I **will have studied** by the time I take the test.
Present progressive:	I **am studying** right now.
Past progressive:	I **was studying** when you called.
Future progressive:	I **will be studying** tomorrow night.

English verbs are of two general types: regular and irregular. Regular verbs form their past and past participle tenses by adding *-d* or *-ed* to the present tense (*work, worked, worked*); irregular verbs form their past and past participle by changing their internal spellings (*give, gave, given*).

Regular Verbs

The following chart lists the forms of a few of the most common **regular verbs.** Notice that each past tense and past participle form ends in *-d* or *-ed*.

PRESENT TENSE First- and Second-Person Singular	Third-Person Singular	PRESENT PARTICIPLE (Use with form of *to be*)	PAST TENSE	PAST PARTICIPLE (Use with *have, has,* or *had*)
ask	asks	asking	asked	asked
look	looks	looking	looked	looked
talk	talks	talking	talked	talked
use	uses	using	used	used
wait	waits	waiting	waited	waited

(*Note:* Because writers don't easily hear the *-d* or *-ed* ending in some regular past tense verbs, they sometimes omit this ending. Remember that the past tense forms of *use* and *suppose* are *used* and *supposed.*)

EXERCISE

24.1

Fill in the appropriate past tense forms of the regular verbs in parentheses.

1. The two teenagers often _____ for hours on the telephone.
   (talk)

2. Mark _____ for an hour while Dr. Lieberman _____
   (wait)   (examine)
   the new patient.

3. Study guides _____ to recommend studying two hours outside
   (use)
   of class for each hour in class.

4. Anitra _____ the house while Anika _____ the lawn.
   (paint)   (mow)

5. My mother _____ so hard that she _____ her teacher's
   (work)   (pass)
   examination in one attempt.

EXERCISE

24.2

Edit the following paragraph, changing the present tense verbs to past tense. All of the verbs in the paragraph are regular verbs.

[1]Every summer, I visit my cousin in the small, sleepy town of Miller's Cove. [2]In good weather we skateboarded down the sidewalk of my cousin's street. [3]In rainy weather, we play Nintendo and computer games. [4]And at night, we watch videos of old horror movies. [5]Year after year, we manage to amuse ourselves so well that I always hate to leave.

Irregular Verbs

Irregular verbs change their forms in both the past and past participle forms. The following list of common irregular verbs will help you choose the correct verb tenses as you write and edit your papers. Notice that each of these irregular verbs changes its internal spelling to form its past and past participle forms.

PRESENT TENSE First- and Second-Person Singular	Third-Person Singular	PRESENT PARTICIPLE (Use with form of *to be*)	PAST TENSE	PAST PARTICIPLE (Use with *have, has,* or *had*)
arise	arises	arising	arose	arisen
awake	awakes	awaking	awoke (awaked)	awoken (awaked)
bear	bears	bearing	bore	borne
beat	beats	beating	beat	beaten
become	becomes	becoming	became	become
begin	begins	beginning	began	begun
bend	bends	bending	bent	bent
bite	bites	biting	bit	bitten
bleed	bleeds	bleeding	bled	bled
blow	blows	blowing	blew	blown
break	breaks	breaking	broke	broken
build	builds	building	built	built
burst	bursts	bursting	burst	burst
buy	buys	buying	bought	bought
catch	catches	catching	caught	caught
choose	chooses	choosing	chose	chosen
cling	clings	clinging	clung	clung
come	comes	coming	came	come
creep	creeps	creeping	crept	crept
deal	deals	dealing	dealt	dealt
dig	digs	digging	dug	dug
dive	dives	diving	dove (dived)	dived
do	does	doing	did	done
draw	draws	drawing	drew	drawn

PRESENT TENSE First- and Second- Person Singular	Third-Person Singular	PRESENT PARTICIPLE (Use with form of *to be*)	PAST TENSE	PAST PARTICIPLE (Use with *have, has,* or *had*)
drink	drinks	drinking	drank	drunk
drive	drives	driving	drove	driven
dwell	dwells	dwelling	dwelt (dwelled)	dwelt (dwelled)
eat	eats	eating	ate	eaten
fall	falls	falling	fell	fallen
feed	feeds	feeding	fed	fed
feel	feels	feeling	felt	felt
fight	fights	fighting	fought	fought
find	finds	finding	found	found
fling	flings	flinging	flung	flung
fly	flies	flying	flew	flown
forget	forgets	forgetting	forgot	forgotten (got)
forgive	forgives	forgiving	forgave	forgiven
freeze	freezes	freezing	froze	frozen
get	gets	getting	got	gotten
give	gives	giving	gave	given
go	goes	going	went	gone
grow	grows	growing	grew	grown
hang	hangs	hanging	hung (hanged)	hung (hanged)
have	has	having	had	had
hear	hears	hearing	heard	heard
hide	hides	hiding	hid	hidden
hit	hits	hitting	hit	hit
hold	holds	holding	held	held
hurt	hurts	hurting	hurt	hurt
keep	keeps	keeping	kept	kept
know	knows	knowing	knew	known
lay	lays	laying	laid	laid
lead	leads	leading	led	led
leave	leaves	leaving	left	left
lend	lends	lending	lent	lent
let	lets	letting	let	let
lie	lies	lying	lay	lain
light	lights	lighting	lit (lighted)	lit (lighted)
lose	loses	losing	lost	lost
make	makes	making	made	made
mean	means	meaning	meant	meant
meet	meets	meeting	met	met
pay	pays	paying	paid	paid
quit	quits	quitting	quit	quit
read	reads	reading	read	read
ride	rides	riding	rode	ridden
rise	rises	rising	rose	risen

PRESENT TENSE First- and Second- Person Singular	Third-Person Singular	PRESENT PARTICIPLE (Use with form of *to be*)	PAST TENSE	PAST PARTICIPLE (Use with *have, has,* or *had*)
run	runs	running	ran	run
see	sees	seeing	saw	seen
sell	sells	selling	sold	sold
send	sends	sending	sent	sent
set	sets	setting	set	set
shake	shakes	shaking	shook	shaken
shine	shines	shining	shone (shined)	shone (shined)
shrink	shrinks	shrinking	shrank (shrunk)	shrunk (shrunken)
sing	sings	singing	sang	sung
sink	sinks	sinking	sank	sunk
sit	sits	sitting	sat	sat
sleep	sleeps	sleeping	slept	slept
slide	slides	sliding	slid	slid
sling	slings	slinging	slung	slung
speak	speaks	speaking	spoke	spoken
spend	spends	spending	spent	spent
spit	spits	spitting	spat (spit)	spat (spit)
split	splits	splitting	split	split
spoil	spoils	spoiling	spoilt (spoiled)	spoilt (spoiled)
spread	spreads	spreading	spread	spread
spring	springs	springing	sprang	sprung
stand	stands	standing	stood	stood
steal	steals	stealing	stole	stolen
stick	sticks	sticking	stuck	stuck
sting	stings	stinging	stung	stung
stink	stinks	stinking	stank (stunk)	stunk
string	strings	stringing	strung	strung
swear	swears	swearing	swore	sworn
swell	swells	swelling	swelled	swelled (swollen)
swim	swims	swimming	swam	swum
swing	swings	swinging	swung	swung
take	takes	taking	took	taken
teach	teaches	teaching	taught	taught
tear	tears	tearing	tore	torn
tell	tells	telling	told	told
think	thinks	thinking	thought	thought
throw	throws	throwing	threw	thrown
wake	wakes	waking	woke (waked)	woken (waked)
wear	wears	wearing	wore	worn
weep	weeps	weeping	wept	wept
win	wins	winning	won	won
wring	wrings	wringing	wrung	wrung
write	writes	writing	wrote	written

24.3

Fill in the correct past tense forms of the irregular verbs in parentheses.

1. I _____ to write my history last night, so I _____ it early
   (forget)   (write)
   this morning.

2. Dora _____ the bus home for spring break last week.
        (ride)

3. The two mallards _____ gracefully from one side of the lake to
                      (swim)
   the other.

4. The ice in the lake _____ two inches thick overnight.
                        (freeze)

5. We _____ the new campus production of *The Crucible*
      (see)
   last week.

6. At the campus store yesterday I _____ my books from last
                                    (sell)
   semester and _____ my books for next semester.
                 (buy)

7. My parents recently _____ a new house two streets away from
                        (build)
   their old house.

8. The man from the moving company _____ all night to get their
                                    (drive)
   furniture delivered.

9. The elderly widow _____ most of her money out of the bank
                      (draw)
   and _____ it to the homeless in her city.
        (give)

10. I _____ I _____ the answers to the test.
       (think)   (know)

Problem Verbs:
Sit/Set, Lie/Lay, Rise/Raise

Three pairs of verbs often give writers special problems. The definitions, forms, and uses of these verbs are given here:

VERB	PRESENT	PAST	PAST PARTICIPLE	PRESENT PARTICIPLE
to sit	sit	sat	sat	sitting

Definition: to assume a seated position
Example: Please *sit* in the chair.

VERB	PRESENT	PAST	PAST PARTICIPLE	PRESENT PARTICIPLE
to set	set	set	set	setting

Definition: to place something
Example: Please *set* the vase on the table.

VERB	PRESENT	PAST	PAST PARTICIPLE	PRESENT PARTICIPLE
to lie	lay	lay	lain	lying

Definition: to recline
Example: The book *lies* unopened on the table
as he *lies* on the couch.

VERB	PRESENT	PAST	PAST PARTICIPLE	PRESENT PARTICIPLE
to lay	lay	laid	laid	laying

Definition: to place
Example: Please *lay* the book on the table.

VERB	PRESENT	PAST	PAST PARTICIPLE	PRESENT PARTICIPLE
to rise	rise	rose	risen	rising

Definition: to ascend; to move upward
Example: As she *rises* in the morning, the sun *rises*
in the east.

VERB	PRESENT	PAST	PAST PARTICIPLE	PRESENT PARTICIPLE
to raise	raise	raised	raised	raising

Definition: to lift or cause something to move upward
Example: Jennifer *raised* the window to let in some air.

Set, lie, and *raise* refer to actions performed on things and thus have objects; *sit, lie,* and *rise* refer to states of being and do not have objects.

In the spaces provided, fill in the correct forms and tenses of the six problem verbs.

1. The carpenter _____ the ladder to the roof.
   (rise, raise)

2. I like to _____ near the front of my history class, but my friend
   (sit, set)

   Haleigh _____ in the back yesterday.
   (sit, set)

3. Did you _____ the alarm for early in the morning?
   (sit, set)

4. Marcy _____ her clarinet on the bleacher while she
   (lie, lay)

   _____ and talked with her friends.
   (sit, set)

5. Because he felt ill when he _____ this morning, Aaron has
   (rise, raise)

   _____ in bed all morning.
   (lie, lay)

6. Jennifer was _____ at her desk when I left, but Stephanie
   (sit, set)

   was _____ on the couch.
   (lie, lay)

Special Uses of the Verbs
To Be and To Have

The verbs *to be* and *to have* are probably the most frequently used verbs in the English language. Each is very irregular and thus has multiple forms. Each of these two verbs may be used alone or as helping verbs to form the special types of verbs discussed in the following sections. The forms of these two verbs are given for you here:

To Be

PERSON	PRESENT TENSE		PAST TENSE	
	Singular	**Plural**	**Singular**	**Plural**
First person	I am	we are	I was	we were
Second person	you are	you are	you were	you were
Third person	he, she, it is	they are	he, she, it was	they were

To Have

PERSON	PRESENT TENSE		PAST TENSE	
	Singular	**Plural**	**Singular**	**Plural**
First person	I have	we have	I had	we had
Second person	you have	you have	you had	you had
Third person	he, she, it has	they have	he, she, it had	they had

EXERCISE

24.5   In the spaces provided, fill in the correct forms of the verbs *to be* and *to have.*

1. So far this year, the Newland Tigers _____ won all their
   (to have)
   games.

2. The quarterback _____ a good candidate for "Most Valuable
   (to be)
   Player in the District."

3. Yes, I heard that he _____ in the running for a scholarship at
   (to be)
   the state university.

4. The local newspaper reported that the team _____ an excellent
   (to have)
   chance of winning state this year.

5. _____ you and your brother seen them play this season?
(to have)

6. No, he and I _____ going to the game last night but we were
(to be)

delayed by an accident on the freeway.

7. The assistant coach _____ a minor accident last night and
(to have)

_____ late for the game.
(to be)

8. Perhaps that _____ the accident we saw.
(to be)

9. Well, we _____ tickets for last night, but we _____ not
(to have)   (to be)

planning to go tonight.

10. I _____ certainly happy to have such an excellent team
(to be)

this year.

Past Participle

The **past participle** is always used with a helping verb, or a form of the
verb *to have:*

SIMPLE PAST: Action has been completed

I **walked** this morning.   (regular verb)

I **gave** a presentation today.   (irregular verb)

PAST PARTICIPLE: Action has gone on in past and is continuing

I **have walked** for 30 minutes.   (regular verb)

I **have given** my best effort.   (irregular verb)

As shown in the next section, the past participle and the helping verb *have*
are used to form the perfect tenses.

24.6

Change the verbs in the following sentences from the simple past to the past perfect, altering the sentence as necessary to show the change in time.

1. The United States exported many automobiles last year.

    _____

2. The new advertising techniques brought in record sales.

    _____

3. The child's mother overlooked his misbehavior.

    _____

4. The conductor gave the orchestra the signal to begin playing.

    _____

5. The visiting lecturer began his lecture.

    _____

Present and Past Perfect Tenses

The **perfect tenses** describe action or events already completed or to be completed before a specific point in time. Forms of the verb *to have* and the past participle are used to form the perfect tenses. The most frequently used perfect tenses are the **present perfect** and **past perfect.** To form the present perfect, use *has* or *have* plus the past participle; to form the past perfect, use *had* plus the past participle.

> PRESENT PERFECT: Action has taken place and is still taking place
>
> I **have cooked** all day.   (regular verb)
>
> I **have beaten** the eggs for several minutes.   (irregular verb)

> PAST PERFECT: Action in past perfect occurs before that in past
>
> I **had cooked** the cake before I made the icing.   (regular verb)
>
> I **had beaten** the eggs before I added the sugar.   (irregular verb)

24.7

Use each of the following verbs to write one sentence in the present perfect tense and another sentence in the past perfect tense:

1. to work

   Present perfect: _____

   Past perfect: _____

2. to know

   Present perfect: _____

   Past perfect: _____

3. to drive

   Present perfect: _____

   Past perfect: _____

4. to wake

   Present perfect: _____

   Past perfect: _____

5. to look

   Present perfect: _____

   Past perfect: _____

Progressive Tenses

The **progressive tenses** of a verb show continuing or ongoing action. The progressive tenses use a form of the verb *to be* with the present participle (*-ing*) form of the verb.

PRESENT PROGRESSIVE:	I **am beating** the eggs now.
PAST PROGRESSIVE:	I **was cooking** the filling earlier.
FUTURE PROGRESSIVE:	I **will be icing** the cake later.

PRESENT PERFECT PROGRESSIVE: I **have been beating** the eggs for ten minutes.

PAST PERFECT PROGRESSIVE: I **had been cooking** all morning.

FUTURE PERFECT PROGRESSIVE: By dinnertime, I **will have been working** in the kitchen all day.

EXERCISE

24.8 Fill in the correct forms of the progressive tenses in the following sentences. In each sentence, you will need to provide a form of the main verb and a form of *to be* or *to have*. (*Note:* You may need to refer to the chart on pages 357–359 for irregular verbs.)

1. _____ you _____ well in your chemistry class?
   (do / present progressive)

2. No, I _____ _____ _____ dropping the course
   (consider / present perfect progressive)
   all semester.

3. I _____ _____ about dropping, but my last exam was
   (think / past progressive)
   much better.

4. Last night, some of the students _____ _____ about
   (talk / past progressive)
   forming a study group.

5. Well, at least we _____ _____ most of our English
   (pass / present progressive)
   compositions!

6. I hope that tomorrow I _____ _____ _____ a good
   (celebrate / future progressive)
   grade on my chemistry test.

Passive Voice

The verb *to be* and the past participle of the verb are used to form the passive voice. In **active voice,** the subject performs the action; in **passive voice,** the subject receives the action.

> ACTIVE VOICE: The pitcher **throws** the ball.   (present tense)
>
> The batter **hit** the ball.   (past tense)
>
> PASSIVE VOICE: The ball **is thrown** by the pitcher.   (present tense)
>
> The ball **was hit** by the batter.   (past tense)

Passive voice is useful when you want to emphasize the receiver of the action rather than the one who performs the action, but active voice is always more vivid and concise.

E X E R C I S E

24.9   Change the following sentences from active to passive voice, using a prepositional phrase that begins with *by* to indicate who performs the action of the verb.

1. The judge convicted the accused woman.

   _____

2. The rebels abducted the priest.

   _____

3. The publisher shipped the books to the campus book store.

   _____

Change the following sentences from passive voice to active voice.

1. The robber was caught by the police officer.

   _____

2. The rock concert was enjoyed by the crowd.

   _____

3. The man on the sidewalk was hit by a drunk driver.

   _____

EXERCISE

24.10

Fill in each blank in the following paragraphs with the appropriate form of the verb in parentheses.

PARAGRAPH A

Yesterday, the weather forecaster _____ a night

(1 / predict)

temperature of twenty degrees, but my roommate and I _____

(2 / ignore)

the warning. My mother had _____ me an electric heater to

(3 / give)

use in our apartment, but I _____ to turn it on. When we

(4 / forgot)

_____ to bed, the temperature was about forty degrees, but

(5 / go)

when we _____ up this morning, it was eighteen degrees. In

(6 / wake)

the night, a water pipe had _____ and _____. When

(7 / freeze)   (8 / burst)

the water _____ this morning, it _____ all over our new

(9 / thaw)   (10 / run)

floor. The water _____ our new VCR that was _____

(11 / ruin)   (12 / sit)

on the floor. Next time the weather forecast _____ the

(13 / say)

temperature will _____ below freezing, my roommate and

(14 / drop)

I will _____ to listen and prepare.

(15 / know)

PARAGRAPH B

Last year's vacation in Galveston _____ delightful.

(1 / is)

I had _____ forward to the trip all year, and I was not

(2 / look)

_____. I have never _____ the water as blue or the sky

(3 / disappoint)   (4 / see)

as clear as it _____ last year. We _____ from the

(5 / is)   (6 / fish)

pier, _____ fresh shrimp every day, _____ every

(7 / eat)   (8 / swim)

afternoon, and then _____ on the beach under the stars at

(9 / lie)

night. I _____ another trip to the coast this year. In fact,

(10 / plan)

I _____ for a reservation just this morning.

(11 / write)

Consistency in Tense

Good writers avoid unnecessary shifts in tense. If you start a paragraph or essay in the present tense, you should keep it in the present; if you start it in the past tense, you should keep it in the past. Awkward shifts in tense, such as the one in the following example, can confuse your reader:

INCONSISTENT: The plumber **installs** the new faucets and **connected** the disposal.

This sentence is confusing because the writer shifts needlessly from the present tense (*installs*) to the past tense (*connected*). Since the following actions occurred at approximately the same time, the tense of both verbs are the same:

CONSISTENT: The plumber **installs** the new faucets and **connects** the disposal.   (present tense)

The plumber **installed** the new faucets and **connected** the disposal.   (past tense)

Changing tenses is permissible, however, if the context indicates that the events or actions occurred at different times.

CORRECT: The plumber **installed** the new faucets yesterday, **is repairing** the drain today, and **will connec**t the disposal tomorrow.   (past, present, and future tenses)

As a rule, do not confuse your readers by changing tenses unless a shift is clearly justified.

EXERCISE

24.11

Underline any needless shifts in tense that you find in the following sentences. Then rewrite the sentences correctly.

1. The war was horrible, and anyone who goes through it had to endure great hardships.

_____

_____

2. The plane passes over the highway and barely missed the tower.

_____

_____

3. The concert started at eight o'clock, will last two hours, and ends at ten o'clock.

_____

_____

4. Out of the jungle creeps a large spotted leopard, which turned suddenly when he sees the hunters on the other side of the river.

_____

_____

5. The planning committee met every Wednesday for three weeks and decides on the projected goals for the next year.

_____

_____

EXERCISE

24.12   Underline the eighteen present tense verbs in the following paragraph. Then edit the paragraph by changing the tense from present to past. (One verb will be in past perfect tense, and the two will be in passive voice.)

¹The game begins promptly at eight o'clock as the teams run out and line up at opposite ends of the field. ²The crowd of cheering fans grows quiet, the official gives the signal, and the two lines of uniformed players begin to run toward each other. ³The ball is kicked by one player so that it arches high above the field before dropping with a decisive thud into the hands of the player who has been waiting for it. ⁴At this point, the receiver begins to fight his way down the field. ⁵As he runs, he is the target of every player on the opposing team. ⁶At the same time, his own teammates attempt to protect him. ⁷After a long run, he is tackled by a large player, and there is a pile-up as players from both teams tangle in a mass of colorfully uniformed arms and legs. ⁸The crowd lets out screams of delight and anguish as another football game gets underway.

Chapter Review

- Regular verbs form their past tense and past participle forms by adding *-d* or *-ed.*

- Irregular verbs form their past tense and past participle forms by changing internally.

- Three pairs of verbs with special usage problems are *sit/set, lie/lay,* and *rise/raise.*

- The most frequently used irregular verbs are *to be* and *to have.*

- The past participle is always used with a form of the verb *to have* or *to be* as a helping verb.

- The present, past, and future perfect tenses use a form of the verb *to have* as a helping verb.

- The present, past, and future progressive tenses use a form of the verb *to be* with a present participle (*-ing*) form of the verb.

- The passive voice, in which the subject receives the action, uses the appropriate form of the verb *to be* and the past participle.

- Good writers avoid unnecessary shifts in tense.

Writing Assignment

Write a paragraph describing one of the most important events in your past. Be sure to use various past tenses correctly in your paragraph.

Participating in the Academic Community

Meet with a group of your classmates to edit your paragraphs. Check each paragraph to be sure it uses the past, past perfect, and past progressive tenses correctly and consistently.

Chapter 25

Modifiers

Modifiers give information about other words in a sentence. A modifier may function as either an adjective or an adverb, and it may be either a single word or a group of words (a phrase or a clause).

Adjective or Adverb?

Sometimes writers have trouble knowing whether to use an adjective or an adverb. Remember that **adjectives** modify nouns or pronouns and explain what kind, which one, or how many.

> ▶ EXAMPLES: The old storekeeper is an **unhappy** person.
> (adjective modifying noun *person*)
>
> As the newest teacher, she was **nervous.**
> (adjective as subject complement modifying noun *teacher*)

As shown in the last example, the linking verb *to be* should always be followed by an adjective. This same rule applies when the verb is a sense verb (such as *feel, taste, smell, hear,* and *look*) that is followed by a modifier describing the subject: *The pizza tastes **awful** (not **awfully**).*

    Adverbs modify verbs or other modifiers—adjectives or adverbs—and tell how, when, in what manner, and to what extent.

> ▶ EXAMPLES: The patient is breathing **normally** again.
> (adverb modifying verb *breathing*)
>
> The new hotel is **extremely** expensive.
> (adverb modifying adjective *expensive*)
>
> The mail came **very** late this morning.
> (adverb modifying adverb *late*)

In the last example, *very* is an adverb **intensifier.** Intensifiers (such as *very, too, really, much,* etc.) add emphasis to the words they modify.

    Remember that *good* is an adjective and *well* is an adverb: *The hamburgers taste **good** but Jim barbecues **well.***

25.1   Underline the correct adjective or adverb in each of the following sentences.

1. The steak was burned _____
   (bad, badly).

2. I slept _____ _____ last night.
   (real, really)   (good, well)

3. She walked _____ into the room and spoke _____ to
   (graceful, gracefully)   (easy, easily)
   the audience.

4. Her walk was _____.
   (graceful, gracefully)

5. Are you _____ that she is _____ _____?
   (sure, surely)   (real, really)   (angry, angrily)

6. The infection made her feel _____.
   (bad, badly)

Comparatives and Superlatives

Adjectives and adverbs have three basic forms: simple, comparative, and superlative. Writers sometimes have difficulty using the comparative and superlative forms. The **comparative** form compares two things; the **superlative** form compares three or more things. To form the comparative of an adjective or adverb, add *-er* or *more* to the simple form; to form the superlative, add *-est* or *most* to the simple form. The following chart illustrates these different forms and the patterns for creating them:

	SIMPLE	COMPARATIVE	SUPERLATIVE
One syllable:	cold	colder	coldest
Ending in y:	easy	easier	easiest
Multisyllable:	famous	more famous	most famous
	gratefully	more gratefully	most gratefully
Irregular:	good, well	better	best
	bad, badly	worse	worst

EXERCISE

25.2

Write the correct form (comparative or superlative) of the adjectives and adverbs in parentheses:

1. One of the _____ stars in the sky is the North Star.
   (bright)

2. Are Wal-Mart stores _____ than K-Mart stores?
   (busy)

3. What is your _____ career goal?
   (important)

4. I watch my diet _____ than I did as a child.
   (carefully)

5. The temperature was _____ today than yesterday.
   (hot)

6. Tracie made a _____ grade on her last essay than on her
   (high)
   previous one, but her grade on her last history quiz is the _____
   (bad)
   she has made all semester.

EXERCISE

25.3

Correct ten errors in adjective/adverb usage in the following paragraph.

¹The campaign started quick. ²One day there were no candidates; the next day six people were compaigning for the nomination. ³All of the candidates wanted to win real bad, so they each tried to convince the voters that he or she was more better than the others. ⁴Some of them didn't do good initially but became popularer as the campaign progressed. ⁵As the campaign became more intense, the candidates became famouser. ⁶Voters became weary of the television ads and inevitable polls as the candidates struggled more hard to become well known. Most of the voters only wanted to live normal again. ⁷In the end, everyone was definite relieved that it was all over for another four years. ⁸It was hard to tell which group was gratefuller—the voters or the candidates.

Misplaced and Dangling Modifiers

Although a writer has options in placing modifiers, sometimes a misplaced or dangling modifier can confuse a reader (see also pages 261 and 384–385).

Misplaced Modifiers

Avoid **misplaced modifiers** by placing each modifier as near as possible to the word it modifies. Otherwise, the meaning may not be clear.

▶ EXAMPLE: The clown entertained the children **wearing baggy pants and an old top hat.**

In this example, it is not clear who is wearing the baggy pants and old top hat. If it is the clown who is dressed in this way, then that phrase should be placed immediately before or after the word *clown*.

▶ EXAMPLES: **Wearing baggy pants and an old top hat,** the clown entertained the children.

The clown, **wearing baggy pants and an old top hat,** entertained the children.

Note that commas separate nonrestrictive modifiers from the rest of the sentence.

EXERCISE

25.4

Rewrite the following sentences by moving each modifier (bolded) next to the word it modifies.

1. The men watched the hockey match **eating sandwiches.**

   _____

   _____

   _____

2. As his playmates continued to tease him, the child was ready to **almost** cry.

   _____

   _____

   _____

3. She found a scorpion **on the floor doing exercises.**

_____

_____

_____

4. **Hanging on a hook in the bedroom closet,** my sister found her lost umbrella.

_____

_____

_____

5. I cautioned the movers **carefully** to carry the dishes.

_____

_____

_____

Dangling Modifers

Sometimes a modifier occurs in a sentence in which there is no antecedent—or word for it to modify. Such modifiers are called **dangling modifiers.**

▶ EXAMPLE: **Sweeping the porch with a straw broom,** the dust filled the air.

In this example, the modifying phrase _sweeping the porch with a straw broom_ is dangling because there is no word in the sentence that it modifies. We need to know _who_ is doing the sweeping.

▶ EXAMPLE: **Sweeping the porch with a straw broom,** the old woman filled the air with dust.

In this corrected example, the modifying phrase describes the old woman.

Participles

Most dangling modifiers are participial phrases that occur at the beginnings of sentences. Since participles are modifiers that derive from verbs (_sweeping_ is the present participle of the verb _to sweep_), they must modify words that can perform the actions implied by the participles. Usually the subject of the sentence is the word modified by the participial phrase. The subject must, therefore, be the person or thing that is performing the action implied by the participle or participial phrase.

25.5

Rewrite the following sentences, correcting the dangling modifier in each one.

1. Using brainwashing techniques, the captives began to weaken in their resolve.

   _____

   _____

   _____

2. Rowing frantically, the boat began to sink.

   _____

   _____

   _____

3. Arriving by ship, Los Angeles looked like an enormous city.

   _____

   _____

   _____

4. By reading late that night, the examination was passed.

   _____

   _____

   _____

5. Driving too fast on a sharp curve, the car had a serious accident

   _____

   _____

   _____

The following paragraph contains eight misplaced or dangling modifiers. Rewrite the paragraph, correcting these errors.

[1]She remembered the stream from her childhood. [2]Then it was a small, clear stream that wound its way in and out of the trees in the wooded area behind her home. [3]Looking at the stream now, it had changed drastically. [4]Her parents had taught her always never to throw anything into the stream. [5]Now it was littered with all kinds of debris obviously. [6]Her parents had cautioned her about contaminating the water repeatedly. [7]Now it was contaminated clearly because dead fish floated on its surface. [8]Flowing sluggishly among the trees, she looked at the stream with tears in her eyes, ready to almost cry. [9]The stream no longer burbled and murmured as it once had. [10]It was silent, sluggish, and stinking. [11]Other people had not been taught to respect and preserve nature evidently as she had. [12]The stream was now dead.

Chapter Review

- Adjectives modify nouns; adverbs modify verbs and other modifiers.
- Comparative forms of adjectives and adverbs compare two things; superlative forms compare three or more things.
- Adjectives and adverbs form their comparative and superlative forms either by changing internally (to -er and -est forms) or by adding more and most.
- To avoid creating a misplaced modifier, a writer should place a modifier as near as possible to the word it modifies.
- To avoid creating a dangling modifier, a modifier should have a clear antecedent that it modifies.

■ Writing Assignment

Write a paragraph comparing and contrasting two people or places. Be sure to use adjectives and adverbs correctly in your paragraph—including comparative and superlative forms.

■ Participating in the Academic Community

Meet with a group of your classmates and edit your paragraphs for correct usage of adjectives and adverbs.

Chapter 26

Sentence Style

Good writing goes beyond mere correctness. To grow as a writer, you also need to develop a clear, concise, vivid, and original **style** of writing. This chapter will provide you with suggestions for improving your writing style by helping you avoid wordiness, triteness, and awkwardness and by helping you achieve effective sentence variety, comparisons, and parallelism.

Avoiding Wordiness

An age-old maxim says "Never use two words when one will do." Like most old sayings, this one is not completely true. You know from experience that you often need to develop your writing by adding details and examples. However, this old saying does suggest the important principle that writers should not use empty, meaningless words. Every word in a sentence or paragraph or essay should be necessary to express the writer's meaning. No words should be wasted.

The writing problem that results from using unnecessary and meaningless words is called **wordiness.** Following are some suggestions to help you avoid wordiness:

1. *Avoid using several words where one will do.* Also, avoid meaningless phrases such as *have a tendency to, because of the fact that, due to the fact that, at this point in time,* and *in my opinion.*

   WORDY: I have a tendency to be bashful around people.

   REVISED: I am shy.

2. *Use words that are clear, direct, and to the point.* Although you should use complex vocabulary words when you need them to make a particular point, avoid using big words for the sake of using such words.

WORDY: As for my own self, I have always had a preference for people of diminutive stature.

REVISED: I like short people.

3. *Avoid the passive voice.* Active voice is much more direct and less wordy than passive voice. (See Chapter 24, page 368, for additional explanation of the passive voice.)

WORDY: The assignment was finally completed by Bill.

REVISED: Bill finally completed the assignment.

4. *Avoid verb forms taken from the root* to be. Try to use more specific verbs.

WORDY: My sister **is** a parent who demands good behavior from her children.

REVISED: My sister **demands** good behavior from her children.

5. *Avoid clauses with postponed subjects.* Sentences with postponed subjects are often introduced by *it* or *there.*

WORDY: It was a miracle that the groom found his cuff links.

REVISED: Miraculously, the groom found his cuff links.

6. *Change* which, that, *and* who *clauses to participles whenever possible.*

WORDY: The men who were fighting the fire were exhausted.

REVISED: The men fighting the fire were exhausted.

EXERCISE

26.1

Rewrite the following sentences to make them less wordy.

1. What are the basic underlying causes that motivate students to affiliate with a fraternity or sorority?

_____

_____

2. At this point in time, I have been overcome by a strong desire to sleep.

_____

_____

3. The reason he went was that he wanted to meet Rosemary.

_____

_____

4. It can truly be said that this is a great university.

_____

_____

5. The rumor was told by her ex-boyfriend.

_____

_____

Achieving Sentence Variety

One hallmark of an effective writing style is **sentence variety.** Although achieving sentence variety may not come easily, you can achieve this goal by applying the following strategies to your own writing.

1. *Alternate longer sentences with shorter ones.* Achieving variety and avoiding wordiness often go hand in hand. Because student writers are concerned about punctuating long sentences correctly, they often write series of short, choppy sentences. As shown in the following example, this practice usually results in both unnecessary repetition of information, or wordiness, and a lack of sentence variety:

WEAK

One time I remember was on Christmas Eve. An angry man knocked on our door. He was the chief of police. He told us that someone had reported seeing a man on our roof. Supposedly, this man wore a red and white suit.

REVISED

One Christmas Eve an angry chief of police knocked on our door because someone had reported a man in a red and white suit on our roof.

As shown in this example, you can often achieve sentence variety and avoid unnecessary wordiness by combining short, choppy sentences into longer ones.

You should not take this advice to mean, however, that all short sentences are bad. Indeed, sometimes a very short sentence intermixed with longer ones can be quite effective in emphasizing a point or varying the rhythm of a passage. For example, one of the most effective sentences in the Bible is the two-word sentence *Jesus wept,* which is interwoven among longer verses.

2. *Vary ways of joining ideas.* Ideally, your writing will be composed of a mixture of simple, compound, and complex sentences. Also, within these types of sentences, many different ways exist for joining ideas. A few of these methods (and their punctuation) are illustrated here:

▶ COMPOUND SUBJECT OR VERB

ORIGINAL: Haleigh studied all night. Lynn studied all night too.

REVISED: **Haleigh** and **Lynn** studied all night.   (compound subject)

ORIGINAL: Haleigh studied all night. Haleigh passed her exam.

REVISED: Haleigh **studied** all night and **passed** her exam.
(compound verb)

▶ COMPOUND SENTENCE

ORIGINAL: Both girls studied all night. Lynn failed her exam.

REVISED: **Both girls studied all night, but Lynn failed her exam.**

▶ PRESENT OR PAST PARTICIPLE
OR PARTICIPIAL PHRASE

ORIGINAL: Haleigh prepared for her exam. She studied
all night.

REVISED: **Preparing for her exam,** Haleigh studied all
night.   (present participial phrase)

ORIGINAL: Haleigh was exhausted from studying all night.
Haleigh still made an A on her exam.

REVISED: **Exhausted from studying all night,** Haleigh still
made an A on her exam.   (past participial phrase)

▶ APPOSITIVE PHRASE

ORIGINAL: Haleigh is one of the best students in the class. Haleigh made an A on her exam.

REVISED: **One of the best students in her class,** Haleigh made an A on her exam.

▶ DEPENDENT CLAUSE

ORIGINAL: Haleigh was exhausted from studying all night. Haleigh still made an A on her exam.

REVISED: **Although she was exhausted from studying all night,** Haleigh still made an A on her exam.   (adverb clause)

ORIGINAL: Haleigh is one of the best students in her class. Haleigh made an A on her exam.

REVISED: Haleigh, **who is one of the best students in her class,** made an A on her exam.   (adjective clause)

▶ INFINITIVE PHRASE

ORIGINAL: Haleigh studied all night. She made an A on her exam.

REVISED: **To make an A on her exam,** Haleigh studied all night.

(See Chapters 18, 19, and 20 for more detailed explanations of ways to combine short sentences and for more sentence-combining practice.)

3. *Vary sentence beginnings.* In addition to varying the types of sentences that you use, you may also vary the way you begin your sentences. The most common way to write a sentence is to begin with the subject and then add the verb and various modifiers.

ORIGINAL: **The band** performed skillfully during the game.

However, you may add variety and emphasis to your writing if you begin with one of the following types of modifiers (note punctuation):

PREPOSITIONAL PHRASE: **During the game,** the band performed skillfully.

PARTICIPIAL PHRASE: **Performing skillfully,** the band played during the game.

ADVERB: **Skillfully,** the band performed during the game.

26.2

The following paragraphs are composed of short, choppy sentences. Using several of the preceding suggestions, rewrite these paragraphs for greater sentence variety.

[1]My grandfather was a real cowboy. [2]His life made him hard. [3]It also made him set in his ways. [4]He taught me honesty. [5]He also taught me respect. [6]My grandfather was a big influence on my life. [7]He was not tall. [8]He was only five feet and 9 inches. [9]But he was built like a bulldog. [10]He was strong willed. [11]He demanded respect. [12]I sometimes thought he was hard. [13]I thought he was mean. [14]I realize now that I was seeing him as a child would see him. [15]Now I respect him for his role in my life.

[16]My grandfather told stories of his youth. [17]He told about riding fences for days under the hot sun. [18]He was checking the cows. [19]He often spent the nights under the stars. [20]He kept his pistol under his head. [21]His stories reminded me of western movies. [22]He never got to ride off into the sunset. [23]He never rode with the pretty lady. [24]My grandfather remains a strong, positive memory for me.

Writing Effective Comparisons

We all use figurative comparisons without realizing it. Have you ever heard of *the eye of a hurricane* or gossip that spreads *like fire?* Statements that use the words *like, as*, or *than* to make a comparison are called **similes;** statements that make a comparison without using *like, as*, or *than* are called **metaphors.**

SIMILE: The policeman butted through the crowd **like a bull.**

METAPHOR: The policeman was a real **bull charging through the crowd.**

Simply saying that your friend is a stubborn person or that the floor is slippery is not as expressive as saying that your friend is *as stubborn as a cork in a bottle* or that *the floor is as slippery as egg white.* As these examples show, the keys to effective comparisons are vividness and originality.

Avoiding Triteness in Comparisons

Although original comparisons can make your writing more effective, you should avoid using comparisons that have become **trite,** or overused. For example, expressions such as *cold as ice* were once effective but are now so worn out by overuse that they are no longer interesting. Unoriginal and overused expressions such as *stubborn as a mule* or *slippery as an eel* are called **clichés,** from an old French word meaning "stereotype." When you use a comparison, be sure it is fresh and original.

Also, be sure the comparison is consistent in tone and nature with the thing being compared. For example, the sentence *The athlete went as fast as a paycheck in the supermarket* may be original, but it is not as effective as the sentence *The athlete raced down the field like a comet through space.* Though both "go fast," the image of the comet suggests the actual movement of the athlete more than the image of the paycheck does.

EXERCISE

26.3

Rewrite each of the following ordinary comparisons into a fresh new one. Use each comparison in a sentence.

▶ EXAMPLE: as light as a feather

New Comparison: as light as an empty eggshell

Sentence: Old Buck nonchalantly picked up the 300-pound crate as if it were as light as an empty eggshell.

1. as quiet as a mouse

   New Comparison: _____

   Sentence: _____

   _____

2. as old as the hills

   New Comparison: _____

   Sentence: _____

   _____

26.3 continued

3. as big as a house

    New Comparison: _____

    Sentence: _____

    _____

4. as red as a beet

    New Comparison: _____

    Sentence: _____

    _____

5. as pretty as a picture

    New Comparison: _____

    Sentence: _____

    _____

Achieving Parallelism

You can achieve effective rhythms and avoid awkwardness in your writing by using parallel structures. Parallel structures express similar ideas so that their similarity is emphasized. **Parallelism** is achieved by balancing words with similar words—nouns with nouns, adjectives with adjectives, adverbs with adverbs, and so forth. Parallelism also balances groups of words with similar groups of words—prepositional phrases with prepositional phrases, participial phrases with participial phrases, infinitives with infinitives, main clauses with main clauses, subordinate clauses with subordinate clauses, and sentences with sentences. In simple terms, parallelism is the balancing of one grammatical structure with another of the same kind.

Some specific types and examples of parallelism are illustrated for you in the following examples (see also Chapter 6, pages 76–79):

PARALLEL WORD FORMS

Jennifer's favorite hobbies are **reading, painting,** and **swimming.**
(parallel *-ing* words)

Note: To be parallel, words must be in the same grammatical form.

PARALLEL PHRASES

Winter visitors to Reno, Nevada, like **to shop, to gamble,** and **to ski.** (parallel infinitive phrases)

PARALLEL CLAUSES

Kari prayed **that the war would end soon** and **that her father would return safely.**   (parallel noun clauses)

PARALLEL SENTENCES

Good students are involved. **They ask questions. They do their homework.** And **they apply their knowledge.**   (parallel sentences)

When a writer uses similar ideas in structures that are not parallel, the result is usually awkward, as shown in this example:

AWKWARD: I like **bowling** better than **to swim.**

PARALLEL: I like **bowling** better than **swimming.**

EXERCISE

26.4   Identify the awkward and unparallel structures in the following sentences. Then revise the sentences to make these structures parallel.

1. When I lean back and closing my eyes, I hear the lap of the waves.

   _____

   _____

2. I hear the seagulls that sing above me, the fish splashing as they swim, and the toads burp on the shore.

   _____

   _____

3. I resolved my problems involving family, with my friend, and my conscience.

   _____

   _____

26.4 continued

4. Make your choices with the future in mind, keeping the present in control, and because you have the past to guide you.

_____

_____

5. At the lake, I have a chance to enjoy the silence, and I have gathered my thoughts.

_____

_____

EXERCISE

26.5

The following two paragraphs have serious weaknesses in sentence style. Read these paragraphs carefully and then rewrite them. In your revision, try to achieve sentence variety and parallelism and to avoid wordiness and triteness.

PARAGRAPH A

¹Needless to say, most people agree that in today's world a great influence can be exerted by a good teacher. ²It is unfortunate that there are not many good teachers available. ³In fact, one is lucky to have five or six top-notch instructors in an entire academic career. ⁴One of the best teachers I have ever had the privilege of studying under was Dr. Glenn Foster, who was a biology professor who taught at Perrine University, which is in Oxford, Alabama. ⁵It can be said without any exaggeration that he was as sharp as a tack. ⁶At the same time he was one of those rare geniuses who could also communicate with undergraduate college students at their own level. ⁷On a few occasions in his biology class, his students were left behind by his powerful intellect. ⁸However, when the class was perceived to be having trouble following the lesson, Professor Foster stopped in the middle of his sentence, would throw up his hands, cross his eyes, and making unintelligible jabbering sounds until

everyone cracked up. [9]It was in this amusing manner that he offered his apologies to the class for going too fast. [10]He also apologized for being too obscure in his explanations. [11]Then he would retrace his steps. [12]He would find out at what point in time he had lost us in the course of the day's lesson. [13]Being popular was not something that he ever worried about. [14]Popularity was something that came naturally as a result of his concern for students. [15]Popularity also resulted from his ability to explain difficult concepts in an entertaining and memorable way.

PARAGRAPH B

[1]In today's modern society many married women must go above and beyond the call of duty because they are trapped between a rock and a hard place. [2]This trap is between the old-fashioned notion that the responsibilities of keeping the house and rearing the children are primarily woman's work and the financial reality that requires women in the United States to work outside the home in order to supplement their husband's income in order to make ends meet. [3]Too many husbands expect their wives to live up to the ideals of the past as well as meeting the challenges of the present. [4]These husbands aren't willing to accept their fair share of the household chores or helping with child-care duties. [5]Any modern American husband worth his salt should recognize the inequities of the present system. [6]The husband should be willing to meet his wife half way or even go the extra mile in order to relieve his spouse of the extra burden of holding down a job outside the home. [7]The wife also has the burden of keeping the home fires burning. [8]At this point in time, the high divorce rate in this country today is a scourge upon our land, and one of the major contributing factors is the unrealistically high expectations that are placed on women at the sacred altar of marriage.

Chapter Review

- Strategies for avoiding wordiness include the following:
  1. Omitting unnecessary words and meaningless phrases
  2. Using clear and direct language
  3. Avoiding the passive voice, the verb *to be*, and postponed subjects
  4. Changing *which, that,* and *who* clauses to participles.
- Strategies for achieving sentence variety include the following:
  1. Alternating longer sentences with shorter ones
  2. Varying ways of joining ideas
  3. Varying sentence beginnings
- A good writer uses effective figurative comparisons (similes and metaphors) and avoids trite language and clichés.
- A good writer uses parallel structure to avoid awkwardness.

■ Writing Assignment

Pick one of the following topics and write a short descriptive paragraph using fresh comparisons (similes and metaphors) to describe that object or event.

1. Rain falling
2. Fire crackling
3. Wind blowing
4. A child laughing
5. The smell of fresh bread

■ Participating in the Academic Community

Make copies of your descriptive paragraph and work with a small group of your classmates to revise your paragraphs for effective sentence style. Edit carefully to avoid wordiness and triteness and to achieve sentence variety and parallel structure.

Chapter 27

Punctuation and Capitalization

Conventions are standards, or rules, that speakers and writers of a language agree to use to communicate effectively. In order to proofread your writing effectively, you need to be familiar with the conventions of **punctuation** and **capitalization.** This chapter explains rules for using the most common marks of punctuation and rules for capitalization.

Punctuation

The common marks of punctuation are the apostrophe, the comma, the colon, the dash, the period, the question mark, quotation marks, and the semicolon. The primary uses of each of these marks of punctuation are explained in the following sections.

Apostrophe

1. Use an apostrophe to indicate the possessive form of the noun.

   The giraffe's neck is too long.

2. Use an apostrophe for a contraction (examples: *it's, can't, doesn't, wasn't, couldn't*).

(See Chapter 28, pages 421–422, for rules about forming the possessives of nouns.)

Comma

1. Use a comma to *separate* the following:

   a. Two independent clauses connected by a coordinating conjunction

      I took my giraffe for a walk, but my cousin stayed at home with his elephant.

   b. Items in a series

      I would like to adopt an aardvark, a walrus, and a crocodile.

   c. Coordinate adjectives that precede a noun

      A neat, courteous rhinoceros would not be a bad pet either.

   d. An introductory modifier from the main clause, especially if it is long or loosely connected to the rest of the sentence

      Wandering through the zoo last week, I saw several animals that I liked.

   e. Nouns of direct address

      Mary, will you please set the table and put the rolls in the oven.

   f. An introductory adverbial clause from the main clause

      Until we move to a larger house, I guess I'll have to be satisfied with my giraffe and kangaroo.

   g. Items in dates and addresses

      Until then, we'll continue to live at 4321 Animal Crackers Avenue, Beastville, Iowa.

      But by January 1, I hope to move to New York, New York, and rent a large penthouse that will hold as many as fifteen new animals.

2. Use commas to *enclose* the following:

   a. A nonrestrictive adjective clause

      My cousin, who also owns a buffalo, lives in a smaller house.

   b. An appositive

      The buffalo, a large male with an impressive hump on its back, stays in the back yard.

    c. A parenthetical expression or interrupter

       My cousin, of course, is not married.

    d. A noun used in direct address

       "Don't worry, Cousin George. Someday you will find a woman who loves animals."

    e. Expressions designating the speaker in direct quotations

       "I'm not worried," he said, "just lonely."

Colon

1. Use a colon at the end of a sentence to direct attention to a list, summary, or appositive.

    Eventually, George and I would like to own a park that has the following animals: a walrus, a rhinoceros, a crocodile, a sea lion, an aardvark, and a laughing hyena.

2. Use a colon after the salutation of a business letter.

    Dear Ms. Wolf:

3. Use a colon between a title and subtitle, between figures indicating the chapter and verse of a biblical reference, and between the hour and minute of a time reference.

    Adopting Animals: Theory and Practice

    Luke 2:13

    Monday at 4:30 p.m.

Dash

1. Use a dash to mark a sudden break in thought or tone.

    Most animals—notice that I said *most*, not *all*—are friendly and gentle.

2. Use a dash to set off a brief summary or an appositive that is loosely related to the sentence in which it appears.

    My giraffe—the animal I have had longest and that I love best—is named Alfred.

3. Use a dash to set off a parenthetical element or appositive that has commas within it.

I have never met an ugly animal—an animal that I couldn't love, admire, and enjoy.

Period

1. Use a period after a declarative sentence.

A zebra cannot change its stripes.

2. Use a period after an abbreviation (examples: *Mr., Ms., U.S., approx., p.m., a.m.*).

Question Mark

Use a question mark after a direct question.

Does this elephant belong to you?

Quotation Marks

1. Use quotation marks to enclose a direct quotation.

My cousin asked, "Can my elephant get through the door?"

2. Use quotation marks to enclose the title of a short work (story, essay, song, or poem) to which you are referring.

I like the song "Giraffes Are a Man's Best Friend."

(*Note:* Italicize, or underline, the titles of longer works such as books, plays, and movies.)

Dances with Wolves is my favorite movie.

Semicolon

1. To join the two independent clauses, use a semicolon in a compound sentence.

The elephant belongs to my cousin; the giraffe is mine.

2. Use a semicolon with a conjunctive adverb to join two independent clauses in a compound sentence.

The elephant is too wide; however, the giraffe is too tall.

3. Use a semicolon to separate items in a series if the items include internal commas.

The awards were presented to Big Foot, the elephant; Crooked Tusk, the walrus; and Long Neck, the giraffe.

EXERCISE

27.1

Correct the following sentences, providing appropriate punctuation where it is needed.

1. My offer and its my final bid is $200.

2. Please mail the order form to Discount Records 4206 Beverly Street Albany New York 60639.

3. Mr B. W Swanson who was defeated for governor last year will speak at the Boy Scout Annual Banquet

4. Even though Mr Brinkley the most successful salesman insisted on a raise in salary the boss replied Its out of the question.

5. John what is the subject of your paper

6. Ms Cheevers purchased a water hose garden shears and plant food.

7. Before setting a time for the trial Judge Thompsons clerk checked a calendar for a day when his case load was light.

8. Most of the old books were worthless but a first edition of *The Scarlet Letter* turned out to be quite valuable.

9. Mr. Johnson the chief of Fire Station 109 will hold a press conference on Wednesday June 9 at 2 00 p m.

10. The defense lawyer argued a brilliant convincing case but the jury found his client guilty anyway.

27.2

Correct the following sentences, providing appropriate punctuation where it is needed.

1. On July 20 1987 the First National Bank of Orion Tennessee will have been in business for fifty years.

2. After answering the phone Professor Reynolds secretary stated that the report was due today.

3. Dr L M Weber who won the Lions Club Award last year will give the major address.

4. Please address your response to Liz Keller 2208 Peachtree Street Atlanta Georgia 30309

5. The labor organizations usually support the Democratic nominees for national state and local offices

6. When Ms. Russell the new personnel manager asked about the afternoon mail Hal responded Its already here.

7. We lost the Miller account however we gained two new accounts Morton Department Store and the Security National Bank.

8. We have branch offices in the following cities San Francisco California Denver Colorado and Houston Texas.

9. Jason wrote his paper on Stephen Cranes short story The Open Boat.

10. Sharon what score did you make on your last examination

Capitalization

The major rules of capitalization apply to (1) sentences and direct quotations; (2) names of specific people, places, organizations, things, and times; and (3) titles and specific elements of letters.

Sentences and Direct Quotations

1. Capitalize the first word of every sentence.

   The repairman took the television set with him.

2. Capitalize the first word of a direct quotation.

   I said, "We'll leave for the game from my house."

Names of Specific People, Places, Organizations, Things, and Times

1. Capitalize proper nouns. A *proper noun* is the name of a specific person, place, or thing.

   During the 1940s, Ernest Hemingway lived in a village near Havana, Cuba, and often fished from his boat the *Pilar.*

   The Mississippi River is the longest river in the United States.

2. Capitalize adjectives and nouns that are derived from proper nouns.

   The former Soviet Union was dominated by Stalinism during the 1940s.

   She was an expert in Marxist philosophy.

3. Capitalize titles of persons when they precede proper names.

   Senator Smith and Admiral Lacy came to the party for Professor Andrews.

   Ms. Murray called Dr. Brinkman for an appointment.

4. Capitalize names of family members only when used in place of proper names.

   Today Mother called to tell me about my father's trip.

   My mother gave Dad a new fishing rod for his birthday.

5. Capitalize names referring to the people or language of a nation, religion, or race.

   Most of the French and the Spanish who settled Louisiana were Catholic.

   Mary took German and Russian courses to satisfy her foreign language requirements.

6. Capitalize cities, states, and countries and adjectives derived from them.

   On vacation we flew to Paris, France, and then to London, England.

   The bus broke down in Denver, Colorado, on its way to Amarillo, Texas.

   We hope to take an Alaskan cruise next summer.

7. Capitalize organizations such as clubs, churches, corporations, governmental bodies and departments, and political parties.

   The members of the Senate passed a resolution praising the American Cancer Society.

   The J. P. Stone Insurance Company made large contributions to both the Democratic and Republican parties.

8. Capitalize geographical areas. Do not capitalize directions.

   Mark Twain writes about his boyhood adventures in the South.

   Go north when you get to Lee Street.

9. Capitalize brand and commercial names.

   I bought a can of Right Guard deodorant spray at Wal-Mart.

   The Safeway store received new shipments of aspirin, including Bayer and St. Joseph's.

10. Capitalize days of the week and months.

    My birthday, June 9, will fall on a Tuesday this year.

    The annual company Christmas party will be held on Friday, December 23.

    Notice that the names of seasons are *not* capitalized.

    The first Monday in January was the coldest day of winter.

    Last Thursday marked the end of summer and the beginning of autumn.

11. Capitalize abbreviations when the words they stand for would be capitalized.

    My brother transferred to UCLA (University of California, Los Angeles).

    The USMC (United States Marine Corps) has a long, proud tradition.

12. Capitalize only the official title of a particular course unless the course refers to a nationality or language.

My history class for next semester will be History 122.

I hate math and science, but I enjoy my French class.

13. Capitalize the pronoun *I*.

I passed my examination.

Although I worked until two o'clock in the morning, I didn't finish my paper.

Titles and Letters

1. Capitalize the first word and all nouns, verbs, adjectives, and adverbs in the titles of books, plays, articles, movies, songs, and other literary or artistic works. Do not capitalize articles (*a, an,* and *the*), conjunctions, and prepositions.

To Kill a Mockingbird is a famous novel by Harper Lee.

The professor wrote an article entitled "Too Far from the Shore" about Hemingway's *The Old Man and the Sea*.

2. Capitalize the first word in the greeting and complimentary close of a letter. Also capitalize names and titles in the greeting.

Dear Madam, Dear Mr. President, Dear Sir

Sincerely yours, Yours very truly

EXERCISE

27.3

Correct the following sentences, adding capital letters wherever needed and deleting capitals if necessary.

1. The international students organization is planning a pancake sale to raise funds for the victims of the turkish earthquake.

2. The cities of new york, london, and madrid are all popular vacation sites.

3. Some people prefer pepsi or coca-cola, but my favorite soft drink is dr. pepper.

4. Mother cried out, "shut that door, and be quick about it!"

27.3 continued

5. If you begin in san diego, go north to los angeles, head east to st. louis, and then go down to baton rouge, you will be in the south.

6. When I finally got my children to bed, I settled down to read larry mcmurtry's book *lonesome dove.*

7. I live in berry hall, but I spend most of my time in the hall of languages, which is where the english, spanish, and french classes are held.

8. The battle of gettysburg was an important battle for both the north and the south.

9. As we studied in my history 121 class, the mexican war was very important to american history, but it is one of the least studied events in history today.

10. My interest in going to college at the university of Oklahoma is to major in business and computer science.

EXERCISE

27.4

Correct the following sentences, adding capital letters wherever needed and deleting capitals if necessary.

1. The university of Wisconsin played a football game against the nebraska cornhuskers last fall on saturday, october 27, at memorial stadium lincoln, nebraska.

2. Bill doesn't like his french class or his history class, but he enjoys sociology 111.

3. Members of the U.S. house of representatives will fly south on a fact-finding mission to brasília, brazil, and then east to volgograd, russia.

4. When my grandfather was a young man, he and grandma traveled throughout the west selling bottles of a homemade medicine called "fountain of youth serum and colic chaser."

5. Roberta wasn't sure if she should begin her letter to the white house in washington with "Dear sir" or "Dear mr. president."

6. My mother's article about her vacation, which she entitled "Around the world in eight days," was printed in *reader's digest*.

7. "The picnic will be held tomorrow," said ms. wilson, "unless it rains."

8. "Come over and watch the game," Sam said. "the Dallas cowboys are playing football."

9. The winter p.t.a. meeting will be held at jefferson high school on wednesday, january 5, at eight o'clock.

10. My father made A's in english and in math as a freshman in college, and mom got A's in chemistry and european history 251.

EXERCISE

27.5   Correct the following paragraph by adding capitals wherever necessary. (You will need to capitalize twenty-four letters.)

[1]People in the southern part of texas can visit old mexico and stay as long as they wish, but citizens of mexico often find it difficult to visit texas. [2]Because many mexican citizens like to come to south texas not only to visit but also to work, the united states border patrol checks visiting permits very carefully—particularly in the summer months of june, july, and august. [3]why do you suppose this is so? [4]One reason is that during these months many mexican citizens try to stay in texas illegally in order to work for the farmers during this busy season. [5]through its recent amnesty program and its officials, the government discourages such illegal labor because many american citizens believe that these migrant workers deprive them of jobs. [6]Also, although many farmers treat all workers fairly, migrant workers are often the objects of discrimination and cruelty. [7]Such cruelty is described by john steinbeck in his novel *the grapes of wrath*.

Chapter Review

- Effective writers know and use the basic conventions of punctuation and capitalization.

- The common marks of punctuation are the apostrophe, the comma, the colon, the dash, the period, the question mark, quotation marks, and the semicolon.

- Basic rules of capitalization apply to the following:
  1. Sentences and direct quotations
  2. Names of specific people, places, organizations, things, and times
  3. Titles and specific elements of letters

Writing Assignment

Review the rules for punctuation and capitalization in this chapter. Then edit one of your essays, focusing on your punctuation and capitalization. You may also want to write a journal entry identifying the areas of punctuation and capitalization on which you need to concentrate as a writer.

Participating in the Academic Community

After you have revised your essay, work with a small group of your classmates to edit and proofread one another's essays. Focus especially on punctuation and capitalization.

Chapter 28

Spelling

Many talented writers struggle with poor spelling skills, but they work to improve their spelling because they know that misspelled words are distracting to readers. Because misspelled words may even give the impression that the writer is careless or irresponsible, more experienced writers develop ways to improve their spelling and to compensate for their problems. If you have difficulty with spelling, you need to learn how to minimize spelling errors so that your reader is not unduly distracted by them.

Strategies that can help you become a better speller include using your dictionary, using your spell checker, improving your vocabulary, concentrating on your own personal spelling problems, learning the most commonly misspelled words, and learning spelling rules and patterns.

- *Using your dictionary.* You should accept the fact that you will always need to check on the spellings of some words and learn to rely on your dictionary. Remember that you can use a **dictionary** to check a word's definition as well as its spelling so that you can be sure you have both used the word appropriately and spelled it correctly. Keep your dictionary handy and use it during the editing and proofreading stages of your writing process.

- *Using your spell checker.* The **spell checker** that is a feature on most word processors is a fast and convenient way to check the spelling in your document. If you write your papers on a word processor, you should *always* run the spell checker as a part of your final proofreading. Be careful, however, about relying too heavily on this feature. Most spell checkers simply identify words not listed in the computer's database of correct words and then give you options for editing these words. You are still responsible, however, for selecting the correct options. Remember, too, that spell checkers cannot determine when you have used a word with an inappropriate meaning for the context (e.g., *there* for *their*).

- *Improving your vocabulary.* Your spell checker cannot identify misspellings of words that look or sound alike or other misuses of **vocabulary.** Hence, being aware of the meanings of words as you read and write is also important to developing your spelling skills. Each time you learn a new word, be sure that you master its spelling as well as its meaning. You can often determine the meaning of a word from its context, but remember that you can also consult your dictionary when you are unsure of the definition of a word that you encounter in your reading or that you want to use in your writing.

Using your dictionary, using your spell checker, and developing your vocabulary should all help you to improve your spelling. The following techniques, however, will be most helpful in improving your spelling:

- Concentrating on your personal spelling problems
- Learning how to spell the most commonly misspelled words
- Learning basic spelling rules and patterns

The remainder of this chapter concentrates on these three strategies.

Personal Spelling Problems

Students often misspell the same words over and over again. One of the most helpful strategies for improving your spelling is to concentrate on your personal spelling problems. To do this, follow these steps:

1. Keep a list in which you record each misspelling that you discover in your own writing as you edit and proofread your work and as you review your instructor's comments. (If you misspell the same word more than once, record it each time you misspell it.)
2. After you have recorded twenty or more words, review your list.
3. Circle any words that you have misspelled more than once and study these words regularly until you master them.
4. Study each word and its misspelling individually to try to determine why you misspelled it and write a note to help you remember how to spell it correctly. Can you think of a memory device to help you remember the correct spelling? (For example, the adverb of place *there* includes the word *here.*) Does it fit into one of the categories of words listed in the chart on page 408? If so, record the word under the appropriate category.
5. Review your list each week to identify words that you misspell frequently and to analyze the reasons you misspell them.

28.1   The following exercise sheet will help you begin your list, but you will need to continue it in a section of your notebook or journal.

Personal Record of Misspelled Words

CORRECT SPELLING	YOUR MISSPELLING	NOTES

▶ EXAMPLE:

there — *their* — adverb *there* includes *here*

1. _____ _____ _____
2. _____ _____ _____
3. _____ _____ _____
4. _____ _____ _____
5. _____ _____ _____
6. _____ _____ _____
7. _____ _____ _____
8. _____ _____ _____
9. _____ _____ _____
10. _____ _____ _____
11. _____ _____ _____
12. _____ _____ _____
13. _____ _____ _____
14. _____ _____ _____
15. _____ _____ _____
16. _____ _____ _____
17. _____ _____ _____
18. _____ _____ _____
19. _____ _____ _____
20. _____ _____ _____

28.2

Each time you record your misspelled words, analyze the type of error you have made. If the error corresponds to one of the categories on this chart, write the word in the appropriate block. You should soon begin to see a pattern of the types of spelling errors you are making. Study especially those parts of this spelling unit that apply to the types of errors that you make consistently. (*Note:* You may not be able to complete your initial analysis of your spelling errors until you have studied the later sections of this chapter.)

Spelling Error Profile

LOOK-ALIKE/ SOUND-ALIKE WORDS	PROBLEM WORDS	COMPOUND WORDS
PLURALS	**POSSESSIVES**	**FINAL *e* WORDS**
FINAL *y* WORDS	***ei/ie* WORDS**	**DOUBLING FINAL CONSONANT**
OTHER WORDS		

Commonly Misspelled Words

Almost everyone misspells words occasionally, especially difficult words. However, educated people do not misspell common, frequently used words. You can improve your spelling ability by studying the following alphabetized list of words that look and sound alike. In addition, you can improve your spelling by memorizing the lists of commonly misspelled problem words and compound words provided on pages 416–418.

Words That Look and Sound Alike

Some commonly misspelled words are especially difficult because they look or sound like other words with which they can easily be confused. Misuse of some of these words occurs because writers do not know the meanings of the words they are using and therefore use the wrong one, as in using *affect* (verb, meaning "to influence") for *effect* (noun, meaning "result"). Misuse of other look-alike and sound-alike words occurs because writers confuse possessive pronouns, such as *its,* with contractions, such as *it's (it is).*

WORD	CORRECT MEANING/USE
a	article used before a consonant sound *(a* book, *a* lamp)
an	article used before a vowel sound *(an* onion, *an* hour)
accept	to receive (I *accept your* apology.)
except	not included (Everyone *except* the teacher laughed.)
advice (noun)	an opinion as to what should or should not be done (Your *advice* was helpful.)
advise (verb)	to recommend or suggest; to inform or notify (Please *advise* your employer that his *advice* was appreciated.)
affect (verb)	to have an influence on (The illness *affected* his mind.)
effect (noun)	a result or consequence (What *effect* will the new law have?)
a lot	a large amount, many (two words; not *alot)*
already	previously or by this time; one word (Summer is *already* here.)
all ready	completely prepared; two words (I am *all ready* to go.)

WORD	CORRECT MEANING/USE
are	present tense form of *to be;* used with you, *we*, and *they* and plural nouns (You and they *are* free to go, but we *are* required to stay.)
our	possessive pronoun (We lost *our* way.)
or	coordinating conjunction (Joe *or* I will stay with you.)
capital (noun)	a city; a sum of money (Legislators in Austin, the *capital* of Texas, control the flow of *capital* in the state.)
capital (adjective)	chief or excellent (What a *capital* suggestion!)
capitol	a building where legislative sessions are held (The state *capitol* has a large dome.)
conscience	knowledge of right and wrong (Your *conscience* should hurt you.)
conscious	aware or alert (Was he *conscious* after the accident?)
complement	to make complete (Her blond hair *complemented* her tan.)
compliment (verb)	to praise (He *complimented* her tan.)
compliment (noun)	an expression of praise (She gave him a *compliment.*)
council	an assembly of persons called together for consultation or deliberation (The student *council* met with the faculty.)
counsel	advice or guidance, especially from a knowledgeable person (She sought the *counsel* of her minister and school counselor.)
coarse	low or common, of inferior quality or lacking in refinement; not fine in texture (That cake has a *coarse* texture.)
course	route or path taken; regular development or orderly succession; a prescribed unit of study (In the *course* of a year, twelve new buildings were built.)
of course	naturally, without doubt (*Of course, I* will.)
dessert	what is eaten at the end of a meal (I like ice cream for *dessert.*)
desert (verb)	to leave; to abandon (The father *deserted* his son.)
desert (noun)	land area characterized by sand and lack of water (The camel is used for transportation in the *desert.*)

WORD	CORRECT MEANING/USE
fill	to make full (Please *fill* the dog's water dish.)
feel	to experience; to touch (I didn't *feel* very happy.)
fourth	number 4 in sequence (We are *fourth* in line.)
forth	onward; in view; forward in place or time (Please step *forth*.)
idea (noun)	a thought, mental image, or conception (My *idea* would be helpful.)
ideal (adjective)	perfect; without flaw (The gulf is an *ideal* place to fish.)
ideal (noun)	a standard or model of perfection (Her teacher was her *ideal*.)
imply	to suggest; to express indirectly (The candidate *implied* that the opponent had lied.)
infer	to conclude, as on the basis of suggestion or implication (A reader *infers* from what has been written.)
its	possessive pronoun meaning "belonging to it" (Virtue is *its* own reward.)
it's	contraction meaning "it is" or "it has" (*It's* a shame you are sick.)
knew	past tense of *to know* (He *knew* the name of the song.)
new	not old (She was *new* in town.)
know	to be mentally aware of (Do you *know* the answer?)
no	opposite of *yes;* not any (That is *no* way to treat a lady.)
lie	to recline (The book *lies* unopened on the table.)
lay	to place (Please *lay* the book on the table.)
	Note: The past tense of *lie is lay;* the past tense of *lay is laid.*
loose (adjective)	not tight; unfastened (The car has a *loose* wheel.)
lose (verb)	to allow to get away; to misplace (Did you *lose* your umbrella?)
mine (pronoun)	possessive pronoun meaning "belonging to me" (That book is *mine.)*
mind (noun)	mental capacity (Your *mind* can play tricks on you.)
mind (verb)	to obey (You should *mind* your mother.)

WORD	CORRECT MEANING/USE
passed (verb)	past tense of *to pass* (The train *passed* through the town.)
past (noun)	former times or belonging to former times (It is easy to forget the *past*.)
past (preposition)	beyond in time or position (The burglar slipped *past* the guard.)
peace	opposite of war; tranquillity (The U.N. was determined to keep the *peace*.)
piece	a part of something (May I have a *piece* of cake?)
personal (adjective)	of or pertaining to a particular person; private (Is this a *personal* call?)
personnel (noun)	those employed by an organization or business (He was referred to the *personnel* department.)
principal (noun)	a governing officer of a school (The *principal* of our high school is Mr. Drake.)
	a sum of money on which interest is calculated (I was able to pay the interest on my loan but not the *principal*.)
principal (adjective)	first in importance (The *principal* actor in the play was ill.)
principle	a fundamental truth, law, or doctrine; a rule of conduct (Mr. Adams is a man of *principle*.)
quiet	not noisy (The library was unusually *quiet.)*
quite	somewhat or rather (The girl was *quite* shocked by the remark.)
rise	to ascend; to move upward (The sun *rises* in the east.)
raise	to lift or cause something to move upward (He wants to *raise* his grades in French class.)
sight	a spectacle; view; scene (The *sight* of the mountains awed him.)
site	a location (They chose a new *site* for the building.)
cite	to quote or use as evidence (He *cited* me as an authority.)
sit	to assume a seated position (Please *sit* in that chair.)
set	to place something (Please *set* the chair by the window.)
than	used in a comparison (Ray is faster *than* George.)
then	at that time (Can you leave *then?*)

WORD	CORRECT MEANING/USE
there	an adverb of place (*There* is our room.)
their	possessive pronoun meaning "belonging to them" (Where is *their* living room?)
they're	contraction of *they are* (*They're* in that room.)
threw	past tense of *to throw* (They *threw* the frisbee across the room.)
through	in one side and out the other; by way of (It went *through* the rear window.)
though	despite; commonly used with *as* or *even* (He looked as *though* he were exhausted.)
to	used as a preposition (*to* the stars) or with a verb as an infinitive (*to* go)
too	also; to an excessive degree (The car was *too* crowded for him to go, *too*.)
two	the number 2 (The child was *two* years old.)
weather	the state of the atmosphere (The *weather* is expected to turn cold.)
whether	if it is the case that; in case (I'm not sure *whether* he is going.)
who's	a contraction meaning "who is" or "who has" (*Who's* there?)
whose	a possessive pronoun meaning "belonging to whom" (*Whose* car are we taking?)
your	possessive pronoun meaning "belonging to you" (I like *your* idea.)
you're	contraction meaning "you are" (*You're* wrong about that!)

EXERCISE

28.3   Choose the correct word in parentheses to complete each of the following sentences.

1. Your (conscious, conscience) should hurt you for defending the robber. The motorists were still (conscious, conscience) after the accident.

2. There's (a, an) antelope in my yard. I was expecting (a, an) moose. The antelope has eaten (alot, a lot) of grass.

28.3 continued

3. The letter (implied, inferred) that he had not paid his phone bill.

   I (implied, inferred) from that remark that he wouldn't be able to balance the budget.

4. My pet elephant (rises, raises) slowly in the mornings.

   She has (risen, raised) two baby elephants.

5. A rabbit is (lose, loose) in my garden.

   I would hate to (lose, loose) all that lettuce.

6. He asked a (personal, personnel) question about my love life.

   He asked if I ever dated any of the (personal, personnel) at the office.

7. If (your, you're) not careful, she'll make you a member of her committee.

   Why didn't you answer (your, you're) phone when he called?

8. (Who's, Whose) elephant is this?

   (Who's, Whose) going to feed it and housebreak it?

9. (Its, It's) difficult to make up for lost time.

   Can a zebra change (its, it's) stripes?

10. I will eat any vegetable (accept, except) okra.

    Will you (accept, except) a collect call from your son?

EXERCISE

28.4

Choose the correct word in parentheses to complete each of the following sentences.

1. She always pays her bills on the (fourth, forth) day of the month.

   The soldier stepped (fourth, forth) eagerly.

2. That (knew, new) song is simply atrocious.

   The student (knew, new) all the answers.

3. Be sure to (site, sight, cite) the source of your quotation.

   The sunset was a beautiful (site, sight, cite).

   The architect will meet us at the building (site, sight, cite).

4. Even (through, threw, though) the boy (through, threw, though) the ball with force, it did not go (through, threw, though) the window.

5. The actress gave (quiet, quite) a performance.

The audience was (quiet, quite) throughout the play.

28.5

Choose the correct word in parentheses to complete the following sentences.

1. The zoo had more monkeys (than, then) it knew what to do with.

First he took out his harmonica; (than, then) he began to play.

2. (There, They're, Their) fun-loving people.

The fishermen mended (there, they're, their) nets every night.

(There, They're, Their) is the spot where I had my wreck.

3. I went (too, two, to) the store (too, two, to) buy some candy for Uncle Monroe.

Uncle Monroe eats (too, two, to) much candy; Aunt Sophie does (too, two, to).

The (too, two, to) of them really love candy.

4. I will (lie, lay) my books on the sofa.

Then I will (lie, lay) down and rest for a while.

5. My pet monkey was (sitting, setting) in my favorite chair.

He was watching me (sit, set) the table for dinner.

28.6

Choose the correct spelling of each word in parentheses to complete the following letter:

Dear Mr. Jones:

We regretfully (accept, except) (you're, your) resignation, which you plan to submit to our (personal, personnel) office next month.

(You're, Your) leaving will (effect, affect) our entire organization.

I hope that your (advice, advise) and (council, counsel) will continue to be available to us after your retirement.

28.6 continued

I realize that (personal, personnel) reasons force you (to, two, too) take this step, but I certainly do hate to (loose, lose) such an (idea, ideal) employee. Your (principal, principle) contribution has been your patience and (conscience, conscious) effort to be a good employee. Of (coarse, course), I will miss your (personnel, personal) friendship also.

Many years have (past, passed) since you first came to work at Smith & Smith, Inc. (Your, You're) going to miss our organization, and we are certainly going to miss you.

(Its, It's) with sincere regret that I see you leave.

Sincerely yours,

J. R. Smith

J. R. Smith
President

Additional Problem Words

Although, as a rule, spelling lists are practically useless in improving spelling skills, a few words are so consistently misspelled by students that it is worth your time to master them. Notice, as you look at this list of problem spelling words, that many are misspelled because they are often not pronounced correctly. The words are divided into syllables, with the accented syllables marked so you can check your pronunciation. Say the words aloud as you study them. If you are saying the words incorrectly, try to correct your pronunciation. Pay particular attention to the boldfaced letters because that is the part of the word that usually causes the spelling error.

athlete (ath´ lete)—two syllables, not three, not ath**e**lete
diff**er**ent (dif´ fer ent)—three syllables, not two
enviro**n**ment (en vi´ ron ment)—notice the *n*
Feb**r**uary (Feb´ ru ar y)—notice the *r*
fin**a**lly (fi´ nal ly)—three syllables, not two
gover**n**ment (gov´ ern ment)—notice the *n*
gramm**ar** (gram´ mar)—ends in *ar* not *er*
int**e**rest (in´ ter est)—three syllables, not two
lib**r**ary (li´ brar y)—notice the *r*
list**e**ning (lis´ ten ing)—three syllables, not two
prob**a**bly (prob´ a bly)—three syllables, not two
qu**ie**t (qui´ et)—two syllables, not one; do not confuse with *quite*

recognize (rec´ og nize)—notice the *g*

sep**a**rate (sep´ a rate)—middle vowel is *a* not *e*

simil**ar** (sim´ i lar)—last syllable is *lar* not *ler* or *liar*

soph**o**more (soph´ o more)—three syllables, not two; notice the *o*

suppos**ed** (sup posed´)—don't forget the *d* if you are using past tense (*He was supposed to call.*)

us**ed** (used)—don't forget the *d* if you are using past tense (*I used to sing.*)

EXERCISE

28.7   Underline each of the twelve misspelled words and write the correct spelling above it.

1. Mrs. Rodriguez is suppose to speak at the city council meeting.

2. The coaches at our college are establishing a program to promote scholarship among our atheletes.

3. I detest grammer, don't you?

4. Are you going to the libary to study tonight?

5. Yes, I probly will study for my history test in the study room where it is quite.

6. I will be a sophmore next semester if I pass all of my final exams.

7. The speaker at the symposium next week will talk about enviromental problems.

8. I hope he gives an intresting lecture.

9. Wasn't last year's symposium theme similiar to this year's?

10. Yes, but this year we are focusing on what the goverment and separate individuals can do to solve these problems.

Compound Words

Many words are formed in English by a process known as *compounding.* That is, a new word is made by combining two familiar words. *Truck stop,* for example, is a relatively new compound that is still written as two words.

The tendency, however, is for compound words to be written (eventually) as one word, as in *hangover, handbook, babysitter,* and *typewriter.* Historically, a compound word is initially written as two words, then as a hyphenated word, and finally as one word. For example, *week end* became *week-end* and then *weekend.* Recently, the trend has been for compound words to change from two words to one without going through the hyphenated stage.

Most compound words are easy to spell because they are made up of two familiar words. However, it is sometimes difficult to remember whether the compound is written as one word or two. Occasionally, also, the spelling of the compound word is altered slightly when it becomes one word. Thus, the word *although* is spelled with one *l* in *all* rather than two.

The following categories of compound words will help you remember whether the compounds in them should be written as one word or two. However, you should consult your dictionary if you are in doubt.

1. Compound words spelled as two words

   a lot, all right (These two words are frequently misspelled as one word rather than two.)

2. Hyphenated compound words
   a. *mother-in-law, son-in-law,* etc.
   b. *self-concept, self-image, self-hypnosis* (all compounds beginning with *self*)
   c. *ex-husband, ex-wife, ex-president,* etc.
   d. *pro-Communist, pro-abortion,* etc.

3. Compound words spelled as one word
   a. *everybody, somebody, anything, everyone, someone, something, anybody, sometime, anyplace, someplace,* etc.
   b. *whenever, wherever, whatever, whichever,* etc.
   c. *although, altogether, always, already, almost* (Note that each of these compound words has only one *l*.)
   d. *moreover, therefore, however, nonetheless*

EXERCISE

28.8   Ten compound words are misspelled in the following sentences. Underline these words and correct them in the spaces provided.

1. Do you remember the old song "Every body Loves Some body Some time"?

2. Yes, my exhusband Robert used to sing it to me when ever we had a quarrel.

_____

3. You all ways had alot of trouble with that marriage, didn't you?

_____

4. Yes, I hated his singing, and he hated his mother in law.

_____

5. Well, your self concept certainly has improved all right since your divorce!

_____

EXERCISE

28.9

Proofread the following paragraph for problems with commonly misspelled words. Underline each misspelled word and write the correct spelling above it. (You will find twenty-two different misspelled words in the passage. Two words are each misspelled twice, for a total of twenty-four mispellings.)

[1]The school and city goverment officials that are choosing the cite for the new football stadium are involved in a serious controversy. [2]The principle, the coaches, the atheletes, and alot of parents want to put the stadium on the edge of the city where it's enviroment will be pieceful and quite. [3]However, every body on the city counsel, including the exmayor, would like to put the field beside the high school and save the residential area for a new public libary. [4]The city counsel members argue that increased traffic will have a negative affect on the residential area, but the school officials argue that the new cite will have more room for a seperate parking lot that will be better in bad whether conditions. [5]Before a decision is reached, both groups are suppose to ask the advise of the city zoning officer. [6]At that point, the too groups will have to meet and determine what is in the best intrest of the city as a whole. [7]Their calling a meeting for tomorrow night in the Civic Center to announce there decision.

Spelling Rules and Patterns

Although some spelling rules are so complicated or have so many exceptions that they are not worth learning, a few spelling rules and patterns actually do work most of the time and can therefore be quite helpful. Included in this section are the rules for forming the plurals of nouns, the rules for forming the possessives of nouns and pronouns, and four of the most useful spelling patterns.

Forming the Plurals of Nouns

By far the most common way to change a singular noun to a plural noun is to add *s* (*car, cars; feeling, feelings; note, notes*). Several other rules for the formation of plurals, however, can be helpful.

1. To form the plurals of words that end with an *s* sound (*s, x, z, ch, sh*), add *es* (*boss, bosses; fox, foxes; buzz, buzzes; ditch, ditches; dish, dishes*).

2. To form the plurals of words that end in *y* preceded by a single vowel, add just an *s* (*tray, trays; key, keys; toy, toys; guy, guys*). But to form the plurals of words that end in *y* preceded by a consonant, change the *y* to *i* and add *es* (*baby, babies; enemy, enemies*).

3. To form the plurals of words that end in *is*, change the *is* to *es* (*basis, bases; analysis, analyses; synopsis, synopses*).

4. To form the plurals of some words that end in *f* or *fe*, change the *f* to *v* and add *es* (*leaf, leaves; knife, knives; wife, wives; loaf, loaves; self, selves*).

5. To form the plurals of words that end in *o*, add *s* or *es*. The plurals of many of these words can be formed either way; with some, however, there is no choice. The following clues are helpful in determining which ending some words require:
   a. To form the plurals of words that end in a vowel plus *o* (*ao, eo, io, oo, uo*), add just an *s* (*stereo, stereos; duo, duos; studio, studios*).
   b. To form the plurals of musical terms that end in *o*, add just an *s* (*piano, pianos; solo, solos; combo, combos; cello, cellos*).
   c. To form the plurals of *tomato* and *potato*, add *es* (*tomato, tomatoes; potato, potatoes*).

   To determine whether other words that end in *o* require an *s* or *es*, check your dictionary.

6. Some words form the plural irregularly by changing internally rather than by adding *s* or *es* (*man, men; woman, women; child, children; mouse, mice; foot, feet*).

7. Some words have the same form in both the singular and the plural (*fish, moose, sheep, deer*).

EXERCISE

28.10   Change the following singular nouns to plural nouns. (Check your dictionary if in doubt.)

1. radio   _____
2. teacher   _____
3. dish   _____
4. beauty   _____
5. leaf   _____

6. thesis   _____
7. fox   _____
8. alley   _____
9. theory   _____
10. foot   _____

EXERCISE

28.11   Change the following singular nouns to plural nouns.

1. friend   _____
2. joy   _____
3. tomato   _____
4. ally   _____
5. industry   _____

6. church   _____
7. thief   _____
8. crisis   _____
9. dress   _____
10. wife   _____

Forming Possessives

Both nouns and pronouns have possessive forms, but the rules for forming possessive nouns and pronouns differ.

Possessive Nouns

Failure to indicate correctly that a noun is possessive causes many needless spelling errors. The rules for forming the possessive are regular and easy to apply.

1. To form the possessive of a singular noun, add an apostrophe and an *s* (*'s*) to the noun.

   George's car was in the garage.

   My **boss's** hat is ridiculous.

   Today's mail needs to be sorted.

   Notice that it does not matter what letter the noun ends in; all singular nouns form the possessive by the addition of an apostrophe and an *s* to the noun.

Note: The rule for forming the singular possessive is presently in some dispute. If the singular noun ends in an *s,* some writers add just an apostrophe after the *s.* Others believe that only if the singular noun is a proper noun of one syllable may you omit the *s* and add just the apostrophe. To avoid confusion and controversy, it is better to apply the simple rule of adding *'s* to all singular nouns, regardless of their final letter or whether they are common or proper.

2. To form the possessive of a plural noun that does not end in an *s,* also add an apostrophe and an *s* (*'s*) to the noun.

The **children's** coats were unbuttoned.

He looked into the **deer's** eyes.

The **women's** club is meeting in the auditorium.

3. However, to form the possessive of a plural noun that ends in *s,* add just an apostrophe after the *s* (*'s*).

The **cats'** tails have all been cut off.

Dust covered the **books'** covers.

The **boys'** teachers were invited to the meeting.

Now review the steps in forming the possessive of a noun:

1. Determine if the noun is possessive.
2. Determine if the noun is singular or plural.
3. Apply the appropriate rule.

Possessive Pronouns

The possessive pronouns are *my, mine, your, yours, our, ours, his, her, hers, their, theirs, its,* and *whose.*

My dress is torn.

That book is **hers.**

The tree has shed **its** leaves.

Do they want **their** papers returned?

Notice that possessive pronouns *do not* require apostrophes. Rather than adding an apostrophe and *s* or just an apostrophe, as you do in forming the possessive of nouns, you form the possessive of pronouns by changing the word itself. Thus the pronoun *I* changes to *my* or *mine; we* becomes *our* or *ours; you* becomes *your* or *yours,* and so on.

Note: Four possessive pronouns (*its, your, their,* and *whose*) are pronounced exactly the same as four contractions (*it's, you're, they're,* and *who's*), which do require apostrophes. *It's* is a contraction of *it is: you're* is a contraction of *you are; they're* is a contraction of *they are;* and *who's* is a contraction of who is. Be careful in your writing not to confuse the contraction with the possessive form. (See also pages 347 and 410–413.)

EXERCISE

28.12   Some nouns in the following sentences should be possessive. Rewrite correctly any noun that requires the possessive form. Write *C* if no nouns in the sentence need to be changed to the possessive form.

1. My sisters have all gotten married.

   _____

2. My brothers wife was in a terrible accident yesterday.

   _____

3. My brothers wives are both in school.

   _____

4. The realities of the situation must be faced.

   _____

5. My fathers attitudes about education differ from mine.

   _____

6. All politicians promises are worthless.

   _____

7. The waiters served the food skillfully.

   _____

8. Several students papers had been plagiarized.

   _____

9. Is this car yours or your best friends?

   _____

10. Dr. Johnsons secretary took the message.

   _____

28.13

Use each of the following nouns in three sentences. In the first sentence use the noun as a singular possessive; in the second sentence use the same noun as a plural possessive; in the third sentence make the noun plural but not possessive.

1. uncle

   a. *singular possessive* _____

   _____

   b. *plural possessive* _____

   _____

   c. *plural* _____

   _____

2. nation

   a. *singular possessive* _____

   _____

   b. *plural possessive* _____

   _____

   c. *plural* _____

   _____

3. child

   a. *singular possessive* _____

   _____

   b. *plural possessive* _____

   _____

   c. *plural* _____

   _____

4. waitress

   a. *singular possessive* _____

   _____

b. *plural possessive* _____

_____

c. *plural* _____

_____

5. newspaper

a. *singular possessive* _____

_____

b. *plural possessive* _____

_____

c. *plural* _____

_____

EXERCISE

28.14   Choose the correct word in parentheses to complete each of the following sentences.

1. (Its, It's) (their, they're) car that was in the accident.

2. (Its, It's) body was in need of repair.

3. Where are (your, you're) books?

4. (Their, They're) there on the chair.

5. (They're, Their) not very happy about being there.

6. This is (they're, their) last visit; you can be sure of that.

7. (Your, You're) going to have to stay up late tonight to finish (your, you're) paper.

8. (Their, They're) teacher is Mr. Jones.

9. (Their, They're) in big trouble about taking (their, they're) father's car without permission.

10. (Its, It's) an important meeting for the entire university.

28.15

Add apostrophes where needed in the following sentences. Write *C* if no apostrophes are needed.

1. The boys hat was on the chair.

2. Its not her fault.

3. Two weeks vacation is provided by our company.

4. The Continental Mens Shop is having a sale on sport coats.

5. The childrens section of the library is always crowded.

6. Viewing the Pacific Ocean with Balboas crew would have been exciting.

7. Grandmothers new house was designed by a famous architect.

8. Was the colonists desire for equal representation the cause of the American Revolution?

9. The expansion of Napoleons army over Europe posed a threat to England in the nineteenth century.

10. His novels are widely read by the general reading public.

11. A students study time is often reduced by the pressure of social activities.

12. The reward is ours.

13. Theyre late again.

14. The snake has shed its skin.

15. The Filipinos government is based on that of the United States.

28.16

Proofread the following paragraph for problems with the spellings of plurals and possessives. Underline each misspelled word and write the correct spelling above it. You will find fifteen different misspelled words.

[1]Local police officers' announced on the 10:00 p.m. news last night that a series of attempted robberys and arsones had taken place in our cities high school. [2]The superintendents statement will be printed in tomorrow mornings' newspapers, but he wants to reassure parents that all student's books and other belongings' will be safe. [3]Thus far, the thiefs have only broken into the hall of the building, so they haven't been able to get inside the teachers classrooms. [4]A few matchez were found beside one group of lockers' but the night guard scared the vandal's away into the back alleys before any harm was done. [5]Several theorys are being considered to determine the cause of the problem, but until the situation is resolved, students should take they're valuables home each afternoon.

Useful Spelling Patterns

There are no simple rules that will eliminate all spelling problems, but knowing the following spelling patterns will help you improve your spelling.

Dropping or Keeping Final e

1. To add a suffix beginning with a vowel to a word ending in a final *e*, drop the silent *e* (*usage, safest, caring*).

   EXCEPTIONS

   Words that have a *c* or *g* before the final *e* keep the *e* before the suffixes *-able* and *-ous* (*noticeable, courageous, changeable, advantageous, peaceable*).

2. To add a suffix beginning with a consonant to a word ending in a final *e*, keep the silent *e* (*lovely, useless, safely*).

   EXCEPTIONS

   a. Words ending in *ue* drop the final *e* before a suffix beginning with a consonant (*argument, duly, truly*).
   b. awe + ful = awful
   c. whole + ly = wholly

28.17

Apply the spelling pattern for dropping or keeping final *e* to the following words. Some of the words are exceptions to the pattern.

1. change + able   _____
2. come + ing   _____
3. service + able   _____
4. shine + ing   _____
5. fame + ous   _____
6. scarce + ly   _____
7. write + ing   _____
8. use + ing   _____

9.   simple + ly   _____
10. resource + ful _____
11. argue + ment   _____
12. care + less   _____
13. complete + ly   _____
14. love + ly   _____
15. guide + ance   _____

Final y

1. To add a suffix not beginning with an *i* to a word that ends in *y* preceded by a consonant, change the *y* to *i* (*happiness, copier, cried*).

2. To add a suffix to a word that ends in *y* preceded by a vowel (*a, e, i, o, u*), do not change the *y* to *i* (*employer, keys, enjoyment*).

3. To add a suffix beginning with an *i* to a word that ends in *y*, do not change the *y* to *i* (*copying, fortyish, playing*).

EXCEPTIONS: *daily, gaily, paid, said, laid, shyly, shyness, slyly, slyness, dryly, dryer* (the machine), all proper nouns (*Kennedy + s = Kennedys; Harry + s = Harrys*)

28.18

Apply the spelling pattern for final *y* to the following words. Watch for exceptions.

1. survey + ed   _____
2. pity + ed   _____
3. monkey + s   _____
4. happy + ness   _____
5. accompany + es   _____
6. shy + ly   _____
7. enjoy + able   _____
8. study + ing   _____

9.   hurry + ed   _____
10. defy + ance   _____
11. lay + ed   _____
12. day + ly   _____
13. beauty + ful   _____
14. wealthy + er   _____
15. twenty + ish   _____

ei/ie *Words*

1. The *i* comes before the *e* if a *c* does not immediately precede it (*believe, niece, yield*).

2. The *e* comes before the *i* if these letters are immediately preceded by a *c* (*receive, deceit, ceiling*).

3. If the sound of *ei/ie* is a long *a*, the *e* comes before the *i* (*vein, weight, neighbor*).

This pattern is most often stated in the form of this familiar rhyme:

Write *i* before *e*
Except after *c*
Or when sounded as *a*
As in *neighbor* and *weigh*.

EXCEPTIONS: There are a number of exceptions to this rule. Concentrate on remembering the five most common: *either, neither, seize, weird,* and *leisure.*

EXERCISE

28.19

Apply the spelling pattern for *ei/ie* words to the following sentences. Again, watch for exceptions.

1. I cannot be____ve that she is so conc____ted.

2. The fr____ght train was long and slow.

3. The president is also commander in ch____f of our armed forces.

4. Will the parents y____ld to the kidnappers' demands?

5. They will s____ze him when he returns.

6. How much do these apples w____gh?

7. His reputation as a th____f followed him everywhere.

8. She gave a p____ce of candy to her little brother.

9. The victims were nearly dead when rel____f came.

10. The blood in his v____ns ran cold at the sight.

28.19 continued

11. The r_____gn of the queen was br_____f.

12. They ach_____ved more than _____ther had expected.

13. In the darkness, she could barely perc_____ve the wire strung across the c_____ling.

14. The for_____gn students attended the rally.

15. N_____ther of the students who failed the course was allowed to graduate.

Doubling the Final Consonant

Double the final consonant when adding a suffix beginning with a vowel if the word ends in a single consonant preceded by a single vowel and meets either of the following additional criteria:

1. It consists of only one syllable (examples: *bigger, dimmer*).
2. It is accented on the last syllable (examples: *referred, occurred*).

Note: Some exceptions exist for this pattern (*beginning*), and some words have two acceptable spellings (*benefited, benefitted*).

EXERCISE

28.20

Apply the rule for doubling the final consonant to the following words.

1. forgot + ten   _____
2. counsel + ing   _____
3. drop + ed   _____
4. commit + ment   _____
5. begin + ing   _____
6. hope + ing   _____
7. occur + ence   _____
8. plan + ing   _____

9. equip + ment   _____
10. compel + ed   _____
11. hit + ing   _____
12. refer + ence _____
13. honor + able _____
14. refer + ed   _____
15. hinder + ed   _____

28.21

Underline each misspelled word in the following paragraph and write the correct spelling above it. If you are unsure whether a word is spelled correctly, review the four useful spelling patterns on pages 427–430. You will find twenty different misspelled words in the passage.

[1]Last summer when I visited Walden Pond in Concord, Massachusetts, I was shocked at what has happened to the place. [2]In writting his book *Walden*, Henry David Thoreau had produced a classic arguement for living simply. [3]As I was driveing to Concord, I beleived I would find a beautyful, clear, and peacful lake. [4]I expected this body of water to be several miles from the closest nieghbor or other intruder, just as Thoreau had described it in his book. [5]As I hurryed to veiw this literary shrine, I remembered Thoreau's description of the battle and seige of the ants, the playfullness of the loon on the pond, and the beauty of the ice cakes as they were loaded onto horse-drawn sledes. [6]I also remembered the lovly arrangment of the viens of the leafs caught in the ice. [7]I was totaly shocked to find the pond filled with bathers and swimers who didn't even know who Thoreau was. [8]I left Walden Pond angryer than I had been in a long time.

Chapter Review

- Misspelled words are distracting to readers and may give a negative impression of the writer.

- Strategies for improving your spelling include using your dictionary, using your spell checker, and improving your vocabulary.

- The three most helpful strategies to improve your spelling are the following:
  1. Concentrate on your own personal spelling problems by keeping a list of the words you misspell and analyzing this list to determine the kinds of spelling problems you have.
  2. Learn to spell the most commonly misspelled words, including words that look and sound alike, special problem words, and compound words.
  3. Use the spelling rules for forming plurals and possessives of nouns.
  4. Apply the spelling patterns for final silent *e*, for final *y*, for *ei/ie* words, and for doubling the final consonant;

Writing Assignment

Edit one or more of your essays for spelling problems. Then review the spelling problems that you and your instructor have discovered in your work. Record your misspelled words on the sheets provided for you in this chapter, and then analyze your spelling habits, strengths, and weaknesses in a journal entry. What spelling problems occur regularly in your own writing? Before reading this chapter, how did you handle these problems? In your opinion, which of the suggestions in this chapter will be most helpful to you? Which will be the least helpful?

Participating in the Academic Community

Meet with a small group of your classmates to analyze and discuss your spelling problems and compare your ideas about which strategies will be most helpful to you in improving your spelling. You might even compare your personal spelling list with those of your classmates. What spelling problems do you have in common? What spelling problems are unique to each of you?

Part Four

Critical Reading Strategies

While this book has focused primarily on writing skills thus far, as a college student, you will discover that reading and writing skills go hand in hand. That is, you cannot be a good writer unless you are a good reader or a good reader unless you are a good writer. Thus, this unit focuses on critical reading skills.

You use critical reading skills in almost every college course. Reading critically means being an active reader who engages in a dialogue with the text. It means being aware of the writer who produced the text and identifying main ideas, distinguishing between fact and opinion, evaluating sources and evidence, and reaching your own conclusions about what you read.

In order to be an effective critical reader, you must first be able to comprehend what you read. You can improve your reading comprehension by using the following strategies:

- Preview the selection to be read, focusing on the introduction, topic sentences, headings, illustrations, and conclusion. This preview will not only provide you with an overview of the selection but will also enable you to form a general idea of its important points.
- Read the selection carefully, annotating the text freely as you read.
- Review the selection to reinforce your comprehension and to be sure you have identified the writer's main points.
- Respond to the selection in some way—ideally, in writing.

In order to read critically you must also be able to outline and summarize what you read. Part Four includes chapters that address these important skills. Finally, because success in essay examinations demands strong reading and writing skills, Part Four ends with a chapter on strategies for taking essay exams.

Chapter 29

Strategies for Reading Critically

Being a good reader involves more than comprehending and retaining what you read. In addition, you need to be able to *evaluate* what you read—in other words, to read critically. Reading critically means reading not only the words on the page but between the lines and even beyond the page.

Developing Critical Reading Skills

Reading critically is primarily a habit of mind acquired through years of practice. To read critically, you must become a skeptic, evaluating the accuracy, value, and relevance of what you read and questioning the intentions and credibility of the author. Although no simple rules exist for becoming an effective critical reader, the following strategies will guide you in learning to read more critically and will help you develop the skills essential to critical reading:

1. *Understand the writer's purpose.* It has been said that "learning to read is learning that you have been written to" (Deborah Brandt, *Literacy as Involvement: The Acts of Writers, Readers, and Texts* [Carbondale, IL: Southern Illinois UP, 1990], p. 5). In other words, readers become *critical* readers when they realize that the writer behind the text is as important as the text itself. Of course, you may not always know much about the writers of the texts you read. Your textbooks, for example, are probably written by people you have never heard of. How can you know a writer who is just a name to you?

All writers reveal themselves in certain ways in their texts. It is up to you to discover the clues that will tell you what you need to know about the author of the text you are reading. First, you need to identify the writer's purpose—why he or she is writing this particular text. People obviously write for lots of different reasons, but some of the more common purposes for writing include the following:

- To express themselves
- To remember information
- To learn
- To amuse
- To reconstruct past experiences
- To communicate
- To inform
- To instruct
- To record information
- To evaluate
- To persuade

Knowing *why* someone wrote something—what he or she hoped to accomplish by writing a particular text—will help you evaluate it. For example, if a writer's purpose is to instruct, you should not complain if the text is not entertaining. On the other hand, if a writer's purpose is to amuse or entertain, you should not expect the text to be informative or useful. Determining the writer's purpose is a good first step when you are doing a critical reading of a text.

Although people write for a variety of purposes, in one sense all writing is persuasive. Some writing is clearly and openly persuasive (editorials, propaganda, recommendation reports). Other writing is less obviously persuasive but still includes arguments (narratives, instructions, textbooks). It is up to you as a reader to recognize the persuasive nature of a text whether or not the writer states this purpose overtly.

2. *Understand the writer's main idea.* Inexperienced readers often confuse a writer's purpose with his or her thesis, but the two are not the same. A writer's *purpose* is the reason the text was written; a writer's *thesis* is the controlling argument of the text. For example, a writer's purpose may be to persuade, but his or her thesis may be something like *Technology has robbed us of our privacy as individuals and citizens.*

Although not all writers place the thesis statement in the introduction, most writers—especially writers of textbooks, newspapers, magazines, and reports—include in their introduction a thesis statement that explains clearly the point they wish to make. It is a good idea, therefore, to read the introduction very carefully, looking especially for the thesis statement. Since everything else in the essay will be related to the thesis, you must identify it before you can understand the essay as a whole.

Occasionally, a writer will not include a thesis statement. Just as a paragraph may have an implied rather than a stated topic sentence, an essay may have an implied rather than a stated thesis. Nevertheless, every essay has a controlling idea. If there is no stated thesis, you should formulate in your own words what you think the writer's thesis is.

29.1

Read the following paragraph carefully, and then state the main idea in your own words.

> Once upon a time, college students needed little more than a pen or pencil and some paper to be prepared for class. Now, students need to own or at least have access to a computer. In addition, they must purchase computer disks, plastic envelopes or boxes for the disks, various types of folders and notebooks, and miscellaneous tools such as hole punchers and staplers. In the past, students bought only a few relatively inexpensive textbooks. Now, it is not unusual for each course to require three or more texts, each of which may cost $30 to $50. And these expenses are just considered the necessities. Many college students also expect to be provided with cell phones, televisions, refrigerators, and, of course, cars of their own. It's difficult to imagine how much it will cost to send the next generation of students to college!

Main idea: _____

_____

_____

Although this paragraph does not have a stated main idea or topic sentence, each sentence is an important detail that suggests or implies the main idea.

When you encounter a text that has an implied rather than a stated thesis, you must use the supporting details to help you determine—or *infer*—the thesis. The thesis you formulate from these details is an **inference.** The process of inferring the thesis of a text from the supporting details is similar to the process of inferring the main idea of a paragraph that does not include a topic sentence. In both situations, you use the information given to help you infer what the writer implies.

29.2

The following paragraphs have been taken from college textbooks. Read each paragraph carefully. The main idea is stated in some of these paragraphs; in others it is implied. In each paragraph underline the main idea statement or words that give clues to the main idea. Then, in the space provided, write the main idea in your own words.

29.2 continued

PARAGRAPH A

Some of the resources you have read about—air, water, soil, plants—have been important to people for thousands of years. Some mineral resources have also been important for a long time. For example, early hunters used a certain kind of rock (flint) to make their spearpoints and arrowheads. And people have long valued gold for its beauty. But many other minerals were not resources for early people. They did not know how to use coal or oil. They did not know how to process iron to make tools from it. Therefore none of these minerals were resources for them. Many of the minerals people use today have only become important resources in the past century or two.

—Arthur Getis and Judith M. Getis, *Geography*

Main idea: _____

_____

_____

Is the main idea stated or implied? _____

PARAGRAPH B

As we read a work of literature, at some point we develop a sense of its quality. In the case of fiction, we may decide that the story it tells is "great," "good," or just "so-so," and thus we begin to evaluate. Often our initial response is subjective, based largely on personal tastes and prejudices. Such a reaction is natural; after all, we must start somewhere. No doubt many professional critics first come to an assessment of an author's work by way of preference and bias. But sheer curiosity might get the better of us and make us ask: Why? Why is this story so enjoyable or moving, and that one not quite satisfying? To find out, we need to probe the elements of fiction and study its techniques. We need to examine the parts so that we might gain a fuller understanding and appreciation of the whole.

—Anthony Dubé et al., *Structure and Meaning: An Introduction to Literature*

Main idea: _____

_____

_____

Is the main idea stated or implied? _____

PARAGRAPH C

Obviously, beyond the very necessities for life itself, the distinction between needs and wants is not clear, at least not for society as a whole. . . . If you live in the suburbs or in a rural area where there is no public transportation, you may believe that you need a car. Others might need only a bicycle and occasional taxi fares. You may also believe that you need a college education in order "to succeed." Again, others may well reject this idea. Likewise, some families need a washer and dryer, some don't. Most profess the need for a refrigerator and a stove; others need only a cafeteria meal ticket or a hot plate and a cold cellar. The point is that most things an individual or family considers to be needs are not really vital to life but are simply higher-order wants.

—Daniel McGowan, *Contemporary Personal Finance*

Main idea: _____

_____

_____

Is the main idea stated or implied? _____

PARAGRAPH D

The Court is neither free to rule on all controversies in American society nor capable of correcting all injustices. Not only do institutional obstacles prevent the Court from considering certain major questions, but even when it has the authority, the Court exercises considerable self-restraint. Judicial restraint can be based on philosophical as well as practical considerations. Many justices believe certain types of questions should not be considered by the Court. Furthermore, the Court often evades those issues on which it can expect little political or public support. John P. Roche states that the Court's power "has been maintained by a wise refusal to employ it in unequal combat."

—Robert S. Ross, *American National Government*

Main idea: _____

_____

_____

Is the main idea stated or implied? _____

29.2 continued

PARAGRAPH E

[During the Middle Ages] London's narrow streets were lined with houses and shops, most of them built of wood. Fire was an ever-present danger. The streets were mostly unpaved and during the day were crowded with people, dogs, horses, and pigs. . . . But from the perspective of the twelfth century, London was a great, progressive metropolis. The old wooden bridge across the River Thames was being replaced by a new London Bridge made entirely of stone. Sanitation workers were employed by the city to clear the streets of garbage. There was a sewer system—the only one in England—consisting of open drains down the centers of streets. There was even a public lavatory.

—C. Warren Hollister, *Medieval Europe: A Short History*

Main idea: _____

_____

_____

Is the main idea stated or implied? _____

3. *Distinguish between fact and opinion.* As a reader, you must be careful to distinguish between fact and opinion. A **fact** may be defined as a statement that can be proved or disproved by concrete evidence. An **opinion** is a statement that may be generally accepted but cannot be proved or disproved.

▶ EXAMPLE

FACT: The *New York Times* has the largest circulation of any newspaper in the country.

OPINION: The *New York Times* is the best newspaper in the country.

A fact is an objective statement about a person, place, act, or thing. Although some factual statements are erroneous, they are still factual because they can be disproved. An opinion is a subjective belief, feeling, or judgment about a person, place, act, or thing. Opinions may be based on facts, but they can never be proved conclusively because they are personal and subjective.

Both facts and opinions have valid purposes, and most experienced writers use both. If a writer makes a statement that appears factual, you as a reader should be able to verify it. If a writer states an opinion, you should expect arguments to support that opinion.

Study the following statements carefully and indicate which are statements of fact and which are statements of opinion by marking an *F* or *O* beside each.

_____ 1. Students of today are smarter than those of ten years ago.

_____ 2. More high school students attend college today than did ten years ago.

_____ 3. Franklin D. Roosevelt founded the March of Dimes.

_____ 4. Franklin D. Roosevelt was a great president.

_____ 5. It is better to save than to spend.

_____ 6. As a rule, women are poor drivers.

_____ 7. Alaska is the largest state in the union.

_____ 8. The Washington Monument is taller than the Statue of Liberty.

_____ 9. Christmas was on Sunday in 1957.

_____ 10. Schools spend too much money on athletic programs.

4. *Evaluate the writer's evidence.* Another way to determine the validity of a text is by evaluating the writer's evidence—the material he or she uses to support arguments. One writer may use a personal example to support an argument while another may conduct or cite a large statistical study. Both of these types of evidence are valid, but the personal example is clearly less impressive than the large statistical study. Statistical evidence can be seriously flawed, however, if not downright inaccurate. For this reason, you should examine statistics as critically as you do other types of evidence.

No evidence is totally convincing and valid, but some is clearly more convincing and valid than others. As a critical reader, you should always determine what kind of evidence a writer is using and then evaluate that evidence as best you can. If the writer has done his or her job well, you will have enough information to judge the evidence that is included. For example, statistical studies should always be identified precisely in terms of who or what the study involved (subjects), when it was conducted, and what the conclusions were. This type of information can then be used by readers to evaluate the quality of the evidence.

Beware of writers who cite too many unidentified examples to support their assertions or who use studies and statistics that are not really pertinent. Some unscrupulous writers have been known to make up examples or cases that conveniently support their arguments. A responsible writer will include only evidence that is clearly identified and relevant to his or her thesis.

It is also important to distinguish between *logical* and *emotional* arguments. Read the following paragraphs, both of which support the idea that technology is robbing us of our privacy, and decide which uses logical arguments and which uses emotional arguments:

PARAGRAPH A

Phones ringing, beepers beeping, cursors blinking—all of these intrusions into our privacy are the result of modern technology, which is out of control. Our lives are no longer our own; our homes are no longer places of refuge. Technology has invaded every aspect of our lives, leaving us at the mercy of anyone who can learn our telephone or Social Security numbers.

PARAGRAPH B

More people own cellular phones, computers, and pagers than ever before. And in the near future, even more people will be purchasing these types of communication devices. As a result, our peace and privacy are becoming increasingly compromised, and more of us are becoming aware of the price we pay for these conveniences.

It is not difficult to see that the first example is more emotional than the second. Although some emotional arguments are perfectly valid and can be extremely effective, as a critical reader you should know when a writer is appealing to you emotionally. Reasonable, logical arguments are not always better or even more ethical, but you certainly want to recognize emotional appeals for what they are and to evaluate them on the basis of their fairness and appropriateness. In general, you should suspect the motives of a writer who uses only emotional arguments or who uses arguments that appeal to negative emotions such as fear, prejudice, and hate. (For more on evaluating evidence, see Chapter 17, Persuasion.)

5. *Evaluate the writer's sources.* To read critically, you must also evaluate a writer's sources—the other people that a writer cites to support his or her arguments. All sources are not equal. Someone who once received welfare may be a good source for a writer who is arguing in favor of the traditional welfare system, but someone who has written an article or book on the subject is usually considered a more knowledgeable, unbiased source. Writers should identify their sources clearly and should include sources who have experience or credentials and who are not obviously biased. A writer

arguing against gun control, for example, should not depend entirely on sources that have been published by the National Rifle Association. And a writer who is arguing that national forests should be preserved should include sources other than those produced by the Sierra Club.

In general, a writer's sources should be

- clearly identified and acknowledged
- qualified by experience or credentials
- unbiased
- relatively current

6. *Arrive at your own conclusions.* Although it is important for you to focus on the writer when you read critically, you must also be able to separate yourself from the writer and reach your own conclusions. You should not accept without question the conclusions of the writer.

While a writer's conclusions may be stated in the introduction or conclusion of the text, they may also be implied and not stated at all. In this case, you must infer from the text the conclusions that the writer wants you to reach and also determine your own thinking on the subject. In effect, you must figure out what the writer is saying, evaluate his or her arguments, and arrive at your own conclusion.

EXERCISE

29.4

In the following two paragraphs, the main ideas are not stated. Read each one, studying the information that is given to draw an appropriate conclusion.

PARAGRAPH A

Hands stained and brow dripping perspiration, the young man struggled to complete the task before him. He had been working for hours, and his body ached with exhaustion. His back hurt from hours of bending over his task; his head hurt from the intense concentration and mental effort he had expended; and his hand hurt from gripping the tool with which he was working. Furthermore, his mind had never felt so fatigued—so utterly depleted. Moaning to himself, he picked up his leaking pen and bent once more over his smudged paper. He must go on. The essay was due in the morning.

Conclusion: _____

_____

29.4 continued

PARAGRAPH B

Henry VIII became king of England in 1509. His first wife was Catherine of Aragon, who was unable to give him a male child. Dissatisfied with Catherine, Henry became interested in Anne Boleyn, for whom he challenged the Church and divorced Catherine. Ann, too, failed to bear him a male child, so she was charged with adultery and beheaded. Next, Henry married Jane Seymour, who gave him a male heir, Prince Edward, and then conveniently died. Later, Henry married Anne of Cleves on the strength of her portrait. Being disappointed in the real Anne, however, he bought her off and sent her away to a remote castle. He then married Catherine Howard, a pretty young woman who was unfaithful to him and who, not surprisingly, was beheaded for her infidelity. Finally, Henry married Catherine Parr, a young widow to whom he remained happily married until his death.

Conclusion: _____

_____

EXERCISE

29.5

In the following reading selection, the main idea is not stated in a thesis statement. However, the writer provides the information needed to draw a conclusion about the main idea.

[1] They didn't say anything about this in the books, I thought, as the snow blew in through the gaping doorway and settled on my naked back.

[2] I lay face down on the cobbled floor in a pool of nameless muck, my arm deep inside the straining cow, my feet scrabbling for a toe hold between the stones. I was stripped to the waist and the snow mingled with the dirt and the dried blood on my body. I could see nothing outside the circle of flickering light thrown by the smoky oil lamp which the farmer held over me.

[3] No, there wasn't a word in the books about searching for your ropes and instruments in the shadows; about trying to keep clean in a half bucket of tepid water; about the cobbles digging into your chest. Nor about the slow numbing of the arms, the creeping paralysis of the muscles as the fingers tried to work against the cow's powerful expulsive efforts.

[4] There was no mention anywhere of the gradual exhaustion, the feeling of futility and the little far-off voice of panic.

⁵My mind went back to that picture in the obstetrics book. A cow standing in the middle of a gleaming floor while a sleek veterinary surgeon in a spotless parturition overall inserted his arm to a polite distance. He was relaxed and smiling, the farmer and his helpers were smiling, even the cow was smiling. There was no dirt or blood or sweat anywhere.

⁶That man in the picture had just finished an excellent lunch and had moved next door to do a bit of calving just for the sheer pleasure of it, as a kind of dessert. He hadn't crawled shivering from his bed at two o'clock in the morning and bumped over twelve miles of frozen snow, staring sleepily ahead till the lonely farm showed in the headlights. He hadn't climbed half a mile of white fell-side to the doorless barn where his patient lay.

—James Herriot, *All Creatures Great and Small*

Using the facts and details given in this reading selection, draw a conclusion about the author's main point.

_____

_____

_____

_____

Guidelines for Critical Reading

Reading critically means that you engage in a dialogue with the writer, questioning, evaluating, and responding to the ideas and arguments he or she presents. Although critical reading cannot be reduced to a formula, the following guidelines will help you evaluate what you read:

1. Read the introduction carefully to identify the writer's thesis and purpose, and preview the entire selection before beginning to read.
2. As you read, identify the writer's primary arguments, evaluating the evidence and sources used to support the arguments and distinguishing between facts and opinions.
3. After you read, review the selection, deciding your own position on the issues addressed by the writer. On what points do you agree and disagree? If you disagree, what are your counterarguments?
4. Finally, arrive at your own conclusions on the subject.

These guidelines should be useful to you in any assignment that requires critical reading and writing. However, the skill of reading and writing critically is one that is developed slowly as you gain experience. There is no formula or set of rules that can automatically give you these complex skills. Most of all, critical reading and writing require *thinking*—a skill that cannot be acquired instantly. The more you think seriously about what you read and write, the more accomplished you will become as a critical reader and writer.

The following essay has been annotated to show you how a critical reader might respond to a text:

[1]BALTIMORE MARYLAND. I was waiting for breakfast in a coffee shop the other morning and reading the paper. The paper had sixty-six pages. The waitress brought a paper place mat and a paper napkin and took my order, and I paged through the paper.

What does this term mean?

[2]The headline said, "House Panel Studies a Bill Allowing Clear-Cutting in U.S. Forests."

[3]I put the paper napkin in my lap, spread the paper out on the paper place mat, and read on: "The House Agriculture Committee," it said, "is looking over legislation that would once again open

Fact

national forests to the clear-cutting of trees by private companies under government permits."

[4]The waitress brought the coffee. I opened a paper sugar envelope and tore open a little paper cup of cream and went on

Evidence?

reading the paper: "The Senate voted without dissent yesterday to allow clear-cutting," the paper said. "Critics have said clear-cutting in the national forests can lead to erosion and destruction of wildlife

Is this fact or opinion?

habitats. Forest Service and industry spokesmen said a flat ban on clear-cutting would bring paralysis to the lumber industry." And to the paper industry, I thought. Clear-cutting a forest is one way to get a lot of paper, and we sure seem to need a lot of paper.

[5]The waitress brought the toast. I looked for the butter. It came on

More evidence

a little paper tray with a covering of paper. I opened a paper package of marmalade and read on: "Senator Jennings Randolph, Democrat of West Virginia, urged his colleagues to take a more restrictive view and permit clear-cutting only under specific guidelines for certain types of forest. But neither he nor anyone else voted against the bill, which was sent to the House on a 90 to 0 vote."

Fact

⁶The eggs came, with little paper packages of salt and pepper. I finished breakfast, put the paper under my arm, and left the table with its used and useless paper napkin, paper place mat, paper salt and pepper packages, paper butter and marmalade wrappings, paper sugar envelope, and paper cream holder, and I walked out into the morning wondering how our national forests can ever survive our breakfasts.

Writer's conclusion

—Charles Kuralt, "Down with the Forests," *Dateline America*

The first paragraph of the following response summarizes Kuralt's essay, identifying his thesis and his two major points. The second paragraph evaluates the essay, giving the reader's reasons for agreeing with Kuralt's stand but pointing out an omission, or weakness, in the essay.

Main idea

Summary

¹In his essay "Down with the Forests," Charles Kuralt points out that **our widespread use of paper products is a serious threat to our national forests.** He argues that Americans use huge, and probably unnecessary, quantities of paper products; he also implies that this dependence on paper is one reason the government is reluctant to pass laws that prohibit the destruction of entire forests. Kuralt not only implicitly argues against legislation that allows "clear-cutting" in U.S. forests but also indirectly blames American consumers for their thoughtless overuse of paper.

Agreement

Reasons for agreement

Overall strength/ weakness

²I agree with Kuralt's basic argument that our forests are in danger and with his implied argument that Americans use too many paper products. By describing in detail how much paper we use in a typical breakfast served in a restaurant, Kuralt dramatically illustrates how we waste paper. Because my own experience confirms that of Kuralt, I too realize that we use a lot of paper products— probably more than we need. Moreover, since paper is made from trees, it is obvious that our extravagant use of paper is directly related to the destruction of forests and perhaps specifically to the loss of our national forests. However, although Kuralt's essay does identify a potentially serious problem, it does not go beyond identification to suggest possible solutions.

29.6   Read the following selection from *Future Shock* by Alvin Toffler. Annotate the selection as you read, identifying the author's purpose and thesis and evaluating his arguments, evidence, sources, and conclusions.

[1]Our attitudes toward things reflect basic value judgments. Nothing could be more dramatic than the difference between the new breed of little girls who cheerfully turn in their Barbies for the new and improved model and those who, like their mothers and grandmothers before them, clutch lingeringly and lovingly to the same doll until it disintegrates from sheer age. In this difference lies the contrast between past and future, between societies based on performance, and the new, fast-forming society based on transience.

[2]That man-thing relationships are growing more and more temporary may be illustrated by examining the culture surrounding the little girl who trades in her doll. This child soon learns that Barbie dolls are by no means the only physical objects that pass into and out of her young life at a rapid clip. Diapers, bibs, paper napkins, Kleenex, towels, non-returnable soda bottles—all are used up quickly in her home and ruthlessly eliminated. Corn muffins come in baking tins that are thrown away after one use. Spinach is encased in plastic sacks that can be dropped into a pan of boiling water for heating, and then thrown away. TV dinners are cooked and often served on throw-away trays. Her home is a large processing machine through which objects flow, entering and leaving, at a faster and faster rate of speed. From birth on, she is inextricably embedded in a throw-away culture.

[3]The idea of using a product once or for a brief period and then replacing it runs counter to the grain of societies or individuals steeped in a heritage of poverty. Not long ago Uriel Rone, a market researcher for the French advertising agency Publicis, told me: "The French housewife is not used to disposable products. She likes to keep things, even old things, rather than throw them away. We represented one company that wanted to introduce a kind of plastic throw-away curtain. We did a marketing study for them and found the resistance too strong." This resistance, however, is dying all over the developed world.

⁴Thus a writer, Edward Maze, has pointed out that many Americans visiting Sweden in the early 1950's were astounded by its cleanliness. "We were almost awed by the fact that there were no beer and soft drink bottles by the roadsides, as, much to our shame, there were in America. But by the 1960's, lo and behold, bottles were suddenly blooming along Swedish highways. . . . What happened? Sweden had become a buy, use and throw-away society, following the American pattern." In Japan today throw-away tissues are so universal that cloth handkerchiefs are regarded as old fashioned, not to say unsanitary. In England for sixpence one may buy a "Dentamatic throw-away toothbrush" which comes already coated with toothpaste for its one-time use. And even in France, disposable cigarette lighters are commonplace. From cardboard milk containers to the rockets that power space vehicles, products created for short-term or one-time use are becoming more numerous and crucial to our way of life.

⁵We develop a throw-away mentality to match our throw-away products. This mentality produces, among other things, a set of radically altered values with respect to property. But the spread of disposability through the society also implies decreased durations in man-thing relationships. Instead of being linked with a single object over a relatively long span of time, we are linked for brief periods with the succession of objects that supplant it.

—From Alvin Toffler, *Future Shock*

Chapter Review

- Critical reading involves the following:
    1. Understanding the writer's purpose
    2. Understanding the writer's thesis
    3. Distinguishing between fact and opinion
    4. Evaluating the writer's evidence
    5. Evaluating the writer's sources
    6. Arriving at one's own conclusions

Writing Assignment

Using the guidelines on page 445, reread the selection from *Future Shock* by Alvin Toffler and write a response in which you summarize and evaluate Toffler's ideas. The annotations you wrote in Exercise 29.6 may be helpful.

Participating in the Academic Community

Discuss with your classmates your response to the selection by Alvin Toffler, comparing your summary and evaluation with theirs.

Chapter 30

Strategies for Outlining and Summarizing

Two of the most important strategies for improving your textbook reading skills are outlining and summarizing. You may know how to outline and summarize in general, but in this chapter you will learn specifically how these two strategies can reinforce reading.

Outlining to Study

Outlining can be an important aid to reading when your purpose is to learn the material being read. If you outline what you read, you force yourself to focus on your reading task and to analyze the content and structure of what you are reading. Because it involves writing, outlining also reinforces learning and retention. Furthermore, an outline provides a written record of the most important ideas from your reading—a record that can be invaluable when the time comes for a written assignment or a test.

Study outlines are informal outlines that help you understand and remember what you read. Study outlines, like planning outlines, do not have to conform to any one format or any specific restriction. They can be as informal and individual as you want to make them. (See the examples of informal planning outlines on pages 20–23 in Chapter 2.)

A useful study outline is one that is still comprehensible to you weeks or even months after you have written it, so your outline needs to be clear and complete. A useful study outline is also comprehensive and accurate; it includes all of the important ideas and does not distort their meaning.

Guidelines to Follow in Outlining

If you have not previously constructed study outlines, you may find the following general guidelines helpful:

1. Read the *entire* passage carefully.
2. Determine the author's main idea and state it in your own words.
3. Decide on the major subdivisions. (Be sure that all of the major supporting points are of equal importance.)
4. Under each major division, list the more specific supporting points. (Do not include too many minor details.)

EXERCISE

30.1

Use the preceding guidelines to outline the following paragraph:

1. Read the entire passage carefully.

> [1]Comedy is usually defined as the opposite of tragedy. [2]One reason definitions of comedy are rarely given is that there are two distinct types of comedy, and these two types are very different. [3]The first type, low comedy, is loud, uninhibited, occasionally physical, and often vulgar. [4]For example, slapstick comedy is considered low comedy. [5]The second type, high comedy, is sophisticated, subtle, and usually romantic. [6]The situation comedies so popular with television viewers are an example of high comedy. [7]Because these two types of comedy are so different, it is difficult to define comedy.

2. Determine the author's main idea and state it in your own words.

_____

3. Decide on the major subdivisions. (Be sure these major points are of equal importance.)

   First major point: _____

   _____

   Second major point: _____

   _____

4. Now list the more specific supporting points. (Do not include minor details or, as a rule, examples.)

Specific supporting points under first major point: _____

_____

_____

Specific supporting points under second major point: _____

_____

_____

You probably did not include information from either the first or last sentence of the paragraph. Since the first sentence is not the topic sentence but merely an introduction to the main idea (which is stated in the second sentence), it has no information that needs to be included. The last sentence serves as a conclusion and restates the main idea, so it, too, contains no new information. You may have also omitted the examples of the two types of comedy. However, if these examples helped you understand the difference between the two types, you may have included them as minor supporting points.

Now you are ready to construct your outline. Use any format or arrangement with which you are comfortable, but be sure that you (1) indicate the order in which the points on your outline occur and (2) show the appropriate relationships among major and minor supporting points.

When you have completed your outline, you may want to compare it with those of your classmates. Notice that the same basic outline can assume many different forms.

EXERCISE

30.2

Read the following paragraphs from a chemistry textbook. The main idea of this selection could be as follows: *The origins of modern chemistry can be traced back to ancient civilizations.* As you read, identify the major supporting points in annotations in the margins.

[1]The earliest attempts to explain natural phenomena led to fanciful inventions—to myths and fantasies—but not to understanding. Around 600 BC, a group of Greek philosophers became dissatisfied with these myths, which explained little. Stimulated by social and cultural change as well as curiosity, they began to ask questions about the world around them. They answered these questions by constructing lists of logical possibilities. Thus, Greek philosophy was an attempt to discover the basic truths of nature by thinking things through, rather than by running laboratory experiments. The Greek philosophers did this so thoroughly and so

30.2 continued

brilliantly that the years between 600 and 400 BC are called the "golden age of philosophy."

[2]During this period, the Greek philosophers laid the foundation for one of our main ideas about the universe. Leucippus (about 440 BC) and Democritus (about 420 BC) were trying to determine whether there was such a thing as a smallest particle of matter. In doing so, they established the idea of the atom, a particle so tiny that it could not be seen. At that time there was no way to test whether atoms really existed, and more than 2,000 years passed before scientists proved that they do exist.

[3]While the Greeks were studying philosophy and mathematics, the Egyptians were practicing the art of chemistry. They were mining and purifying the metals gold, silver, and copper and were making embalming fluids and dyes. They called this art *khemia,* and it flourished until the seventh century AD, when it was taken over by the Arabs. The Egyptian word *khemia* became the Arabic word *alkhemia* and then the English word *alchemy.* A major goal of the alchemists was to transmute (convert) "base metals" into gold. That is, they wanted to transform less desirable elements such as lead and iron into the element gold. The ancient Arabic emperors employed many alchemists for this purpose, which, of course, was never accomplished. The alchemists also tried to find the "philosopher's stone" (a supposed cure for all diseases) and the "elixir of life" (which would prolong life indefinitely). Unfortunately they failed in both attempts, but they did have some lucky accidents. In the course of their work, they discovered acetic acid, nitric acid, and ethyl alcohol, as well as many other substances used by chemists today.

[4]The modern age of chemistry dawned in 1661 with the publication of the book *The Sceptical Chymist,* written by Robert Boyle, an English chemist, physicist, and theologian. Boyle was "skeptical" because he was not willing to take the word of the ancient Greeks and alchemists as truth, especially about the elements that make up the world. Instead, Boyle believed that scientists must start from basic principles, and he realized that every theory had to be proved by experiment. His new and innovative scientific approach was to change the whole course of chemistry.

—From Alan Sherman, Sharon Sherman, and Leonard Russikoff,
Basic Concepts of Chemistry

EXERCISE

30.3

Using the guidelines on page 452, outline the selection from the chemistry textbook that you have just read and annotated.

Summarizing

Many of the skills you use in outlining are also used in writing a summary—a concise restatement of a reading selection. To summarize, you must have a good understanding of what you have read and be able to identify clearly the main idea and the major supporting points. Then you must restate these ideas in your own words. Thus, **summarizing,** like outlining, requires both reading and writing skills.

Guidelines to Follow in Summarizing

Summarizing requires two important reading skills: (1) finding the main idea and (2) determining major supporting points. Neither of these skills is new to you. You simply need to see how they apply to summarizing. Following are some suggestions for how to read a selection you plan to summarize:

1. *Read through the entire selection before you start to summarize.* If you try to summarize as you read, you will very likely fail to recognize the major ideas, and your summary will be too long and inclusive.

2. *Identify the author's main idea.* If the main idea is expressed in a topic sentence or thesis statement, underline this sentence.

3. *Determine the major supporting points and their relationship to the main idea.* Again, underlining may be helpful.

After you have read the selection carefully and have gone back over it to determine the main idea and major supporting details, you are ready to begin writing your summary. The length of a summary depends on the length of the original selection. For example, a summary of a thirty-page textbook chapter might be several pages long. In summarizing a paragraph, however, you would probably write only one sentence, or two or three at most. A good rule of thumb is that your summary should be approximately one-third the length of the text you are summarizing.

Writing a summary requires all of the writing skills you have studied so far. In addition, here are several specific suggestions that may prove helpful:

1. *If you know the title and author of the selection you are summarizing, include them in your summary.* You may combine this information and the main idea statement in one sentence. (See page 456, the summary of the selection by Langacker.)

2. *Include only the author's main ideas and the important supporting details.* Do not insert your own ideas or unimportant details.

3. *Write in your own words.* Use the author's ideas but not the author's words unless you include a direct quotation.

4. *Be brief and to the point.* The idea of summarizing is to condense the main ideas of the original work into as few words as possible.

To summarize, you first need to read through the entire passage and then go back and identify the main idea and major supporting points. The main idea is bolded in the following paragraph:

> **Children display an amazing ability to become fluent speakers of any language consistently spoken around them.** Every normal human child who is not reared in virtual isolation from language use soon comes to speak one or more languages natively. The child's learning of his native language is not dependent on special tutoring. Parents may spend many hours "reinforcing" every recognizable bit of their child's verbal activity with a smile or some other reward, or trying by means of "baby talk" to bridge the gap between their mature language competence and the child's immature one. But there is no particular reason to believe that such activity has any bearing on the child's ultimate success in becoming a native speaker of his parents' language. Children can pick up a language by playing with other children who happen to speak it just as well as they can through the concentrated efforts of doting parents. All they seem to need is sufficient exposure to the language in question.
>
> —From Ronald W. Langacker, *Language and Its Structure*

One possible summary of this passage follows:

> In *Language and Its Structure*, Ronald W. Langacker points out that children learn to speak any language that is spoken around them without any special instruction.

EXERCISE

30.3   Read the following paragraphs and write a summary of each:

PARAGRAPH A

Good written instructions are easy to read, easy to follow, and easy to remember. Unfortunately, they are also rare. Everyone has had the frustrating experience of trying to follow badly written instructions that are open to different interpretations, leave out important information, assume too much knowledge on the part of the reader, or do not explain what needs to be done in a straightforward manner. When you read instructions, your primary purpose is usually to accomplish something—to improve your vocabulary, dress more stylishly, save money, find a job, lose or gain weight, and so on. Thus reading instructions is usually a means to an end, a way of accomplishing some goal. Few other types of reading are so focused and specific in purpose.

—Adapted from Jeanette Harris and Donald Cunningham,
The Simon & Schuster Guide to Writing, 2nd ed.

Summary: _____

_____

_____

_____

_____

PARAGRAPH B

Let me put this in another way. It is true that there are bad teachers—teachers who do not prepare for class, who are arbitrary, who subject their students to sarcasm, who won't tolerate (let alone encourage) questions and criticism, or who have thought little about education. But there are also bad students. By "bad students" I do not mean students who get low grades. Instead, I mean students who do not participate sufficiently in their own education and who do not actively demand enough from their teachers. They do not ask questions in class or after class. They do not discuss the purposes of assignments with their teachers. They do not make the teacher explain the importance and significance of the subject being studied. They do not go to office hours. They do not make the teacher explain comments on papers handed back to the student. They do not take notes on the readings. They just sit in class, letting the teacher do all the work. Education can only be a cooperative effort between student and teacher. By actively participating in these and other ways, you play your proper and necessary part in this cooperative process.

—Jack W. Meiland, *College Thinking: How to Get the Best Out of College*

Summary: _____

_____

_____

_____

_____

30.3 continued

PARAGRAPH C

The best means of benefiting the community is to place within its reach the ladders upon which the aspiring can rise—free libraries, parks, and means of recreation, by which men are helped in body and mind; works of art, certain to give pleasure and improve the public taste; and public institutions of various kinds, which will improve the general condition of the people; in this manner returning their surplus wealth to the mass of their fellows in the forms best calculated to do them lasting good.

—Andrew Carnegie, "The Gospel of Wealth"

Summary: _____

_____

_____

_____

_____

Summarizing Essays

Writing a summary of a longer composition, such as an essay or a textbook chapter, is similar to writing a summary of a paragraph. Whether you are summarizing a paragraph or a longer passage, you must read through the entire selection and identify both the author's main idea and major supporting details. In summarizing a paragraph, you look for a stated or implied *topic sentence*. In summarizing an essay or chapter, you look for a stated or implied *thesis statement*. In writing a summary of a paragraph, you determine the major supporting details; in writing a summary of an essay, you determine the main ideas of each paragraph.

In the following passage, the thesis is identified and the main supporting points are bolded:

THESIS: Word-processing programs are useful writing tools but have several limitations.

[1]Word-processing programs are tools that facilitate writing much as the fountain pen and the typewriter have in the past: They make writing easier and faster. Numerous word-processing programs are available, and more are being developed all the time. Each program differs in execution and function, but most programs offer essentially the same assistance: They enable a writer to make changes in a text—insertions, deletions, substitutions, and rearrangements—without having to retype the manuscript repeatedly. In addition, most word-processing programs are

supplemented by programs that check spelling and help writers edit and proofread their texts. As marvelous as such assistance is to a writer, these programs have limitations.

[2]**First, word-processing programs do not improve a person's writing.** Writing with the aid of word processing does encourage writers to revise what they have written, but writers must still know how to revise. Revision, which involves reseeing and rethinking, involves substantive modifications in a text. Inexperienced writers will frequently produce several drafts when they use a word processor, but the modifications they make are often minor changes in word choice or punctuation rather than substantive changes in content and organization.

[3]**A second limitation is that the editing programs** that frequently accompany word-processing programs usually **focus on problems with spelling or punctuation and thus reinforce the idea that revising involves making small changes rather than substantive modifications in content and organization.** Furthermore, these text-editing programs **give inexperienced writers a false sense of security.** For example, writers who use spell-check programs usually feel confident that they have eliminated all spelling errors. However, if a writer has written *their* instead of *there* or *effect* instead of *affect*, the spell-check program will not identify the error. Existing programs simply cannot determine if the writer has used the correct word. All they can do is alert the writer if he or she writes a word that is not in its dictionary.

[4]Word processing does offer writers some real advantages, but writers should not assume that their writing will magically be more coherent or convincing or even more correct simply as a result of their using word processing.

EXERCISE

30.4   In your own words, write a one-paragraph summary of the passage you have just read. If you include specific phrases from the passage, be sure to enclose them in quotation marks. Begin your summary as follows: *The author of this passage points out that . . .*

_____

_____

_____

_____

_____

30.4 continued

_____

_____

_____

_____

_____

_____

_____

_____

_____

_____

_____

_____

_____

Chapter Review

- Outlining and summarizing include the following steps:
  1. Read the *entire* piece.
  2. Determine the writer's main idea.
  3. State it in your own words.
  4. Identify major supporting points.

Writing Assignment

Write an informal study outline of a textbook reading selection that is required reading for you. Then use that outline to write a brief summary of the same reading selection.

Participating in the Academic Community

Discuss outlining and summarizing with your classmates and instructor, focusing on their usefulness and/or limitations as reading strategies.

Chapter 31

Strategies for Taking Essay Exams

Many of the courses you take in college will require you to take **essay exams.** Although students often dread this type of exam, you should view it as an opportunity to demonstrate for your instructor what you have learned. Because an essay exam requires both reading and writing skills, the previous chapters in this book have prepared you for this type of examination. The chapters on writing effective paragraphs and essays have taught you how to structure an essay exam (which is, in effect, simply an essay). The chapters on methods of development have provided you with terminology and patterns that are commonly used in essay exams. And the chapters on reading have taught you to read more critically and to outline and summarize—skills that will be extremely useful to you when you take an essay exam. For example, essay exam questions often ask you to outline the steps in a process or summarize something you have read.

Most instructors assume that your response to an essay question will be based on a critical reading of a text. So your preparation for taking an essay exam should, of course, include a careful, critical reading of the material on which the test will be based. This reading should include extensive annotation of the text; careful notes on lectures and what you have read; possibly an outline and/or summary; a thoughtful evaluation of the writer's arguments, evidence, and sources; and your own conclusions.

Understanding Essay Exam Terminology

Following is a list of the common types of instructions you may encounter when taking an essay exam and their definitions:

Analyze. Identify and discuss the various elements of an issue or an event, as in analyzing causes or effects.

Compare. Examine specific events, beliefs, individuals, qualities, or problems to show similarities. (Differences may also be mentioned.)

Contrast. Examine specific events, beliefs, individuals, qualities, or problems to show differences.

Discuss. Examine and analyze in detail a specific issue or problem, considering all sides.

Enumerate. Although you may answer this type of question in paragraph form, you should answer concisely, listing items instead of discussing them thoroughly. Some instructors prefer items listed and numbered in columns.

Explain. Clarify and interpret fully, showing how and why a certain event occurred or a certain belief developed. Often this requires a discussion of causes and effects, as in the question *Explain the causes* . . .

Illustrate. Present a clear, complete example to clarify your answer.

Relate. Show connections and relationships among ideas, individuals, or events.

Summarize. Present the main ideas in concise summary form.

Trace (Narrate). Describe the progress, sequence, or development of events or ideas.

Guidelines for Taking Essay Exams

Understanding the terms in the preceding list will help you get started on your essay. The following guidelines can also help you perform more successfully on essay examinations:

1. *Read through the entire examination.* Pay close attention to the directions and note whether you are to answer all questions or only a specified number. Reading through the entire test gives you an overview of the information to be covered and may prevent unnecessary and time-consuming overlapping in your answers. As you read each question, you may want to jot down ideas and examples in the margin so you will not forget them later.

2. *Budget your time.* After reading through all of the questions, determine the total time for the test, the total number of questions to be answered, and the point value for each question. Then quickly plan how you will use your time, allowing a short planning period and a review period but saving the bulk of your time for actually answering the questions. Consider the point value of each question and divide your total time into blocks. The following illustration shows how you might budget your time for a one-hour examination with four test questions of different point values:

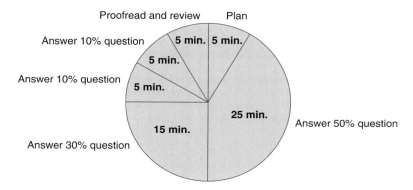

3. *Analyze the question carefully.* Circle or underline key words such as *compare, explain,* or *summarize,* and think carefully about what each key word requires of you. Also be sure to notice whether the question contains more than one part.

4. *Follow directions.* Be sure you understand the directions, and then follow them closely. If you have been asked to list, don't discuss; if you have been asked to discuss, don't list.

5. *Plan your answer to each question.* Use scratch paper or the inside cover of your test booklet to make a rough outline of the ideas you intend to include in your answer.

6. *Answer each question clearly, directly, and completely.* Give your thesis or main idea in the first sentence. If there are two or more subpoints to your answer, you may indicate this in your thesis. (Example: *The Native Americans of North and South America differed in their civilizations, their governments, their religions, and their property concepts.*) As you develop your thesis, include specific and thorough support, but don't ramble. In a short essay question, your thesis can probably be developed in a paragraph; a longer essay question may require three or more paragraphs. In either case, pay close attention to transitions and include a concluding statement.

7. *If you don't remember the answer to a question, leave a blank space for it.* Return to it after you have finished the other questions. You might

remember the answer before you finish the exam. (Sometimes there are clues in other questions.) It is also a good idea to leave wide margins and blocks of blank space after each answer so you can add information you remember later.

8. *Proofread your answers.* Rereading your answers will give you a chance to catch careless mistakes in spelling and punctuation. Reviewing your answers may also jog your memory and help you think of points that did not occur to you earlier. If so, you will be glad you left extra time and space to add to your answers.

EXERCISE

31.1

The following passage is from a college history textbook. Remember to preview the passage before you read it and to annotate it as you read.

The European Background

What drove Europeans to leave their native lands and explore unknown parts of the globe? Why did some of them stay in the New World? This surge of activity was part of a complex process of change which had been building in Europe for centuries. These changes—economic, political, and religious—were to shape the destiny of the New World. They deserve a closer look.

The Commercial Revolution

Before Columbus's voyages, there was little interest in colonizing far-off territories. The excitement which began in 1492 can be explained in part by economic changes in Europe between the eleventh and fifteenth centuries.

In AD 1000, when Leif Ericson was exploring the northern coastal areas of Canada, Europe was divided into countless small duchies, principalities, and estates. The chief economic unit was the manor, a virtually self-supporting landed estate ruled by a hereditary nobility. All food and labor required to sustain the community were supplied by its serfs, servants who were in permanent bondage to the soil and who were never permitted to leave the manor. In return for a guarantee of personal safety, the serfs devoted much of their time to serving the lord of the manor. This meant plowing and tilling the fields, repairing the castle, and fighting as foot soldiers in the periodic battles with neighboring lords.

The dominant role of the manor in European life began to change slowly during the Crusades. Between 1095 and 1291 the Christian church of western Europe attempted to recover Palestine from the Moslems and to liberate Middle Eastern Christians from Islamic authority. These efforts were ultimately unsuccessful, but most modern historians believe that the Crusades helped transform the European way of life by increasing commercial activity.

During and after the Crusades long-distance trade became safer and cheaper. Money in the form of gold and silver coins also came into widespread use, providing the means for more people to buy goods without relying on the barter system.

As a result, the small amount of trade between the towns of southern Italy and the eastern Mediterranean was enlarged to include Venice, Genoa, and other port cities in the western Mediterranean. Since the exchange of goods took place mainly in towns, these trading centers grew larger and more influential as commercial activity increased.

In addition, to raise funds for the long voyage to the Holy Land, feudal knights often sold towns the right to incorporate. Townsfolk were able to buy from their ruling baron or bishop a charter granting them the right to levy taxes, enroll a militia, and name their own officials. The growth of cities in turn encouraged the expansion of commerce. Nobles, eager to buy new products, raised money by selling freedom to their serfs. More and more of these freed serfs moved into the towns, increasing their populations and swelling the number of people engaged in producing goods for trade. This further heightened the demand for manufactured goods and for luxury items from the eastern Mediterranean.

Merchants

As trade between towns, countries, and even continents increased, the merchant became an increasingly important figure. Emphasis slowly shifted from making goods for local consumption to producing for distant markets. This trend was accelerated during the fifteenth century, when the new sea routes to the Orient and the Americas brought a great upsurge in trade, especially in such bulk commodities as lumber, rice, tea, and sugar. Heavy industries such as ship-building and cannon manufacture were also stimulated. This intercontinental trade, as well as trade within Europe, enlarged the role of the middleman. The merchants of this period often functioned as bankers and manufacturers, too. If they did not make the goods they were selling, they frequently financed their production.

These successful European merchants directly affected the development of America in at least two ways. First, the merchants had made international trade such a vital part of the European economy that the New World provided necessary new raw materials as well as a potentially large new market. Second, the rise of the merchant class enabled some European countries to colonize the New World, for it was the merchants, not the government, who financed the first English colonies.

31.1 continued

Laborers

As merchants steadily improved their position in European society, the gap between the wealthy middle class and the impoverished laborers widened year by year. One reason was the great inflation of the sixteenth and seventeenth centuries, caused in part by the importation of vast amounts of precious metal from the Spanish colonies in America. Inflation caused prices to rise while wages lagged far behind. In 1560 workers in Spain, France, Germany, and England had 50 percent less purchasing power than their great grandparents had had a hundred years earlier.

At the same time, the guild system—and thus the opportunity to improve one's station in life—was declining. In the twelfth and thirteenth centuries any worker could rise from apprenticeship to journeyman status and eventually become a master craftsman. But by the sixteenth century master craftsmen tended to hand their positions down to their sons, so that journeymen had little hope of ever improving their status. Thus for many laborers the only way to share in the New World's wealth was to actually go there.

—Rebecca Brooks Gruver, *An American History,* Brief ed., Vol. I

EXERCISE

31.2

The following essay exam question is based on the passage from the history textbook in Exercise 31.1. Analyze the question, thinking about what the instructor is asking you to do and how you would answer the question.

QUESTION: Trace the major economic and social changes that took place in Europe between the eleventh and fifteenth centuries. Explain how these changes affected colonization in America.

Now read the following analysis of the question to see if you have considered all aspects of the question:

ANALYSIS OF QUESTION: This question consists of two parts. In the first part, you are asked to trace the major economic and social changes that occurred in Europe between the eleventh and fifteenth centuries. To *trace* is to narrate the progress of an event, historical sequence, or development. Thus the first part of your answer will be largely narrative in organization (see Chapter 10, Narration).

In the second part of the question you are asked to explain or show how and why these events affected American colonization. Explanation often requires discussion of causes and effects. Thus the second part of your answer will follow the pattern for cause and effect (see Chapter 15, Cause and Effect).

Now read the following answer to this question. As you read the answer, try to determine if it follows the instructions given in the question and whether it effectively answers the question. Then read the analysis of the answer that follows and compare it to your own analysis.

ANSWER: [1]Between the eleventh and fifteenth centuries, the economic and social situation in Europe evolved from a feudal system to a middle-class or "merchant's" system. [2]In AD 1000 the major economic unit was the feudal manor, which was ruled by a hereditary noble and peopled with serfs bound to the soil. [3]These serfs were given a guarantee of personal safety in return for working the soil and serving in the lord's army. [4]The Crusades of the twelfth and thirteenth centuries, however, began to change this system. [5]Money was in more frequent use, and nobles released some of their feudal power by selling towns the right to incorporate and by selling freedom to many of the serfs, who then moved to the new towns. [6]As these towns and cities grew, so did trade and the economy.

[1]As trade grew, the merchants became more and more important and began to look for new products and new markets. [2]The New World provided both a source of raw materials for products and, through the practice of colonization, sources for investment and new markets. [3]As the middle class rose, however, the position of the laborer declined. [4]His buying power decreased in the sixteenth and seventeenth centuries when Spanish gold created an inflation, and his hope of improving his social and economic status was reduced when the guild system declined. [5]Thus, the New World became a source of investment for merchants and a last source of hope for the laborers who moved there.

ANALYSIS OF ANSWER: This answer is developed by narration and by cause and effect relationships. The thesis, which is stated in the first sentence of the first paragraph, is that between the eleventh and fifteenth centuries the economic and social situation in Europe changed from a feudal system to a middle-class system. Sentences 2 and 3 describe the feudal system, and sentences 4 and 5 show how the Crusades began to alter this system so that the manors were superseded in power by the growing towns. Sentence 6 concludes this paragraph and looks forward to the next paragraph. (This question could have been answered in one paragraph, but a logical break occurs here between the end of the feudal system and the growth of the middle class.)

Sentence 1 in paragraph 2 introduces the idea of the importance of the merchants, and sentence 2 explains how the New World helped this new merchant class. Sentences 3 and 4 explain the position of the laborers in Europe, and sentence 5 sums up the effects of the New World on both merchants and laborers. Thus, the entire answer is well organized, including a stated thesis, clear transitions between ideas, and a concluding sentence.

Read the following passage on memory from a psychology textbook. Preview the passage before reading it; then, as you read, annotate the text by identifying the main idea and major supporting points.

Basic Memory Processes

Most people have a favorite story about forgetfulness. For example, one of the authors sometimes drives to work and sometimes walks. On one occasion he drove, forgot that he had driven, and walked home. When he failed to find his car in its normal spot the next morning, he called the police to report the car stolen. After about twenty-four hours, the police called to let him know that they had found the car parked next to the psychology building on campus and that it had been towed to a storage area. When he went to retrieve the car, it was embarrassing enough for the author to explain that he had made a mistake, but particularly so when he realized that he was once again stranded because he had forgotten to bring his car keys. What went wrong? There are several possibilities, because remembering the contents of episodic, semantic, or procedural memory requires the flawless operation of three fundamental processes—encoding, storage, and retrieval. . . . A breakdown of any one of these processess will produce some degree of forgetting (Melton, 1963).

First, information must be put into memory, a step that requires *encoding.* Just as incoming sensory information must be coded so that it can be communicated to the brain, information to be remembered must be put in a form that the memory system can accept and use. In the memory system, sensory information is put into various memory codes, or mental representations of physical stimuli. As discussed in Chapter 9, on thought, mental representations can take many forms. For example, people sometimes put information into *acoustic codes,* which represent information as sequences of sounds. *Visual codes* represent stimuli as pictures. *Semantic codes* represent an experience by its general meaning. Thus, if you see a billboard that reads "Huey's Going Out of Business Sale—50% Off Everything in Stock," you might encode the sound of the words as if they had been spoken (acoustic coding), the image of the letters as they were arranged on the sign (visual coding), or the fact that you saw an ad for Huey's (semantic coding). The way stimuli are coded can influence what is remembered. For example, semantic coding might allow you to clearly remember seeing a car parked in your neighbors' driveway just before their house was robbed, but because there was little or no other coding, you might not be able to remember the make, model, or color (Bahrick & Boucher, 1968).

The second basic memory process is *storage*, which simply means maintaining information in the system over time. Episodic, semantic, and procedural memories can be stored for a very long time. When you find it possible to use a pogo stick or perform some other "rusty" skill or to recall facts and events from many years ago, you are depending on your memory's storage capacity.

Retrieval is the process of finding information stored in memory and bringing it into consciousness. Retrieving stored information like your address or telephone number is usually so fast and effortless as to seem automatic. Only when you try to retrieve other kinds of information—such as the answer to a quiz question that you know but cannot quite recall—do you become aware of the searching process.

Encoding, storage, and retrieval are all vital links in the memory chain. The author's forgetfulness might thus be traced to information about his car's location being (a) never properly encoded, (b) encoded but never stored, or (c) stored but never retrieved.

—Douglas A. Bernstein et al., *Psychology*

Chapter Review

- Essay exams require both reading and writing skills.

- Understanding the terms commonly used in essay exams is essential.

- Following these suggestions will improve your performance on essay exams:

  1. Read through the entire examination.
  2. Budget your time.
  3. Analyze each question carefully.
  4. Follow directions.
  5. Plan your answer to each question.
  6. Answer each question clearly, directly, and completely.
  7. If you don't remember the answer to a question, leave a blank space and return to it later.
  8. Proofread your answers.

■ Writing Assignment

Following the guidelines for taking essay exams given in this chapter, answer the following question about the psychology passage in Exercise 31.3:

> Identify and explain each step of the mental process that allows a person to store and retrieve information.

■ Participating in the Academic Community

Compare your answer with those of your classmates, discussing the strengths and weaknesses of each. As a group, come to a conclusion about what information is essential to a "correct" answer.

Part Five

Reading Selections

The reading selections in Part Five provide you with an opportunity to practice the writing and reading skills you have learned in Parts One through Four of this book. As you read each selection, try to apply what you have learned about both reading and writing. For example, **preview** each selection before you read it, **annotate** the text as you read, and **review** the selection after you have finished reading it. In addition, you should analyze each selection to determine the writer's main idea and purpose. The questions at the end of each selection will guide your understanding and evaluation of it.

The selections are grouped into four units, each of which addresses a different theme or issue. The first unit focuses on identity issues—a person's sense of who he or she is and how that identity is formed. The second explores several issues related to education, and the third focuses on media issues, especially the role of television in our society. The fourth unit includes three selections that address racial issues. At the end of each unit, you will find cumulative discussion and writing assignments that focus on the theme and emphasize the connections among the reading selections in the unit.

Identity Issues

The three essays in this unit focus on identity issues—especially on how young people establish a sense of identity. Maya Angelou writes about how home and family shape individual identity. Amy Tan not only focuses on the influence of family but also explores the role that language plays in establishing a sense of identity. Finally, Kevin Davis considers the ways in which attending college changes a person.

■ Reading Preview

In the first essay, Maya Angelou tells about her decision to leave home just after graduating from high school, giving you insight into not only Angelou's feelings but also those of her mother. Angelou, a well-known African American writer, is perhaps best known for her autobiography, *I Know Why the Caged Bird Sings*, and for her poem "On the Pulse of the Morning," which she read at President Bill Clinton's first inauguration. This selection is taken from a collection of stories entitled *Even the Stars Look Lonely*.

■ Predicting and Questioning

On the following lines, predict how Angelou's mother reacts when she learns that her daughter is leaving home.

_____

_____

Now write a question about what it is like to leave home for the first time.

_____

_____

■ Reading Strategy

This essay is easy to read because it is short and is essentially a narrative. However, like most stories, Angelou's has a thesis, which is not stated but is clearly implied. As you read, try to formulate in your own words the main point she is making.

Mother and Freedom

Maya Angelou

She stood before me, a dolled-up, pretty yellow woman, seven inches shorter than my six-foot bony frame. Her eyes were soft and her voice was brittle. "You're determined to leave? Your mind's made up?"   1

I was seventeen and burning with passionate rebelliousness. I was 2
also her daughter, so whatever independent spirit I had inherited had been
nurtured by living with her and observing her for the past four years.

"You're leaving my house?" 3

I collected myself inside myself and answered, "Yes. Yes, I've found a 4
room."

"And you're taking the baby?" 5

"Yes." 6

She gave me a smile, half proud and half pitying. 7

"All right, you're a woman. You don't have a husband, but you've got 8
a three-month-old baby. I just want you to remember one thing. From the
moment you leave this house, don't let anybody raise you. Every time you
get into a relationship you will have to make concessions, compromises,
and there's nothing wrong with that. But keep in mind Grandmother Hen-
derson in Arkansas and I have given you every law you need to live by. Follow what's right. You've been raised."

More than forty years have passed since Vivian Baxter liberated me 9
and handed me over to life. During those years I have loved and lost, I have
raised my son, set up a few households and walked away from many. I have
taken life as my mother gave it to me on that strange graduation day all
those decades ago.

In the intervening time when I have extended myself beyond my 10
reach and come toppling Humpty-Dumpty-down on my face in full view of
a scornful world, I have returned to my mother to be liberated by her one
more time. To be reminded by her that although I had to compromise with
life, even life had no right to beat me to the ground, to batter my teeth
down my throat, to make me knuckle down and call it Uncle. My mother
raised me, and then freed me.

And now, after so many eventful years of trials, successes and fail- 11
ures, my attention is drawn to a bedroom adjoining mine where my once
feisty mother lies hooked by pale blue wires to an oxygen tank, fighting
cancer for her life.

I think of Vivian Baxter, and I remember Frederick Douglass's 12
mother, enslaved on a plantation eleven miles from her infant son, yet who,
after toiling a full day, would walk the distance to look at her child hoping
that he would sense a mother's love, then return to the plantation in time
to begin another day of labor. She believed that a mother's love brought
freedom. Many African Americans know that the most moving song created during the centuries of slavery was and remains "Sometimes I Feel
Like a Motherless Child."

As a mother and a daughter myself, I have chosen certain songs and 13
poems to take to my mother's room, and there we will laugh and cry together.

I pray I shall have the courage to liberate my mother when the time 14
comes. She would expect that from me.

■ Summarizing
What You
Have Read

Write a brief summary of this essay, focusing on not only the events in the story but also the point that Angelou is making.

_____

_____

_____

_____

_____

■ Responding to
What You
Have Read

Respond to this essay by describing how you felt when you left home and/or started to college.

_____

_____

_____

_____

_____

■ Discussing
What You
Have Read

Discuss this essay with your classmates and instructor, focusing on the following questions:

1. How would you characterize the relationship between Angelou and her mother? (You might be interested to know that Angelou lived with her grandmother as well as her mother when she was a young child.)

2. How can a mother both raise and free a child? Why are both necessary?

3. Explain what Angelou means when she writes at the end of the essay that she hopes she will "have the courage to liberate [her] mother when the time comes."

4. At the end of the story, how have Angelou's and her mother's roles become reversed?

5. What is Angelou suggesting in this essay about how a person establishes a sense of identity?

■ Writing about
What You
Have Read

Write an essay based on a single experience you have had that helped you establish your sense of who you are. Be sure you make a point as well as tell a story. You need not state your thesis explicitly, but be sure that your readers understand the point you are making.

■ Reading
 Preview

Amy Tan, author of *The Joy Luck Club* and *The Kitchen God's Wife*, tells in this essay about "all the Englishes" she knows. As a successful Asian American writer, Tan uses all of these "Englishes" in her writing. In this essay she analyzes the effect that her mother's version of English has had on her own speaking and writing and suggests how both her relationship with her mother and her mother's language have shaped her own identity.

■ Predicting and
 Questioning

On the following lines, predict why Tan has more than one English.

_____

_____

Now write a question about what the title of this essay might mean.

_____

_____

■ Reading
 Strategy

Although Tan does not state her thesis at the beginning of her essay, she gives a broad clue to her main point when she states that, as a writer, she uses all the "Englishes" she grew up with. Tan then explains this statement as she develops her ideas in the essay. As you read, underline clues that reveal her thesis.

Mother Tongue

Amy Tan

I am not a scholar of English or literature. I cannot give you much more than personal opinions on the English language and its variations in this country or others.

I am a writer. And by that definition, I am someone who has always loved language. I am fascinated by language in daily life. I spend a great deal of my time thinking about the power of language—the way it can evoke an emotion, a visual image, a complex idea, or a simple truth. Language is the tool of my trade. And I use them all—all the Englishes I grew up with.

Recently, I was made keenly aware of the different Englishes I do use. I was giving a talk to a large group of people, the same talk I had already given to half a dozen other groups. The nature of the talk was about my writing, my life, and my book, *The Joy Luck Club*. The talk was going along well enough, until I remembered one major difference that made the whole talk sound wrong. My mother was in the room. And it was perhaps the first time she had heard me give a lengthy speech, using the kind of English I have never used with her. I was saying things like, "The intersection of memory upon imagination" and "There is an aspect of my fiction that relates to thus-and-thus"—a speech filled with carefully wrought grammatical phrases, burdened, it suddenly seemed to me, with nominalized forms, past perfect tenses, conditional

1

2

3

phrases, all the forms of standard English that I had learned in school and through books, the forms of English I did not use at home with my mother.

Just last week, I was walking down the street with my mother, and I again found myself conscious of the English I was using, the English I do use with her. We were talking about the price of new and used furniture and I heard myself saying this: "Not waste money that way." My husband was with us as well, and he didn't notice any switch in my English. And then I realized why. It's because over the twenty years we've been together I've often used that same kind of English with him, and sometimes he even uses it with me. It has become our language of intimacy, a different sort of English that relates to family talk, the language I grew up with.

So you'll have some idea of what this family talk I heard sounds like, I'll quote what my mother said during a recent conversation which I videotaped and then transcribed. During this conversation, my mother was talking about a political gangster in Shanghai who had the same last name as her family's, Du, and how the gangster in his early years wanted to be adopted by her family, which was rich by comparison. Later, the gangster became more powerful, far richer than my mother's family, and one day showed up at my mother's wedding to pay his respects. Here's what she said in part:

"Du Yusong having business like fruit stand. Like off the street kind. He is Du like Du Zong—but not Tsung-ming Island people. The local people call putong, the river east side, he belong to that side local people. That man want to ask Du Zong father take him in like become own family. Du Zong father wasn't look down on him, but didn't take seriously, until that man big like become a mafia. Now important person, very hard to inviting him. Chinese way, came only to show respect, don't stay for dinner. Respect for making big celebration, he shows up. Mean gives lots of respect. Chinese custom. Chinese social life that way. If too important won't have to stay too long. He come to my wedding. I didn't see, I heard it. I gone to boy's side, they have YMCA dinner. Chinese age I was nineteen."

You should know that my mother's expressive command of English belies how much she actually understands. She reads the *Forbes* report, listens to *Wall Street Week,* converses daily with her stockbroker, reads all of Shirley MacLaine's books with ease—all kinds of things I can't begin to understand. Yet some of my friends tell me they understand 50 percent of what my mother says. Some say they understand 80 to 90 percent. Some say they understand none of it, as if she were speaking pure Chinese. But to me, my mother's English is perfectly clear, perfectly natural. It's my mother tongue. Her language, as I hear it, is vivid, direct, full of observation and imagery. That was the language that helped shape the way I saw things, expressed things, made sense of the world.

Lately, I've been giving more thought to the kind of English my mother speaks. Like others, I have described it to people as "broken" or "fractured" English. But I wince when I say that. It has always bothered me that I can think of no way to describe it other than "broken," as if it were damaged and needed to be fixed, as if it lacked a certain wholeness and soundness. I've heard other terms used, "limited English," for example. But they seem just as bad, as if everything is limited, including people's perceptions of the limited English speaker.

I know this for a fact, because when I was growing up, my mother's "limited" English limited my perception of her. I was ashamed of her English. I believed that her English reflected the quality of what she had to say. That is, because she expressed them imperfectly her thoughts were imperfect. And I had plenty of empirical evidence to support me: the fact that people in department stores, at banks, and at restaurants did not take her seriously, did not give her good service, pretended not to understand her, or even acted as if they did not hear her. 9

My mother has long realized the limitations of her English as well. When I was fifteen, she used to have me call people on the phone to pretend I was she. In this guise, I was forced to ask for information or even to complain and yell at people who had been rude to her. One time it was a call to her stockbroker in New York. She had cashed out her small portfolio and it just so happened we were going to go to New York the next week, our very first trip outside California. I had to get on the phone and say in an adolescent voice that was not very convincing, "'This is Mrs. Tan.'" 10

And my mother was standing in the back whispering loudly, "Why he don't send me check, already two weeks late. So mad he lie to me, losing me money." 11

And then I said in perfect English, "Yes, I'm getting rather concerned. You had agreed to send the check two weeks ago, but it hasn't arrived." 12

Then she began to talk more loudly. "What he want, I come to New York tell him front of his boss, you cheating me?" And I was trying to calm her down, make her be quiet, while telling the stockbroker, "I can't tolerate any more excuses. If I don't receive the check immediately, I am going to have to speak to your manager when I'm in New York next week." And sure enough, the following week there we were in front of this astonished stockbroker, and I was sitting there red-faced and quiet, and my mother, the real Mrs. Tan, was shouting at his boss in her impeccable broken English. 13

We used a similar routine just five days ago, for a situation that was far less humorous. My mother had gone to the hospital for an appointment, to find out about a benign brain tumor a CAT scan had revealed a month ago. She said she had spoken very good English, her best English, no mistakes. Still, she said, the hospital did not apologize when they said they had lost the CAT scan and she had come for nothing. She said they did not seem to have any sympathy when she told them she was anxious to know the exact diagnosis, since her husband and son had both died of brain tumors. She said they would not give her any more information until the next time and she would have to make another appointment for that. So she said she would not leave until the doctor called her daughter. She wouldn't budge. And when the doctor finally called her daughter, me, who spoke in perfect English—lo and behold—we had assurances the CAT scan would be found, promises that a conference call on Monday would be held, and apologies for any suffering my mother had gone through for a most regrettable mistake. 14

I think my mother's English almost had an effect on limiting my possi-   15
bilities in life as well. Sociologists and linguists probably will tell you that a
person's developing language skills are more influenced by peers. But I do
think that the language spoken in the family, especially in immigrant families
which are more insular, plays a large role in shaping the language of the child.
And I believe that it affected my results on achievement tests, IQ tests, and
the SAT. While my English skills were never judged as poor, compared to
math, English could not be considered my strong suit. In grade school I did
moderately well, getting perhaps B's, sometimes B-pluses, in English and
scoring perhaps in the sixtieth or seventieth percentile on achievement tests.
But those scores were not good enough to override the opinion that my true
abilities lay in math and science, because in those areas I achieved A's and
scored in the ninetieth percentile or higher.

This was understandable. Math is precise; there is only one correct an-   16
swer. Whereas, for me at least, the answers on English tests were always a
judgment call, a matter of opinion and personal experience. Those tests were
constructed around items like fill-in-the-blank sentence completion, such as,
"Even though Tom was _____, Mary thought he was _____." And the correct
answer always seemed to be the most bland combinations of thoughts, for example, "Even though Tom was shy, Mary thought he was charming," with the
grammatical structure "even though" limiting the correct answer to some
sort of semantic opposites, so you wouldn't get answers like, "Even though
Tom was foolish, Mary thought he was ridiculous." Well, according to my
mother, there were very few limitations as to what Tom could have been and
what Mary might have thought of him. So I never did well on tests like that.

The same was true with word analogies, pairs of words in which you   17
were supposed to find some sort of logical, semantic relationship—for example, "*Sunset* is to *nightfall* as _____ is to _____." And here you would be presented with a list of four possible pairs, one of which showed the same kind of
relationship: *red* is to *stoplight, bus* is to *arrival, chills* is to *fever, yawn* is to
boring. Well, I could never think that way. I knew what the tests were asking,
but I could not block out of my mind the images already created by the first
pair, "*sunset* is to *nightfall*"—and I would see a burst of colors against a dark-
ening sky, the moon rising, the lowering of a curtain of stars. And all the other
pairs of words—red, bus, stoplight, boring—just threw up a mass of confusing
images, making it impossible for me to sort out something as logical as saying:
"A sunset precedes nightfall" is the same as "a chill precedes a fever." The
only way I would have gotten that answer right would have been to imagine
an associative situation, for example, my being disobedient and staying out
past sunset, catching a chill at night, which turns into feverish pneumonia as
punishment, which indeed did happen to me.

I have been thinking about all this lately, about my mother's English, about   18
achievement tests. Because lately I've been asked, as a writer, why there are
not more Asian Americans represented in American literature. Why are there
few Asian Americans enrolled in creative writing programs? Why do so many
Chinese students go into engineering? Well, these are broad sociological ques-

tions I can't begin to answer. But I have noticed in surveys—in fact, just last week—that Asian students, as a whole, always do significantly better on math achievement tests than in English. And this makes me think that there are other Asian-American students whose English spoken in the home might also be described as "broken" or "limited." And perhaps they also have teachers who are steering them away from writing and into math and science, which is what happened to me.

Fortunately, I happen to be rebellious in nature and enjoy the challenge of disproving assumptions made about me. I became an English major my first year in college, after being enrolled as pre-med. I started writing nonfiction as a freelancer the week after I was told by my former boss that writing was my worst skill and I should hone my talents toward account management. 19

But it wasn't until 1985 that I finally began to write fiction. And at first I wrote using what I thought to be wittily crafted sentences, sentences that would finally prove I had mastery over the English language. Here's an example from the first draft of a story that later made its way into *The Joy Luck Club,* but without this line: "That was my mental quandary in its nascent state." A terrible line, which I can barely pronounce. 20

Fortunately, for reasons I won't get into today, I later decided I should envision a reader for the stories I would write. And the reader I decided upon was my mother, because these were stories about mothers. So with this reader in mind—and in fact she did read my early drafts—I began to write stories using all the Englishes I grew up with: the English I spoke to my mother, which for lack of a better term might be described as "simple"; the English she used with me, which for lack of a better term might be described as "broken"; my translation of her Chinese, which could certainly be described as "watered down"; and what I imagined to be her translation of her Chinese if she could speak in perfect English, her internal language, and for that I sought to preserve the essence, but neither an English nor a Chinese structure. I wanted to capture what language ability tests can never reveal: her intent, her passion, her imagery, the rhythms of her speech and the nature of her thoughts. 21

Apart from what any critic had to say about my writing, I knew I had succeeded where it counted when my mother finished reading my book and gave me her verdict: "So easy to read." 22

■ Summarizing What You Have Read

Summarize this essay, focusing on the author's explanation of how she uses all the "Englishes" she grew up with and the significance of this insight.

_____

_____

_____

_____

_____

■ Responding to Identify at least two different versions of English that you speak.
   What You
   Have Read
_____

_____

_____

_____

■ Discussing Discuss this essay with your classmates and instructor, focusing on the fol-
   What You lowing questions:
   Have Read

1. The title of this essay has two meanings. Can you explain both meanings?
2. In what type of writing does Tan use her mother's version of English?
   Why does she not use this version in writing the essay you have just
   read? In what oral situations does she use her mother's English?
3. Tan discovered that she writes better fiction when she envisions her
   mother as her audience. What effect does thinking of her mother as
   her audience have on her writing?
4. Tan does not mention that she also knows Chinese—a language that is
   very different from English. Why do you think she focuses on the different "Englishes" she knows rather than this other language? What
   are some of the effects of having a second language and of writing in a
   language that is not your native tongue?
5. How does the language a person uses help shape that person's cultural
   identity? Does language also affect a person's personal identity? If so,
   in what way?

■ Writing about Write a letter to a member of your family telling him or her what you
   What You learned from reading this essay. Then expand the brief summary you wrote
   Have Read earlier, writing this time for your instructor. After you have completed both
   assignments, compare the language and tone you used in the letter with the
   language and tone of the summary.

■ Reading Kevin Davis teaches writing and directs the writing center at East Central
   Preview University in Ada, Oklahoma. But he is also an avid baseball fan, bicycle
   rider, pasta maker, and poet. In this essay, which appeared in a collection entitled *The Subject Is Writing*, Davis uses his own experiences as a student to
   explore the idea that college changes a person. The essay will also help you
   understand more clearly your identity as a student writer.

■ Predicting and Questioning

On the following lines, predict whether Davis believes that students change in the process of acquiring a college education.

_____

_____

Now write a question about this issue—something you would like Davis to answer in this essay.

_____

_____

■ Reading Strategy

The term *discourse community*, which appears in this essay, may be a new concept for you. Davis attempts to define the term, but it is a difficult concept to explain, so he cannot give you a simple definition. As you read, underline everything in the essay that will help you understand this concept.

Does Coming to College Mean Becoming Someone New?

Kevin Davis

As an undergraduate English major, I felt like an outsider. I originally chose to major in English because of my love for reading and writing, but the reading and writing college expected of me was not the reading and writing I was prepared to do. Sure, I could read the assigned literature, and I could make my own good sense of it. Yet that was not enough for my English professors. They wanted me to make their sense of the literature, to understand the texts as they understood them. Not only that, they expected me to write about this alien sense-making in turgid, impersonal, passive-voiced prose. When I became an English major, I didn't just learn certain understandings of what I read; I also had to learn a particular way of reading and writing. Right from the start, it was clear that if I was to become a member of the English-majors community, I had to do more than read and think and write; I had to turn into someone new. 1

Perhaps that is why I was never a very successful English major and why, eventually, I left the academic world and joined the business community. I was living on the boundary between academic and home communities, between maintaining my identity and accepting another. I found I didn't like the someone new I was being asked to become. 2

Eventually, I returned to the academic world and discovered I fit into the community of outsiders known as rhetoricians (people who study the way other people effectively communicate). I'm not sure if I fit into this community because I wanted to join it more than I had wanted to join the English studies community, because it was willing to accept me as I already was, or 3 because I had matured enough to be willing to become someone new. I do know, however, that this second attempt at entrance into the academic community has been as successful as my earlier attempt was a flop.

As a rhetorician and because of my past experience, I have become interested in issues of community membership. Everyone is a member of several discourse communities (the term rhetoricians use to describe groups of people who share patterns and strategies of communication). We're all members of a home discourse community, based on our family's regional, social, and economic lifestyles. And many of us are members of other discourse communities because we are familiar with particular language communities through experiences such as jobs or hobbies. But entering the academic discourse communities present on college campuses can produce problems and anxieties for students who are attempting the transitions.

In the rest of this essay, I want to use my own experiences and research to answer several questions: What happens as students try to become members of new academic discourse communities? What special writing and thinking abilities are required? What personal investments must be made?

When I was 18, my writing was an extremely personal activity. I didn't just throw words on pages; I invested myself into the work. Everything I wrote was full of personal insights, personal style, and voice. A good writer, I was regularly praised and awarded for my high school writing efforts. I was totally unprepared for the shocking comments that my college professors would place on my writing.

Part of the problem came from a natural maturing process: The valued and original insights of a high school senior were suddenly the trite and common repetitions of a college student. And part of the problem came from style: The original, personal, whimsical voice of a young writer was not enough to assure my spot in the academic community. . . .

I didn't know what academic writing sounded like, and I didn't know how to present my ideas in the lingo that would bring the ideas recognition and acceptance. I was not thinking like members of the academic world are supposed to think. I didn't process my thoughts in appropriate academic ways, and I wasn't positively involved with my studies.

Several composition scholars have completed research studies that try to understand more fully what happens with students trying to enter academic discourse communities. Recently, for example, . . . Lucille McCarthy (1987) studied one student as he learned to negotiate his way through new discourse communities in several different freshman and sophomore courses. McCarthy made several conclusions from her work. First, she found that her subject used the same writing process to figure out how to complete a variety of writing tasks; this would imply that a student who can write in one situation, like I could, can extrapolate a process for writing into other situations. Second, she found that the purpose for the writing task and the student's involvement with the task were important to the writer's success; this implies that students write better if they are actively involved in the topic they are writing about, which is certainly true in my own experience. Finally, McCarthy concluded that writing tasks that are familiar in one situation were considered different when the student encountered them in a different situation; this implies that epistemic knowledge of a discourse community is important for a writer to succeed. . . .

By looking at . . . studies and at my experience, then, I can begin to make 10
some conclusions about how students have to adapt their writing and thinking to succeed in a college's unfamiliar academic discourse community. First, we have to recognize and accept the forms of the community; we have to make our writing look and sound like that of the field. Second, we have to learn to think in the ways that are valued by the field we are entering; we have to be personal or impersonal, focused on ideas or numbers, as the field demands. Third, we have to have a reliable, comfortable writing process that we can take with us from task to task, community to community; once established, the process will probably serve us in a variety of settings. Finally, we have to become personally and intellectually involved with the community, wanting to be a part of it; without personal involvement, the formalistic and epistemic changes are merely window dressing.

As I look back on my own experience, I can clearly identify that last 11
change as the most problematic for me. As an undergraduate English major, I never completed the personal commitment important for my success in the field. Eventually, I learned to mimic the writing and thinking activities that the field valued, but I remained unwilling to submit to the authority of those form and thought patterns. To personally endorse the English studies discourse community I would have had to abandon much of what I believed about life. Later, when I returned to graduate school to study rhetoric, however, I easily endorsed the field, finding it much more palatable to my native ways of being.

As I began my own research into discourse community membership, I 12
was particularly interested in the personal involvement issues. Did other people reject communities, as I had done, because they were hesitant to make the personal commitments necessary for success? Could individuals only join communities that endorsed their native ways of thinking? Or did other people accept the communities and, in the process, give up something of their native ways of being in the world?

To investigate the personal changes students make as they enter new 13
discourse communities, I interviewed, several times over six months, two undergraduates who were taking their first courses toward a degree and eventual licenses in social work.

Stella (the names are changed) was in her early twenties and in college 14
for the second time, having delayed her education for a marriage. As Stella engaged the social work community, she became more accepting of differences in others, developing a new sense of open-mindedness. As she put it, "I try to see people as they are and not make judgements. . . . Through my social work classes, I've learned that everybody should be treated that way." But sometimes this open, nonjudgmental attitude caused problems for Stella who suddenly found that her husband was prejudiced in several ways: "My husband is racially prejudiced, and I'm real open and have no problem with that"; "My husband's family thinks welfare people are lazy. I really stand up for people

they don't understand." Through her entrance into the new community, her attitudes toward others changed, and she adopted a socially accepting world view even when that new world view was in direct conflict with her family. In the process, she became more committed to the community of social workers.

The other participant in the study, Charlotte, had graduated from high   15
school in 1957. After raising a family and working as both a cosmetologist and a practical nurse, Charlotte was finally returning to college to get the degree she had long cherished. Charlotte, too, was willing to make the personal commitment that membership in the social work community required. As she put it, "This course is really making a difference in my thoughts. I had not recognized that I was biased in my way of thinking." Further, Charlotte suggested that self-awareness and open-mindedness were mandatory for a social worker: "If you don't understand yourself, you can't help anyone else. Not in the way that will help people take control of a situation." Her studies in social work, she said, changed her overall view of people and communities and culture. And, like Stella, Charlotte tried to become a change agent for those around her: "Just this weekend my husband made a comment, and I said 'Now just a minute; that's not the way it is at all.'"

In attempting to enter the social work discourse community, both Stella   16
and Charlotte underwent a great deal of self-realization. Both acknowledged their native social world view, critiqued it, began to develop new social world views, and even tried to become change agents for their spouses' world views. Through this progression, both women began to develop what their instructor described as the "social work frame of reference," a socially accepting world view that is necessary for an individual to help members of diverse social groups try to improve their position in life. In the process, they became increasingly estranged from their home communities.

Research—my own and others'—exploring discourse communities veri-   17
fies what my personal experiences taught me: Learning to write within an academic discourse community is not a simple procedure.

First, we have to learn to put down words and ideas in community ac-   18
ceptable ways. We have to internalize and apply the form limitations of the discourse community; our writing has to look like writing in the community is supposed to look. In my own experience, this formalistic community entrance was easy to master, quick to develop; I learned to sound like an English major early in my education.

But there is more. We also have to learn to explore ideas by employing   19
the intellectual manners that are important to a particular field. We have to accept and use the epistemic processes of the discourse community. This can be more difficult than the forms, but new ways of thinking usually develop easily through repeated contact. In my own experience, the epistemic knowledge developed a bit more slowly than the formalistic, but it, too, grew rapidly; I was soon thinking and sounding like an English major.

Finally—and I think most importantly—personal commitment to a par-   20
ticular community is involved in entering that new discourse community. Students can develop the sound of a community and apply the thought processes of the community without adopting the world views of the community, with-

out truly accepting membership in that community. In my own case, I was unwilling to become the person the literary studies community required me to be and to develop the world view the community expected. As a result, I pursued careers in two different communities, business and rhetoric. Literary studies expected me to become somebody new, somebody I was unwilling to become. I was willing to become a business manager and, later, a rhetorician.

In my research, however, I found that Stella and Charlotte were willing   21
to make the total transition, to write in social worker ways, to solve problems using social worker methods, and finally to adopt a social worker world view, no matter how alien it was to their native communities. In the process of coming to college, Stella and Charlotte found themselves becoming someone new.

Works Cited

McCarthy, Lucille. "A Stranger in Strange Lands: A College Student Writing across the Curriculum." *Research in the Teaching of English 21* (1987): 233–265.

■ Summarizing What You Have Read

Write a brief summary of this essay, focusing on the conclusions Davis draws "about how students have to adapt their writing and thinking to succeed in a college's unfamiliar academic discourse community."

_____

_____

_____

_____

■ Responding to What You Have Read

Now respond to this essay by drawing a diagram of the discourse communities to which you belong.

■ Discussing What You Have Read

Discuss this essay with your classmates and instructor, focusing on the following questions:

1. Davis uses not only his own experiences but also library research (professional books and journals) and field research (interviews with students) to develop his essay. Which of these sources do you find most interesting? Which do you find most convincing?

2. What do you see as the risks of joining a new discourse community?

3. Why is language such an important part of who you are and how you define yourself?

4. Do you agree with Davis that success in college requires you to join new discourse communities? Why or why not?

5. Compare this essay to the one by Amy Tan ("Mother Tongue"). Is Tan also explaining the concept of discourse communities and how they function in our lives? Do she and Davis agree or disagree? Explain your answer.

■ Writing about What You Have Read

Use the question posed in the title to survey five students in your class. Then, using the results of your survey plus your own experiences, write an essay that answers the question: "Does Coming to College Mean Becoming Someone New?"

CUMULATIVE ASSIGNMENTS FOR IDENTITY ISSUES

■ Discussion Assignment

The three reading selections you have just read by Maya Angelou, Amy Tan, and Kevin Davis suggest several different ways a person forms a sense of identity. Angelou suggests that a person's relationship with his or her family plays an important role in the formation of identity but also emphasizes the importance of independence. Tan reinforces the idea that family shapes identity but adds the element of language—how the language a person uses influences both cultural and personal identities. Finally, Davis explores the issue of how college shapes professional identity and ultimately personal identity. Using these three readings as well as your own experiences and observations, discuss the following questions with your classmates:

1. Why is a strong sense of identity essential to a healthy personality?
2. What elements and forces other than those suggested by these three reading selections affect a person's sense of identity?
3. Why is conflict often instrumental in forging a clear sense of identity?

■ Writing Assignment

Using the three essays you have just read and your own experiences, write an essay describing your own sense of identity—who you think you are—and identifying the forces you think shaped this image you have of yourself.

Education Issues

The selections in this unit focus on issues in education. Mike Rose questions the value of remedial education, while Mary Sherry suggests that the possibility of flunking can be an effective means of motivating some students. Finally, Ethan Bronner reports on the trend among college freshmen to view a college education primarily as a means of preparing for a career.

■ Reading Preview

In this essay, Mike Rose describes the journey that one remedial student made to success. Rose is a respected authority on remedial education. In fact, his book *Lives on the Boundary*, from which this reading is taken, has received several awards from academic organizations. But the book is not written in an academic style. Rather, Rose uses his own experiences as his major source of information and writes in a style that is personal and direct. In this selection, he describes an interview with a young woman named Lilia, who grew up in the same Los Angeles neighborhood where Rose spent his youth.

■ Predicting and Questioning

Before you read, write your prediction of what type of experience led to Lilia's success—to her "crossing the boundary" from remedial classes to honors classes.

_____

_____

Next, write a question about remedial education that you would like to have answered.

_____

_____

■ Reading Strategy

To understand this selection, you must occasionally *infer* the author's point of view from what he says. As you read, focus not only on what Rose states but also on what he is *implying* about our education system in general and remedial education in particular.

Lives on the Boundary: Lilia

Mike Rose

I sit with Lilia, the tape recorder going. "We came from Mexico when I was four years old. When I went into school, I flunked the first grade. The first grade! I had to repeat it, and they put me in classes for slow learners. I stayed in those classes for five years. I guess there was a pattern where they put me in those really basic classes and then decided I would go through my elementary school years in those classes. I didn't learn to read or write. My parents got my cousins—they came here prior to us, so they knew English really well—and they had me read for them. I couldn't. They told my parents I didn't know anything. That's when my parents decided they would move. They moved to Tulare County. My aunt was there and told them that the schools were good and that there was work in agriculture. I picked grapes and cotton and oranges—everything—for six straight summers. I kinda liked it, out there with all the adults, but I knew it wasn't what I wanted for the future. The schools *were* good. The teachers really liked me, and I did very well. . . . Between the eighth and ninth grades I came to UCLA for six weeks in the summer. It was called the MENTE program—Migrants Engaged in New Themes of Education—I came here and loved the campus. It was like dreamland for me. And I made it my goal to come here."

The school that designated Lilia a slow learner is two miles from my old neighborhood on South Vermont. She arrived as a child about eight years after I left as an adult. The next generation. We make our acquaintance in an office of the University of California at Los Angeles. Lilia is participating in an unusual educational experiment, one developed by some coworkers of mine at UCLA Writing Programs. Lilia and fifteen other freshmen—all of whom started UCLA in remedial writing courses themselves—are tutoring low-achieving students in Los Angeles area schools. The tutoring is connected to a special composition class, and Lilia and her partners write papers on their tutorial work and on issues of schooling. Lilia is writing a paper on the academic, social, and psychological effects of being placed in the remedial track. Her teacher suggested she come to see me. I can't stop asking her questions about growing up in South L.A. 2

Desire gets confused on South Vermont. There were times when I wanted so much to be other than what I was, to walk through the magical gate of a television cottage. But, strange blessing, we can never really free ourselves from the mood of early neighborhoods, from our first stories, from the original tales of hope and despair. There are basic truths there about the vulnerability and power of coming to know, about the way the world invites and denies language. This is what lies at the base of education—to be tapped or sealed over or distorted, by others, by us. Lilia says the tutoring makes her feel good. "Sometimes I feel that because I know their language, I can communicate. I see these kids and I see myself like I was in elementary school." Lilia stops. She asks me what it was like in South L.A. when *I* was there, when I was going to school. Not much different then, I say. Not as tough probably. She asks me if I've ever gone back. I tell her I did, just recently. . . . 3

The place was desolate. The power plant was still standing, smaller than I remembered it, surrounded now by barbed wire. All the storefront businesses were covered with iron grating; about half of them, maybe more, were shut down. The ones that were open had the grating pulled back the width of 4 the door, no further. The hair and nails shop was closed. The Stranger's Rest Baptist Church was closed. Teddy's Rough Riders—an American Legion post—was battered and closed. The Huston Mortuary looked closed. My house had been stuccoed over, a dark dirty tan with holes in the walls. 9116 South Vermont. My old neighborhood was a blighted island in the slum. Poverty had gutted it, and sealed the merchants' doors. "It's worse now," I tell Lilia, "much worse. No one comes. No one goes." At Ninety-sixth Street two men were sitting on the curb outside a minimart. East on Ninety-first a girl sat in the shadows of steps tucked back from the pavement. At Eighty-ninth Street, a woman walked diagonally in front of me, moving unsteadily in a tight dress, working the floured paper off an X-L-NT burrito. As I drove back by my house, I saw a little boy playing with two cans in the dirt. Imagination's delivery. Fantasy in cylinders and tin.

Lilia is telling me about one of her fellow classmates who had also been designated a slow learner. "She said it was awful. She had no friends because everyone called her dumb, and no one wanted to be seen with a dumb person. . . . Because they were calling her dumb, she started to believe she was really dumb. And with myself and my brother, it was the same thing. When we were in those courses we thought very low of ourselves. We sort of created a little world of our own where only we existed. We became really shy." 5

What we define as intelligence, what we set out to measure and identify with a number, is both in us and out of us. We have been socialized to think of intelligence as internal, fixed, genetically coded. There is, of course, a neurophysiology to intelligence, but there's a feeling to it as well, and a culture. In moving from one school to another—another setting, another set of social definitions—Lilia was transformed from dumb to normal. And then, with six powerful weeks as a child on a university campus—"opening new horizons for me, scary, but showing me what was out there"—she began to see herself in a different way, tentatively, cautiously. Lilia began the transition to smart, to high school honors classes, to UCLA. She could go back, then, to the schools, to the place where, as she says, she "knows the language." 6

The promise of community and equality is at the center of our most prized national document, yet we're shaped by harsh forces to see difference and to base judgment on it. The language Lilia can speak to the students in the schools is the language of intersection, of crossed boundaries. It is a rich language, filled with uncertainty. Having crossed boundaries, you sometimes can't articulate what you know, or what you know seems strange. What is required, then, is for Lilia and her students to lean back against their desks, grip the firm wood, and talk about what they hear and see, looking straight ahead, looking skyward. What are the gaps and discordances in the terrain? What mix of sounds—eerie and compelling—issues from the hillside? Sitting with Lilia, our lives playing off each other, I realize that, finally, this is why the current perception of educational need is so limited: It substitutes terror for awe. But it is not terror that fosters learning, it is hope, everyday heroics, the power of the common play of the human mind. 7

■ Summarizing
What You
Have Read

Write a brief summary of this selection, focusing on what Rose believes the primary purpose of remedial education should be.

_____

_____

_____

_____

_____

■ Responding to
What You
Have Read

Write a response to what you have read, focusing on your own views about the effectiveness of remedial courses.

_____

_____

_____

_____

_____

■ Discussing
What You
Have Read

Discuss this selection with your instructor and classmates, focusing on the following questions:

1. What positive and negative effects do remedial courses have on students?
2. Is placement in remedial classes the best way to help students who are academically underprepared? If so, why? If not, what alternatives for remedial classes can you suggest?
3. What types of courses does Rose advocate for academically underprepared students?
4. How did Lilia's experience in her remedial class change her sense of identity?

■ Writing about
What You
Have Read

Write an essay in which you propose the type of remediation you think would be most effective for academically underprepared students. Use your own experiences as well as the reading selection by Rose to support your proposal.

■ Reading
  Preview

In this guest editorial for *Newsweek*, Mary Sherry, who is both a mother and a teacher, argues that our educational system would be more effective if teachers and administrators were not reluctant to fail students. In defending the practice of flunking students, she cites her own son's experience in a high school English class to support her argument. Sherry, who lives near Minneapolis, Minnesota, believes that "flunking as a regular policy has just as much merit today as it did two generations ago."

■ Predicting and
  Questioning

On the following lines, predict the reason Sherry might be in favor of schools' flunking students.

_____

_____

Now ask a question about the practice of flunking that you would like to have answered.

_____

_____

■ Reading
  Strategy

As you read, identify and number the arguments that Sherry includes to support her thesis.

In Praise of the F Word

Mary Sherry

Tens of thousands of 18-year-olds will graduate this year and be handed meaningless diplomas. These diplomas won't look any different from those awarded their luckier classmates. Their validity will be questioned only when their employers discover that these graduates are semiliterate.   1

Eventually a fortunate few will find their way into educational-repair shops—adult-literacy programs, such as the one where I teach basic grammar and writing. There, high school graduates and high school dropouts pursuing graduate-equivalency certificates will learn the skills they should have learned in school. They will also discover they have been cheated by our educational system.   2

As I teach, I learn a lot about our schools. Early in each session I ask my students to write about an unpleasant experience they had in school. No writers' block here! "I wish someone would have made me stop doing drugs and made me study." "I liked to party and no one seemed to care." "I was a good kid and didn't cause any trouble, so they just passed me along even though I didn't read well and couldn't write." And so on.   3

I am your basic do-gooder, and prior to teaching this class I blamed the poor academic skills our kids have today on drugs, divorce, and other impedi-   4 ments to concentration necessary for doing well in school. But, as I rediscover each time I walk into the classroom, before a teacher can expect students to concentrate, he has to get their attention, no matter what distractions may be at hand. There are many ways to do this, and they have much to do with teaching style. However, if style alone won't do it, there is another way to show who holds the winning hand in the classroom. That is to reveal the trump card of failure.

I will never forget a teacher who played that card to get the attention of one of my children. Our youngest, a world-class charmer, did little to develop his intellectual talents but always got by. Until Mrs. Stifter. 5

Our son was a high school senior when he had her for English. "He sits in the back of the room talking to his friends," she told me. "Why don't you move him to the front row?" I urged, believing the embarrassment would get him to settle down. Mrs. Stifter looked at me steely-eyed over her glasses. "I don't move seniors," she said. "I flunk them." I was flustered. Our son's academic life flashed before my eyes. No teacher had ever threatened him with that before. I regained my composure and managed to say that I thought she was right. By the time I got home, I was feeling pretty good about this. It was a radical approach for these times, but, well, why not? "She's going to flunk you," I told my son. I did not discuss it any further. Suddenly English became a priority in his life. He finished out the semester with an A. 6

I know one example doesn't make a case, but at night I see a parade of students who are angry and resentful for having been passed along until they could no longer even pretend to keep up. Of average intelligence or better, they eventually quit school, concluding they were too dumb to finish. "I should have been held back," is a comment I hear frequently. Even sadder are those students who are high school graduates who say to me after a few weeks of class, "I don't know how I ever got a high school diploma." 7

Passing students who have not mastered the work cheats them and the employers who expect graduates to have basic skills. We excuse this dishonest behavior by saying kids can't learn if they come from terrible environments. No one seems to stop to think that—no matter what environments they come from—most kids don't put school first on their list unless they perceive something is at stake. They'd rather be sailing. 8

Many students I see at night could give expert testimony on unemployment, chemical dependency, abusive relationships. In spite of these difficulties, they have decided to make education a priority. They are motivated by the desire for a better job or the need to hang on to the one they've got. They have a healthy fear of failure. 9

People of all ages can rise above their problems, but they need to have a reason to do so. Young people generally don't have the maturity to value education in the same way my adult students value it. But fear of failure, whether economic or academic, can motivate both. 10

Flunking as a regular policy has just as much merit today as it did two generations ago. We must review the threat of flunking and see it as it really is—a positive teaching tool. It is an expression of confidence by both teachers and parents that the students have the ability to learn the material presented 11 to them. However, making it work again would take a dedicated, caring conspiracy between teachers and parents. It would mean facing the tough reality that passing kids who haven't learned the material—while it might save them grief for the short term—dooms them to long-term illiteracy. It would mean that teachers would have to follow through on their threats, and parents would have to stand behind them, knowing their children's best interests are indeed at stake. This means no more doing Scott's assignments for him because he might fail. No more passing Jodi because she's such a nice kid.

This is a policy that worked in the past and can work today. A wise   12
teacher, with the support of his parents, gave our son the opportunity to succeed—or fail. It's time we return this choice to all students.

■ Summarizing
What You
Have Read

Summarize this essay, focusing on the arguments you identified and numbered as you read.

_____

_____

_____

_____

_____

■ Responding to
What You
Have Read

Write about how it feels to fail or to fear failing a particular assignment or course.

_____

_____

_____

_____

_____

■ Discussing
What You
Have Read

Discuss this essay with your instructor and classmates, focusing on the questions that follow:

1. How did Sherry's own experiences as a mother and teacher shape her conviction that flunking is a useful policy? Do you think she would have felt the same had her son actually flunked the English class rather than making an A?

2. Do you think her son's fear of flunking was the only factor in his success? What other factors might have been involved?

3. Do you agree or disagree with Sherry that our schools would be more effective if students knew they would fail if they did not meet the school's academic standards? Why or why not?

4. What are the positive and negative effects of flunking students?

■ Writing about
What You
Have Read

Write a letter to your local school board arguing for or against the policy of flunking students who do not meet certain standards.

■ Reading
Preview

Ethan Bronner, a writer for the *New York Times*, reports in this article on a nationwide poll by researchers at the University of California at Los Angeles. The results of the poll suggest that most students now view getting an education as a way to gain financial security rather than as an opportunity to develop "a meaningful philosophy of life." The article also reveals several interesting trends among college freshmen nationwide.

■ Predicting and
Questioning

On the following lines, predict the author's answer to this question: Is college valued less for learning than for earning?

_____

_____

Now write a question about the value of an education.

_____

_____

■ Reading
Strategy

Skim the information about "Freshman Opinions" included with this article before you read the article itself. Then, after you have read the article, reread—this time more carefully—these "Freshman Opinions" and mark any that surprise you.

College Valued Less for Learning Than for Earning

Ethan Bronner

A survey of college freshmen confirms what professors and administrators said they have been sensing: that students are increasingly disengaged and view higher education less as an opportunity to expand their minds and more as a means to increase their incomes.

1

The annual nationwide poll by researchers at the University of Califor-   2
nia at Los Angeles shows that two suggested goals of education—"to be very
well off financially" and "to develop a meaningful philosophy of life"—have
switched places in the past three decades.

In the survey taken at the start of the fall semester, 74.9 percent of   3
freshmen chose being well off as an essential goal and 40.8 percent chose developing a philosophy. In 1968, the numbers were reversed, with 40.8 percent
selecting financial security and 82.5 percent citing the importance of developing a philosophy.

It is a matter of using education more as a means to an end, rather than   4
valuing what you are learning, said Linda Sax, director of the survey at the
Higher Education Research Institute at UCLA. The survey was first taken 32
years ago.

The trend has long been in the making, with students' strong interest in   5
high incomes rising to a plateau in the mid-1980s. But the desire edged down
a bit through the 1990s, rising again slightly with this latest survey.

Sax said the trend took on more significance when added to the fact that   6
incoming students showed unprecedented levels of academic and political disengagement.

The percentage of students who said that during their last year in high   7
school they had been frequently "bored in class" hit a record high of 36 percent, compared with 26.4 percent in 1985, the second year the question was
asked.

At the same time, a record 34.5 percent said they had "overslept and   8
missed class," compared with a low of 18.8 percent in 1968.

Despite that, a record high of 39.4 percent said they aspire to obtain a   9
master's degree and 49.7 percent said they expect to earn a B average.

Some professors expressed little surprise at the seemingly contradictory   10
mix of boredom and ambition.

"Schooling has become more about training and less about transforma-   11
tion," said Mark Edmundson, a professor of English at the University of Virginia who wrote of the growing consumerist view of education by students in
the September issue of *Harper's* magazine.

"You go there to prepare yourself for the future," Edmundson said, "to   12
learn a skill, a capacity that you can convert into dollars later on. And being
trained is boring. Being educated is not, but that is going on less and less."

The disengagement was also reflected in attitudes toward politics.   13

A record low 26.7 percent of freshmen thought that "keeping up to date   14
with political affairs" is a very important or essential life goal, compared with
29.4 percent in 1996 and a high of 57.8 percent in 1966.

Similarly, an all-time low 13.7 percent said they frequently discuss   15
politics, compared with 16.2 percent last year and a high of 29.9 percent in
1968.

Freshman Opinions

Some highlights of the UCLA annual survey of college freshmen nationwide. The fall 1997 survey analyzed data from 252,082 students at 464 institutions. The first survey was taken in 1966.

Politics

- A record low 27 percent believe that "keeping up to date with political affairs is an important life goal compared with the record high of 58 percent in 1966.
- 14 percent said they frequently discuss politics down from 30 percent in 1968.
- Some 55 percent consider themselves as "middle of the road," compared with 53 percent last year and a high of 60 percent in 1983.

Academics

- A record-high 36 percent reported being frequently bored in class during their last year of high school, compared with the all-time low of 26 percent in 1985.
- A record high 39 percent plan to obtain master's degrees and a record 15 percent plan to obtain doctorates.

Social attitudes

- Support for legal abortion declined for the fifth straight year to 54 percent, compared with a high of 65 percent in 1990. This is the lowest level of support for legal abortion since 1979.
- The percentage of those who believe "it is important to have laws prohibiting homosexual relationships" increased to 34 percent, the second increase in a row. Fifty percent, however, said that "same sex couples should have the right to legal marital status."

Alcohol, drugs, tobacco

- Percentage of freshman smokers is at its highest level in 30 years, with 16 percent saying they smoke frequently. That compares with 9 percent a decade earlier.
- Support for legalizing marijuana again rose, with 35 percent agreeing that marijuana should be legalized. That compares with a low of 17 percent in 1989.
- Fifty-three percent acknowledged frequent or occasional beer drinking, compared with a high of 75 percent in 1981.

Source: The Associated Press.

■ Summarizing What You Have Read

Briefly summarize the article you have just read, focusing on the survey and its results rather than the quotations that are included.

_____

_____

_____

_____

_____

■ Responding to
What You
Have Read

Identify one finding of the survey that does not reflect your opinions or attitude toward education. Then write a brief response in which you make the point that statistical surveys do not accurately represent everyone.

_____

_____

_____

_____

_____

■ Discussing
What You
Have Read

Discuss the results of this survey with your instructor and classmates, focusing on the questions that follow:

1. Which of the results do you find most surprising and why?

2. Do an informal survey of your class to determine if you and your classmates agree with the students who participated in the poll about the purpose of an education. Discuss why the results of a survey may vary depending on who is surveyed.

3. Notice the quotes by Linda Sax, director of the survey, and Mark Edmundson, a professor who has written an article on the same topic for *Harper's* magazine. What effect do these quotations have on you as a reader?

4. Do you agree or disagree with Edmundson's statement that "Schooling has become more about training and less about transformation"?

5. The author of this article, Ethan Bronner, does not give his opinion of the survey and its results, but he suggests his opinion by what he chooses to report and the people he quotes. In addition, the inclusion of the other highlights from the survey ("Freshman Opinions") indicates something about the conclusion that the author has drawn. Can you infer Bronner's opinion from the clues that are provided? Do you agree or disagree with his opinion?

■ Writing about
What You
Have Read

Write an essay in which you explain what you think the purpose of a college education should be.

CUMULATIVE ASSIGNMENTS FOR EDUCATION ISSUES

■ Discussion Assignment

The three reading selections you have just read by Mike Rose, Mary Sherry, and Ethan Bronner focus on different issues in education. Rose addresses the issue of remedial courses while Sherry argues that flunking is an effective strategy in motivating students. Bronner points out that many students attend college, not because they want an education but to prepare for a career. Using these three readings as well as your own experiences and observations, discuss the following questions with your classmates:

1. What do you think motivates students to learn?
2. Should colleges admit anyone who wants to attend or only those who have good high school records and excellent test scores? What obligation do colleges have to help underprepared students if they choose to admit them?
3. How do you measure the quality of an education? What factors are involved?
4. Evaluate your own education thus far.

■ Writing Assignment

Choose one of the issues addressed in these three reading selections: remediation, flunking students, or the purpose of a college education. Survey the students in one of your classes about this issue. Next, interview one of your professors, focusing the interview on the same issue. Then, write an essay in which you report on the results of your survey and interview, and conclude with your own opinion on this issue.

The three essays in this section all focus on media issues. From magazines and newspapers to movies and television, the mass media not only *reflect* society but also help *shape* it. John Vivian provides three models of the mass media that are useful in analyzing the media. Robert MacNeil looks at the negative effects of television, while Anna Quindlen suggests that television isn't harmful and can even be educational.

■ Reading Preview

John Vivian's *Mass Media Models* is an excerpt from a communication textbook. In it, Vivian introduces three common models of the mass media: hot versus cool, entertainment versus information, and elitist versus populist. In discussing each model, Vivian points out its potential for explaining the mass media.

■ Predicting and Questioning

On the following lines, predict which forms of media will be classified as hot rather than cool or as entertainment rather than information.

_____

_____

Now write a question about the meaning of the term *mass media*.

_____

_____

■ Reading Strategy

As you read this selection, underline sentences that help you define each model.

Mass Media Models

John Vivian

Hot versus Cool

Marshall McLuhan
Devised hot-cool media model.

hot media Print media, which requires intimate audience involvement.

Theorist **Marshall McLuhan** developed an innovative model to help 1 explain the mass media. To McLuhan's thinking, books, magazines and newspapers were **hot media** because they require a high degree of thinking to use. To read a book, for example, you must immerse yourself to derive anything from it. The relationship between medium and user is intimate. The same is true with magazines and newspapers. McLuhan also considered movies a hot medium because they involve viewers so completely. Huge screens command the viewers' full attention, and sealed, darkened viewing rooms shut out distractions.

In contrast, McLuhan classified electronic media, especially television, as cool because they can be used with less intellectual involvement and hardly any effort. Although television has many of the sensory appeals of movies, including sight, motion and sound, it does not overwhelm viewers to the point that all else is pushed out of their immediate consciousness. When radio is heard merely as background noise, it does not require any listener involvement at all, and McLuhan would call it a **cool medium.** Radio is warmer, however, when it engages listeners' imaginations, as with radio drama.

cool medium Can be used passively.

McLuhan's point is underscored by research that has found people remember much more from reading a newspaper or magazine than from watching television or listening to the radio. The harder you work to receive a message from the media, the more you remember.

Entertainment and Information

Many people find it helpful to define media by whether the thrust of their content is entertainment or information. By this definition, newspapers almost always are considered an information medium, and audio recording and movies are considered entertainment. As a medium, books both inform and entertain. So do television and radio, although some networks, stations and programs do more of one than the other. The same is true with magazines, with some titles geared more for informing, some for entertaining.

Although widely used, the entertainment-information dichotomy has limitations. Nothing inherent in newspapers, for example, precludes them from being entertaining. Consider the *National Enquirer* and other supermarket tabloids, which are newspapers but which hardly anybody takes seriously as an information source. The neatness of the entertainment-information dichotomy doesn't work well with mainstream newspapers either. Most daily newspapers have dozens of items intended to entertain. Open a paper and start counting with Calvin and Hobbs, Garfield and the astrology column.

The entertainment-information dichotomy has other weaknesses. It misses the potential of all mass media to do more than entertain and inform. The dichotomy misses the persuasion function. . . . People may consider most movies as entertainment, but there is no question that Steven Spielberg has broad social messages even in his most rollicking adventure sagas. In the same sense, just about every television sitcom is a morality tale wrapped up in an entertaining package. The persuasion may be soft-peddled but it's everywhere.

infotainment Melding of media role as purveyor of information and entertainment.

Dividing mass media into entertainment and information categories is becoming increasingly difficult as newspapers, usually considered the leading information medium, back off from hard-hitting content to woo readers with softer, entertaining stuff. For better or worse, this same shift is taking place also at *Time* and *Newsweek*. This melding even has a name that's come into fashion: **infotainment.**

While the entertainment-information model will continue to be widely 8
used, generally it is better to think in terms of four media functions—to entertain, to inform, to persuade, and to bind communities—and to recognize
that all media do all of these things to a greater or lesser degree.

Elitist and Populist

An ongoing tension in the mass media exists between advancing social 9
and cultural interests and giving broad segments of the population what they
want. This tension, between extremes on a continuum, takes many forms:

- Classical music versus pop music.
- Nudes in art books versus nudes in *Playboy* magazine.
- The New York *Times* versus the *National Enquirer.*
- A Salman Rushdie novel versus pulp romances.
- Ted Koppel's "Nightline" versus "Oprah Winfrey."
- A Public Broadcasting Service documentary on crime versus Fox Televi-
  sion's "Ten Most Wanted" re-creations.

elitists Focuses on
media responsibility to
society.

populists Applauds
media that attract large
following.

At one end of the continuum is serious media content that appeals to 10
people who can be called **elitists** because they feel the mass media have a responsibility to contribute to a better society and a refinement of the culture,
regardless of whether the media attract large audiences. At the other end of
the continuum are **populists,** who are entirely oriented to the marketplace.
Populists feel the mass media are at their best when they give people what
they want.

The mass media have been significant historically in shaping social and 11
cultural values. Media committed to promoting these values generally forsake
the largest possible audiences. In New York City, the serious-minded *Times,*
which carries no comics, has generally lagged in circulation behind the *Daily
News,* a screaming tabloid that emphasizes crime and disaster coverage, loves
scandals and sex, and carries popular comics. The *Times* can be accused of
elitism, gearing its coverage to a high level for an audience that appreciates
thorough news coverage and serious commentary. The *Daily News,* on the
other hand, can be charged with catering to a low level of audience and providing hardly any social or cultural leadership. The *Daily News* is in the populist tradition.

A lot of media criticism can be understood in the context of this elitist- 12
populist continuum. People who see a responsibility for the mass media to
provide cultural and intellectual leadership fall at one extreme. At the other
extreme are people who trust the general population to determine media content through marketplace dynamics. Certainly there are economic incentives
for the media to cater to mass tastes.

Most mass media in the United States are somewhere in the middle of 13
the elitist-populist continuum. Fox Television offers some serious fare, not
only hyped crime re-creations, and the New York *Times* has a sense of humor
that shows itself in the wit of its columnists and in other ways.

■ Summarizing
What You
Have Read

Summarize this reading selection in a single sentence.

_____

_____

_____

_____

_____

■ Responding to
What You
Have Read

Briefly explain which one of the three media models you find most useful in understanding the role of media.

_____

_____

_____

_____

_____

■ Discussing
What You
Have Read

Discuss this essay with your classmates and instructor, focusing on the following questions:

1. Do you think the power of the media has increased or declined in recent years? Support your answer with specific examples and details.
2. What form of media do you think is the most powerful and why?
3. Do you believe some forms of media have a negative influence on children? Support your answer.
4. Do you agree with McLuhan that "The harder you work to receive a message from the media, the more you remember"? Explain your answer.
5. What are some of the problems with the entertainment versus information model?
6. Do you prefer "elitist" or "populist" forms of mass media? Why is this model a useful way of classifying different types of media?

■ Writing about
What You
Have Read

Write an essay based on cause and effect in which you discuss the effect that a particular type of media has had on you or other people.

■ Reading
Preview

In the following essay, Robert MacNeil, former anchor of the *MacNeil/Lehrer NewsHour* on the Public Broadcasting Service, discusses the negative effects that he fears television has on its viewers. The essay was originally a speech that MacNeil delivered at the President's Leadership Forum at the State University of New York at Purchase, New York.

■ Predicting and
Questioning

Before you read, write your prediction of what MacNeil thinks is wrong with television.

_____

_____

Next, write a question you have about the effects of television on viewers.

_____

_____

■ Reading
Strategy

Although MacNeil begins his essay with a general statement that looks and sounds like a thesis, his real thesis is implied rather than stated. As you read, underline the phrases that suggest his thesis.

The Trouble with Television

Robert MacNeil

It is difficult to escape the influence of television. If you fit the statistical averages, by the age of 20 you will have been exposed to at least 20,000 hours of television. You can add 10,000 hours for each decade you have lived after the age of 20. The only things Americans do more than watch television are work and sleep.   1

Calculate for a moment what could be done with even a part of those hours. Five thousand hours, I am told, are what a typical college undergraduate spends working on a bachelor's degree. In 10,000 hours you could have learned enough to become an astronomer or engineer. You could have learned several languages fluently. If it appealed to you, you could be reading Homer in the original Greek or Dostoyevsky in Russian. If it didn't, you could have walked around the world and written a book about it.   2

The trouble with television is that it discourages concentration. Almost anything interesting and rewarding in life requires some constructive, consistently applied effort. The dullest, the least gifted of us can achieve things that seem miraculous to those who never concentrate on anything. But television encourages us to apply no effort. It sells us instant gratification. It diverts us only to divert, to make the time pass without pain.   3

Television's variety becomes a narcotic, not a stimulus. Its serial, kaleidoscopic exposures force us to follow its lead. The viewer is on a perpetual guided tour: 30 minutes at the museum, 30 at the cathedral, 30 for a drink,   4 then back on the bus to the next attraction—except on television, typically, the spans allotted are on the order of minutes or seconds, and the chosen delights are more often car crashes and people killing one another. In short, a lot of television usurps one of the most precious of all human gifts, the ability to focus your attention yourself, rather than just passively surrender it.

Capturing your attention—and holding it—is the prime motive of most 5
television programming and enhances its role as a profitable advertising vehicle. Programmers live in constant fear of losing anyone's attention—anyone's. The surest way to avoid doing so is to keep everything brief, not to strain the attention of anyone but instead to provide constant stimulation through variety, novelty, action and movement. Quite simply, television operates on the appeal to the short attention span.

It is simply the easiest way out. But it has come to be regarded as a given, 6
as inherent in the medium itself; as an imperative, as though General Sarnoff, or one of the other august pioneers of video, had bequeathed to us tablets of stone commanding that nothing in television shall ever require more than a few moments' concentration.

In its place that is fine. Who can quarrel with a medium that so brilliantly packages escapist entertainment as a mass-marketing tool? But I see 7
its values now pervading this nation and its life. It has become fashionable to think that, like fast food, fast ideas are the way to get to a fast-moving, impatient public.

In the case of news, this practice, in my view, results in inefficient communication. I question how much of television's nightly news effort is really 8
absorbable and understandable. Much of it is what has been aptly described as "machine-gunning with scraps." I think the technique fights coherence. I think it tends to make things ultimately boring and dismissible (unless they are accompanied by horrifying pictures) because almost anything is boring and dismissible if you know almost nothing about it.

I believe that TV's appeal to the short attention span is not only inefficient communication but decivilizing as well. Consider the casual assumptions 9
that television tends to cultivate: that complexity must be avoided, that visual stimulation is a substitute for thought, that verbal precision is an anachronism. It may be old-fashioned, but I was taught that thought is words, arranged in grammatically precise ways.

There is a crisis of literacy in this country. One study estimates that 10
some 30 million adult Americans are "functionally illiterate" and cannot read or write well enough to answer a want ad or understand the instructions on a medicine bottle.

Literacy may not be an inalienable human right, but it is one that the 11
highly literate Founding Fathers might not have found unreasonable or even unattainable. We are not only not attaining it as a nation, statistically speaking, but we are falling further and further short of attaining it. And, while I would not be so simplistic as to suggest that television is the cause, I believe it contributes and is an influence.

Everything about this nation—the structure of the society, its forms of 12
family organization, its economy, its place in the world—has become more

complex, not less. Yet its dominating communications instrument, its principal form of national linkage, is one that sells neat resolutions to human problems that usually have no neat resolutions. It is all symbolized in my mind by the hugely successful art form that television has made central to the culture, the 30-second commercial: the tiny drama of the earnest housewife who finds happiness in choosing the right toothpaste.

When before in human history has so much humanity collectively surrendered so much of its leisure to one toy, one mass diversion? When before has virtually an entire nation surrendered itself wholesale to a medium for selling? 13

Some years ago Yale University law professor Charles L. Black, Jr., wrote: ". . . forced feeding on trivial fare is not itself a trivial matter." I think this society is being force-fed with trivial fare, and I fear that the effects on our habits of mind, our language, our tolerance for effort, and our appetite for complexity are only dimly perceived. If I am wrong, we will have done no harm to look at the issue skeptically and critically, to consider how we should be resisting it. I hope you will join with me in doing so. 14

■ **Summarizing What You Have Read**

Write a brief summary of this essay, beginning with a statement of what you think MacNeil's thesis is and then focusing on the main problems that MacNeil identifies to support his thesis.

_____

_____

_____

_____

_____

■ **Responding to What You Have Read**

Now write a response to what you have read, focusing on whether you agree or disagree with MacNeil.

_____

_____

_____

_____

_____

■ **Discussing What You Have Read**

Discuss MacNeil's essay with your instructor and classmates, focusing on the following questions:

1. The figures that MacNeil gives about average television viewing times suggest that television is addictive, or habit forming. Do you agree that television is addictive? If so, what are the immediate effects of television addiction? What are the long-range effects?

2. According to MacNeil, television news can be described as "machine-gunning with scraps." Explain this metaphor. What effect does this type of news reporting have on viewers?

3. MacNeil believes that television's tendency to sell "neat resolutions to human problems" is symbolized by the television commercial. In your opinion, what effects do these commercials have on their viewers? Do commercials present an unrealistic and stereotyped view of life? Give examples to support your answer.

■ Writing about What You Have Read

Write an essay in which you identify and discuss the effects of television viewing on a certain audience, such as young children, adolescents, economically deprived adults, mature adults, and so on.

■ Reading Preview

Well-known columnist and novelist Anna Quindlen states in this reading selection that she likes television, even though such an admission is unfashionable. She points out that "sniping at TV has become a kind of pedigree, a guarantee of superiority." Unlike Robert MacNeil, she argues that watching television is at worse a harmless activity and at best educational.

■ Predicting and Questioning

Before you read, write your prediction of why Quindlen thinks watching television is harmless.

_____

_____

Now write a question about the educational value of television.

_____

_____

■ Reading Strategy

As you read, underline the arguments Quindlen includes in her defense of television.

TV or Not TV

Anna Quindlen

Ten years ago at some awards banquet I sat next to an actress who was   1
bored out of her gourd (and probably high as a kite) and who proceeded to perform a medley of television theme songs. She did "Gilligan's Island," "The

Flintstones," "The Patty Duke Show" and "Rawhide," making a very convincing whip sound by whistling between her front teeth. She did "Green Acres," "The Beverly Hillbillies" and, as her finale, the theme from "The Mickey Mouse Club." Though she'd grown up in the hills of Beverly, I felt we were neighbors.

I like television. This is unfashionable. Sniping at TV has become a kind 2 of pedigree, a guarantee of superiority. One woman said to me proudly not long ago, "We don't even own a TV." Great—so you missed "The Civil War," the Challenger explosion, the "Who Shot J.R.?" episode of "Dallas," the World Series, and a considerable part of American culture over the last 10 years. We have a generation of parents who were raised on a steady diet of red meat, Pez and "The Brady Bunch" and who now pride themselves on denying their kids sugar and television.

I like television. "Nova." "Masterpiece Theater." "Sesame Street." Ah, 3 public television, you say, the green vegetables of video viewing—they are exempt from censure. But I also like the channel that shows old movies, and "Headline News," and Nickelodeon, with reruns of most of the sitcoms from my own childhood. (Watch your kids marvel at the fact that you are personally familiar with "Mr. Ed"!) I love a good trashy miniseries, with lots of diamonds and a pint of ice cream.

I think television can be educational even when it doesn't come from the 4 sanctified Corporation for Public Broadcasting. Not long ago a sitcom called "Dinosaurs," which is basically "The Honeymooners" except that the fat guy in the flannel shirt is a megalosaurus, did an episode called "I Never Ate for My Father." Plot line: Son thinks he may be herbivorous instead of carnivorous; dad finds broccoli in son's room, is horrified. I watched this show with my sons and there ensued spirited discussion of parental expectations and prejudices. A friend with an adolescent, which is a little like saying a friend with a grenade, says they often watch "Roseanne" together, using exchanges on that program between mother and daughter as talking points, kind of an electronic mediator.

In our black/white, good/bad world, we've focused on all the ways TV can 5 be abused, all the kids glassy-eyed before the tube for six hours a day, all the 4-year-olds watching "Nightmare on Elm Street 10—Freddy Maims the Homecoming Queen," all the bad programming. (Although sometimes we seem to forget that we are children of "The Three Stooges," which is not exactly Chekhov.) We focus on the either/or: either they'll read, or they'll watch television. And we respond with a blanket condemnation: No television. TV is bad.

I can still remember when TV was a kind of miracle that simultaneously 6 enveloped us all in Ed Sullivan and "The Wonderful World of Disney." Now we trash our own technology almost as soon as we've invented it, worried that the machines have the upper hand. The only good explanation I've ever heard for that comes from the comedian Rita Rudner, who says she's not buying a CD player until someone promises her they're not going to invent anything else. I get an enormous kick out of writers who talk about the "tactile sensation" of rendering a novel in longhand. I like tactile sensation, but I've got laundry to do. Pass the word-processing software, please.

(I believe, however, that everyone is permitted one refusal to change   7
with the times. Mine is the microwave oven. I prefer to prepare food by applying heat to it rather than by rearranging molecules.)

I like technology; I like being able to watch "Duck Soup" whenever I   8
please on the VCR. And I like popular culture; it's where I come from. I want
my kids to recognize Mozart, Sinatra and Madonna: I want them to know the
world, not some bottled-water version of it. And that world includes television, some of it educational, some of it harmless. My kids have learned to spell
Mickey Mouse as I did, by singing it: "M-I-C, K-E-Y, M-O-U-S-E." It's the new
"Mickey Mouse Club"; Annette and Cubby are long gone and at the end they
do a rap version of the old theme song. To be honest, it's an improvement.

■ Summarizing   Write a brief summary of this selection, focusing on the arguments Quind-
What You   len includes in her defense of television.
Have Read

_____

_____

_____

_____

_____

■ Responding to   Write a response to what you have read, focusing on whether you agree or
What You   disagree with Quindlen's arguments.
Have Read

_____

_____

_____

_____

_____

■ Discussing   Discuss this selection with your instructor and classmates, focusing on the
What You   following questions:
Have Read

1. Do you agree with Quindlen that we are "worried that the machines
   have the upper hand"? Support your answer.

2. Are there other concerns about television viewing that are not addressed by Quindlen? If so, what are they?

3. Do you find Quindlen's or MacNeil's arguments more convincing?
   Why?

4. Quindlen points out that issues like this are often seen as black and
   white. That is, people want to see television as either good or bad.
   What is Quindlen suggesting our attitude should be toward this issue
   and others like it?

■ Writing about
What You
Have Read

Write an editorial, letter to the editor, or essay stating and supporting your position on this issue. You may want to use information from this reading selection or the one by MacNeil to develop your own arguments. If so, be sure to acknowledge your use of these sources. (See Chapter 8 for instruction on documenting sources.)

CUMULATIVE ASSIGNMENTS FOR MEDIA ISSUES

■ Discussion Assignment

The three reading selections you have just read by John Vivian, Robert MacNeil, and Anna Quindlen explore some issues related to the mass media. Vivian provides three mass media models that can be used effectively in thinking about different types of media. MacNeil points out the negative effects of television, while Quindlen argues that television is not harmful and can even be educational. Using these three readings as well as your own experiences and observations, discuss the following questions with your classmates:

1. Do the different forms of mass media reflect or create social values? Support your answer.

2. Using one or more of the mass media models that Vivian provides, classify the television shows that Quindlen mentions in her essay.

3. Compare and contrast the arguments presented by MacNeil and Quindlen.

4. Think about your own attitude toward television. Do you think watching television is primarily beneficial or harmful? Do you believe that its effects on children are similar to or different from its effects on adults? Why or why not?

■ Writing Assignment

Using the three essays you have just read and your own experiences, write an essay in which you analyze your own television viewing habits. Base your analysis on one of Vivian's mass media models. Conclude your essay by reaching a general conclusion about yourself as a television viewer.

Racial Issues

In this unit, the selections address the issue of race. The first selection, a speech by Martin Luther King, Jr., is perhaps the best-known statement of the 1960s civil rights movement. The second selection, by Wallace Terry, looks at a current racial issue: challenges to affirmative action. The final selection, by Ferdinand M. de Leon and Sally Macdonald, considers how the language used to refer to different ethnic groups may affect the ways individuals perceive these groups.

■ Reading Preview

Martin Luther King, Jr., delivered this famous speech in 1963, five years before he was assassinated. Throughout his life, King worked with the Southern Christian Leadership Conference to gain for African American citizens the freedom and justice promised all Americans in the Constitution. This speech, with its famous refrain, "I have a dream," played a major role in the civil rights movement of the 1960s and continues to be cited frequently.

■ Predicting and Questioning

In the following lines, predict what King's dream for African Americans was in 1963.

_____

_____

Now write a question about Martin Luther King, Jr., or his speech.

_____

_____

■ Reading Strategy

Because this selection is a speech, it will be more effective if you read it aloud. As you read, notice the rhetorical devices (such as direct address, repetition, parallel structure, and Biblical and historical references) that contribute to the powerful effect of this speech.

I Have a Dream

Martin Luther King, Jr.

I am happy to join with you today in what will go down in history as the greatest demonstration for freedom in the history of our nation. 1

Five score years ago, a great American, in whose symbolic shadow we stand today, signed the Emancipation Proclamation. This momentous decree came as a great beacon light of hope to millions of Negro slaves who had been 2 seared in the flames of withering injustice. It came as a joyous daybreak to end the long night of their captivity.

But one hundred years later, the Negro still is not free; one hundred 3 years later, the life of the Negro is still sadly crippled by the manacles of segregation and the chains of discrimination; one hundred years later, the Negro lives on a lonely island of poverty in the midst of a vast ocean of material prosperity; one hundred years later, the Negro is still languished in the corners of American society and finds himself in exile in his own land.

So we've come here today to dramatize a shameful condition. In a sense 4 we've come to our nation's capital to cash a check. When the architects of our republic wrote the magnificent words of the Constitution and the Declaration of Independence, they were signing a promissory note to which every American was to fall heir. This note was the promise that all men, yes, black men as well as white men, would be guaranteed the unalienable rights of life, liberty, and the pursuit of happiness.

It is obvious today that America has defaulted on this promissory note in 5 so far as her citizens of color are concerned. Instead of honoring this sacred obligation, America has given the Negro people a bad check; a check which has come back marked "insufficient funds." But we refuse to believe that the bank of justice is bankrupt. We refuse to believe that there are insufficient funds in the great vaults of opportunity of this nation. And so we've come to cash this check, a check that will give us upon demand the riches of freedom and the security of justice.

We have also come to this hallowed spot to remind America of the fierce 6 urgency of now. This is no time to engage in the luxury of cooling off or to take the tranquilizing drug of gradualism. Now is the time to make real the promises of democracy; now is the time to rise from the dark and desolate valley of segregation to the sunlit path of racial justice; now is the time to lift our nation from the quicksands of racial injustice to the solid rock of brotherhood; now is the time to make justice a reality for all of God's children. It would be fatal for the nation to overlook the urgency of the moment. This sweltering summer of the Negro's legitimate discontent will not pass until there is an invigorating autumn of freedom and equality.

Nineteen sixty-three is not an end, but a beginning. And those who hope 7 that the Negro needed to blow off steam and will now be content, will have a rude awakening if the nation returns to business as usual. There will be neither rest nor tranquility in America until the Negro is granted his citizenship rights. The whirlwinds of revolt will continue to shake the foundations of our nation until the bright day of justice emerges.

But there is something that I must say to my people, who stand on the 8 worn threshold which leads into the palace of justice. In the process of gaining our rightful place, we must not be guilty of wrongful deeds. Let us not seek to satisfy our thirst for freedom by drinking from the cup of bitterness and hatred. We must forever conduct our struggle on the high plain of dignity and discipline. We must not allow our creative protests to degenerate into physical violence. Again and again we must rise to the majestic heights of meeting physical force with soul force. The marvelous new militancy, which has engulfed the Negro community, must not lead us to a distrust of all white people. For many of our white brothers, as evidenced by their presence here today, have come to realize that their destiny is tied up with our destiny. And they have come to realize that their freedom is inextricably bound to our freedom. We cannot walk alone. And as we walk, we must make the pledge that we shall always march ahead. We cannot turn back.

There are those who are asking the devotees of Civil Rights, "When will   9
you be satisfied?" We can never be satisfied as long as the Negro is the victim of the unspeakable horrors of police brutality; we can never be satisfied as long as our bodies, heavy with the fatigue of travel, cannot gain lodging in the motels of the highways and the hotels of the cities; we cannot be satisfied as long as the Negro's basic mobility is from a smaller ghetto to a larger one; we can never be satisfied as long as our children are stripped of their selfhood and robbed of their dignity by signs stating "For Whites Only"; we cannot be satisfied as long as the Negro in Mississippi cannot vote and a Negro in New York believes he has nothing for which to vote. No! No, we are not satisfied, and we will not be satisfied until "justice rolls down like waters and righteousness like a mighty stream."

I am not unmindful that some of you have come here out of great trials   10
and tribulations. Some of you have come fresh from narrow jail cells. Some of you have come from areas where your quest for freedom left you battered by the storms of persecution and staggered by the winds of police brutality. You have been the veterans of creative suffering. Continue to work with the faith that unearned suffering is redemptive. Go back to Mississippi. Go back to Alabama. Go back to South Carolina. Go back to Georgia. Go back to Louisiana. Go back to the slums and ghettos of our Northern cities, knowing that somehow this situation can and will be changed. Let us not wallow in the valley of despair.

I say to you today, my friends, so even though we face the difficulties of   11
today and tomorrow, I still have a dream. It is a dream deeply rooted in the American dream. I have a dream that one day this nation will rise up and live out the true meaning of its creed, "We hold these truths to be self-evident, that all men are created equal." I have a dream that one day on the red hills of Georgia, sons of former slaves and the sons of former slave owners will be able to sit down together at the table of brotherhood. I have a dream that one day even the state of Mississippi, a state sweltering with the heat of injustice, sweltering with the heat of oppression, will be transformed into an oasis of freedom and justice. I have a dream that my four little children will one day live in a nation where they will not be judged by the color of their skin, but by the content of their character.

I HAVE A DREAM TODAY!   12

I have a dream that one day down in Alabama—with its vicious racists,   13
with its Governor having his lips dripping with the words of interposition and nullification—one day right there in Alabama, little black boys and black girls will be able to join hands with little white boys and white girls as sisters and brothers.

I HAVE A DREAM TODAY!   14

I have a dream that one day every valley shall be exalted, every hill and   15
mountain shall be made low. The rough places will be plain and the crooked
places will be made straight, "and the glory of the Lord shall be revealed, and
all flesh shall see it together."

This is our hope. This is the faith that I go back to the South with. With   16
this faith we will be able to hew out of the mountain of despair, a stone of
hope. With this faith we will be able to transform the jangling discords of our
nation into a beautiful symphony of brotherhood. With this faith we will be
able to work together, to pray together, to struggle together, to go to jail together, to stand up for freedom together, knowing that we will be free one
day. And this will be the day. This will be the day when all of God's children
will be able to sing with new meaning, "My country 'tis of thee, sweet land of
liberty, of thee I sing. Land where my father died, land of the pilgrim's pride,
from every mountain side, let freedom ring." And if America is to be a great
nation, this must become true.

So let freedom ring from the prodigious hilltops of New Hampshire; let   17
freedom ring from the mighty mountains of New York; let freedom ring from
the heightening Alleghenies of Pennsylvania; let freedom ring from the snow-
capped Rockies of Colorado; let freedom ring from the curvaceous slopes of
California. But not only that. Let freedom ring from Stone Mountain of Georgia; let freedom ring from Lookout Mountain of Tennessee; let freedom ring
from every hill and mole hill of Mississippi. "From every mountainside, let
freedom ring."

And when this happens, and when we allow freedom to ring, when we let   18
it ring from every village and every hamlet, from every state and every city,
we will be able to speed up that day when all of God's children, black men and
white men, Jews and Gentiles, Protestants and Catholics, will be able to join
hands and sing in the words of the old Negro spiritual: "Free at last. Free at
last. Thank God Almighty, we are free at last."

■ Summarizing
What You
Have Read

Write a brief summary of this speech, focusing particularly on King's
dream—what he hoped to see happen in the future.

_____

_____

_____

_____

_____

■ Responding to
What You
Have Read

This speech is noted for its poetry and effectiveness as oral discourse, but it
also includes skillful arguments. Respond to King's speech, focusing on his
arguments and how convincing you found them.

_____

_____

_____

_____

_____

■ Discussing
What You
Have Read

Discuss this speech with your classmates and instructor, focusing on the following questions:

1. What was King's purpose in giving this speech? That is, what did he
    hope to accomplish? What effect do you think the speech had on his au-
    dience?

2. It has been nearly forty years since King delivered this speech. Do you
    think his dream is closer to realization today than it was then? Support
    your answer.

3. Notice that King begins his second paragraph with the phrase "Five
    score years ago," echoing Abraham Lincoln's famous Gettysburg Ad-
    dress, which begins "Four score and seven years ago." What purpose
    does this reference to Lincoln serve?

4. What is your dream for the future of this country?

■ Writing about
What You
Have Read

Review this speech as if you were a journalist, beginning with a brief summary and then pointing out its strongest and weakest features.

■ Reading
Preview

This article is based on an interview the author, Wallace Terry, had with
Ward Connerly, the African American political consultant who led the campaign to ban affirmative action at the University of California. Terry, a
contributing editor of *Parade* magazine, covered the civil rights movement
and Vietnam for the *Washington Post* and *Time*. Rather than state his own
opinions on the issue of affirmative action, Terry focuses in this article on
Connerly and his views.

■ Predicting and
Questioning

Before you read, write your prediction of the reasons Connerly, an African
American, opposes affirmative action.

_____

_____

Next, write a question about affirmative action that you would like answered.

_____

_____

■ Reading
Strategy

This article includes a number of words you may not know. As you read, you may want to circle words that are unfamiliar to you. However, you should also try to figure out their meanings from the context in which they occur. After you have finished reading the entire article, you can discuss the words that you did not know with your instructor and classmates.

Racial Preferences Are Outdated

Wallace Terry

"We can continue perpetuating the outdated premise on which race and gender preferences are based," said Ward Connerly, "that blacks, women and other minorities are incapable of competing without a handicap. Or we can resume the journey to a fair and inclusive society. I wouldn't accept a job or college admission based on color. I would not want the stigma, the cloud hanging over me. There could be no greater insult."

Connerly, 58, led the campaign to ban affirmative action at the University of California in 1995. Then, a year later, he headed the Proposition 209 ballot initiative to end the practice in all California state and local government programs. Those victories thrust him into national leadership as the most active opponent of racial and gender preferences.

Proposition 209 was passed at a time when courts were paring down affirmative action and President Clinton was pleading to "mend it, don't end it." Last year Connerly formed the nonprofit American Civil Rights Institute to urge Congress and states to support need-based programs only. And this year he organized a group of mostly conservative scholars and politicians to serve as an alternative panel to Clinton's race initiative.

I met Connerly at his offices in a handsome mansion in Sacramento. He is a cordial man. Until the summer of 1995, he was a behind-the-scenes political operative and land-use consultant. Now he travels across the country speaking about his vision of a color-blind America.

"Thirty years ago, we agreed that racism was morally wrong and we embraced affirmative action to remedy the harm done to black people," Connerly told me. "But somewhere along the line, we became addicted to government and its occupation of our lives."

Under affirmative action, 42% of the blacks at the University of California at Berkeley dropped out in the years 1988–91, as opposed to only 16% of the whites, said Connerly. "Most students will perform in the range that their entering academic credentials suggest," he added.

The first impact of Proposition 209 was felt this spring, when California's prestigious public universities announced huge drops in the admission of black, Hispanic and Native American students. Of 8034 students accepted at Berkeley, for example, only 191 were black—a 66% drop from last year. Connerly said he felt vindicated by the news. 7

"No one can look at the sharp decline in non-Asian minority admissions and not feel saddened," he said, "but I see plenty that is positive." He pointed to the sharp increase in minority admissions to less-competitive universities. "And those blacks who will enter Berkeley today," he explained, "can say with pride that they were admitted on their own." 8

Connerly, who is black, has been the target of the vitriol the black community once reserved for the Ku Klux Klan. Even some relatives have tried to undermine his credibility with reporters. But Connerly holds fast to his convictions and has no regrets. "I would do it again," he said, "in a heartbeat." 9

Wardell Anthony Connerly was born on June 15, 1939, in Leesville, La. Before Ward turned 2, his father, Roy, a handyman, abandoned the family. When Ward was 4, his mother, Grace, died from a brain tumor. Mary Soniea, Ward's maternal grandmother, gained custody of him. She sent Ward to live with her daughter Bertha and son-in-law James Louis in Sacramento. 10

James and Bertha taught Ward about the value of work. He ran errands, helped a carpenter and sold sodas. Ward's grandmother eventually moved to Sacramento, built a two-bedroom house and, in 1951, reclaimed Ward. But her funds soon were spent, and they were on welfare for a few months. "Those were desperate times," Connerly recalled. He worked 27 hours a week as a stock boy for 65 cents an hour to help pay the mortgage and buy food. 11

Connerly went to nearby American River Junior College because it was all he could afford. He transferred to Sacramento State University—where, he said, his teachers (all white) recognized his leadership potential and encouraged his intellectual growth. He became the first black vice president and then president of the nearly all-white student body. But he never thought of himself as a "first." 12

After graduating from college in 1962, Connerly wed a white fellow student. Presently he is under attack in the black community for having a white wife, in part because of his views on affirmative action. "What can be more fundamental to the pursuit of happiness than the freedom to marry whomever you want?" Connerly asked. They have two grown children, a son and a daughter. 13

Two days after graduation, Connerly took a job at a redevelopment agency in Sacramento. In 1966 he joined the California Department of Housing and Community Development, becoming its liaison to the Legislature. In 1968, Connerly met Assemblyman Pete Wilson, who hired him as his chief consultant. Connerly registered with the GOP, and Wilson became his mentor and close friend. "He is the reason I'm a success," said Connerly. 14

In 1973, he opened Connerly & Associates in a 100-square-foot office with his wife, Ilene, as his partner and a single contract of $4000 a month. "I had two children to support," he said. "It was scary." But the business grew rapidly. Today the company helps private interests and local governments 15 comply with state land-use laws, guides businesses through the housing and building regulations Connerly helped to devise and manages the assets of building trade associations. The staff now totals 15 full-time employees.

In 1993, Pete Wilson—who has been governor since 1991—was under pressure to appoint a nonwhite to the University of California Board of Regents. He offered Connerly a 12-year term that paid no fee. Connerly accepted to give something back to his adopted state. In his first months, he was applauded by students and professors for spending time on campus. "I was ready to ask tough questions of the administration," he said.   16

In 1994, Connerly met a white couple from La Jolla, Jerry and Ellen Cook, whose son had been rejected by the medical school in San Diego despite grades so good that he got into Harvard. They showed Connerly statistics suggesting that whites were being passed over for admission in favor of blacks and Latinos with lesser academic records and test scores. Connerly also learned that colleges were advertising jobs by race. "I had never seen this kind of racial engineering," he said. "It was preference, pure and simple."   17

Connerly talked with Governor Wilson, who had been a longtime supporter of affirmative action, about the need to end preferences. Wilson agreed to back Connerly's efforts. On July 20, 1995, the Board of Regents voted to end its 29-year policy of preferences for minorities and women in admissions, jobs and contracting.   18

The new policy's impact was first felt at Berkeley's law school. Only 14 blacks were among 792 accepted, a drop of 81%, and none of them chose to enter. "It shows we have a long way to go," Connerly said. But he is pushing for preferences based on economic need. "It makes sense to give extra consideration to a [qualified] student who is poor," Connerly added. Meanwhile, the regents are sending tutors to low-performing schools to help minority students become more competitive academically.   19

The affirmative action vote led to Connerly's leadership of Proposition 209, to prohibit the State of California and local governments from discriminating or granting preferential treatment on the basis of race, gender, color, ethnicity or national origin in public education, employment and contracting. He traveled across the state, pleading for support. In 1996, Californians voted 54% to 46% to pass Proposition 209. Among blacks, 29% voted for it.   20

To counter Connerly's national efforts, Martin Luther King III, a son of the slain civil-rights leader, has organized a coalition of groups called Americans United for Affirmative Action. "Civil rights in the '90s is about getting decent-paying jobs and competing in corporate America," King said. Anita Perez Ferguson, the president of the National Women's Political Caucus, has joined King.   21

Ward Connerly believes the future of black America lies in assimilating into mainstream organizations like the Chamber of Commerce. "It's not white culture," he noted. "It's *our* culture." And how does he want to be remembered? "As an ordinary American who saw something he considered wrong and had the conviction to pursue a solution," Connerly replied. "You don't have to be an elected official to make a difference. That's democracy."   22

■ Summarizing
What You
Have Read

Write a brief summary of this article, focusing on Connerly's reasons for opposing affirmative action.

_____

_____

_____

_____

_____

■ Responding to
What You
Have Read

Now write a response to what you have read, focusing on one of Connerly's
reasons for opposing affirmative action.

_____

_____

_____

_____

_____

■ Discussing
What You
Have Read

Discuss Terry's article with your instructor and classmates, focusing on the
following questions:

1. Do you think Terry presented Connerly's position clearly and fairly?
   Did he provide enough information about Connerly? Did he provide
   enough background information about the issue of affirmative action
   and what has occurred with regard to this issue in the California university system?

2. Following are four reasons frequently cited by those who favor affirmative action:

   ■ It's a form of reparation for past discrimination.
   ■ It fosters opportunity for minorities and women shut out by the
     "old-boy network."
   ■ Society as a whole benefits from programs that increase participa-
     tion by minorities and women.
   ■ It allows government funding to be allotted fairly.

   Now read the following reasons often used by those who oppose affirmative action:

   ■ It's a form of reverse discrimination.
   ■ Preferences are based on color and gender, instead of solely on merit.
   ■ It says minorities can't earn admission into prestigious schools with-
     out getting extra points.
   ■ It doesn't work. At the University of California at Berkeley, 42 per-
     cent of all black students dropped out, as opposed to only 16 percent
     of whites.

   —*Parade* Magazine, May 31, 1998, p. 4

Which of these opposing arguments do you find most convincing? Why or why not?

3. Do you think minorities should be given preferences in college admissions? Why or why not?

■ Writing about What You Have Read

Write an essay in which you argue for or against affirmative action as it applies to the college admission process. You may want to interview someone in the admissions office of your school or use Terry's article as a source for your essay.

■ Reading Preview

There *is* power in a name. What we call something shapes people's attitudes and feelings about it. Thus, we do not like it when someone mispronounces our name or gives us a nickname that is demeaning or unflattering. Ethnic groups are also concerned about their names, and in recent years many have made it clear that they prefer names other than those that have traditionally been used to designate members of their group. This essay explores this process of naming as it applies to different ethnic groups and also seeks to answer the question: "Why can't we all just be Americans?"

■ Predicting and Questioning

On the following lines, predict which ethnic groups are discussed in this essay.

_____

_____

Now write a question about a name that is used to identify a particular ethnic group.

_____

_____

■ Reading Strategy

As you read this essay, write your responses to the authors' ideas in the margin.

Name Power

Ferdinand M. de Leon and *Sally Macdonald*

All these many years after the nation's wrenching confrontations over   1
civil rights, you can still hear the clenched fist in Rick Olguin's voice as he declares, *"I* am a Chicano." And the firm resolve in Maxine Chan's as she corrects someone who has just called her an Oriental, "I am *not* a rug." And the

calm certainty in Nona Brazier's as she talks about abandoned labels and concludes, "I will *always* refer to myself as an African American." Few things are as fundamental as what we call ourselves.

The labels we use affect how others perceive us and how we see our-2 selves; they shape how we see others and how we want to be seen by them; they are used by those in power to define the rest even as they struggle to define themselves. They shape who we are.

Little wonder then, that when the names we have always used for our-3 selves and for others start to change, as they are doing, we feel a tremor down the spine of our collective national consciousness. Is it *African American* or is it *black?* Should we use *Hispanic* or *Latino? Native American* or *American Indian?* What about *white?* What about *Asian American?* Then comes the underlying question that—depending on who does the asking and what spurred the question—can inspire understanding or provoke outrage: "Why can't we all just be Americans?"

"Language Is Political"

Today, more of us than ever come from somewhere else. More of us than 4 ever have brown or black skins, not white ones. More of us than ever are demanding that the names people call us are respectful ones, ones we have chosen to best describe ourselves. "Language is political," says Guadalupe Friaz, an assistant professor of ethnic studies at the University of Washington. "When we talk about language we're talking about the relationships between people, and what people call each other reflects whatever tension and anxiety that society is going through." We've fought for power among ourselves for generations, and words have been a frequent weapon. We sling epithets that bruise as much as bricks and police batons. Nicknames for whole groups of people slide from slang to slur, gathering the power to maim psychologically. Some labels retain for generations the power to call up a host of stereotypes that dig and slice and kill the spirit. But sometimes the group at the receiving end of that abuse reclaims a label, like "black," effectively changing it from a negative term to a positive and proud one. "Change is constant," Friaz says. "Group relationships always change, so of course terminology is going to change. As people of color we don't have power, and we haven't had the power to name." But that, too, is changing.

Black or African American?

In 1967, Larry Gossett stopped using *Negro* and became *black.* Today, 5 he's *African American.* Gossett, executive director of the Central Area Motivation Program, was then involved in the civil-rights struggle, and the switch came as the black-power and black-pride movement gained steam. "We were defining black as beautiful and not as something ugly," Gossett says. "It had a profound inspirational impact on the youth of the '60s." The new label was a rejection of the labels imposed by whites and the labels of his parents' generation—a radical reclaiming of a word that had been viewed as a slur. "It was revolutionary and emotionally wrenching because we had parents saying,

'We've been Negroes and coloreds all our lives. Why are you calling yourselves black?'" Gossett says. "Black, in America and in the English language, had such a negative connotation that it scared our parents."

The changes in the labels used by or for African Americans over the course of the country's history reflect the struggles between the dominant culture and other groups. For centuries, negro—in the lower case—was the accepted label. But after Reconstruction there was a push by black leaders and the black press to give dignity to the name by capitalizing it—an effort that took 50 years. In the 1900s, "colored" competed with Negro as the preferred group name, and it lives on today in the name of the National Association for the Advancement of Colored People, founded in 1910. Afro-American was first proposed in 1880, but it didn't catch on. Eventually Negro emerged as the preferred name, surviving until the late 1960s, when it was rejected by younger black people because of its associations with slavery.

Three years ago, Gossett decided it was time for him to make another switch—this time to African American. "How you refer to yourselves as a people has social, historical and cultural significance," Gossett says. "I'm from the current school of thought which says that African American comes closest to describing who we are as a people." The change is rooted in the political growth of the African-American community, Gossett says, and was also prompted in part by a sense of identification with Africa—especially the struggles of black South Africans. For Gossett, it was again the reclaiming of a word that had been tarnished. Today Gossett uses *African American* and *black* interchangeably, but he believes *African American* will prevail. Although most people still use black, many community leaders agree.

For Nona Brazier, the switch to African American happened further back. Like Gossett, Brazier used *black* as a reaction to her parents' use of *Negro.* But by the end of the 1960s, she had started to use *African American.* "I often refer to black folks and the black community, but I never refer to myself as a black American," says Brazier, who is co-owner of Northwest Recovery Systems, a recycling firm. Brazier's preference for *African American is* rooted in her direct ties to Africa. She has a business in Nigeria and feels an attachment to the land from which her ancestors came. "The fact that I refer to myself as an African American reflects my time," Brazier says. "It's based on myself, my life and times, and even if other labels emerge, I will always refer to myself as an African American." "It doesn't matter what others call you, but it's very important what you call yourself."

Native Americans or American Indians?

As every child learns in grade school, Christopher Columbus sailed the ocean blue to find India, and when he arrived in the New World, he mistakenly named the people Indians. Yet the name survives today. And to Joseph Brown, a Lakota elder who has worked with the homeless and street kids, Indian is just fine. "The word *Indian* identifies us," Brown says. "*Indian* covers a lot. A lot of Indians don't like to be called Indian because they're trying to be white men and they're prejudiced against themselves."

But for others, especially those who are younger, Native American is the   10
preferred label because it rejects the tragic historical associations that the
word *Indian* carries. "The idea of calling people Native Americans appeals to
me because we are native—more so than any other group," says Allethia
Allen, an assistant professor of social work at the UW. "I would prefer that because the name *Indian* comes from Columbus."

Others say there are no right or wrong choices. "I think the majority   11
feels comfortable with the word *Indian,*" says Cecil James, a resource-man-
agement worker for the Yakima fisheries. "Each individual has their own definition of how they want to be called. When I talk in public, I identify myself
as an Indian of the Yakima Nation, but it should be up to each person to decide." Allen, who is half Native American and part black and white, says she
hasn't eliminated *Indian* from her own vocabulary. "People tend to do what
the majority does," Allen says. "But people are getting much more distinctive
about what they say about their heritage and their customs and very, very
identified with their bloodline."

While there seems to be no overwhelming majority for using either *In-*   12
dian or *Native American,* most agree that using tribal affiliations is usually
preferred. "Traditionally, among Native Americans, we identified each other
by our tribal affiliation, and very often people greet each other that way," says
Allen, who is Mohawk and Mohican. "To me, the more clearly a person is described in terms of heritage, the better it is." Robert Eaglestaff, the principal
of American Indian Heritage School in Seattle says: "Most Indian tribes describe themselves as The People or human beings. The Lakotas, my tribe,
means the friendly people. The others are labels, and I take labels for what
they're worth—with a grain of salt. But I know who I am."

What about Asian Americans?

Not long ago, Ron Chew, director of the Wing Luke Museum in Seattle's   13
International District, was interviewing an elderly woman in Sequim about
some of the Chinese people who settled on the Olympic Peninsula in the early
days. She described them as Chinamen. "I didn't correct her," he says. "She
grew up in another era and was frozen in time. Maybe in her time and her
place that was not a derogatory term. But language evolves. What might be
appropriate at one time might not be at another." *Chinaman* is not OK anymore, and neither is *Oriental,* although it's a term still used by some older
Asians and many whites. *"Oriental* has a negative connotation," says Maxine
Chan, a Chinese American who works with the community for the Seattle Police Department. "It's very much the Fu Manchu, Suzy Wong thing. It speaks
about the 'yellow peril,' and the 'yellow horde.' If someone calls me that, I just
say I'm not a rug."

While *Asian American* is all right, most people of Asian heritage would   14
rather be identified by the country of their origin. "Asian Americans need to
be divided into Japanese Americans or Chinese Americans or Korean Americans—just because they want to be," says Setsuko Buckley, a Japanese language teacher and multicultural education expert at Western Washington
University in Bellingham. "Even Southeast Asians are different from each

other—Vietnamese, Thai, Cambodian—and they should have the option of being called what they want."

Tomie Rogers, a UW medical student, says she's "half Japanese, half Swedish-Irish." When she was younger, new friends often thought—based on her almond-shaped eyes and tall stature—she must be Native American. "I don't really take offense to whatever people call me," she says. "I don't really have much ethnic feeling, and I don't even know how I'm listed as a student. I often mark the 'other' box." 16

Being considered Asian poses a problem for some Filipinos and Pacific Islanders: They aren't from the Asian continent and feel they shouldn't be put in that category. Many Filipinos have the Catholic religion, Spanish surnames and some cultural vestiges of their colonial days. "Our biggest problem in the Filipino community, besides economics, is an identity crisis," says Fred Cordova, a historian, author and manager of the UW information-services office. "We've never had a chance to identify ourselves. The majority of our community here is made up of immigrants now, and they're very different from the ones who have been here a long time." 17

Most of the Asian and Latino groups are trying to deal with the chaos created by large waves of immigrants in recent years. As each new group begins to settle itself in the United States, another new group comes pouring in. Many never come to think of themselves as full-fledged U.S. citizens and neither do their children. They continue to use the ethnic label they arrived with, identifying themselves as, say, Chinese—not Chinese American. "A lot of us just don't put on the American tag," says Chew. "For most of us, it's understood that we're here, and for some, particularly the older generation, when they say American, they mean white." 18

Hispanic, Latino or Chicano?

Like Asians, people whose ethnic roots are in Latin America most often identify themselves by the country of their forebears—Mexican American, Cuban American. If they have to be inclusive, they'll be Latino. Even that is "an umbrella term that will suffer the same complications" with age as the other broad ethnic identifications, says the UW's Guadalupe Friaz. "If you have to have a broad term, it's OK. At least it's not Eurocentric." 19

If Lorenzo Alvarado is given the choice of Hispanic to mark on a document, he'll say that's what he is. But when he marks the box that way, he feels he's losing his real heritage somehow. "I may be in America, but I'm a Mexican," says the Kent School District math teacher. Hispanic—a tag made up by census workers to identify Latin Americans, Caribbean Islanders and Spaniards—is considered by most of those it would describe as too broad, irritatingly bureaucratic or just plain unacceptable. "My understanding is there is no place called Hispanica," says Eduardo Diaz, a social-service administrator. "I think it's degrading to be called something that doesn't exist. Even Latino is a misnomer. We don't speak Latin." 20

Friaz calls herself a Chicana, a term—like a raised fist of defiance—that gathered power during the antiwar and civil-rights movements. Although the term has lost some of its punch, many baby boomers who called themselves 21

Chicanos (or Chicana, the feminine form) in their youth still do today. For some Mexican Americans, the term became a survival tool to replace *Mexican,* which had become tainted with racism, says Rick Olguin, a UW ethnic-studies assistant professor. Now *Mexican* is back in favor.

Javier Almaya, a native Colombian who has been in the United States   22
for 10 years, is reasonably comfortable calling himself a Latino. But, like many Latin Americans, he considers himself a mestizo—a mixture of European and Indian ancestry. It's a term that's used widely in Central and South America but isn't readily recognized in this country.

Such complexity is the rule in discussions of ethnic labels for Latinos.   23
Consider the employees of Diaz's Seattle office: Diaz is the assistant manager of the King County Guardian Ad Litem program, a court advocacy program for children. A Puerto Rican who grew up in the Bronx in New York City, he says he feels degraded if he's called a Hispanic. But Cathy Ortiz, the office's support staff supervisor, whose grandparents still live in Mexicali, Baja California, says although *Hispanic* is OK with her, she'd rather be called an American of Mexican descent. And Rita Amaro, an office worker, is a third-generation Mexican American who says people can call her Latina, although the word reminds her of "kind of an island, like Puerto Rico or Cuba."

Minority, Non-White or People of Color?

When whites were clearly the dominant group in this country, it was   24
easy to divide the population into majority and minority. Not the most sensitive division, but a handy one for whites that reflected the existing power dynamics and neatly summed up who had the power and numbers and who didn't. But as whites lose their numerical dominance, and non-white immigrants continue to come into the country, the racial makeup of the nation becomes even more complex. The balance is shifting. At the current rate of growth, the groups we consider minorities will collectively become the majority in this country in about 2050, according to recent projections by the Population Reference Bureau, a non-profit Washington, D.C., agency that studies demographic trends. The bureau based its projection on 1990 census figures.

There has long been a debate over what to call people who aren't white.   25
In 1962, in *The Negro History Bulletin,* Eldridge Cleaver wrote of the term *non-white:* "The very words that we use indicate that we have set a premium on the Caucasian ideal of beauty. When discussing interracial relations, we speak of 'white people' and 'non-white people.' Notice that that particular choice of words gives precedence to 'white people' . . . making them a center—a standard—to which 'non-white' bears a negative relation. Notice the different connotation when we turn around and say 'colored' and 'non-colored' or 'black' or 'non-black.'"

These days much of the discussion centers on the phrase "people of   26
color," an alternative that has emerged in recent years. It has generated strong reactions—but so far little consensus among those to whom the phrase would be applied. "I don't like the term 'people of color,'" says Almaya, a health educator with the AIDS Prevention Project. "It doesn't give us any definition. It could be a person from Colombia or a person from Samoa, and they

don't really have anything in common at all." But Olguin likes the phrase and argues that it was significantly different from the now discredited "colored people." "It's viewing it from the top instead of the bottom," he says. "'Colored people' says 'inferior,' and to be a colored person is to define a people by their color. But people of color are persons with other attributes."

But the changes won't come easily, and those who would claim the power to name themselves—and do away with long-entrenched labels—should expect resistance, says UW Professor Haig Bosmajian, whose book *The Language of Oppression* explores the power of language. Bosmajian says opposition usually comes from two groups: those who need to be persuaded that there is a problem, and those who have a psychological stake in maintaining their power and not acquiescing to the new labels. "It's more than etiquette, it's power," he says.   27

White, Caucasian or Euro-American?

White people don't tend to think much about what they're called. Since they're already the majority, they see no need to label themselves. "I don't think of it the way a black person would call himself black," says Nick Wilson, a Metro bus driver. "I think my grandparents were Irish, but I don't really even know. The only thing I can tell you about one of my grandfathers is that he was from Texas. Come to think of it, he was a Texan."   28

"I don't think about it at all," says Jerry Edwards, a Seattle yacht broker. "And I guess that's as much an indication of the situation as anything. "It points out how privileged we are compared to other racial groups." When pressed to make a choice between *white* and *Caucasian,* Edwards dislikes both. *"Caucasian is* too antiseptic somehow, and *white is* too racial."   29

"It's easy in America to be white," says Pier van den Berghe, a UW sociology and anthropology professor. "It's easy for whites to forget they're white. But it's impossible for blacks to forget they're black." When van den Berghe is asked to check a box with his ethnic background, he marks "Other" or "African American." He's white, but he can do that, he says, because he was born in South Africa. In the Southwest, whites are used to being called Anglos. But *Anglo,* introduced by Mexicans, means English. And many whites point out that England is not their homeland. Many white people dislike being called Caucasian. Van den Berghe calls it "a pseudo-ethnic label" and he finds it "profoundly objectionable." Most modern scholars no longer use racial divisions. Genetically, people are people, and any differences between them are only skin deep. Friaz, the UW ethnic-studies professor, calls whites Euro-Americans, a term many whites consider contrived and unnecessary and in some cases erroneous.   30

Friaz believes whites should start their own discussion of heritage. "Everyone has an ethnicity," she says. "Euro-Americans have to start seeing themselves as ethnics. Most Euro-Americans are not proud of who they are. I ask my white students about their ethnicity and they say, 'I guess I'm American.' They say it in an apologetic way." This denial of cultural background is something that wasn't widely seen until World War I, Friaz says. Until then, most whites sent their children to language schools after their regular classes   31 to preserve their culture. But with the onset of the war, becoming "American" meant proving your loyalty by rejecting all ties to other lands. "This is one of the few countries in the world that is willfully ignorant—which is a worse kind of ignorance," says the UW's Olguin. "In the rest of the world it's a virtue to speak different languages. Here if you speak three languages you're trilingual, and if you speak two languages you're bilingual, and if you speak one language, you're American."

Why Can't We All Just Be Americans?

It seems like a simple enough question, but it can be fraught with insensitivity and misunderstanding, depending on who hears it and who asks. At best, it's a naive, idealistic attempt to say, "Why can't we quit categorizing each other?" If we call each other the same thing, it insists, other differences will dissolve. But Friaz and some other people of color hear the question this way: "Why do you have to keep emphasizing your ethnicity, your color? Why can't you be white like *us?*" Those questions release a flood of perceived insensitivities: Why don't you adopt white values, white culture? Why don't you dress in Western styles, eat Western foods? Why press universities to offer ethnic studies in a curriculum served perfectly well by the study of Western culture? To many, whites and people of color alike, the questions are a sign of a new imagery. The melting pot is now an ethnic salad. 32

The simplistic solution is to cut ethnic roots. "The day we can just call ourselves Americans comes after the day that we can figure out what we call each other," Olguin says. "After centuries of antagonism, it's naive to think that we can just forget all of that." "God, if we *could* all just be Americans," says Cordova. "But there is such a thing as reality, and it's borne out by the acts of the past weeks. There is racism in this country. As long as we have to call ourselves something, I'm proud to be a Filipino American. What you call yourself, hell, that's up to you." 33

Cecilia Concepcion Alvarez, an artist, believes the white majority and the society it dominates eye the immigrating cultures with suspicion because the country has never been racially homogenous. Some whites fear—singly and collectively, consciously or not—giving any other culture or its people even a sliver of power. Minorities sometimes fear losing their personal identity to a nameless mass. "We have to talk about that. We can't just dismiss it," says Alvarez. "A lot of people have been dismissed in the past. It's not cultural; it's not even necessarily genetics. It's human, and the discussion has to be how we can get together." 34

So how do we get together? One way is to recognize and respect each other's identity, rather than insist everyone adopt the same identify. Nona Brazier argues that clinging to separate labels does not necessarily detract from the idea of a united people. "One of the best things about this country is the variety," she says. "I think people need to accentuate the American, but people also need to accentuate the love of their history and culture." 35

The UW's Bosmajian offers the following anecdote: During the late 1960s, at a panel discussion on the Vietnam War, one of the panelists used the phrase "our colored boys," a phrase that Bosmajian points out is triply offen- 36 sive. The phrase erected a wall that divided the participants along racial lines and blocked further communication. "You're not going to change race relations by changing the language," Bosmajian says. "You're not going to get jobs by changing the language. But changing the language is one of the steps that has to be taken. . . . At least we'd be talking to each other."

■ Summarizing
What You
Have Read

Briefly summarize this essay, focusing on the author's thesis.

_____

_____

_____

_____

_____

■ Responding to
What You
Have Read

Identify the ethnic group that you belong to and state which name you prefer and why.

_____

_____

_____

_____

_____

■ Discussing
What You
Have Read

Discuss this essay with your instructor and classmates, focusing on the following questions:

1. What is meant by the statement "Language is political"? Give an example of an incident or event in your own experience that supports this statement.

2. Do you agree or disagree that "The labels we use affect . . . how we see ourselves" as well as how others see us? Why do you feel as you do?

3. Why do you think there has been so much emphasis recently on the names used by different ethnic groups? Has this emphasis helped or hindered race relations?

4. Do you think it is important for everyone to agree on a single name for each ethnic group or should people just use the names they prefer? Why or why not?

5. Why do the authors of this article argue that we can't "all just be Americans"? Do you agree or disagree with their conclusions?

6. How important is diversity to our society? Would we be a more or less productive society if we all shared the same ethnic background?

■ Writing about
What You
Have Read

Write an essay in which you discuss both the positive and negative effects of diversity on our society.

CUMULATIVE ASSIGNMENTS FOR RACIAL ISSUES

■ Discussion Assignment

The three reading selections you have just read by Martin Luther King, Jr., Wallace Terry, and Ferdinand M. de Leon and Sally Macdonald focus on racial issues. King's famous "I Have a Dream" speech is a classic example of civil rights oratory. Partially as a result of King's efforts, we now have affirmative action laws, but these are being challenged, as the article by Terry makes clear. Finally, the essay by de Leon and Macdonald explores the power of names—especially as they relate to ethnic groups. Using these three readings as well as your own experiences and observations, discuss the following questions with your classmates:

1. What do you think King's reaction would be to Ward Connerly's position on affirmative action (as explained by Wallace Terry in "Racial Preferences Are Outdated")?

2. What progress have we made toward racial equality and harmony since King made his "I Have a Dream" speech in 1963?

3. What racial issues remain to be solved in our society?

4. How does language contribute to both racial problems and solutions? Support your answer with examples.

5. How has ethnic diversity both divided and enriched our society?

■ Writing Assignment

Using the three essays you have just read as well as your own experiences and observations, write an essay in which you argue that diversity either strengthens or weakens our society.

Index

Text Credits

Part One: **p. 39:** From *This Stubborn Soil,* by William A. Owens. Published by N. Lyons Books. Copyright © 1986. Reprinted with permission of Jessie Ann Owens and David Owens.

Part Two: **p. 69:** From Howard B. Wilder, Robert P. Ludlum, and Harriett McCune Brown, *This Is America's Story,* 5th ed. Copyright © 1983 by Houghton Mifflin Company. **p. 73:** From Paul Weisz, *The Science of Biology,* 4th ed. Copyright © 1977 by The McGraw-Hill Companies. Reproduced with permission of the publisher. **p. 75:** Excerpt from *Silent Spring* by Rachel Carson. Copyright © 1962 by Rachel L. Carson, renewed 1990 by Roger Christie. Reprinted by permission of Houghton Mifflin Company. All rights reserved. **pp. 82–83:** From Thomas C. Kinnear and Kenneth L. Bernhardt, *Principles of Marketing* (pages 153–154). © 1995 HarperCollins Publishers. Reprinted by permission of Addison Wesley Longman. **pp. 83–86:** Adapted from Karen O'Connor and Larry J. Sabato, *The Essentials of American Government,* 3rd ed. (pages 203–204). © 1998 HarperCollins Publishers. Reprinted by permission of Addison Wesley Longman. **pp. 123, 151–152, 205, and 215–216:** From Edward J. Tarbuck and Frederick K. Lutgens, *Earth Science,* 7th ed. Copyright © 1994 by Prentice-Hall, Inc. Reprinted by permission of Prentice-Hall, Inc., Upper Saddle River, NJ. **pp. 124–125:** Excerpt from *A Walker in the City,* copyright 1951 and renewed 1979 by Alfred Kazin, reprinted by permission of Harcourt Brace & Company. **pp. 125–126 and 139:** From N. Scott Momaday, *The Way to Rainy Mountain.* Copyright © 1969. Reprinted by permission of University of New Mexico Press. **pp. 127 and 135–136:** Excerpts from "The Inheritance of Tools," copyright © 1986 by Scott Russell Sanders; first appeared in *The North American Review;* from *The Paradise of Bombs;* reprinted by permission of the author and the Virginia Kidd Agency, Inc. **pp. 127–128:** Excerpt from *Pilgrim at Tinker Creek* by Annie Dillard. Copyright © 1974 by Annie Dillard. Reprinted by permission of HarperCollins Publishers, Inc. **p. 137:** Excerpt from *A Thousand Days.* Copyright © 1965 by Arthur M. Schlesinger, Jr. Reprinted by permission of Houghton Mifflin Co. All rights reserved. **pp. 139 and 150:** From "The Spider and the Wasp," by Alexander Petrunkevitch. Copyright © 1952 by Scientific American, Inc. All rights reserved. **p. 140:** Excerpt from *Holy the Firm* by Annie Dillard. Copyright © 1977 by Annie Dillard. Reprinted by permission of HarperCollins Publishers, Inc. **pp. 163, 164, 178, and 204–205:** From Mary Beth Norton, et al., *A People and a Nation: A History of the United States,* Fifth Edition. Copyright © 1998 by Houghton Mifflin Company. Excerpted with permission. **pp. 174, 197–198, and 204:** From Lester Lefton, *Psychology,* 6th ed. Copyright © 1997 by Allyn & Bacon. Reprinted by permission. **p. 202:** From Isak Dinesen, *Out of Africa.* Copyright © 1938 by Random House, Inc. Reprinted with permission of the publisher. **p. 202:** From *My Life and Hard Times,* by James Thurber. Copyright © 1933, 1961 James Thurber. Published by HarperCollins, Inc. **pp. 226–227 and 232:** From Alan Pistorius, "Species Lost," *Country Journal,* vol. 24 (July/August 1997), pp. 36–39. Reprinted with permission of the author. **pp. 228–233:** Excerpts from Martin Luther King, Jr., "Letter from a Birmingham Jail." Reprinted by arrangement with The Heirs to the Estate of Martin Luther King, Jr., c/o Writers House, Inc., as agent for the proprietor. Copyright 1963 by Martin Luther King, Jr., copyright renewed 1991 Coretta Scott King. **p. 230:** Excerpted with permission from "Why Gun-Control Laws Don't Work," by Barry Goldwater, *Reader's Digest,* December 1975. Copyright © 1975 by The Reader's Digest Association, Inc.

Part Three: **pp. 249–250:** From *The Book of Lights,* by Chaim Potok. Copyright © 1981 by Chaim Potok Individually & Adena Potok as Trustee for Rene N. Potok, Naana S. Potok, and Akiva Potok. Reprinted by permission of Alfred A. Knopf, Inc. **pp. 252–253:** Excerpt from *The Water Is Wide,* by Pat Conroy. Copyright © 1972 by Pat Conroy. Reprinted by permission of Houghton Mifflin Company. All rights reserved. **pp. 264–265:** From *The Invisible Man,* by Ralph Ellison. Copyright © 1952 by Random House, Inc. Reprinted with permission of the publisher.

Part Four: **pp. 444–445:** Copyright © 1972 by James Herriot. From *All Creatures Great and Small,* by James Herriot. Reprinted by permission of St. Martin's Press, Incorporated. **pp. 446–447:** "Down with the Forests," from *Dateline America,* by Charles Kuralt, copyright © 1979 by CBS, Inc., reprinted by permission of Harcourt Brace & Company. **pp. 448–449:** From *Future Shock,* by Alvin Toffler. Copyright © 1970 by Alvin Toffler. Reprinted by permission of Random House, Inc. **pp. 453–454:** From Alan Sherman, Sharon Sherman, and Leonard Russikoff, *Basic Concepts in Chemistry,* Third Edition. Copyright © 1984 by Houghton Mifflin Company. Used with permission. **pp. 464–466:** From Rebecca Brooks Gruver, *An American History,* Vol. I. Copyright © 1985 by The McGraw-Hill Companies. Reprinted with permission of the publisher. **pp. 468–469:** From Douglas A. Bernstein, Edward J. Roy, Thomas K. Srull, and Christopher D. Wickens, *Psychology,* First Edition. Copyright © 1988 by Houghton Mifflin Company. Used with permission.

Part Five: **pp. 472–473:** "Mother and Freedom," from *Even the Stars Look Lonesome,* by Maya Angelou. Copyright © 1997 by Maya Angelou. Reprinted by permission of Random House, Inc. **pp. 475–479:** "Mother Tongue," by Amy Tan. Originally appeared in *The Threepenny Review,* Copyright © 1990 by Amy Tan. Used by permission of Amy Tan and the Sandra Dijkstra Literary Agency. **pp. 481–485:** "Does Coming to College Mean Becoming Someone New?" adapted by permission of Kevin Davis. In *The Subject Is Writing,* edited by Wendy Bishop (Boynton/Cook, a subsidiary of Reed Elsevier, Inc., Portsmouth, NH, 1993). **pp. 487–489:** "Lives on the Boundary: Lilia," Reprinted with the permission of The Free Press, a Division of Simon & Schuster, Inc., from *Lives on the Boundary: The Struggles and Achievements of America's Underprepared,* by Mike Rose. Copyright © 1989 by Mike Rose. **pp. 491–493:** "In Praise of the F Word," by Mary Sherry. Reprinted by permission of the author. **pp. 494–496:** "College Valued Less for Learning Than for Earning," by Ethan Bronner. Copyright © 1998 by the New York Times Co. Reprinted by permission. **pp. 499–501:** "Mass Media Models," by John Vivian, from *The Media of Mass Communication,* 4th ed. Copyright © 1996 by Allyn & Bacon. Reprinted by permission. **pp. 503–505:** "The Trouble with Television," by Robert MacNeil. Reprinted with permission of the author from the March 1985 *Reader's Digest.* **pp. 506–508:** "TV or Not TV," by Anna Quindlen. Copyright © 1991 by the New York Times Co. Reprinted by permission. **pp. 510–513:** "I Have a Dream," by Martin Luther King, Jr. Reprinted by arrangement with The Heirs to the Estate of Martin Luther King, Jr., c/o Writers House, Inc., as agent for the proprietor. Copyright 1963 by Martin Luther King, Jr., copyright renewed 1991 Coretta Scott King. **pp. 515–517:** "Racial Preferences Are Outdated," by Wallace Terry. First published in *Parade.* Copyright © 1998 by Wallace Terry. Reprinted by permission of *Parade* and Scovil Chichak Galen Literary Agency on behalf of the author. **pp. 519–527:** "Name Power," by Ferdinand M. de Leon and Sally Macdonald. Copyright © 1997 Seattle Times Company. Reprinted by permission.